ORIGINAL LETTERS

RELATIVE TO

THE ENGLISH REFORMATION.

ORIGINAL LETTERS

RELATIVE TO

THE ENGLISH REFORMATION,

WRITTEN DURING THE REIGNS OF

KING HENRY VIII., KING EDWARD VI.,
AND QUEEN MARY:

CHIEFLY FROM THE ARCHIVES OF ZURICH.

TRANSLATED FROM AUTHENTICATED COPIES OF THE AUTOGRAPHS

AND EDITED FOR

The Parker Society,

BY THE

REV. HASTINGS ROBINSON, D.D. F.S.A.

RECTOR OF GREAT WARLEY, ESSEX;
AND FORMERLY FELLOW OF ST JOHN'S COLLEGE, CAMBRIDGE.

THE SECOND PORTION.

Wipf & Stock
PUBLISHERS
Eugene, Oregon

Wipf and Stock Publishers
199 W 8th Ave, Suite 3
Eugene, OR 97401

Original Letters Relative to the English Reformation, 2 Volumes
Written During the Reigns of King Henry VIII., King Edward VI.,
and Queen Mary: Chiefly from the Archives of Zurich
By Robinson, Hastings
ISBN 13: 978-1-55635-049-8
ISBN 10: 1-55635-049-X
Publication date 11/3/2006
Previously published by Cambridge, 1846

INTRODUCTION.

THE volume now presented to the members of the Parker Society completes the correspondence obtained by the researches of that Society from the archives of Zurich and other similar repositories in Switzerland. It is, however, entirely independent of the two series of letters already published; inasmuch as those series included only the letters written during the reign of Elizabeth, while the present collection belongs to a somewhat earlier period of our history, extending from the latter part of the reign of Henry VIII. through those of his two immediate successors. The dubious character of the English Reformation under the first of these sovereigns, its marked and decided progress under Edward VI., and its temporary overthrow under queen Mary, invest each of these periods with a character peculiar to itself, and which will also be found reflected in the correspondence of each respectively. Among the writers are many of those master-minds, who appear to have been raised up by Divine providence for the necessities of the times in which they lived, to whom it was "given in the behalf of Christ not only to believe on him, but also to suffer for his sake;" to plead for him in the council-chamber, to preach him in the pulpit, to glorify him at the stake. And while the same fervent zeal, and holy energy, and lively faith, that supported Cranmer and Hooper and Barnes in the flames of persecution, may be traced in glowing characters in their respective correspondence; we may observe in that of the less distinguished individuals, whose letters are preserved in this collection, a vein of godly simplicity which affords the surest evidence, that the facts they communicated were (as they every where professed them to be) gathered by them, if not always from personal observation, at least from the general belief and undisputed intelligence of the day. And if the accuracy of subsequent researches has failed to confirm some of the minuter details recorded in their correspondence, such want of confirmation can neither seriously impugn the reality of the facts, nor shake the credibility of the writers. The circumstances under which they wrote did not require them to ascertain absolutely the truth of all the events they communicated; but they were content to transmit them as they themselves received them, from the usual sources of information in the places whence they wrote.

By far the greater portion of the letters both in this and the two preceding series were addressed to that distinguished divine, to whose affectionate regard for the writers we are indebted for the preservation of their correspondence. And truly few persons have been honoured with such correspondents; and few, perhaps, have been more worthy of such distinction, than the Zurich pastor, who with his brother ministers entertained the Marian exiles "with a tenderness and affection that engaged them to the end of their lives to make the greatest acknowledgements possible for it."

When the first portion of the present series was delivered to the members of the Parker Society, in the course of last autumn, it was supposed that the entire collection would prove too extensive to be conveniently contained in one volume. Upon subsequent examination, however, it appeared to be practicable, as it was clearly desirable, to comprise the whole in one volume, only dividing it in the delivery into two portions. The paging of the two portions therefore has been made continuous, and with this latter portion is given an Index to the whole, as well as a general Title-page, so as to meet the wishes of those who may prefer binding the entire series in one volume.

The tabular arrangement of the letters in chronological order has been made as accurate as possible; but as the dates have, in many instances, been omitted by the writers, it was necessary to resort to internal evidence, which has not in every case been so decisive as to exclude all doubt. It was originally intended, in this introduction, to give more extended notices of the writers of the letters, and of the principal characters therein mentioned, than have been afforded in the notes; which, it should be remembered, are simply added by way of illustration and confirmation of the facts and circumstances recorded in the correspondence. When, however, it was determined to confine the whole publication to a single volume, it became necessary to abandon that intention, which would have had the effect of swelling the volume to an inconvenient size, while the materials brought together would have been only a compilation from former writers well known and easily accessible.

A similar consideration has prevented the insertion in this volume of the Latin originals of the letters, which would have been attended with a serious increase of expense to the Society without a corresponding advantage to the great majority of the subscribers. Should it however appear to be the wish of any considerable number of the members of the Society, or others, to become possessed of them, the Council have determined to issue them in a small separate volume in return for an additional subscription of the lowest possible amount.

The editor cannot conclude his labours without offering a sincere tribute of affectionate regard to the memory of one by whose friendly encouragement he was induced to undertake them, and by whose judicious counsel he has been so abundantly aided during their progress. This sheet, indeed, that records the expression of grateful acknowledgement for the valuable assistance afforded to the editor by the late George Stokes, Esq., is almost the only one that has not derived benefit from that assistance: for while it was preparing for the press, it pleased God to remove him from the works and labours of love to which he had so long devoted his time, and talents, and money, and even health itself, in the service of this and other Societies, having for their object the advancement of divine truth. His energy in suggesting means of usefulness, his unwearied perseverance in carrying them into effect, his unostentatious industry, adorned and animated by christian principles, will endear his memory more especially to the members of the Parker Society, which was called into existence by his active and well-directed exertions, and sustained during the first period of that existence by his almost unassisted efforts.

GREAT WARLEY,
July 1, 1847.

CONTENTS.

LET.			PAGE
	John ab Ulmis		
CLXXXIV.	To H. Bullinger	Oxford, Ascension day, 1548	377
CLXXXV.	To the same	London, Aug. 18, 1548	379
CLXXXVI.	To the same	Oxford, Nov. 27, 1548	381
CLXXXVII.	To the same	[Oxford,] March 2, 1549	386
CLXXXVIII.	To the same	Oxford, Aug. 7, 1549	389
CLXXXIX.	To the same	London, Aug. 1549	392
CXC.	To the same	Westminster, Oct. 20, 1549.	395
CXCI.	To the same	Oxford, Jan. 31, 1550	396
CXCII.	To the same	Oxford, March 25, 1550.	398
CXCIII.	To the same	Oxford, April 30, 1550	402
CXCIV.	To the same	Oxford, May 28, 1550	408
CXCV.	To R. Gualter	Oxford, June 1, 1550.	410
CXCVI.	To H. Bullinger	Oxford, June 21, 1550	413
CXCVII.	To the same	Oxford, Aug. 22, 1550	414
CXCVIII.	To R. Gualter	Oxford, Nov. 5, 1550	418
CXCIX.	To H. Bullinger	Oxford, Nov. 11, 1550	421
CC.	To R. Gualter	Oxford, Nov. 26, 1550	424
CCI.	To H. Bullinger	Oxford, Dec. 31, 1550	425
CCII.	To the same	London, March, 1551	428
CCIII.	To the same	Bradgate, May 29, 1551	429
CCIV.	To C. Pellican	Bradgate, May 29, 1551	431
CCV.	To R. Gualter	Bradgate, May 29, 1551	434
CCVI.	To H. Bullinger	Bradgate, July 12, 1551	436
CCVII.	To the same	Oxford, Nov. 7, 1551	437
CCVIII.	To the same	Oxford, Dec. 4, 1551	437
CCIX.	To the same	Oxford, Jan. 10, 1552	443
CCX.	To the same	Oxford, Feb. 5, 1552	446
CCXI.	To the same	Oxford, Feb. 8, 1552	448
CCXII.	To the same	Oxford, March 1, 1552	450
CCXIII.	To C. Pellican	Oxford, before June 19, 1552	451
CCXIV.	To H. Bullinger	Oxford, July 7, 1552	452
CCXV.	To the same	Oxford, July 27, 1552	454
CCXVI.	To the same	Oxford, Aug. 9, 1552	455
CCXVII.	To the same	Oxford, Aug. 16, 1552	457
	Conrad ab Ulmis		
CCXVIII.	To R. Gualter	Oxford, Aug. 10, 1551	458
CCXIX.	To John Wolfius	Oxford, March 1, 1552	459
	John Stumphius		
CCXX.	To H. Bullinger	Oxford, May, 1549	460
CCXXI.	To the same	Oxford, Jan. 29, 1550	462

LET.			PAGE
	John Stumphius		
CCXXII.	To H. Bullinger	Oxford, Feb. 28, 1550	464
CCXXIII.	To the same	s. l. June 1, 1550	466
CCXXIV.	To the same	Oxford, Nov. 12, 1550	467
	Peter Martyr		
CCXXV.	To Martin Bucer	Oxford, Dec. 26, 1548	468
CCXXVI.	To the same	Oxford, Jan. 22, 1549	474
CCXXVII.	To H. Bullinger	Oxford, Jan. 27, 1550	477
CCXXVIII.	To the same	Oxford, June 1, 1550	481
CCXXIX.	To R. Gualter	Oxford, June 1, 1550	484
CCXXX.	To H. Bullinger	Oxford, Jan. 28, 1551	486
CCXXXI.	To C. Hubert	Oxford, March 8, 1551	490
CCXXXII.	To H. Bullinger	Oxford, April 25, 1551	493
CCXXXIII.	To the same	Oxford, Aug. 6, 1551	496
CCXXXIV.	To the same	Oxford, Oct. 26, 1551	498
CCXXXV.	To R. Gualter	Lambeth, March 6, 1552	501
CCXXXVI.	To H. Bullinger	[Lambeth], March 8, 1552	503
CCXXXVII.	To the same	Strasburgh, Nov. 3, 1553	505
CCXXXVIII.	To the same	Strasburgh, Dec. 15, 1553	507
CCXXXIX.	To the same	Strasburgh, Jan. 22, 1554	510
CCXL.	To the same	Strasburgh, Feb. 24, 1554	512
CCXLI.	To the same	Strasburgh, April 3, 1554	515
CCXLII.	To the same	Strasburgh, Dec. 31, 1555	516
CCXLIII.	To J. Wolfius	Strasburgh, Feb. 18, 1556	519
	Martin Bucer		
CCXLIV.	To Archbishop Cranmer	Strasburgh, Oct. 23, 1538	520
CCXLV.	To the same	Strasburgh, Oct. 29, 1539	526
CCXLVI.	To the same	Strasburgh, Sept. 3, 1548	531
CCXLVII.	To the same	Strasburgh, Dec. 23, 1548	533
CCXLVIII.	To Ministers of Strasburgh	Lambeth, April 26, 1549	534
CCXLIX.	To J. Sturmius	Lambeth, May 30, 1549	537
CCL.	To A. Hardenberg	London, Aug. 14, 1549	538
CCLI.	To Edm. Allen	Lambeth, Aug. 27, 1549	541
CCLII.	To John Brentius	Cambridge, May 15, 1550	542
CCLIII.	To John Calvin	Cambridge, s. m. 1550	545
CCLIV.	To Ministers of Strasburgh	Cambridge, Dec. 26, 1550	549
CCLV.	Œcolampadius to Zuinglius	s. l. Aug. 20, 1531	551
	Simon Grynæus		
CCLVI.	To Martin Bucer	s. l. Sept. 10, 1531	552
CCLVII.	To K. Henry VIII.	s. l. Sept. 10, 1531	554
CCLVIII.	Melancthon to Bucer	s. l. Nov. 8, 1531	556
	Martin Micronius		
CCLIX.	To H. Bullinger	London, Sept. 30, 1549	557
CCLX.	To the same	London, May 20, 1550	558
CCLXI.	To the same	London, May 28, 1550	562
CCLXII.	To the same	London, June 4, 1550	564
CCLXIII.	To the same	London, Aug. 28, 1550	566
CCLXIV.	To the same	London, Oct. 13, 1550	570
CCLXV.	To the same	London, Aug. 14, 1551	574
CCLXVI.	To the same	London, Nov. 7, 1551	577

LET.			PAGE
	Martin Micronius		
CCLXVII.	To H. Bullinger	London, March 9, 1552	578
CCLXVIII.	To the same	London, Feb. 18, 1553	581
	John Utenhovius		
CCLXIX.	To H. Bullinger	Strasburgh, July 7, 1549	583
CCLXX.	To the same	London, April 9, 1551	584
CCLXXI.	To the same	London, Aug. 14, 1551	588
CCLXXII.	To the same	London, March 9, 1552	589
CCLXXIII.	To the same	London, Oct. 12, 1552	591
CCLXXIV.	To the same	London, June 7, 1553	592
CCLXXV.	To the same	Basle, March 1, 1554	595
CCLXXVI.	To the same	Wladislaw, June 23, 1557	596
CCLXXVII.	W. Peterson to C. Pulbert	s. l. et a.	604
CCLXXVIII.	J. Finch to C. Humpard	s. l. et a.	605
	Nicolas Partridge		
CCLXXIX.	To H. Bullinger	Frankfort, April 12, 1538	608
CCLXXX.	To the same	Frankfort, Sept. 17, 1538	610
CCLXXXI.	To the same	[Dover], Feb. 26, 1540	614
CCLXXXII.	Robert Barnes to John Æpinus	London, May 21, 1540	616
	Nicolas Eliot		
CCLXXXIII.	To H. Bullinger	s. l. Aug. 21, 1538	617
CCLXXXIV.	To the same	s. l. et a.	619
	John Butler		
CCLXXXV.	To John Calvin	s. l. about 1537	621
CCLXXXVI.	To H. Bullinger	s. l. et a.	623
CCLXXXVII.	To C. Pellican	London, March 8, 1539	624
CCLXXXVIII.	To H. Bullinger	Basle, Feb. 24, 1540	627
CCLXXXIX.	To the same	Basle, March 29, 1540	628
CCXC.	To the same	Basle, April 4, 1540	629
CCXCI.	To the same	[Basle], May, 1540	631
CCXCII.	To the same	Basle, Nov. 10, 1542	632
CCXCIII.	To Thomas Blaurer	[Winterthur], Feb. 16, 1550	635
	John Burcher		
CCXCIV.	To R. Gualter.	Basle, s. m. [1540]	637
CCXCV.	To H. Bullinger	Strasburgh, Dec. 31, 1546	638
CCXCVI.	To the same	Strasburgh, Jan. 30, 1548	640
CCXCVII.	To the same	Strasburgh, Aug. 24, 1548	641
CCXCVIII.	To the same	Strasburgh, Oct. 29, 1548	642
CCXCIX.	To the same	Strasburgh, Jan. 22, 1549	644
CCC.	To the same	Strasburgh, Jan. 28, 1549	646
CCCI.	To the same	Strasburgh, Feb. 15, 1549	647
CCCII.	To the same	Strasburgh, March 12, 1549	649
CCCIII.	To the same	Strasburgh, April 1, 1549	650
CCCIV.	To the same	Strasburgh, May 30, 1549	651
CCCV.	To the same	Strasburgh, June 1, 1549	653
CCCVI.	To the same	Strasburgh, Aug. 25, 1549	654
CCCVII.	To the same	Strasburgh, Sept. 1, 1549	656
CCCVIII.	To the same	Strasburgh, Sept. 25, 1549	657
CCCIX.	To the same	Strasburgh, Oct. 16, 1549	658
CCCX.	To the same	Strasburgh, Dec. 12, 1549	660

LET.			PAGE
	John Burcher		
CCCXI.	To H. Bullinger	Strasburgh, April 20, 1550	662
CCCXII.	To the same	Strasburgh, June 8, 1550	665
CCCXIII.	To the same	Strasburgh, July 10, 1550	667
CCCXIV.	To the same	Strasburgh, Aug. 10, 1550	668
CCCXV.	To the same	Strasburgh, Sept. 1, 1550	670
CCCXVI.	To the same	Frankfort, Sept. 14, 1550	671
CCCXVII.	To the same	Strasburgh, Nov. 21, 1550	672
CCCXVIII.	To the same	Strasburgh, Dec. 28, 1550	674
CCCXIX.	To the same	Strasburgh, Jan. 6, 1551	675
CCCXX.	To the same	Strasburgh, Jan. 21, 1551	676
CCCXXI.	To the same	Strasburgh, Aug. 3, 1551	677
CCCXXII.	To the same	Strasburgh, Aug. 10, 1551	680
CCCXXIII.	To the same	Strasburgh, May 1, 1553	681
CCCXXIV.	To the same	Strasburgh, July 8, 1553	683
CCCXXV.	To the same	Strasburgh, Aug. 16, 1553	684
CCCXXVI.	To the same	Strasburgh, March 3, 1554	685
CCCXXVII.	To the same	Strasburgh, Sept. 3, 1554	686
CCCXXVIII.	To the same	Pinczov, Nov. 4, 1557	687
CCCXXIX.	To the same	Cracow, Feb. 16, 1558	689
CCCXXX.	To the same	Cracow, March 1, 1558	693
CCCXXXI.	To the same	Cracow, March 16, 1558	695
CCCXXXII.	To the same	Cracow, Oct. 27, 1558	698
CCCXXXIII.	To the same	Cracow, Nov. 30, 1558	701
	John Calvin		
CCCXXXIV.	To lady Anne Seymour	Geneva, July 15, 1549	702
CCCXXXV.	To the Protector Somerset	s. l. et a.	704
CCCXXXVI.	To king Edward VI	Geneva, Jan. 1, 1551	707
CCCXXXVII.	To Thomas Cranmer	s. l. et a.	711
CCCXXXVIII.	To K. Edward VI	Geneva, July 4, 1552	714
CCCXXXIX.	To Lord John Grey	s. l. et a.	715
CCCXL.	Council of Berne to Edward VI.	Berne, Dec. 14, 1549	717
	Christopher Froschover		
CCCXLI.	To H. Bullinger	Oxford, Nov. 19, 1550	719
CCCXLII.	To R. Gualter	Oxford, Feb. 21, 1551	721
CCCXLIII.	To the same	Oxford, May 28, 1551	723
CCCXLIV.	To the same	London, Aug. 12, 1551	725
CCCXLV.	To H. Bullinger	s. l. et a.	727
	Francis Bourgoyne		
CCCXLVI.	To John Calvin	London, Dec. 4, 1550	730
CCCXLVII.	To the same	London, Jan. 22, 1552	731
CCCXLVIII.	Valerandus Pollanus to Calvin	London, March 7, 1552	737
	Henry Bullinger		
CCCXLIX.	To John Burcher	Zurich, June 28, 1549	739
CCCL.	To Theodore Beza	Zurich, Aug. 30, 1553	741
CCCLI.	To John Calvin	Zurich, Oct. 15, 1553.	742
CCCLII.	To the same	Zurich, March 26, 1554	743
CCCLIII.	To certain Englishmen	Zurich, Aug. 24, 1554	747
CCCLIV.	To John Calvin	[Zurich], Sept. 9, 1554	750
CCCLV.	To the same	s. l. et a.	751

LET.		PAGE
CCCLVI.	R. Horn, &c. to Magistrates of Zurich .... 1554. ...	751
CCCLVII.	Richard Cox, &c. to J. Calvin ......Frankfort, April 5, 1555. ...	753
	David Whitehead, &c.	
CCCLVIII.	To John Calvin ....Frankfort, Sept. 20, 1555....	755
CCCLIX.	To Henry Bullinger ....Frankfort, Sept. 17, 1557....	763
	William Whittingham	
CCCLX.	To John Calvin ....Frankfort, March 25, 1555 .	764
CCCLXI.	To the same ....Frankfort, Sept. 21, 1555...	766
CCCLXII.	John Foxe to Boniface Amerbach...Basle, Nov. 25, 1556.........	767
CCCLXIII.	Chr. Goodman to P. Martyr.........Geneva, Aug. 20, 1558......	768

APPENDIX.

Account of Certain English Martyrs. 1555. 772
The Latin Original of Letter LIV. p. 114. 774

THE

LETTERS IN THIS SERIES

ARRANGED IN CHRONOLOGICAL ORDER.

The capitals affixed to the titles in the following list indicate the sources from which the transcripts of the original documents were procured.

A denoting the Archives at Zurich.
L ....the City Library at ditto.
S. C. ....the Simler Collection.
Str. ....the Library at Strasburgh.
St Gall ......, Geneva ......, Zofingen ... } the respective libraries in those places.

1531.

LET.				PAGE
CCLV.	Œcolampadius to Zuinglius	Aug. 20	A.	551
CCLVI.	Simon Grynæus to Bucer	Sept. 10	Str.	552
CCLVII.	The same to Henry VIII	Sept. 10	Str.	554
CCLVIII.	Melancthon to Bucer	Nov. 8	Zofingen.	556

1537.

CCLXXXV.	Butler to Calvin		Geneva.	621
CCXLIV.	Bucer to Cranmer	Oct. 23	Str.	520
VII.	Cranmer to Vadian	s. m.	S. C.	11
VIII.	The same to Capito	s. m.	A.	15
CCLXXXVI.	Butler to Bullinger	s. m.	A.	623

1538.

CCLXXIX.	Partridge to Bullinger	April 12	A.	608
CCLXXXIII.	Eliot to the same	Aug. 21	A.	617
CCLXXXIV.	The same to the same	s. m.	A.	619
CCLXXX.	Partridge to the same	Sept 17	A.	610
CCLXXVII.	Peterson to Pulbert	s. m.	Str.	604
CCLXXVIII.	Finch to Humpard	s. m.	Str.	605

1539.

CCLXXXVII.	Butler to Pellican	March 8	A.	624
CCXLV.	Bucer to Cranmer	Oct. 29	Str.	526

1540.

LET.				PAGE
CXLVIII.	Traheron to Bullinger	Feb. 20	A.	316
CCLXXXVIII.	Butler to the same	Feb. 24	A.	627
CCLXXXI.	Partridge to the same	Feb. 26	A.	614
CCLXXXIX.	Butler to the same	March 29	A.	628
CCXC.	The same to the same	April 4	A.	629
CCXCI.	The same to the same	May	A.	631
CCLXXXII.	Barnes to Æpinus	May 21	S. C.	616
CIV.	Hilles to Bullinger	Aug.	A.	196
CCXCIV.	Burcher to Gualter	s. m.	L.	637

1541.

CV.	Hilles to Bullinger	s. m.	A.	200
CVI.	The same to the same	Sept. 18	A.	216
CVII.	The same to the same	Nov. 23	A.	222

1542.

CVIII.	Hilles to Bullinger	May 10	A.	224
CCXCII.	Butler to the same	Nov. 10	A.	632
CIX.	Hilles to the same	Dec. 18	A.	228

1543.

CX.	Hilles to Bullinger	March 24	A.	239
CLXXV.	Warner to the same	July 8	A.	355
CXI.	Hilles to the same	Sept. 26	A.	240
CXII.	The same to the same	Nov. 15	L.	242

1544.

CXIII.	Hilles to Bullinger	Sept. 26	A.	244

1545.

CXIV.	Hilles to Bullinger	April 15	A.	246

1546.

XXI.	Hooper to Bullinger	Jan. 27	A.	33
CXV.	Hilles to the same	Jan. 28	A.	250
CXLIX.	Traheron to the same	Before Feb. 18.	A.	317
XCVI.	Hilles to the same	April 30	A.	252
XXII.	Hooper to the same	s. m.	A.	38
XXIII.	The same to the same	s. m.	L.	40
CCXCV.	Burcher to the same	Dec. 31	A.	638

1547.

LET.				PAGE
CLXXVI.	Knight to Bullinger	Jan. 23	A.	357
CXVII.	Hilles to the same	Jan. 26	A.	255
CXVIII.	The same to the same	Feb. 25	A.	257
CXIX.	The same to the same	May 19	A.	259
XXIV.	Hooper to the same	s. m.	A.	43

1548.

LET.				PAGE
CCXCVI.	Burcher to Bullinger	Jan 30	A.	640
XIX.	Coverdale to Calvin	March 26	Geneva.	31
CLXXXIV.	John ab Ulmis to Bullinger	Ascension day.	A.	377
CXX.	Hilles to Bullinger	June 18	A.	261
XXV.	Hooper to Bucer	June 19	A.	44
IX.	Cranmer to à Lasco	July 4	S. C.	16
CLXI.	Ochinus to Musculus	July 17	S. C.	334
X.	Cranmer to Hardenberg	July 28	S. C.	18
CL.	Traheron to Bullinger	Aug. 1	A.	319
CLXXXV.	John ab Ulmis to the same	Aug. 18	L.	379
CCXCVII.	Burcher to the same	Aug. 24	A.	641
CCXLVI.	Bucer to Cranmer	Sept. 3	Str.	531
CLI.	Traheron to Bullinger	Sept. 28	A.	321
XI.	Cranmer to Bucer	Oct. 2	S. C.	19
XX.	Coverdale to Fagius	Oct. 21	Str.	32
CCXCVIII.	Burcher to Bullinger	Oct. 29	A.	642
LXII.	Oglethorp to the same	Oct. 30	A.	124
CLXXXVI.	John ab Ulmis to the same	Nov. 27	A.	381
CLXII.	Ochinus to Musculus	Dec. 23	S. C.	336
CCXLVII.	Bucer to Cranmer	Dec. 23	Str.	533
CCXXV.	Martyr to Bucer	Dec. 26	S. C.	468
CLII.	Traheron to Bullinger	Dec. 31	A.	322

1549.

LET.				PAGE
CCXCIX.	Burcher to Bullinger	Jan. 22	A.	644
CCXXVI.	Martyr to Bucer	Jan. 22	S. C.	474
CCC.	Burcher to Bullinger	Jan. 28	A.	646
XII.	Cranmer to Melancthon	Feb. 10	S. C.	21
CCCI.	Burcher to Bullinger	Feb. 15	A.	647
CLXXXVII.	John ab Ulmis to the same	March 2	L.	386
CCCII.	Burcher to the same	March 12	A.	649
CLXIII.	Musculus to the same	March 12	A.	336
CLVII.	Alexander to Fagius	March 24	Str.	329
CLXX.	Dryander to Bullinger	March 25	A.	348
XXVI.	Hooper to the same	March 28	A.	48

LET.				PAGE
XXVII.	Hooper to Bullinger	March 31	L.	50
CCCIII.	Burcher to the same	April 1	A.	650
XXVIII.	Hooper to the same	April 8	A.	51
XXIX.	The same to the same	April 14	A.	55
CLVIII.	Fagius to Ulstetter	April 18	Str.	331
CLIX.	The same to the same	April 26	Str.	332
CCXLVIII.	Bucer to ministers of Strasburgh	April 26	Str.	534
XXX.	Hooper to Bullinger	April 26	A.	57
XXXI.	The same to the same	May 3	L.	62
CLX.	Fagius to Hubert	May 7	Str.	333
CCXLIX.	Bucer to Sturmius	May 30	Str.	537
CCCIV.	Burcher to Bullinger	May 30	A.	651
CCXX.	Stumphius to the same	s. m.	A.	460
XXXII.	Hooper to the same	May 31	A.	64
CCCV.	Burcher to the same	June 1	A.	653
CXXI.	Hilles to the same	June 4	A.	265
CLXXI.	Dryander to the same	June 5	A.	350
CLXXII.	The same to Vadian	June 5	St. Gall.	352
XXXIII.	Hooper to Bullinger	June 25	A.	65
CCCXLIX.	Bullinger to Burcher	June 28	Str.	739
CCLXIX.	Utenhovius to Bullinger	July 7	A.	583
II.	Lady Jane Seymour to Bucer	June 12	Str.	2
CCCXXXIV.	Calvin to lady Anne Seymour	July 15	Geneva.	702
XXXIV.	Hooper to Stumphius	Aug. 1	L.	67
CLXXXVIII.	John ab Ulmis to Bullinger	Aug. 7	A.	389
CCL.	Bucer to Hardenberg	Aug. 14	Str.	528
CCCVI.	Burcher to Bullinger	Aug. 25	A.	654
CCLI.	Bucer to Allen	Aug. 27	Str.	541
CLXXXIX.	John ab Ulmis to Bullinger	Aug.	A.	392
CCCVII.	Burcher to the same	Sept. 1	A.	656
CCCVIII.	The same to the same	Sept. 25	A.	657
CCLIX.	Micronius to the same	Sept. 30	L.	557
CCCIX.	Burcher to the same	Oct. 16	A.	658
I.	Edward VI. to Senate of Zurich	Oct. 20	A.	1
CXC.	John ab Ulmis to Bullinger	Oct. 20	A.	395
LVIII.	Cox to the same	Oct. 22	A.	119
XXXV.	Hooper to the same	Nov. 7	A.	69
CXXII.	Hilles to the same	Nov. 17	A.	267
CLXXIII.	Dryander to the same	Dec. 3	A.	353
CLXVII.	Byrchman to the same	Dec. 10	A.	344
CCCX.	Burcher to the same	Dec. 12	A.	660
CCCXL.	Council of Berne to Edward VI	Dec. 14	A.	717
XXXVI.	Hooper to Bullinger	Dec. 27	A.	71
CCCXLV.	Anonymous to the same	s. m. et a.	A.	727

1550.

LET.				PAGE
CXLVI.	Skinner to Bullinger	Jan. 5	A.	313
CCXXVII.	Martyr to the same	Jan. 27	A.	477
CCXXI.	Stumphius to the same	Jan. 29	A.	462
CXCI.	John ab Ulmis to the same	Jan. 31	L.	396
XXXVII.	Hooper to the same	Feb. 5	A.	74
CCCXXXV.	Calvin to the Protector Somerset	s. a.	Geneva.	704
CLXIV.	Peter of Perugia to Bullinger	Feb. 10	A.	338
CCXCIII.	Butler to Blaurer	Feb. 16	St. Gall.	635
CCXXII.	Stumphius to Bullinger	Feb. 28	A.	464
XCVIII.	Hales to Gualter	March 4	L.	184
CXCII.	John ab Ulmis to Bullinger	March 25	A.	398
XXXVIII.	Hooper to the same	March 27	A.	78
CCCXI.	Burcher to the same	April 20	A.	662
CXCIII.	John ab Ulmis to the same	April 30	A.	402
CCLII.	Bucer to Brentius	May 15	Basle.	542
CCLX.	Micronius to Bullinger	May 20	A.	558
CCLIII.	Bucer to Calvin	s. m.	Geneva.	545
XCIX.	Hales to Gualter	May 24	A.	186
CCLXI.	Micronius to Bullinger	May 28	A.	562
CXCIV.	John ab Ulmis to the same	May 28	A.	408
CXCV.	The same to Gualter	June 1	L.	410
CCXXIII.	Stumphius to Bullinger	June 1	A.	466
CCXXVIII.	Martyr to the same	June 1	A.	481
CCXXIX.	The same to Gualter	June 1	S. C.	484
CCLXII.	Micronius to Bullinger	June 4	A.	564
CCCXII.	Burcher to the same	June 8	A.	665
CLIII.	Traheron to the same	June 12	A.	323
C.	Hales to the same	June 12	A.	188
CXCVI.	John ab Ulmis to the same	June 21	A.	413
CXXIII.	Hilles to the same	June 25	A.	268
XXXIX.	Hooper to the same	June 29	A.	86
CCCXIII.	Burcher to the same	July 10	A.	667
CCCXIV.	The same to the same	Aug. 10	A.	668
CXCVII.	John ab Ulmis to the same	Aug. 22	A.	414
CCLXIII.	Micronius to the same	Aug. 28	A.	566
CCCXV.	Burcher to the same	Sept. 1	A.	670
CCCXVI.	The same to the same	Sept. 14	A.	671
CCLXIV.	Micronius to the same	Oct. 13	A.	570
LIX.	Cox to the same	Nov. 1	A.	120
CXCVIII.	John ab Ulmis to Gualter	Nov. 5	L.	418
CXCIX.	The same to Bullinger	Nov. 11	A.	421
CCXXIV.	Stumphius to the same	Nov. 12	A.	467
CCCXLI.	Froschover to the same	Nov. 19	L.	719

LET.				PAGE
CCCXVII.	Burcher to Bullinger	Nov. 21	A.	672
CC.	John ab Ulmis to Gualter	Nov. 26	L.	424
CCCXLVI.	F. Bourgoyne to Calvin	Dec. 4	Geneva.	730
CI.	Hales to Bullinger	Dec. 10	A.	189
CCLIV.	Bucer to ministers of Strasburgh	Dec. 26	Str.	549
CCCXVIII.	Burcher to Bullinger	Dec. 28	A.	674
CCI.	John ab Ulmis to the same	Dec. 31	A.	425

1551.

LET.				PAGE
CCCXXXVI.	Calvin to Edward VI	Jan. 1	Geneva.	707
CCCXIX.	Burcher to Bullinger	Jan. 6	A.	675
CCCXX.	The same to the same	Jan. 21	A.	676
CII.	Hales to Gualter	s. m.	L.	191
CIII.	The same to the same	Jan. 26	L.	195
CCXXX.	Martyr to Bullinger	Jan. 28	Str.	486
CCCXLII.	Froschover to Gualter	Feb. 21	L.	721
CCII.	John ab Ulmis to Bullinger	March	A.	428
CCXXXI.	Martyr to Hubert	March 8	Str.	490
CXXIV.	Hilles to Bullinger	March 22	A.	271
XLIX.	Anne Hooper to the same	April 3	A.	107
CCLXX.	Utenhovius to the same	April 9	A.	584
CCXXXII.	Martyr to the same	April 25	A.	493
LX.	Cox to the same	May 5	A.	121
CCCXLIII.	Froschover to Gualter	May 28	L.	723
CXXVI.	Aylmer to Bullinger	May 29	A.	275
CXXVIII.	Haddon to the same	May 29	A.	279
CCIII.	John ab Ulmis to the same	May 29	A.	429
CCIV.	The same to Pellican	May 29	L.	431
CCV.	The same to Gualter	May 29	L.	434
CLXXVII.	Masters to the same	June 14	L.	358
CCVI.	John ab Ulmis to Bullinger	July 12	A.	436
IV.	Lady Jane Grey to the same	July 12	A	4
XL.	Hooper to the same	Aug. 1	A.	91
CCCXXI.	Burcher to the same	Aug. 3	A.	677
CCXXXIII.	Martyr to the same	Aug. 6	A.	496
CCXVIII.	Conrad ab Ulmis to Gualter	Aug. 10	L.	458
CCCXXII.	Burcher to Bullinger	Aug. 10	A.	680
CCCXLIV.	Froschover to Gualter	Aug. 12	L.	725
CCLXXI.	Utenhovius to Bullinger	Aug. 14	A.	588
CCLXV.	Micronius to the same	Aug. 14	A.	574
CXLIV.	Harding to the same	Oct. 19	A.	309
CCXXXIV.	Martyr to the same	Oct. 26	A.	498
XLI.	Hooper to the same	Oct. 27	A.	95
XLII.	The same to Stumphius	Oct. 27	L.	98

LET.				PAGE
L.	Anne Hooper to Bullinger	Oct. 27	A.	108
CCLXVI.	Micronius to the same	Nov. 7	A.	577
CCVII.	John ab Ulmis to the same	Nov. 7	A.	437
CCVIII.	The same to the same	Dec. 4	A.	437
III.	Duke of Suffolk to the same	Dec. 21	A.	3
CXXVII.	Aylmer to the same	Dec. 23	A.	277
CXXIX.	Haddon to the same	Dec. 28	A.	280
CLXXIX.	Parker to Hubert, &c.	s. m.		361

1552.

LET.				PAGE
LXXVI.	Lever to Ascham	s. m.	Geneva.	150
CCIX.	John ab Ulmis to Bullinger	Jan. 10	A.	443
CCCXLVII.	Bourgoyne to Calvin	Jan. 22	Geneva.	731
CCX.	John ab Ulmis to Bullinger	Feb. 5	A.	446
CCXI.	The same to the same	Feb. 8	A.	448
CCXII.	The same to the same	March 1	A.	450
CCXIX.	Conrad ab Ulmis to Wolfius	March 1	L.	459
CCXXXV.	Martyr to Gualter	March 6	L.	501
CCCXLVIII.	Pollanus to Calvin	March 7	Geneva.	737
CXXXVI.	Martyr to Bullinger	March 8	A.	503
CCLXVII.	Micronius to the same	March 9	A.	578
CCLXXII.	Utenhovius to the same	March 9	A.	589
XIII.	Cranmer to the same	March 20	A.	22
XIV.	The same to Calvin	March 20	A.	24
CCCXXXVII.	Calvin to Cranmer	s. m.	S. C.	711
XV.	Cranmer to Melancthon	March 27	A.	25
CLXXX.	Bucer's widow to Cranmer	s. m.	Str.	363
XVI.	Cranmer to Bucer's widow	April 20	Str.	27
XVII.	The same to Hubert	April 20	Str.	28
CLXXIV.	Dryander to Bullinger	May 2	A.	354
CXLVII.	Willock to the same	May 12	A.	314
CLXXVIII.	Bernher to the same	May 31	A.	360
CCXIII.	John ab Ulmis to Pellican	s. m.	L.	451
CCCXXXVIII.	Calvin to King Edward VI	July 4	Geneva.	714
CCXIV.	John ab Ulmis to Bullinger	July 7	A.	452
V.	Lady Jane Grey to the same	July 7	L.	7
CCXV.	John ab Ulmis to the same	July 27	A.	454
CCXVI.	The same to the same	Aug. 9	A.	455
CCXVII.	The same to the same	Aug. 16	A.	457
CXXX.	Haddon to the same	Aug.	A.	281
CLIV.	Traheron to the same	Sept. 10	A.	324
CXLV.	Sidall to the same	Oct. 4	A.	311
CXXXI.	Haddon to the same	s. m.	A.	288

LET.				PAGE
LXI.	Cox to Bullinger	Oct. 5	A.	123
CCLXXIII.	Utenhovius to the same	Oct. 12	A.	591
CLXV.	Norton to Calvin	Nov. 13	Geneva.	339

1553.

LET.				PAGE
CCLXVIII.	Micronius to Bullinger	Feb. 18	A.	581
XLIII.	Hooper to the same	Feb. 28	A.	99
CCCXXIII.	Burcher to the same	May 1	A.	681
VI.	Lady Jane Grey to the same	s. m.	L.	9
CLV.	Traheron to the same	June 3	A.	326
LXXI.	Cheke to the same	June 7	A.	140
CCLXXIV.	Utenhovius to the same	June 7	A.	592
CLXXXI.	Chelius to Parker	June 20	Str.	364
CCCXXIV.	Burcher to Bullinger	July 8	A.	683
CXXV.	Hilles to the same	July 9	A.	272
CCCXXV.	Burcher to the same	Aug. 16	A.	684
CCCL.	Bullinger to Beza	Aug. 30	A.	741
XLIV.	Hooper to Bullinger	Sept. 3	A.	100
CCCLI.	Bullinger to Calvin	Oct. 15	Geneva.	742
CCXXXVII.	Martyr to Bullinger	Nov. 3	A.	505
CLXXXII.	Julius to J. ab Ulmis	Nov. 20	A.	365
XLV.	Hooper to J. à Lasco	Nov. 25	S. C.	101
CXXXII.	Haddon to Bullinger	Nov. 30	A.	290
CCXXXVIII.	Martyr to the same	Dec. 15	A.	507
CLXVI.	Massarius to the same	Dec. 21	A.	342
CLVI.	Traheron to Calvin	s. a.	Geneva.	328

1554.

LET.				PAGE
CCXXXIX.	Martyr to Bullinger	Jan. 22	A.	510
CCXL.	The same to the same	Feb. 24	A.	512
CCLXXV.	Utenhovius to the same	March 1	A.	595
CCCXXVI.	Burcher to the same	March 3	A.	685
CXLI.	Banks to the same	March 15	A.	303
CCCLII.	Bullinger to Calvin	March 26	A.	743
CCXLI.	Martyr to Bullinger	April 3	A.	515
CCCLVI.	Horn to the magistrates of Zurich	s. m.	A.	751
LXXVII.	Lever to Bullinger	April 11	A.	153
LI.	Anne Hooper to the same	April 20	A.	110
LXXVIII.	Lever to the same	April 23	A.	155
XLVI.	Hooper to the same	May 23	A.	102
XLVII.	The same to the same	May 29	A.	103
LXXIX.	Lever to the same	June 28	A.	156
CXXXIII.	Haddon to the same	July 9	A.	291

LET.				PAGE
CCCLIII.	Bullinger to certain Englishmen	Aug. 24	A.	747
CXXXIV.	Haddon to Bullinger	Aug. 31	A.	292
CCCXXVII.	Burcher to the same	Sept. 3	A.	686
CCCLIV.	Bullinger to Calvin	Sept. 9	A.	750
LII.	Anne Hooper to Bullinger	Sept. 22	A.	111
LIII.	The same to the same	Nov. 12	A.	112
CCCXXXIX.	Calvin to Lord J. Grey	Nov. 13	Geneva.	715
CLXVIII.	Salkyns to Bullinger	Nov. 26	A.	345
CXLII.	Banks to the same	Dec. 9		306
CXXXV.	Haddon to the same	Dec. 9	A.	294
XLVIII.	Hooper to the same	Dec. 11	A.	104
CLXIX.	Salkyns to the same	Dec. 29	A.	346

1555.

LET.				PAGE
XVIII.	Cranmer to Martyr	s. d.	S. C.	29
CXXXVI.	Haddon to Bullinger	Jan. 8	A.	297
CXLIII.	Banks to the same	Jan. 9	A.	308
CXXXVII.	Haddon to the same	Jan. 15	A.	298
LXXX.	Lever to the same	Jan. 17	A.	157
LXXXI.	The same to the same	Feb. 12	A.	159
LXXXVIII.	Sampson to Calvin	Feb. 23	A.	170
CCCLX.	Whittingham to the same	March 25	Geneva.	764
CCCLVII.	Cox and others to the same	April 5	Geneva.	753
LIV.	Anne Hooper to Bullinger	April 11	A.	114
LXXIV.	Morison to Calvin	April 17	Geneva.	147
CXXXVIII.	Haddon to Bullinger	April 24	A.	299
LXXXIX.	Sampson to the same	Aug. 6	A.	172
LXXV.	Morison to the same	Aug. 23	A.	148
CCCLVIII.	Whitehead, &c. to Calvin	Sept. 20	Geneva.	755
CCCLXI.	Whittingham to the same	Sept. 21	Geneva.	766
LXXII.	Cheke to Bullinger	Oct. 20	Geneva.	142
CXXXIX.	Haddon to the same	Dec. 7	A.	300
CCXLII.	Martyr to the same	Dec. 31	A.	516
CCCLV.	Bullinger to Calvin	s. m.	A.	751

1556.

LET.				PAGE
LXXXII.	Lever to Bullinger	Jan. 4	A.	160
LXIII.	Horn to Wolfius	Feb. 2	A.	125
LXIV.	The same to the Senate of Zurich	Feb. 3	L.	126
LXV.	The same to Bullinger	Feb. 3	A.	129
CCXLIII.	Martyr to Wolfius	Feb. 18	A.	519
LXXIII.	Cheke to Bullinger	March 12	A.	145
CXL.	Haddon to the same	March 12	A.	301

LET.				PAGE
XC.	Sampson to Bullinger	April 6	L.	173
LXVII.	Pilkington to Gualter	April 7	A.	134
LV.	Ponet to Bullinger	April 14	A.	115
LXXXIII.	Lever to the same	May 12	A.	162
LXVIII.	Pilkington to the same	June 27	A.	136
XCI.	Sampson to the same	s. d.	A.	175
LVI.	Ponet to the same	June	A.	117
XCII.	Sampson to the same	Aug. 12	A.	176
XCIII.	The same to the same	Sept. 13	L.	177
LXVI.	Horn to the same	Sept. 19	A.	131
XCIV.	Sampson to the same	Oct. 13	A.	179
CLXXXIII.	Reniger to the same	s. d.	A.	374
CCCLXII.	Foxe to Amerbach	Nov. 25	Basle.	767

1557.

LET.				PAGE
XCV.	Sampson to Bullinger	April 23	A.	180
LXIX.	Earl of Bedford to the same	April 26		138
LXXXIV.	Lever to Gualter	May 27	L.	163
CCLXXVI.	Utenhovius to Bullinger	June 23	A.	596
LVII.	Maria Ponet to the same	July 15	L.	118
LXXXVI.	Lever to Gualter	Aug. 11	L.	166
CCCLIX.	Whitehead, &c. to Bullinger	Sept. 17	Geneva.	763
LXXXV.	Lever to the same	Sept. 18	A.	165
LXXXVII.	The same to the same	Oct. 5	A.	169
CCCXXVIII.	Burcher to the same	Nov. 4	A.	687

1558.

LET.				PAGE
LXX.	Sir A. Cook to Martyr	Jan. 20	L.	139
CCCXXIX.	Burcher to Bullinger	Feb. 16	A.	689
CCCXXX.	The same to the same	March 1	A.	693
CCCXXXI.	The same to the same	March 16	A.	695
XCVI.	Sampson to Martyr	April 8	L.	181
XCVII.	The same to the same	July 10	L.	182
CCCLXIII.	Goodman to the same	Aug. 20	A.	768
CCCXXXII.	Burcher to Bullinger	Oct. 27	A.	698
CCCXXXIII.	The same to the same	Nov. 30	A.	701

LETTER CLXXXIV.[1]

JOHN AB ULMIS TO HENRY BULLINGER.

Dated at OXFORD, Ascension-day, 1548.

THAT I have not hitherto written to you, most learned and very dear sir, you must neither attribute to neglect, than which nothing can be farther from my wishes, nor to forgetfulness of your deserts towards me, the remembrance of which no time shall ever efface. It must be ascribed partly to my inability, in the short time that I have been residing at this place, to give you any intelligence either as to the state of England, or of my own individual concerns; and partly, because I was waiting to tell you of the result of your [letters of] commendation: so that if this intermission of my correspondence should excite your displeasure, which I do not however expect will be the case, I earnestly entreat you for the sake of your affectionate regard to me and of my respect to you that you will forgive me this once. And now, since the state of affairs is such, that I can furnish you with some certain and undoubted information, I am unwilling any longer to delay my correspondence.

You must know then that England, which I have entered under favourable auspices, but yet not without very great pecuniary expense, is adorned and enlightened by the word of God; and that the number of the faithful is daily increasing in vast multitudes more and more. The mass, that darling of the papists, is shaken, and in many places its condition corresponds with its name[2]; that is, by the best of rights, namely, a divine right, it is condemned, and with a safe conscience entirely abolished. The images too are extirpated root and branch in every part of England; nor is there left the least trace which can afford a hope or handle to the papists for confirming their error respecting images, and for leading away the people from our Saviour. Holy wedlock, too, is now free to the clergy[3], and sanctioned by the king himself. It has been proved by Peter Martyr to the great satisfaction

[1 The original of this letter is printed in Fueslin, p. 243.]

[2 Multis in locis jam missam factam esse missam. Orig.]

[3 The bill for allowing the marriage of the clergy was sent up to the lords, Dec. 13th, 1548, and was agreed to, Feb. 19th, 1549. Burnet, II. 141. The dates of some of these letters appear very uncertain.]

[of his hearers], both from the writings of the orthodox, as well as from the holy scriptures, that there is no other purgatory[1] than the cross to which we wretched beings are exposed in this life. He has also maintained in like manner the cause of the eucharist and holy supper of the Lord, namely, that it is a remembrance of Christ, and a solemn setting forth of his death, and not a sacrifice. Meanwhile, however, he speaks with caution and prudence (if indeed it can be called such) with respect to the real presence, so as not to seem to incline either to your opinion, or to that of Luther. But the public preachers for the most part openly and candidly confute, according to their ability, the notion of a carnal partaking [of the Lord's supper], and have brought over a considerable number to this their opinion. The Capernaites, papists, and this class of sarcophagists, are not sleeping, by whose weapons the truth is attacked; but, by the grace of God, it is never wounded; nay, rather they themselves are perishing miserably and pierced through by their own swords and sophisms. But enough of this.

I have nothing to write to you about the effect of your [letters of] commendation, except that Eliot has been long dead and gone to heaven; and that Traheron has either not yet returned[2], or else your letter has had but little weight with him. If therefore you should think proper to renew your introduction, which I greatly desire, I would wish you to write very earnestly respecting me; I mean, that you should commend me to him in very favourable terms: or, should not this seem good to you, I could wish, that since the opinion of all respecting me, as well as your own, is, I trust, exceedingly favourable, you would write a letter to the archbishop of Canterbury, who has a great regard for you, in which you might commend me to him by some testimony of your approbation. For you are not unacquainted with the exceeding narrowness of my circumstances, and in what solitude I am living in this place; so as when I put my foot out of doors, I do not meet a single individual who is known to me either personally or even by name: you are aware too of how much service you may be to me in this matter by your aid and exertions. I therefore most earnestly request and entreat

[1 See P. Martyr's Common Places, Part III. Ch. 9, p. 233.]
[2 See above, Letter CL. p. 321.]

you, by your love to Christ and regard for his church, that you will shew yourself compliant and ready to serve me in this respect: which favour should I obtain from you, I will endeavour with all my power so to conduct myself, that you may know that the obligation has been conferred by you upon one who is neither unmindful nor ungrateful.

I have nothing to write about this university, and the course of my own studies, except that it every where abounds with excellent and most agreeable writers, and is adorned with great numbers of men who are most distinguished in every kind of learning; and as to myself, that I can enjoy in this place to my heart's content both sacred and profane studies, with the entire liberty of a most delightful and honourable leisure; and indeed with the hope and opinion that the heads of my family will some time or other understand and acknowledge that I have not left Germany without sufficient reason. Farewell, then, and, if convenient, salute from me most affectionately in Christ masters Pellican, Theodore, Gualter, and Ammian, men of the greatest piety and learning, together with others who deserve so well of me; and desire them to ask of God to consecrate my studies solely with a view to his glory and the salvation of my soul. Farewell, my master, again and again, and continue to love me as you have begun. Dated at Oxford, in England, in the year of our Lord 1548, on the very day of the ascension of the Lord.

Your most attached pupil,
JOHN AB ULMIS.

LETTER CLXXXV.

JOHN AB ULMIS TO HENRY BULLINGER.

Dated at LONDON, *Aug.* 18, [1548].

As I am about to send you this Interim[3], I cannot do otherwise, very learned and dear sir, than write you some-

[3 Sir Philip Hoby, the king's ambassador to the emperor Charles V. at Augsburgh, wrote a letter to the protector, in July 1548, of the news then stirring in reference to religion; sending at the same time certain articles of the Interim to which the protestants would not agree. They are given in Strype, Mem. II. i. 175, and may possibly be referred to in the text.]

thing of a letter myself; though I really cannot tell what to write about, unless it be the commemoration of your kindness to me. And yet I think you must have long been tired of such commemoration: I am certainly ashamed at having so often laboured to express those thanks which my very thoughts are unable to comprehend; and I am afraid too of coming under the suspicion of flattery, as though this eulogistic mention of your favours were to be attributed rather to circumstances, than to a sense of duty. But must I then cease from mentioning them? What then can I write, or in what way can I shew that I am both mindful and grateful? This indeed I must do, and then will relate such news, should there be any, as it may be necessary for me to inform you of; for I am well assured that you cannot doubt of my manifesting towards you, even when absent, the duty, good-will, and respect that I owe you. I write indeed to some others yonder, even when I have no occasion to do so; but it is only to those who are connected with me by domestic ties or familiar intercourse; but I dare not interrupt by a very frequent correspondence a man of so much weight, dignity, and learning, as yourself, and one too, who is overwhelmed as it were in a sea of business. Do you, my master, love me, and farewell: for I exceedingly love and reverence you, and am well, and engaged to my great delight in literary pursuits, (than which I never accounted any thing more agreeable or more honourable,) and with this view, that my relatives may some time or other understand and be convinced, that I have not quitted Germany to no purpose. Dated in London, the noble metropolis of England, the third day after the festival of [the Assumption of] Mary. August.

After I had written this very short letter, lo! your letter was delivered to the archbishop of Canterbury, which I fully understand from master Peter Martyr that you had written to him with the greatest courtesy and respect. The first part, if I remember right, was a grave and learned admonition as to his episcopal duties; the remainder was a subtle transition to the eucharist. But, to tell you all in few words, although your letter (for it was constantly being copied) afforded pleasure to every one, and to the bishop himself a full and gratifying exhortation to his duty; yet I would have you know this for certain, that this Thomas has fallen into so heavy a slumber, that we entertain but a very cold hope that he will be aroused even by your most learned letter. For he has lately published a Catechism[1], in which he has not only approved that foul and sacrilegious transubstantiation of the papists in the holy supper of our Saviour, but all the dreams of Luther seem to him sufficiently well-grounded, perspicuous, and lucid[2]. Oh, how lamentable is it, and to be deplored in the discourse, letters, and records of every nation, that the flock of Christ are now-a-days surrounded by some persons with error; nor will any of those who are most influential both from learning and authority, boldly stand up against these herdsmen, that is, holzböcken, and send them into exile! Farewell again and again, and receive the salutation of your very loving friend in Christ, William Peterson.

Your most attached,

JOHN AB ULMIS. *Helvetius.*

LETTER CLXXXVI.

JOHN AB ULMIS TO HENRY BULLINGER.

Dated at OXFORD, *Nov.* 27, 1548.

THOUGH I never doubted, most learned and very dear sir, but that you still cherished the same regard for me when

[1 The title of this Catechism is: *A short Instruction into the Christian Religion; for the syngular commoditie and profite of children and young people. Set forth by the most Reverend Father in God, Thomas, Archbyshoppe of Canterbury.* It is said in the title page to be "overseen and corrected by the archbishop. It was written originally in German, and translated into Latin by Justus Jonas, junior, who was entertained in Cranmer's family." Strype, Mem. II. i. 51, Cranmer, 227. A letter from Burcher to Bullinger, dated Oct. 29, 1548, speaks of the discord occasioned by the publication of this Catechism, and that fightings frequently took place among the common people, even in sermon time, by reason of their diversity of opinion.]

[2 Cranmer indeed disclaimed this inference, maintaining that the language of the Catechism was to be understood spiritually: and it is remarkable that many of the strong expressions of the original were studiously softened in the translation, for the sake, as it appears, of admitting such a sense. Jenkyns' Pref. to Cranmer, p. LXXIX. See Soames, III. 69.]

absent, as you had entertained when I was present with you; yet I could not but rejoice exceedingly, when I understood from Augustine that this was the case: for he told me that such was the force and extent of your affection for me, that if he could have waited upon you before his departure, you had purposed to commend me to the archbishop of Canterbury by your favourable testimony in my behalf. How gratifying this would have been to me in this my time of difficulty and trial, I can neither express in words, nor in writing; nor, what is worse, even in thought. I should have considered indeed, and I beg you will give credit to my assertion, that a happier day had scarce shone upon me of a long time. But though Augustine, most unfortunately in my opinion, did not pass through Zurich, yet as I know you by experience to be endued with such equability and firmness of mind, as that you grant no favours as such, but with your singular judgment and uprightness are wont to consider, not what persons desire, but what is demanded by the nature of the case; I would have you know therefore, that such is my position in regard to my studies and condition of life, that unless you aid me by that your valuable commendation, I shall greatly fear that it will be all over with them. Traheron indeed, a good and learned man, has most readily afforded me his friendship and assistance; but in such a way, as that I not only think myself, but I am sure you will think with me, that but little provision appears to have been made for my studies; for he considers that it would be better for me to live entirely at court, where he informs me that he has already obtained for me a large and ample salary: but I repeat again and again, that this step cannot be taken without the greatest detriment to my studies. On you therefore rest all my hopes, as I am well assured of your power to aid me in this matter; for I well know your activity and diligence, as well as the weight and influence of your authority and advice, which if you will exert in this business, I shall consider you to have performed the duty of a real Christian. I entreat you again and again, by your singular good-will towards me, that should any thing occur to you, which may seem to be for my comfort and advantage, you will take it into your consideration and carry it into effect. I should write more at length, only that I do not doubt your favourable inclination to me, and that the thing speaks sufficiently for itself. Only bear in mind, that should I learn that my case has been undertaken by you at this time, you will some time derive great satisfaction from this your kind office; nor will it be the least of your praises, that you alone, out of all others, have brought me safe into harbour with the favourable gale of your commendation, when I was not only carried out to sea by the instrumentality of others, but was miserably forsaken in the very midst of the waves. But enough of this.

I have nothing to write respecting England, except that she is flourishing in all the glory of the gospel, and labouring and exerting herself that she may daily and unceasingly be delivered from all wickedness and error. The general council, which they call a parliament[1], is assembled, and begun, but not yet finished. I will send you by the first opportunity a careful and distinct account of the principal acts, and of whatever other information I may know to be correct. The bishops entertain right and excellent opinions respecting the holy supper of Jesus Christ. That abominable error and silly opinion of a carnal eating has been long since banished and entirely done away with. Even that Thomas [Cranmer] himself, about whom I wrote to you when I was in London, by the goodness of God and the instrumentality of that most upright and judicious man, master John a Lasco[2], is in a great measure recovered from his dangerous lethargy. The emperor's ambassadors arrived here the day before yesterday, with great pomp and display, as they thought. I do not affirm it for certain, (for it is only what I hear,) that they are desirous of presenting to the king of England their *Interim*[3],

[1 The second session of this parliament began Nov. 24, and ended not before March 14 ensuing. Strype, Mem. II. i. 210.]

[2 "John ab Ulmis," observes Dr Jenkyns, (in his Pref. to Cranmer, p. LXXX.) "is a competent witness respecting the time when the change in Cranmer's opinions became known, though he was mistaken with regard to the person by whom it was effected." This was Dr Ridley, afterwards bishop of Rochester, and his fellow-martyr. See Strype, Cranmer, 97, and above, p. 13, *n.* 1.]

[3 The system of doctrine, known by the name of the *Interim*, because it contained temporary regulations which were to continue no longer in force than till a general council could be held, was compiled by Pflug, Helding, and Agricola, and upon the model of the articles

that offering, forsooth, worth all the gospel! What present the king will make in return, is still undetermined; not a great one, certainly,—I wish it may resemble theirs. These same legates are reported to intercede suppliantly with the king on behalf of the bishop of Winchester[1] and the rest of the pretended doctors: what advantage they will gain by their puffing, I leave to God, whose cause it is; you may be sure of this, that in proportion as the truth is more studiously oppressed and concealed by them, the more it is manifested and shines forth; for at this very time those privileged altars are entirely overthrown in a great part of England, and by the common consent of the higher classes altogether abolished. Why should I say more? Those idolatrous altars[2] are now become hogsties, that is, the habitations of swine and beasts.

Cox, the king's tutor, a man of noble disposition, and of great influence, and possessed of great acuteness and weight of character, entertains and expresses most excellent and correct notions respecting every article of the christian faith. Had he not so liberally taken me into his friendship when I was distressed, and destitute of all hope, and afforded me both relief and consolation, I must long since have followed the advice of Traheron; for he was the only remaining friend I had, and offered me the royal patronage and support: for which great and lasting benefit, deterred as I am by a strange kind of bashfulness, I am unable to find any language or means whereby to express my thanks. It is in your power therefore to do me a most especial favour: I feel some difficulty in mentioning it, and you know what I mean; nevertheless let it be stated. I could wish then that in a letter to him you would expressly offer him your thanks on my behalf, and request him to regard me, whom he has now received into his friendship, with his continual favour and affection: which indeed he alone is best able to do, as well on account

presented in 1541 to the diet of Ratisbon. It was conformable in almost every article to the tenets of the Romish church, though expressed for the most part in the softest words, or in scriptural phrases, or in terms of studied ambiguity. See Robertson's Charles V. B. ix. and the authorities there quoted.]

[1 Bishop Gardiner was committed to the Fleet in June 1547 for refractoriness to the king's proceedings. Strype, Cranmer, 213.]

[2 Aræ factæ sunt haræ. *Orig.*]

of the power and influence which he possesses in this place[3]; as by reason of the judgment and authority by which he is every where so distinguished. I earnestly entreat you again and again, to undertake this service. But how, you ask, am I to act? In any way you please; for whatever may be your object, your letter will be more gratifying to him than your silence: for as he delights in the friendship of learned men, so likewise does he rejoice in the remembrance and testimony of good men concerning him; and you cannot take up any subject for writing upon, that will not be suitable and adapted to one or other of his excellent qualities. If you write familiarly and about your own concerns, you will seem to have regard to his exceeding courtesy; if in an honourable and grave style, to his eminent dignity. Which will please him best, it is hard to say; but of this there is no doubt, that a letter from you, of whatever kind, will be most gratifying to him. Farewell, most excellent and worthy sir, and commend me to you by reason of your love to Christ, for whose sake you are, I hope, ready to do any thing.

After I had written thus much, before I concluded my letter, I received the most horrid intelligence of the destruction of the city of Constance[4]. O lamentable condition, and most difficult of endurance! For they say that it was again attacked by the Spaniards on the 18th of October, taken by storm, and at length entirely levelled with the ground, and destroyed. O wicked men, foaming with crime, and breathing out cruelty from their inmost soul! Words are altogether wanting to me to express my grief, which perhaps ought to be restrained. For I know, I know, I say, that you have felt so much sorrow at this event, as no time can ever exhaust, nor the greedy Charybdis of the poets ever absorb. I will not therefore be guilty of adding my own sorrow to the infinite distress experienced by yourself. I will only request, what indeed you do most diligently of your own accord, that you will bear in mind, that these events incident to humanity, of whatever

[3 Dr Cox was dean of Christ Church, and chancellor of the university of Oxford.]

[4 The inhabitants of Constance, who had taken arms in their own defence, were not only compelled to receive the Interim, but were deprived of their privileges as a free city, and placed under the ban of the empire. See Sleidan, 474. Robertson's Charles V. B. ix.]

nature, should be wisely and firmly endured by you, who are devoted beyond others to the pursuit of wisdom, and endued with such strength of mind, that whatever the vulgar may admire or dread, you are able, if you so determine, to look down upon and despise. And you will very readily do this, if you always bear in mind, what I know you to practise and to teach, that theology itself is nothing else but a constant remembrancer of death. The time truly will arrive, and that day at last will dawn, when these most foolish men shall suffer in hell the punishment of their wickedness, while we shall attain with the greatest praise and glory the abode and habitation of the godly, filled in every part with great and excellent men. For God delivers his enemies to destruction, and will not suffer them to exalt themselves. O happy day and long expected hour, when, delivered from all the assaults of our enemies, we shall arrive in heaven, as it were our abode and resting-place; where the blessed are in the enjoyment of everlasting life, and where, the journey once accomplished, there will be no more care nor anxiety! Again farewell, and see that you act with firmness and decision. Oxford, Nov. 27, 1548.

I wish you would take care that the letter which you see addressed to John Wolf be given to him at the first opportunity; and also give my cordial salutation to master Rodolph Gualter.

LETTER CLXXXVII.

JOHN AB ULMIS TO HENRY BULLINGER.

Dated *March* 2, 1549.

Although I had no doubt whatever of your good-will towards me, since I have always experienced your stedfastness and constancy, as well in all other respects as especially in preserving friendship; you must know, notwithstanding, that your letter was most gratifying to me even on this account, inasmuch as you thought fit to assure me of your continued affection for me: for thus, wherever I turn, the traces of your regard appear expressed in such soothing and affectionate terms, that I think more numerous or more evident ones could never be conveyed by letter. But that I am now replying to your letter for the first time, must by no means be attributed to my negligence, or forgetfulness of what you deserve at my hands; but partly, because I had most fully written to you respecting almost every thing that I thought it would interest you to know, three days before I received your letter; partly too, because I was aware that master Traheron, a man most distinguished by every kind of learning, and one too endued with an incredible integrity and firmness of mind, had informed you of the discussion of the council respecting the eucharist. I hope therefore, that with your accustomed kindness and benevolence you will hold me excused. I now come to your letter.

It is certain that the queen[1] of Scotland has been carried away by her friends into France: but as to what the French are boasting of their own glory, and making a display of their valour, and bragging that two thousand English have perished by their arms, you must know that it is a great and most impudent falsehood, and most unworthy of France; for it has been clearly ascertained that not more than two hundred soldiers were slain. But that you may understand in few words what changes have been made by the English in Scotland, take them as follows. The castles, fortresses, islands, promontories, and towns, which have been seized by the English either by force of arms or treachery during the war, are Jedburgh, Kelso, Roxburgh, Hume[2], a citadel most strongly fortified by nature and position, and which the Scots recovered back again by stratagem and treachery; but beyond doubt they will be forced to surrender it to the English by reason of the long and continual blockade, and the want of provisions. Besides, as Broughty castle, Dundee, Douglas, and the islands of St Connis, are kept by the English in a state of siege; all the country, from the fortress of Berwick, which is strengthened by the walls and harbours of the English, as far as Edinburgh, the metropolis of all Scotland, is taken and delivered into their power. Last year, on the 15th of October, the Scots, in conjunction with a very numerous French army, vigorously

[1 The queen of Scots was sent to France, and delivered to her uncles, the princes of Lorraine, in July 1548.]

[2 At Hume castle, the Scots, under the guidance of some who were acquainted with all the secret passages, climbed up a steep rock, slew the English garrison, and made themselves masters of the place.]

laid siege to a town of the name of Haddington, which had been most impetuously stormed by the English, and which they had scarcely fortified; in which siege four thousand Scots and French were cruelly slaughtered and butchered. This you may receive as a certain fact, and give credit to it without any hesitation.

As to what they have reported respecting religion, namely, that there are great differences of opinion, I admit that such has been the case to a considerable extent; but I can now assert that by the goodness of God the minds of all good men are disposed to harmony and peace. For the cause of these dissensions is removed in this present parliament; namely, the babbling and dogmas of antichrist, which are now positively and effectually banished. I would here write you word what has been done and determined respecting the Lord's supper, only that your most excellent and loving friend, master Traheron, has already acquainted you with every particular. From him therefore you will learn the whole matter more completely, and from me these few things very briefly. The archbishop of Canterbury, a man of singular worth and learning, has, contrary to the general expectation, delivered his opinion upon this subject learnedly, correctly, orderly, and clearly; and by the weight of his character, and the dignity of his language and sentiments, easily drew over all his hearers to our way of thinking. His opponent was that lying and subtle Cerberus, the bishop of Winchester, together with a number of other babblers who were brought in, men who knew nothing else beyond a few quiddities, and those silly and false. Peter Martyr has openly declared to us all, on this very day on which I write this letter, what was his opinion upon this subject; and he seemed to all of us not to depart even a nail's breadth from that entertained by yourself. Nay more, he has defended that most worthy man, Zuingle, by the testimony of your opinion, and taken part with him against his adversaries, who falsely object to him that he makes the sacrament a mere sign: he moreover declares that those persons are out of their senses, who make the body of Christ to be without any local habitation, uncircumscribed, in many places at once, void of shape, and other matters of the like kind. The rest you will know from the bearer.

One only subject remains, which I desire you to know;

and that is, that by the aid and assistance of that most excellent man, Cox, I was chosen and admitted into the king's college[1] on the first of January. To this means of subsistence must be added the great munificence of the marquis of Dorset, a most courteous and discreet personage, who immediately, on my first waiting upon him, ordered eight crowns to be given me on the instant, and faithfully promised me the same or a larger sum every year. How wonderfully, or rather how providentially, this has happened, I cannot at present explain to you: I only request you to offer especial thanks to Almighty God in my behalf, and this I earnestly entreat of you again and again. The last thing I have to say is this, that you also express your enduring thanks by letter on my account to master Cox, the king's tutor, for having so promptly afforded me his assistance. You must therefore beg of him, that as he has of his own accord admitted me into his confidence and friendship, he will persevere in the same inclination and disposition to love me, if not on account of my studious mode of living, at least for the sake of his own consistency. As to myself, I will take care that no duty or respect shall be ever wanting on my part to either of your reverences; and my services at least shall be exerted, and to the utmost of my power, that no one shall at any time have occasion to feel the want of them. Farewell, most learned sir, and receive this Englishman with your wonted kindness. Farewell, again and again. March 2, 1549.

Your most devoted,

JOHN AB ULMIS.

LETTER CLXXXVIII.

JOHN AB ULMIS TO HENRY BULLINGER.

Dated at OXFORD, *Aug.* 7, 1549.

As to your gratifying and delightful letter, so full of love, and affection, and regard, I never met with any thing that occurred more opportunely. For your commendation was brought to me at the very moment of time when an

[[1] Wood, in his Fasti Oxon. mentions John Abulinis an Helvetian of Christ Church, whom he considers to be identical with John ab Ulmis, as admitted B. A. 1549, M. A. 1552.]

order was being issued against the admission of foreigners into college; and I was beginning to entertain no little doubt as to my own situation and means of subsistence. But you, most excellent and very dear sir, have not only removed from me all fear and apprehension, but have so confirmed the favour and good opinion of doctor Cox and many other learned men respecting me, that, if I choose, I may be quite sure of my income here for some years without any obligation whatever. Therefore, for this your truly valuable and fatherly commendation, I hold myself obliged to you in every possible way: but neither letters nor language can suffice to express my gratitude. I thank you however as much as I am able. You will, with your wonted acuteness, perceive the greatness of the favour you have conferred upon me in this my mediocrity of attainment; for you have not only far excelled me in that courtesy which I always admired in you, but I can perceive nothing in myself which could justly induce a person of your dignity and learning to write to men of such exalted rank on my behalf. In this indeed you have no associate: it all arises from the goodness and graciousness of your character, and from your courtesy to a man of no esteem or reputation. But all these things, as I have just said, and ever shall say, have so bound me to you, that I am quite unable to express in any terms whatever, how greatly I value you, how much I owe you, and how exceedingly I shall endeavour in every respect to make you perceive that I am grateful, and ever mindful of your kindness. I would have you be altogether persuaded, that I am so encouraged by your letter, as that I shall now welcome with greater satisfaction my prospects of independence, which I did not expect would ever be realized; and also regard you with such respect and reverence as that individual ought to be regarded by me, whom I not only know to be most kindly disposed towards myself, but also by reason of his singular and distinguished pursuit of useful learning and virtues, and the character he has acquired for divine eloquence, to be placed in the most honourable position in all Switzerland. But these things are more conveniently said at their own place and season. I now come to those events which I think it right you should be made acquainted with.

You must know, in the first place, that our excellent and most godly king Edward is still in good health, and that he is most diligently and studiously advancing the gospel of Jesus Christ, and restoring the true use of holy things. In the next place, there has been a sharp disputation[1] at Oxford respecting the eucharist, where the subject was made so clear and easy of comprehension, in the very presence of the king's commissioners, that any person of ordinary capacity might easily understand on which side the truth lay, and detect the absurdities of our opponents. I have thought proper to forward you a copy of these discussions, of which the two former have been written out by your attached young friend John Rodolph Stumphius, and the two latter by myself; in which if any thing should be written inelegantly, you must not attribute it to us, but to our want of time and the impatience of the bearer. There is one thing which I will write to you more cautiously; your sagacity will smell it out.

[2]The countrymen are every where in rebellion[3], and have already committed some murders. The enemies of religion are rampant, neither submitting to God nor to the king. They would give a good deal to renew and confirm the act of the Six Articles respecting celibacy, images, divine worship, and some other things which are now repealed. The king is now sending a large army against them. But all these things will not continue long: for we all of us expect that they will be put an end to by the next month. The Oxfordshire[4] papists are at last reduced to order, many of them having been apprehended, and some gibbeted, and their heads fastened to the walls. But king Edward six days

[1 For an account of this disputation, see Foxe, Acts and Mon. VI. 298. The commissioners were, Henry Holbeach, bishop of Lincoln, Dr Cox, Dr Haines, dean of Exeter, R. Morison, and Dr Christopher Nevinson.]

[2 This paragraph in the original is in Greek, and in the latter part is either corrupt or at least obscure.]

[3 This rebellion was ostensibly occasioned by the numerous inclosures of the lands formerly belonging to the monasteries; and fomented by the popish priests, who industriously fanned the flame of popular discontent. See Burnet, II. 181. Strype, Cranmer, 264. Foxe, V. 731. Soames, III. 434, &c.]

[4 The rebels in Oxfordshire were dissipated by a force of 1500 men, led against them by the lord Grey of Wilton. Burnet, II. 183. iv. 205.]

ago (I mention only what is whispered about) having sent to the better part of the popish camp a book (the liturgical mass they call it), is grievously slandered, though not consenting to annul even the smallest part of his own laws about such things.

You will hear the whole of this affair more accurately and minutely from your friend Butler, to whom I have sent the book above mentioned, on condition that he should read over to you every particular. Lastly, will you send to that excellent and learned man, Ambrose Blaurer[1], this copy of the disputations, for him to read, at the first opportunity? I most earnestly entreat you to do this. Farewell. Oxford, Aug. 7, 1549.

Cordially salute from me those worthy men, masters Pellican, Gualter, and Bibliander, and promise them every thing that may be expected from a man altogether devoted to our religion, and one too who is most grateful. I will take care that you shall make no rash promises respecting me. Once more farewell.

JOHN AB ULMIS.

LETTER CLXXXIX.

JOHN AB ULMIS TO HENRY BULLINGER.

Dated at LONDON, [*August*, 1549].

IF you hear from me less frequently than from others, you must not, I beg of you, impute it either to my negligence, or even to my engagements; which, numerous as they might be, could never become of such consequence as to interrupt the intercourse of my love and duty. For as I am now in London, I have again ascertained that there is a person to whom I can confide my letters; and I have therefore given him this second one. In my last I told you what had been the result of your commendatory letter; and what was the state of England, as well as that of my individual concerns, how changeable in prosperity, and good in adversity. The writing of that letter was followed by the exceeding liberality of the marquis of Dorset towards me; for he faithfully promised to allow me a yearly pension of twenty crowns, and

[1 Ambrose Blaurer was of a noble family at Constance, where he was minister in 1548, till the Interim, forced upon the city by Charles V, drove him away, when he retired to Bienne. He died in 1568.]

paid me down twelve at the time. I have now been visiting at his house for three days in this hot and dusty weather, when there are no lectures at Oxford. I am living with masters Skinner and John Wullock, most excellent men, and so exceedingly attached to you, that nothing more holy, nothing more learned, nothing, in fine, can be said or imagined by them to shew greater attachment to yourself and to our religion. For as soon as they discovered, from the letter that you sent me last month, that you were safe and well, they most solemnly expressed how much they rejoiced with me; and they asked me again and again as to the circumstances of Switzerland and of your honoured self. I replied that the general state of Switzerland was good, and favourable, and happy, and prosperous; and that you were preaching and setting forth, without any grudging of labour, or time, or exertion, and with great success, the most holy name of Jesus the Almighty God. Then Wullock, who is well skilled in Greek and Latin, went off into the conversation which in our mirth we had had together respecting you a few months since. "Do you know," says he, "the news that has lately been circulated among us every where at Oxford? As you have long and often told us a great deal about the good-will of Bullinger towards us, and as I have learned the same also from his letters sent both to yourself and many others; I have been thinking with myself by what means we can obtain from him the favour of his dedicating and inscribing some of his writings to our patron the marquis; for I think that he will thus procure, not only the entire esteem of all godly persons, but also the eternal recompence of this service from God. Now you appeared entirely, and in a manner positively, to promise us that Bullinger would do this. If you wish to ascertain more certainly the inclination and opinion of the marquis in this matter, you must know that the whole subject has been fully explained to him by me, and that it is so approved of and commended by him that nothing at this time will be more acceptable to him than to receive some book dedicated to him by Bullinger. Now therefore, it is your business, my friend John, to keep your promises, and fulfil the engagement you have made in this matter." Thus far he. As to myself, therefore, since it seemed very ungracious to me to refuse one whom I esteemed so much, and to whom I felt that I was very dear, and especially when he demanded the performance of my promise, and that for a becoming object; I thought it best, my master, immediately to write to you upon the subject, that you may be enabled to take an impartial and correct judgment respecting this duty. If you should perform that which I have promised on your behalf, you will not so much seem to regard [the wishes of] all godly persons, as your own dignity. I know, my excellent and very dear friend, that it is not the part of a wise man to affirm any thing as to the disposition of another; but yet if the feelings and disposition of any individuals can be gathered from their appearance, their look, their conversation, in a word, from long experience, and an honourable life, I dare assure you that this nobleman, so greatly distinguished by all liberal learning, will afford such manifestations of his good feeling and gratitude as shall be most worthy of himself, and most honourable to you and all your friends. Thomas Caius, a man eminent for his knowledge of languages, and a great friend of the marquis, had intended to write to you on this subject in confirmation of this my opinion, had not the distance by which we are now separated prevented his doing so. But of this at another time. I wish the subject to be made known to you by myself, and you will use your judgment respecting it: for I have no doubt but that you will accomplish, at the earliest opportunity, whatever with your acknowledged prudence and discretion you may consider most expedient; and that you will take this my request in good part, as is required both by my entire respect for you, and by your favourable inclination towards myself.

I think of soon returning to Oxford, whence I will write you word of any new intelligence I may have to communicate. The king is alive and well: the rebellion of the peasantry has been marvellously subdued; about five thousand papists have been slain; all the others are, for the most part, quiet. It now remains for me to bid you farewell, and to request you most affectionately to salute from me all my friends. I am devoting myself entirely to this one object, that neither you, nor my excellent master, John Wolfius, shall seem to have made any rash promises or vain assurances respecting me; and should I not altogether be able to redeem your pledges on my behalf, this at least I will certainly effect by diligence, labour, and assiduity, that both friends and enemies may be persuaded, some time or other, that fortune has rather envied my exertions, than that they have been wanting to do justice to your authority. Do you only continue to love me, and occasionally to write to me. At this present time you cannot do me a greater favour. Once more farewell.

Your most attached,

JOHN AB ULMIS.

LETTER CXC.[1]

JOHN AB ULMIS TO HENRY BULLINGER.

Dated at WESTMINSTER, *October* 20, 1549.

RICHARD Cox, tutor to the king's majesty, and high-chancellor of Oxford, desires me to attest by this my subscription, that he has penned this letter to you in great haste, being occupied by matters of the highest importance; which I solemnly assure you is the case. Besides, most reverend father in Christ, I wish you to receive from me the certain assurance, that the religion given us by Christ is making a satisfactory and successful progress. I am able to write to you as a most certain fact, that antichrist in these difficult and perilous times is again discomfited by the general sentence of all the leading men in England; and that not only is the religion adopted last year decided by them to be the true one, but a doubly severe penalty is now imposed upon all who neglect it. The godly therefore have nothing to fear from the idolatrous mass, and the papists have nothing to hope from it. The Lord is present with his church, and will not suffer her to be disturbed or afflicted beyond what she is able to bear. If this had not been the case in these turbulent times, what mischief and confusion would the papists have occasioned us! But enough of this. Peter Martyr, and Bernardine Ochinus, with Skinner also, and Wullock, desire me to send their kindest salutations. Fare-

[1 This letter was added as a postscript to that of Cox given above, p. 119.]

well, and excuse the shortness of this letter. I have hastily written it in Cox's chamber. Oct. 20, 1549.

JOHN AB ULMIS,
Yours to serve, but Christ's to own.

Some books[1] written by you have lately been translated into English. Bucer is silent. If it be not too much trouble, I wish you would briefly reply to what I mentioned in my last letter. Woe betide me, if the marquis of Dorset has not this very day treated me with the greatest kindness, upon hearing that I had been commended by you to Cox. What will he not do for your sake! But Thomas Caius, a most excellent Greek and Latin scholar, will shortly write to you more fully upon this subject. October 20.

LETTER CXCI.

JOHN AB ULMIS TO HENRY BULLINGER.

Dated at OXFORD, *Jan.* 31, 1550.

I LATELY wrote to you, with all the earnestness in my power, concerning Alexander Schmutz[2]; not that I distrusted either your memory or your stedfastness; for I was well aware how you maintained your own dignity, and that you were by no means given to forgetfulness, especially when the interests of your friends are concerned; but that request

[1 The following works may perhaps be referred to: "An epistle on the mass, 1548." "An epistle of H. Bullinger wyth the consent of all the learned men of the church of Tygurie, whether it be lawfull for a chrysten man to communicate or be partaker of the mass of the papistes, without offending God and hyes neygbour, or not. Lond. 1548." "A treatise or sermon much fruitfull and necessary for this tyme, concernynge magistrates and obedience of subjects, also concernynge the affayres of warre and what scryptures make thereof, &c. Lond. 1549."]

[2 Cecil and Cheke had gotten this youth into the king's school at Westminster. A letter was afterwards, in 1552, procured from the king to St John's college, Oxford, to grant him the fellowship there which John ab Ulmis had resigned on his return to Switzerland. See Strype, Mem. II. i. 534.]

was then made me by Alexander, who was most exceedingly importunate for me to commend him to you. But I am again addressing you, and of my own accord, to the same purport, as being not only desirous to stimulate your willing exertions, but also, because I am so greatly distressed at the miserable situation in which he is placed. But really I want words whereby to commend him to you; for I have already stated all that I could say, in my two former letters upon the same subject. I will therefore content myself for the present with this single observation, that you are now the only one upon whom depend all his hopes of obtaining a livelihood; which hopes I most earnestly implore you again and again, by your zeal for the members of Christ, not to disappoint. The way and means of accomplishing this object I have, I think, sufficiently explained to you in my former letters. For to whichever party you write, whether to Henry Grey, marquis of Dorset, or to John Dudley, earl of Warwick, I know to a certainty that the business will turn out according to your wish, that is, most successfully: but should you have thought upon any other plan, you can avail yourself of my assistance: the one I have proposed is both ready of execution, and not without a most hopeful prospect; but this I leave to your discretion. Oh, if you could but know and see what great hopes there are of this youth, you would exceedingly regret that he has been so long deprived of your fatherly help; for you might with little exertion on your part be of great service to him in matters of importance. I confess indeed, that it is not the part of a wise man to affirm any thing respecting the disposition of another, especially when that other is still a boy, of whom it cannot be known beforehand how he will turn out; but yet I have such judgment in the discernment of character and the selection of my friends, as to warrant you that this youth will not only satisfy the favourable opinion of his friends, and retain their good offices, but that he will also recompense and do honour to their kindness. If therefore you love me, or rather if you love Christ himself, use your exertions in this matter, and endeavour that I may shortly learn from you that something has been done agreeably to my wishes, by your addressing a letter either to the marquis of Dorset or the earl of Warwick. For you must bear in mind that I am not at this time in so much anxiety about any thing whatever, as I am about this subject upon which I have already written to you three or four times. But enough of this. I have not any news to communicate. The parliament is still sitting. Some persons are of opinion that a peace[1] will be made between the English and French. I suspect there is nothing in it; but should it take place, I shall say it has happened contrary to expectation. But you know this better than I do, or rather, I should say, than any one. There is no need for me to write at length respecting the reciprocity of my affection, or rather of my respect for you. For I should be altogether unfitted for those studies and pursuits to which I have devoted myself from my childhood, and quite a barbarian, unless I not only reciprocated your regard, but also repaid it with interest; which though I perceive to be difficult, yet I trust that I shall be able ultimately to accomplish it. Do you love me as you have begun, and farewell. Master Peter Martyr desires me to salute you. I write this at Oxford. Jan. 31, 1550.

[JOHN AB ULMIS.]

LETTER CXCII.

JOHN AB ULMIS TO HENRY BULLINGER.

Dated at OXFORD, *March* 25, 1550.

To that letter of yours dated on the 21st of December, and received by me on the 15th of March, when I was in Hooper's house at London, I wrote a short and hasty answer while I was at dinner, as I had not at that time either any convenient place or opportunity for writing. Now, however, that I have returned to my studies, and obtained a little more leisure, I will again write to you, and somewhat more at length, upon the same subject. You must know then, that I received your letter with the greatest expectation and delight, and that I especially noticed therein what I most earnestly

[1 This treaty was made about the end of February; by the terms of which Boulogne was to be surrendered to the French, on the payment of 400,000 crowns. Burnet, II. 236. Strype, Mem. II. i. 358.]

wished, namely, that you intend to dedicate some one of your lucubrations to that most noble personage, the marquis of Dorset. I cannot express the gratification this has afforded me: you must only suppose that nothing has ever occurred to me more delightful or of greater importance, than what you declare your intention of shortly carrying into effect. This alone was wanting, that I did not send you his title or style sufficiently plain and distinct: you must know, however, that this was not from any fault of mine, but of a servant of the marquis, who copied it out so awkwardly. But since what is done cannot be undone, I again send you the title now given me by the marquis himself, in this form: "To the Lord Henry Grey, marquis of Dorset, Baron Ferrers of Groby, Harrington, Bonville, and Astly, one of his majesty's most honourable privy council, his right courteous master, &c." He told me indeed that he had the rank of prince, but that he did not wish so to be styled by you; so that you must judge for yourself whether to keep it back or not. For my own part, I always use this title, and shall henceforth do so with much greater freedom, now that I perceive him at this time raised to the highest and most illustrious dignity. For this honour is given by the English to one who is descended from the royal family[2], and is one of the king's council, and also a lord of parliament; which latter office he has so filled to the great admiration and applause of the whole kingdom, that he and John Dudley, earl of Warwick, are considered the two most shining lights of the church of England: for they alone have exerted, far more than the rest, all their power and influence in the restoration of the church. They have utterly and entirely repressed and extinguished that dangerous and deadly conspiracy and rebellion so foully agitated last year. They are, and are considered to be, the terror and thunderbolt of the Roman pontiff. These very men exerted their influence and good offices on behalf of the king's uncle, who had been miserably plotted against, and restored him, from being in the utmost danger of his life, out of darkness to light and life. And now, if you consider the magnificent establishment which he maintains,

[[2] Henry Grey, marquis of Dorset, married Frances, daughter of Charles Brandon, duke of Suffolk, by Mary Tudor, sister of Henry VIII.]

you would even thence derive just and sufficient materials for commending him: for this prince is learned, and has with him all the most learned men, with whom he mutually compares his studies. Moreover, he is not so mighty and powerful as he is kind and liberal; for on that very day on which I took your letter, he really seemed to be transported with joy on account of your intended commendation of him. He has also liberally increased my stipend, which is now annual: and when I was about to take my departure, he offered me his hand, and presented me, by a domestic, with six pounds for my journey; whereas at first he had only given me two, afterwards five, to which he has now added six, in a letter. I am aware, and readily acknowledge, that he has manifested this good-will and generosity towards me especially for your sake; for when he sometimes sees a letter addressed to me from you, so distinguished and eminent a character, he thinks that his kindness and assistance is due to me as it were of right. I wish therefore, that he may incidentally learn from you, not only that his courtesy and favour and attention have been most gratifying to me, but also that I have most warmly expressed my obligation in my letters to you. For you are aware that men of this sort are supported as it were, and retained in constant good-will, by the nourishment of gratitude. But why am I teaching a dolphin to swim? You know the whole matter, and far better than any one else.

Lastly, I entreat of you to keep in mind with diligence and kindness the remembrance of that young man of excellent promise, Alexander Schmutz. I have already written to you about him almost ten times, in the full hope and persuasion that from your recommendation he would derive some assistance towards his studies; and I feel assured that this object cannot be effected in any better way, than by your causing the book which you have dedicated to the marquis to be delivered to him by means of this young man and myself. For the marquis himself expects to receive it from no one but me. It would certainly be the most gratifying to me of all your favours, great and numberless as they are, and most worthy of yourself and of your long experienced kindness, if you would take upon yourself to assist in the education of this youth. This, believe me, (such is the favour and influence which you possess with the nobleman in question,) you may accomplish by a mere nod, much more by an express request. If you will effect this object, my master, you will confirm my opinion of your good-will towards that excellent and learned man his father; and will also, by this exceeding favour, have brought Alexander himself, a most grateful and dutiful and worthy young man, to an intimacy with me and respect for you. I have written upon this subject more fully, that you might perceive that I am not writing in a customary or ostentatious manner, but for a most intimate friend, and, as he really is, a member of Jesus Christ; and I am fully assured that your kind and benevolent disposition will believe this to be the case.

But enough of this. I have no news whereof now to write. All things are safe and quiet. The meeting of parliament is prorogued till the first of April. What has been done and determined, I am altogether ignorant. Hooper's letter, I suppose, will bring you much intelligence. The religion of antichrist is universally despaired of and laid aside. The sarcophagy[1] is neglected and despised by every one. Master Peter Martyr has undertaken to lecture upon the Epistle to the Romans. Bucer had entered upon the exposition of the sixth chapter of St John, but is now, at the very threshold of his work, confined to his bed by a severe and dangerous illness. God, our merciful Father, knows what will be the result. We have almost entirely abandoned all hopes of his recovery.

Many reports are spread abroad here respecting a peace between the English, French, and Scots, but they rest on no certain authority. As soon as I obtain any positive intelligence, and which I think it will interest you to be informed of, I will diligently and dutifully let you know. Do you only take care of your health, and shortly effect that object, than which you cannot at this time do any thing more agreeable to me.

Andrew Wullock and Robert Skinner, the principal domestics of the marquis, salute you: they are not so learned and discreet as they are dutiful and affectionate towards you. Make, I entreat you, honourable mention of them, either in your letter to the marquis, or in a private letter written jointly to them both; and recommend either me or Alexander

[[1] Σαρκοφαγία, carnal eating.]

to them. This will not be of so much advantage to our affairs, as it will be a suitable accompaniment to your little present. Besides, their singular probity, learning, and intimate friendship with the marquis, as well as the courtesy and benevolence which they diligently manifest and attentively exhibit to me for your sake, will give you confidence in writing to them. Peter Martyr salutes you, as does also my friend Rodolph [Stumphius], a young man who entertains the greatest respect for you, and with whom I live upon the most pleasant and agreeable terms, and derive much advantage both from his attainments, and also from his virtue and probity. Again and again, excellent sir, farewell.

I have written this at Oxford on the day of the annunciation of [the Virgin] Mary, in the month of March.

Your most attached son in Christ,

JOHN AB ULMIS.

LETTER CXCIII.

JOHN AB ULMIS TO HENRY BULLINGER.

Dated at OXFORD, *April* 30, 1550.

I RECEIVED your letter after eight o'clock this evening, which although it was most agreeable to me as manifesting what I most desired, your paternal regard; yet it nevertheless occasioned me some anxiety, as it shewed that you suspected me, partly of negligence, and partly of I know not what kind of shuffling and deceit. Indeed, my master, I am very greatly distressed on this account, and most earnestly desire your forgiveness. For I must ingenuously confess the truth of what she[1] has told you, namely, that by my letters I have enticed her son hither. But as I do not find that she has acquainted you with the reason and object of my doing so, I pray you to hear from me, in few words, the whole state of the case. On my departure from [Zurich], the mother of Alexander, a most worthy and religious woman, most earnestly entreated me, even with tears, to repay the kindness I owed to her deceased husband: I perceived too that she was labouring

[1 Namely, the mother of Alexander Schmutz, mentioned in p. 352. See p. 348, *n.* 2.]

under such poverty and indigence, as to be compelled to withdraw her sons from literary pursuits, and place them in the work-shop of some artificer. Under these circumstances therefore, I promised her most faithfully and solemnly, as it was my duty to do, that I would use all my diligence, endeavour, and labour in her service, without any exception either of place, or time, or occupation. And I performed this promise shortly after: for as soon as the supremely great and good God had made sufficient provision for me in this country, I immediately wrote to the boy's mother to entreat her not to degrade her son by any illiberal and mean employment, but rather to send him hither to me, where, by God's help, I would either enable him to go on with his studies, or at least, far more conveniently than she could do at home; I would place him with a bookseller here of my acquaintance, a man most thoroughly acquainted with his business, and favourably disposed towards religion. And if you will seriously consider the matter, you will say that I was not so much guilty of imprudence in thus acting, as I piously performed the promise I had made her; for the boy, had he remained at home, would most certainly have been condemned long since to the work-shop either of a tailor or a smith.

With me, however, in this country, he is engaged in learning, and applies himself to those studies, than which nothing more desirable, nothing more excellent, either has or will be bestowed upon mankind by the gift and bounty of God; namely, to that all-powerful and glorious philosophy, yea, that most ancient and honourable profession: and had I not been able to have brought him over to so beautiful and excellent a study, or to have continued him in the pursuit of it, the shop would still have been at hand, and the master also, who would most readily have received him without any expense. He could also have applied himself to learning trade in a remote and foreign nation with greater reputation and advantage than he could at home. I do not therefore perceive with what propriety I can be accused by you either of rashness or imprudence, and much less with what justice I have received this sort of thanks and kindness from the boy's mother.

I now therefore come to your other charge, in which you tell me that you have heard that I am not applying myself to my studies and learning, but that I am perpetually running backwards and forwards to and from London[1]. I cannot sufficiently wonder at this accusation; for I am quite sure you have no sufficient evidence of my negligence from any good authority. But, say you, your letters betray you; for you have of late written to me much more frequently when you were in London. I admit this; but what certain proof, I would ask, either of industry or negligence can be derived from this? Surely none. Besides, I most solemnly assure you that I have never been in London except for most urgent and necessary reasons. I have ridden there twice with my very dear and most attached master, Peter Martyr, to the palace of the archbishop of Canterbury, where I shewed the primate the confession of the church at Strasburgh, which, at the request and advice of Peter Martyr and Utenhovius, I had translated into Latin, and received some angels as a reward. A third time, last summer, when the discussion took place here concerning the eucharist, I constantly took notes of that disputation, and presented a copy to the marquis of Dorset, in whose palace I passed some days most agreeably with those excellent men Wullock and Skinner. When I left him, he kindly promised me for my labour and pains an annual stipend of twenty crowns, and he has most abundantly performed his promise: for within these ten months he has presented me with more than thirty-four crowns in hand. On a fourth occasion I was called [to London] by a letter from my excellent and most constant patron Traheron, being requested by him to present to the earl of Warwick some lectures of Peter Martyr, which I had copied out, concerning divorce[2]. From this also I derived some emolument. Then, lastly, I went to London by the advice of Peter, to shew the marquis of Dorset the letter which you wrote to me in December; and I most dutifully informed him of your respect and good-will, which was of all things most gratifying to him. At that time also, contrary to all expectation, he spoke in the highest terms of my zeal and benevolence in so kindly lending a helping hand to my countryman Alexander. He added that he should on this account more readily exercise his liberality

[[1] This was Hooper's complaint respecting John ab Ulmis. See above, p. 70.]

[[2] For Peter Martyr's opinions respecting divorce see his common places, Part II. ch. 10, p. 457.]

towards myself. And in fine, to speak all in one word, if one's object be to procure the patronage of any man of rank, I think that I must not be content with walking, but must use all possible speed. Thus then you have the motives and reasons of my various journeys: they are not fictitious or pretended, but real, and connected with what is virtuous and praise-worthy. But with respect to my studies, if you entertain any doubt, make inquiry either of master Cox or master Peter Martyr, with whom I pass at least three or four hours every day, and very often half a day at a time, in comparing the writings of the fathers, and copying out lectures and disputations. I do not feign or invent any thing in making this statement; the labour itself affords certain and abundant testimony to the fact. Let those persons therefore go and tell there what falsehoods of me they please. I, for my part, shall not consider such groundless calumnies worth a straw. Your discretion, my master, will lead you not to give credit at first sight to men of that sort, until you have well and accurately ascertained the facts. But enough of this. I now come to things of too great importance to be committed to the Latin language: take them therefore as follows[3].

It was not my fortune to be either a citizen or a resident [of Zurich]: for I was born in a village far distant from your city; so that, as far as I can learn upon due investigation, there is nothing either to hinder me from accepting any presents from other quarters, or you from commending me to your townsmen. But I do not desire you to ask them for any favour or benevolence to myself, but only that they will shew some kindness to those who have formerly done me some service. I can solemnly assure you that I have never either said or left unsaid any thing to flatter or pay court to any one: least of all would I attempt this with you, whom I well know to have such practices in especial abhorrence. No one indeed can deny that I have passed all my life in Thurgau, and that I have never lived under the eye of your magistrates, excepting only two years, in which I resided in your immediate neighbourhood, though, for all that, I was not during that time an inhabitant of your city. You have no occasion therefore to be under any anxiety or distress concerning me.

But I am not able to conjecture how far your commen-

[3 The two following paragraphs in the original are in Greek.]

datory letter respecting Alexander would avail with Hooper and Traheron: for it is wonderful how very far they disagree respecting God's predestination of men; and I would not wish you to set them at variance, or bring them into collision by letter. But this is a profound secret, which you must not disclose or mention to a single individual.

What therefore I must do in this matter, I cannot tell. I lately called upon master Peter Martyr, and asked him what he thought best to be done. He briefly replied, "Since master Bullinger has resolved to dedicate a book to these noblemen, I certainly am of opinion that the matter should be put off till that time; nor would I advise him to solicit any stipend either for yourself or any one else, but only take care that the book should be presented by Alexander: the thing will then probably succeed better of its own accord, without any prejudice to the honour of Bullinger, or any shock to your modesty." This is what he said, and I think we should acquiesce in this advice, which is full of prudence and fidelity. It will now be a kind and friendly service on your part, to bring the thing itself, which you so kindly and courteously promised me, shortly to an end. You cannot indeed do any thing more gratifying to the marquis, more worthy of your illustrious reputation, and more advantageous to myself.

I have fully pointed out to you, in my former letters, the materials and subject of a suitable address to this personage. I will now state them in few words. He is descended from the royal family, with which he is very nearly connected; and is the most honourable of the king's privy council. He has exerted himself up to the present day with the greatest zeal and labour courageously to propagate the gospel of Christ. He is the thunderbolt and terror of the papists, that is, a fierce and terrible adversary. He spoke most nobly in defence of the eucharist in the last parliament. He is very much looked up to by the king. He is learned, and speaks Latin with elegance. He is the protector of all students, and the refuge of foreigners. He maintains at his own house the most learned men: he has a daughter, about fourteen years of age, who is pious and accomplished beyond what can be expressed; to whom I hope shortly to present your book on the holy marriage of Christians, which I have almost entirely translated into Latin. You may adopt this form of dedication to the book: "To Henry Grey, marquis of Dorset, Baron Ferrers of Groby, Harrington, Bonville and Astley, one of his majesty's privy council, and my most honoured lord, &c. &c." I am unable to write to you more plainly or expressly. I write nothing now respecting Dudley, earl of Warwick, with whom you are an especial favourite. For I am daily expecting his chaplain, a most worthy and accomplished man, from whom I shall very fully ascertain my lord's wishes, and will then write to you forthwith. I must mention lastly, that in your letter to the marquis of Dorset you should incidentally offer your warmest acknowledgments for his kindness in honouring me with his friendship and patronage for your sake. You may also diligently and earnestly recommend Alexander in your private letter to Andrew Wullock and Robert Skinner, persons who are much attached to your church: I do not mean that you should solicit any stipend for us, but only that they may be aware of your commendation of us. They are well acquainted with Alexander's necessities, and on that account are more ready to help me. I only wish you to thank them. They will soon find out afterwards the state of the case, or, if need be, I will fully explain it to them; and this may be done without prejudice to your dignity, or the modesty of this excellent youth. The letter, believe me, which you wrote to me in December last, was most gratifying to them. For you seemed therein both to speak and think most honourably respecting them. I wish you would send a copy to each, or at least request me here by letter to do so. Do you understand me? If you send one here, my letter will be sufficient for them; if you expressly request me in your letter, I will deliver it to them here.

It now remains for me, my very dear and much loved master, to bid you farewell, and pray you to continue for me your wonted regard. Master doctor Peter Martyr salutes you all, and desires me to return his best thanks to you for your kindness and good-will towards himself. He will write to you within this present month, but is now employed in matters of great importance. He entertains a very great regard for us. Again, farewell. April 30, 1550. Oxford, from the king's college.

Your excellence's most attached,

JOHN AB ULMIS.

P.S. The very careless courier departed on the 15th.

LETTER CXCIV.

JOHN AB ULMIS TO HENRY BULLINGER.

Dated at OXFORD, *May* 28, 1550.

IF you are in health, it is well; so also am I. Although I wrote you a long letter very few day since, wherein I informed you of the motives upon which I acted, and what I also thought right should be done by you; yet as Peter Martyr, one who is very much attached to you, was writing to Zurich, I was unwilling that his letter should reach you without a few lines from myself. I therefore most earnestly and repeatedly exhort you, my master, with regard to the subject of my last letter, that you diligently proceed in the execution of that office you have so kindly undertaken. Indeed, I told the marquis that you would not any longer keep our expectation in suspense, than till the next Frankfort fair. Wherefore, most excellent sir, you must be abundantly careful not to defer this matter any longer, especially in paying off that debt, of which as a great part is cancelled by you already, the remainder may very easily be got rid of. What need is there of many words? Can you bear the just complaints of those persons, who, I say, do not simply ask, but positively demand it of you, and that too very justly? since in your former publication to the king you pledged your faith to them, which you also most courteously confirmed in your letter to me, that you would pay to the last farthing whatever you had at any time promised to perform. Will you then suffer this expectation, nay, rather, this glory which you have in your hands, to be either shamefully wrested from you, or to be lost in a way yet more disgraceful? You will not, I think, suffer it, if I am well acquainted with all your feelings. For I both know your unwillingness to be deficient in duty and consistency of character, and also by what virtues and accomplishments you have already commended your name to immortality, and wish yet further to commend it: I know too the gravity of your mind; I know your high feelings, which can neither be induced in any way to inflict an injury, nor easily persuaded to return one. But if you write to the marquis, take care, I entreat you, to make honourable mention of those excellent men, Robert Skinner and Andrew Wullock. I do not mean in the preface to your book, (although that would be very gratifying to me,) but in your private letter to the marquis, in which I would have every one to understand that I have expressed to you my warmest thanks for their kindness to me. I do not ask, neither indeed am I altogether desirous, that you should make any other request than that they will continue to regard me.

But especially with respect to the commendation of Alexander, I would that the just and legitimate authority of your name should bear testimony also to his father, that most excellent and godly man; which indeed will be of the greatest advantage to his affairs and studies. This you can do with a safe conscience, and it will be a great commendation of the youth: if you send the book to me, (as I hope you will do,) I shall take it to Traheron, my most excellent patron; he is constantly employed at court with that nobleman, and regards your concerns, and therefore mine also, with as much attention as his own. But I leave all this to your judgment and discretion. You have, I think, abundant materials to write in praise of the marquis. He is a most honourable member of the king's council, and descended from the royal family: he is very learned, and a favourer of the gospel, the scourge of the papists, and one who is very partial to your church. I again send you his title, altogether in this form: "To Henry Grey, marquis of Dorset, Baron Ferrers of Groby, Harrington, Bonville, and Astley, king's councillor, &c.;" unless you would add the name of the marquis: this will be at your own discretion, and altogether a matter of choice.

I have no more certain intelligence of Henry[1] Dudley, [earl of] Warwick, than that he is very dangerously ill. I am daily expecting his chaplain here. You may be thoroughly assured that you will gratify him very much, if you will write a joint letter to them both. I am not, however, quite certain as to his full address. Nor do I think it matters much; for you can always at any future time dedicate to him some one of your lucubrations, which also will be more agreeable to them both. But enough of this.

A peace has been entirely concluded between the French, Scots, and English. The people of Devonshire are now re-

[1 So the original; but it should be *John*.]

duced to submission after great loss on their part. The Irish are becoming in all respects conformed to the English. Boulogne, a sea-port, is given up, but an annual tribute is paid by the French: the English ambassadors and hostages are reported to have brought away as much as sixteen hundred thousand crowns, by means of which it is universally hoped that the English coinage will be renewed and purified. A great number of the bishops now entertain right views respecting religion. Our friend Hooper, who was at Zurich, was made a bishop on the day of our Lord's ascension. The king's uncle, the duke of Somerset, carried this in the council against the opposition of almost all the bishops. I hear that great contests took place on each side respecting ceremonies, and the vestments of the popish priests—I should have said, of the stage-players and fools. Hooper at length gained his cause. I never saw or heard any one who spoke more piously and with greater kindness respecting Switzerland, and especially your church. Our schools here are in a most flourishing state, with most useful lectures and disputations. I have dedicated my time in the morning to Galen and Aristotle, but so as to refer all that I learn to theology alone. I must tell you that I am most intimate with Peter Martyr, not as a pupil, but as a son; for as I delight to hear him, so I ardently love his peculiar suavity. I pass whole hours with him, so that I have henceforth no occasion for any introduction. If you desire to read any of the lectures or disputations of Peter Martyr, I will send them to you; for I have them all written out, and with Martyr's own corrections. Farewell, most excellent sir. In haste, at Oxford, May 28, 1550.

Your honour's most devoted,

JOHN AB ULMIS.

LETTER CXCV.

JOHN AB ULMIS TO RODOLPH GUALTER.

Dated at OXFORD, *June* 1, 1550.

THE same reason that induced me to write to master Bibliander now induces me to write to you. I desire to shew myself grateful to you, and mindful of your kindness. I should have done so indeed long since, most readily and at greater length, could I have supposed that a letter of mine would have been acceptable to a man of your learning and distinction, and one too, who is so much engaged in so many public and private affairs. Now, however, that a learned friend has requested me to write to you, I hope you will pardon my ignorance. You must know therefore, very learned and dear sir, that I entertain for you the same respect as a scholar ought to do towards his master, an unlearned man towards a learned one, in fine, as a son towards his father; and that is, of the most affectionate character, and full of admiration both of your learning and virtue. I omit all mention of that singular kindness and regard for me, which induced you to make me a partaker in all your researches: there is nothing so abstruse in the most important, that is, in divine subjects, which you have not investigated with a learning and discernment almost peculiar to yourself, and most kindly communicated the same to me; which obligation indeed, great as it is, yet certainly, when I consider it more and more, appears greater and more conspicuous every day; and I may add too, is, both in reality and in my estimation of it, increasingly acceptable to myself. And I wish again and again that the day may sometime dawn upon me, when I shall frequently hear you preach, or at least when I may be able to offer my duty and services to so great and distinguished a person in the manner most agreeable to my feelings. Should I be permitted to attain either of these objects, I shall indeed regard myself as fortunate and happy. I ardently and earnestly wish and implore of Almighty God, for yourself and the whole church, grace and perpetual peace in Christ. Moreover, do you have me commended to you, and persevere in this your favourable disposition and desire to love me: I will certainly endeavour that you shall have no cause to repent of your kindness; for though my condition is such as to prevent my equalling a man so distinguished as yourself, yet in duty and zeal and affection I will so contend with you, as that you shall not easily carry off the prize of friendship.

But enough of this. I have no news to communicate at this time. Every thing here is safe and quiet. Our

Oxford papists are discomfited to a man; for turn wherever they will, they see that an end is put to their sacrilegious mass. Some useful disputations were set on foot here about six months since, in which Peter Martyr was often attacked, but, as I would have you believe upon my assertion, is not yet slain: these jangling sophists have many complete arguments, and more incomplete; they have too their wonderful intentions, and execrable restrictions, to say nothing of their eccities and quiddities, which are all destitute of common sense, and quite abhorrent to the nature of things. The solutions, divisions, and distinctions of Peter Martyr are simple and clear. Besides, his opponents can no longer lean upon Duns Scotus, or any other of the schoolmen; for they are all of them driven away to a man by the force and authority of an oath. But the most ancient fathers occupy their place, and especially the holy scriptures, to which, as to a touchstone, every argument is referred. You may all of you, therefore, be bold and confident, let persons among you yonder tell what lies they please; provided only you pay no regard to those worthless fellows. Your warfare is of a noble and distinguished character; the contest is not for the riches or honours of this world, nor for a thing of no value, but for eternal happiness. Think again and again that it is reserved for you, not here, but in heaven.

But I must now conclude. Farewell, therefore, most excellent sir, and salute most cordially in my name your wife, and that very learned and worthy man Zuingle. All your friends here most respectfully salute you, and especially Masters, my most excellent friend and patron. The others are more remiss than they should be; but he is a man of distinguished learning, and one who has a very great regard for you. He would have written to you, had he not been confined to his bed by a severe and long continued indisposition. He very often affords me his friendly services for your sake; so that you will much oblige me if you incidentally give him to understand by letter both that his kindness, and zeal, and assiduity are most gratifying to you, and that I have abundantly expressed my obligations to him in my letters to yourself. I earnestly entreat you, again and again, to do this.—When I had written thus far, the youth Stumphius came in: he has a great respect for you, and desired me to send you his cordial salutations. He will write to you by the next opportunity. Dated at Oxford, June 1.

Your most devoted,

JOHN AB ULMIS,

A native of Switzerland, and your constant disciple.

LETTER CXCVI.

JOHN AB ULMIS TO HENRY BULLINGER.

Dated at OXFORD, *June* 21, [1550.]

ALTHOUGH I had nothing whatever to write about, most learned and very dear sir, yet I could not but give the courier, who is about to journey into Switzerland, a mere nothing of a letter to you rather than none at all. In truth there is nothing new to communicate respecting myself. I am still engaged in those literary pursuits which you have at all times especially recommended to me. And although I hear less of you than I wish, yet I hear what I desire, that you are adorning and defending Switzerland with so much piety and prudence, that none of her enemies, howsoever inveterate, dare to attack her. You will easily understand how gratifying to me is this intelligence, even though I say nothing. I offer my prayers indeed for your safety, (which is the only thing I can and ought to do while I am absent,) and I desire most earnestly that I may some time behold you established in your ancient liberty. I am not able to describe the religion now received in England more fully than I have done in my former letters; for all things are now in a safe and prosperous condition, nor does any godly person think of looking back. We are devoutly hoping that both Ireland and Wales will shortly come over to our mind, or rather, to speak more correctly, to the mind of Christ, with all their power. We have full confidence too respecting Scotland, that when she has been thoroughly subdued, she will embrace the true and wholesome doctrine of Christ with her whole heart: but of this I will write to you at another time, when I shall have something more certain to communicate. You must understand that that excellent divine, Peter Martyr, is engaged in the same kind of teaching, and will not concede any thing to the papists; and that he has recently declared his mind more openly respecting the eucharist, in which, if I understand his language, he differs very little, if at all, from you. There are very many, I mean of those who are regenerate, who are not only not opposed to your opinion, but who support it, according to their ability, from holy scripture and maintain it as the true one. The transubstantialists are on the opposite side; for one of their number, and of notoriously bad character, holding forth in a public discourse that the bread was substantially the body of Christ, pulled to pieces with his impure mouth that most learned and pious man John Œcolampadius, and bespattered him with falsehoods, asserting that he was driven to such extremity of madness as that he attempted to destroy himself. O pestiferous, shameless and virulent tongue, which relies upon no other arguments than cheats and barefaced trickery! But why do I talk so impertinently? for you have things of this kind at home. Take care of your health: I am both enjoying the best health, and am most diligent in my studies. Salute in the kindest terms your most amiable wife, and Gualter, a most learned man, and very dear to me, together with all others who deserve well of me. Dated at Oxford, in England, three days before the feast of John the Baptist.

Your most attached,

JOHN AB ULMIS.

LETTER CXCVII.

JOHN AB ULMIS TO HENRY BULLINGER.

Dated at Oxford, *Aug.* 22, 1550.

As I have an opportunity of sending you a letter, I will not let it pass, although I have not any thing to write about. For there is no change in my circumstances and pursuits, and I am still going on in the same way of living as I long have done. I am in daily expectation of a letter from you, and with it also the fulfilment of your promise, in which I heartily pray that I may not be disappointed. I shewed your letter to our marquis, in which you desired to convey to him, through me, the expression of your respect and good-will. No circumstances, believe me, could have been more gratifying or honourable to him, or more agreeable to his wishes than this your message; whereby you may easily conceive how greatly it concerns both of us, who have clearly pledged our promise to him. I have repeatedly sent you a suitable form of dedication, namely, one that is plain and proper for the occasion. I have no doubt but that you have already received it more than once, so that I shall not make any farther mention of it. Your discourses lately dedicated to the king are now rendered into English by Thomas Caius[1], a first-rate scholar and divine. He is the head schoolmaster of this city, and a great lover and admirer of you: he has long too been highly esteemed throughout this whole island by reason of his numerous and valuable publications; and he wishes to regard me, for your sake, on the most intimate and friendly terms. The duke of Somerset is now five miles from this city. He has caused the book of our friend Otho[2] to be translated into English at his own expense: it is considered most excellent, and is universally read by persons of the highest rank and learning. It would, in my opinion, be well worth his while to turn it into Latin; for I have no doubt but that the uncorrupted purity of the Latin language will throw more light upon it than an English translation can do.

Cox, who most highly esteems you, was here a few days since. I waited upon him, and asked whether he had any message for you. He replied that he would write to you at the same time with the king: I suppose they have, both of them, written by this time. The king himself, as you must have long since learned from Hooper, is exceedingly well disposed toward your church. Last week, when he confirmed Hooper in his bishoprick, and demanded from him the oath

[1 This Thomas Caius was "an eminent Latinist, Grecian, poet, orator, excellent for all kinds of worth, and at length *antiquitatum Oxoniensium plane helluo.*" He was elected fellow of All Souls in 1525, and master of University College in 1561. He died in 1572. See Wood's Athen. Oxon.]

[2 Otho Wermullerus. The book referred to seems to be the "Spiritual and Most Precious Pearl," translated by Coverdale. See "Writings and Translations of Myles Coverdale," Park. Soc. edit. p. 86.]

[of supremacy], he chanced to notice that the saints[1] were mentioned by the bishops in such sort, as though they were to swear and be confirmed by them. His majesty became much excited, and said, "What wickedness is here, Hooper? Are these offices ordained in the name of the saints, or of God?" As soon as Hooper had declared his opinion, the king immediately erased with his own hand the error of the bishops. This I had from Peter Martyr as an undoubted fact. Hooper's dispute[2] with Traheron, thank God, is now settled, and almost forgotten, although one of the parties, namely, Hooper, has fallen into far greater and more dangerous circumstances with certain other persons. He is reported to have stated, a short time since, in a sermon[3] before the king, that the marriage bond once broken and violated can neither be restored and renewed by the interference of the magistrate, nor by the will of the parties, so as to be holy wedlock; and to be regarded as such. These words have occasioned great disturbance to many worthy persons: he has very few defenders of his opinion, nor do I think that Peter Martyr will ever agree with him upon this point. For his opinion seems to every one to be too harsh and extreme. But I will write more upon this subject at another time, when I shall have attained more accurate information: meanwhile I wish that what I have stated and written should be confined solely to yourself.

Bucer is alive and well. He has preached here twice. The substance of what he said you will fully learn from the letter of Stumphius. We dined with him, and he was exceedingly kind to us. It happened that while he was here, he received a letter from France, in which it was told him that the Sorbonists and some others were disputing in the presence of the king about the Hebrew language. The Sorbonists wish the professorship of that language to be entirely abolished; the others have a different object in view. It is easy to perceive what these most impure knaves and sacrilegious robbers are driving at; for the bird is known by its singing. On that same day Arnold Byrkman came here,

[1 See above, p. 81, n. 3.]

[2 This dispute was respecting the doctrine of predestination. See above, p. 358.]

[3 See Hooper's Early Writings, Park. Soc. edit. p. 378, &c.]

and told us that articles of inquiry[4] into heretical wickedness (for so they commonly term the doctrine of Christ) has been published by our Antiochus, or, if you choose, our Julian, by which he has delivered over all those in lower Germany, who entertain right views of Christ, to be sacrificed and slaughtered by his mass-priests, who are to have from henceforth free liberty of examining and harassing any individual, whether a citizen or a stranger. These articles, he says, were printed in the slaughter-house of the mass-priests at Louvaine, and sent over twenty days since to the magistrates at Antwerp; and as soon as they were seen by the citizens, they were exclaimed against and execrated by persons of all ranks throughout all Belgium. He states that they threw the bearer of them into prison. What is to be the result, God only knows: it is most certain that the order is not yet complied with. But it is to be feared, and that greatly, that the pope's executioner will at length obtain it; and if that should be the case, this mischief will doubtless spread and make progress.

It remains for me, my very dear and much longed for master, to wish you well, and request you to take in good part the familiarity of this letter. That weak and enervated style of writing I neglect and despise after your example. Peter Martyr salutes you all, and promises you, through me,

[4 "At this time there appeared another placard about the business of Heresy, dated the 29 April, at Brussels, which not only confirmed all the former placards, but was much more severe, and gave plainer hints of a design to set on foot the Inquisition." It commanded "all justices and other officers, on being requested and desired by the Inquisitors of the Faith, and by the ordinary Judges of the Bishops, to give them all favour, countenance, and encouragement, help and assistance in the seizing, apprehending, and securing all such as appear defiled or infected, and that they should proceed against the offenders by execution, notwithstanding any privileges to the contrary, which were abrogated and annulled by the Edict." Brandt. Hist. of Ref. in the Low Countries, Vol. I. Book III. It appears that the city of Antwerp opposed this placard, and the introduction of the Inquisition, and the chief merchants and burghers prepared to leave the town. The Regent Mary went to her brother Charles V. at Augsburg, and represented to him that the state would receive such a shock as it could never recover, if he insisted upon establishing the Inquisition in the Netherlands. The placard was a little softened as to the words, but the persecutions went on with increased severity.]

his continual service and exertions. Salute much in my name master Otho, and his son-in-law Zuingle, and especially that worthy and learned man, master Ambrose Blaurer. I would have written to him now, were I not prevented by want of time. Aug. 22. Oxford, from the king's college.

Your excellence's most devoted,

JOHN AB ULMIS.

LETTER CXCVIII.

JOHN AB ULMIS TO RODOLPH GUALTER.

Dated at OXFORD, *Nov.* 5, 1550.

THOUGH I entertained no doubt whatever, most learned sir, of your kind disposition towards me, as I have always experienced your consistency as well in all other matters, so especially in retaining friendship; you must know, nevertheless, that your letter was most gratifying to me even on this account, that you thought fit to assure me therein of your favourable regard. For though I had been long since persuaded, that you were not only distinguished in every branch of learning, but also remarkable for your exceeding integrity and firmness of character; yet I was altogether unaware of your being endued with so much courtesy and sweetness of disposition. For I used to suppose, that in proportion as any one was pre-eminent for gravity, moderation, dignity, and learning, he would be less inclined to condescend to these familiar offices of friendship. But now, after the perusal of that most excellent and delightful letter, which you wrote to me without even being invited to do so by any letter on my part, you have indeed far exceeded my expectation, and procured for yourself not only as heretofore my praise and veneration, but my cordial affection from this time forward. For in the first place, when you state that my letter (to mention yours in the mean time) was gratifying and acceptable, you do this out of the abundance of your kindness, which leads you to regard with complacency those services, which if I did not willingly render, I should not certainly answer to the character you have so greatly commended in your letter, namely, that of being grateful to those who have deserved well of me, and ever regardful of the virtues and reputation of distinguished characters. In the next place, the loving, and as it were brotherly commendation of me, from a man so renowned and illustrious as yourself, to your friend, or rather our friend, Masters, was exceedingly gratifying to me, and exactly what I wished. For as soon as he heard that there was a letter to him from you, though he was ill of a fever at the time, he seized it with such avidity as if he were about to satisfy a long-continued thirst: I have therefore no doubt but that this your commendation of me will have its due weight and influence. May God grant that this worthy man may at length be delivered from his long attack of fever! He has now been confined to his bed more than eighteen months by this pestilent disease, and there is at present no hope of a speedy recovery. A few days since he was carried by his friends in a litter into Kent, for change of air and scene; but God alone knows what benefit he will derive from it: the season is certainly inefficacious and altogether ill-adapted for restoring to the diseased parts of the body their proper strength. He therefore prays you to excuse the invalid state of his body, which has hitherto prevented his writing to you; which however he promises to do so soon as the paroxysm of the fever shall have abated.

But enough of this. You must learn from me a few connected particulars respecting our lectures on physic, and the study of medicine. In the morning then, immediately after morning prayer, namely, from six to seven o'clock, are read the eight books of Aristotle on Physics; from seven to eight, the common-places of Galen upon diseased parts; from eight to nine the books which he [Aristotle] wrote upon morals, and his Republic or treatise on civil government; from nine to ten Peter Martyr lectures upon the epistle to the Romans; from ten to eleven Galen's treatise upon natural qualities is lectured upon. These subjects occupy us till dinner-time; but at twelve o'clock some questions in moral and natural philosophy are proposed for our discussion. On Mondays and Wednesdays the masters [of arts] hold disputations; and on Thursdays the students in divinity, physic and law dispute among themselves in regular and alternate turns. Lastly, on the Fridays and Saturdays the bachelors of arts exercise themselves in acts and declamations. Every disputation has a fixed moderator of its own to preside over it. In theology Peter Martyr presides; in physic or medicine Thomas Francis[1], a man of distinguished learning, and formerly an intimate friend and companion of yours, when you resided here; and in civil law Weston, a man of pleasing elocution and considerable erudition. The masters of arts choose their annual proctors, and the bachelors choose to themselves some leading man from among the masters. All their disputations take place in public, and may be heard and attended by any one. The private, or, as they call them, extraordinary lectures, are very numerous. There are, I think, sixteen colleges, which are distinguished by various studies and pursuits. Greek is taught in one, Hebrew in another. Here the mathematicians flourish, there the poets; here divines and physicians, there students of music and civilians: in all of them, however, the elements and rules of rhetoric and logic are impressed with especial diligence and accuracy upon the minds of the scholars. You will readily consider, with your usual discernment, from the above facts, what will be most expedient for your kinsman, I mean, that excellent young man Cellarius: for my own part, when I bear in mind the advantages of the place, the nature of the climate, and the distinguished character of our learned men, I cannot but most earnestly recommend him to come over as soon as possible. The English are really a good-natured and shrewd people, and very fond of strangers; though not a few of them are false and subtle knaves; but this is common to other nations as well as to them. For the expenses and all things necessary for him to pursue his studies with comfort, there will be required not less than fifty florins, unless a man choose to live in a very sordid and penurious manner. I conversed with some persons, a few days since, upon this very subject, and especially with an honest and worthy citizen of this place, who tells me that he will arrange with us on sufficiently moderate terms; and there is no doubt but that we shall meet with a good and comfortable lodging, provided he comes, or rather flies to us as soon as possible. As to myself, I am, and always shall be, ready to render him

[[1] Thomas Francis had been an inmate in cardinal Wolsey's family: he became regius professor of physic at Oxford, where he was afterwards, in 1561, appointed by queen Elizabeth provost of Queen's College. Strype, Grindal, 92.]

every service by my endeavours and assistance; nor will I ever desist from advancing and aiding him in his studies, whenever I can. But I had rather be seen to have performed these promises in reality, than content myself with mere professions.

To conclude, I beg you to preserve your health, and to continue to love me as you have begun. Salute, I pray you, in my name those excellent men, masters Huldric Zuinglius, and Ammian and Colin; and especially commend me to the family of Roustius. You know the rest; and I earnestly entreat you to do this, for I well know how greatly it is for my advantage to be commended by you to my friends. Peter Martyr salutes you, as does also your true and pious friend the younger Bull. Most of your friends have become papists since you returned home; but I will tell you more about this when I have more leisure. I shall write very soon to Bullinger, that most faithful patron of all students. I am daily expecting the letter of the marquis of Dorset, which he desires to be forwarded together with my own. Every thing is (God be praised!) according to our wishes. Oxford, 1550, Nov. 5. Written by torch-light, from the king's college.

Your true disciple,

JOHN AB ULMIS.

LETTER CXCIX.

JOHN AB ULMIS TO HENRY BULLINGER.

Dated at OXFORD, *Nov.* 11, 1550.

I RECEIVED your letter on the eleventh of October, and delivered it to the marquis on the twenty-seventh. To sum up all in one word, it was exceedingly gratifying to him; for it was written by you with great judgment and politeness, and in such a way that I do not think any thing could have been written by you more discreetly, or managed more honourably: I read it to the marquis myself, and soon easily discovered the opinion entertained respecting you by great and distinguished men; wherefore you may be assured of having acted most properly. The reason that I so long detained the letter in my possession is this. At the end of last summer, for the sake of improving my style, I wished to translate into Latin the treatise written by you in German some time since upon the holy marriage of Christians; and when it had been copied afresh, to present it to the lady Jane Grey, daughter of the marquis, who is exceedingly well informed both in Greek and Latin literature. Both Skinner and Wullock warmly approved my design: as soon therefore as I came to London, I took your letter, together with the book, to the marquis, (for his daughter was then from home,) and in effect I ascertained that the business was going on well. The marquis will write to you in a few days, and desires his letter to be forwarded together with mine. You need not doubt but that I shall take care of its being properly and carefully delivered; only do you shortly accomplish the fulfilment of your promise. But there is no occasion for my farther pressing this upon you, since I have no doubt but that you are now fully occupied with it. I wish your intention respecting the earl of Warwick may be carried into effect, for our marquis much approves of it; and as they are united together by an intimate friendship, they will, by this means, be more firmly joined together in a regard for religion. I have not yet obtained the title of the earl full and complete; but when Skinner sends it me, together with his letter, I will take care that it shall be forwarded to you immediately. There are many and conspicuous proofs of the kindness and good-will of Warwick towards you. First of all he undertook that your works, numerous as they are, should be translated into English at his own expense. He also positively assured Hooper, that my friend (or rather yours) Alexander[1] should be, and indeed was already, exceedingly esteemed by him for your sake; although nothing had been done at present, on account of some most important business which had been long in progress between himself and Hooper. But the matter will at length be effected, and, as I hope, very speedily and satisfactorily. For the controversy[2] between Hooper and the bishops, respecting divorce, seems likely to have a good and favourable issue, and the bishops will have no cause on that ground for railing against that most excellent man. For Hooper maintains no other opinion than that which you have all approved, both by your pen, and by your discourses. The report therefore that has got abroad concerning him is a false one, namely,

[1 See Strype, Mem. Eccl. II. 1. 533.]

[2 See above, p. 64, n. 1, and p. 368.]

that he considers a marriage once violated can neither be renewed nor recontracted by the intervention of the magistrate, nor at the will of the parties. But enough of this.

I have not any news at present to communicate. For every thing here is safe and quiet, except that there is some rumour of an attack by the French upon Calais. There is no doubt indeed, but that they attempted to raise an earthwork at the very outposts of the English, by whom they were most bravely repulsed and prevented. The French king sent over an ambassador to offer an apology the day before I came to London. He was admitted to an audience, and treated, as I hear, with courtesy; but the private opinion was by no means favourable either to his sincerity or uprightness. The English therefore know well enough, or rather, I should say, more than enough, what credence is to be given to the French.

It now remains for me, most excellent and learned sir, to bid you farewell. The earl of Ireland[3], a youth of the same age with the king, is very fond of you, and salutes you, as do likewise Skinner and Wullock, men of exceeding learning and piety. You would do well, in my opinion, to send a copy of your forthcoming decade to the marquis's daughter: besides other things you will elicit a letter from her, and that a very learned one. The form of address should be thus: "To the lady Jane Grey, daughter of the marquis of Dorset, &c." But you will easily determine, as your prudence may suggest, what may be most expedient for you to do. I wish you would deliver the accompanying copy of the disputations to M. Otho Wermuller. He is altogether a man of that kind, to whom I desire to shew myself friendly and attentive. Respecting the order of our studies and lectures, you will more accurately obtain from my letter to Gualter whatever information you may desire. Oxford. In haste, on St Martin's day, 1550.

In truth your son and
scholar in Christ,
JOHN AB ULMIS.

[3 This was Barnaby Fitzpatrick, called Comes Hiberniæ in the text. He was bred up with Edward VI. and afterwards made baron of Upper Ossory by queen Elizabeth. See Burnet, II. 358.]

LETTER CC.

JOHN AB ULMIS TO RODOLPH GUALTER.

Dated at Oxford, *Nov.* 26, 1550.

Greeting. You are perfectly informed by my last letter of all circumstances relating to yourself and to your kinsman[1]; with all that has been done by me, and also with what should be determined upon by you. I then wrote you an account of all the lectures and studies in particular; but I shall now only give you a summary view of the study of medicine, lest, if my former letter should chance to have miscarried, that information which you consider the most interesting to you should seem to have been neglected. These then, generally speaking, are the lectures in the faculty of medicine. In the morning, from seven to eight, the subject of the lecture is Galen on diseased parts; then, from ten to eleven, upon natural qualities; and lastly, from three in the afternoon to four, the same author upon simple remedies. The professors of medicine lecture very learnedly, accurately, and intelligently; they are also very courteous, and take very great pleasure in the progress of their pupils. You are, I think, well acquainted with the climate and advantages of this place: to me indeed the atmosphere seems mild and clear, and of an equable temperature. Not less than fifty florins are required for necessary expenses; and you need not doubt but that I will in the mean time provide a comfortable lodging, if only he will come over and reside here with us. I feel assured too that it will greatly promote his interests, if he bring a letter of recommendation from master Bibliander to my fellow collegian, master Cadwell, a man exceedingly distinguished for his learning and knowledge of medicine. He has too, believe me, an especial regard for Bibliander, though they are not personally acquainted with each other; but the band, namely that of religion, by which they are intimately united, is very firm between them. You will act therefore with much propriety and prudence, if you will take care that a letter be written either by yourself or at

[1 Cellarius: see above, p. 372.]

least by our friend Bibliander; you will certainly never repent it. For my own part, I solemnly and positively promise him by you every service in my power, without any exception as to time, or labour, or occupation; in the assured hope that on this condition no slight opportunity will be afforded me of shewing myself grateful to, and mindful of, yourself. But more conveniently of this subject in its own place and time. Do you continue to love me as you do, and feel assured that you are loved and reverenced by me. Your friends in this place most dutifully salute you: do you, on the other hand, cordially salute my friends in my name, which I earnestly entreat you to do. I have repeatedly written to Huldric Spon, but so far from answering my letters, he has never once sent me his salutation: he must not therefore expect any from me; yet I wish him safe and well.

Farewell, most worthy sir, again and again, and take in good part this insignificant letter. A few days since there was published an English translation of Zuingle on the duty of a good pastor, together with some letters written by him and by Œcolampadius: I hope your Antichrist will shortly follow. Dated at Oxford, from the king's college, Nov. 26, 1550.

Your true disciple,

JOHN AB ULMIS.

Every thing still continues in perfect quiet.

LETTER CCI.

JOHN AB ULMIS TO HENRY BULLINGER.

Dated at OXFORD, *Dec.* 31, 1550.

THOUGH I am in bad health, and tormented with a severe and dangerous pain in my side, yet, having procured a confidential messenger, I cannot allow the letter of doctor Peter [Martyr] to be sent you unaccompanied by one from myself. You will therefore, I trust, excuse its plainness. The letter of the marquis of Dorset, as well as that of Oglethorpe, will be conveyed to you by Reniger, a man of great learning, and much attached to you; who is going to Zurich in a few days for the sake of printing the English bible. You have, I hope, before this received the style of the earl of Warwick full and complete. It will be very gratifying to both parties, if your book be addressed to them in common. But I must recommend and exhort you again and again, carefully to consider with yourself, how far it may be expedient that the copy of the forthcoming decade should be presented to Warwick by Hooper. For my friend Martyr declares it as an undoubted fact, that he has lost all influence with almost all the nobility, and especially with Warwick; and that his affairs are consequently in that precarious state, that unless the excellent marquis of Dorset and the archbishop of Canterbury had humbly petitioned for him in parliament, he would long ere this have been committed to prison; chiefly for being too urgent in doing away with the ministerial habits, and rashly pronouncing as impious and wicked all who are content to wear them. The archbishop of Canterbury and the bishop of London recommend equally with himself the entire abolition of the habits; but they consider that it ought to be effected by the general consent of the whole kingdom, and not by the random authority of an individual, or that of the council only. I lately ascertained this to be the case from master Skinner, and yesterday from Dr Peter; so that you will use your own discretion as to what is best to be done in this matter. In my opinion it will be much more advisable that it should be presented to Warwick by Skinner or Traheron, who of all men are among your greatest admirers. When I gave your letter to Traheron last year, he rejoiced exceedingly on reading it; but complained to me bitterly of Hooper respecting his books, and also some letters formerly addressed in common to both, not having been returned to him. This seems to me an evident proof that they are not yet properly reconciled. You are acquainted, I think, with the subject of their dispute, as also with the learning and piety of each. It is on this account very much to be lamented.

Cox, the chancellor of the university, was here on the 9th of January, and remained some days. Just as I had made up my mind to wait upon him, his servant came to invite me to him. I waited upon him immediately. He first of all inquired about you and Alexander, whom you had recommended to him, and thus apologized for not having spoken to me about that matter before; namely, that he had long been vainly expecting Hooper, with the view of ascertaining from him the circumstances of the youth; but as he had been waiting to no purpose, he would forthwith learn the whole state of the case from ourselves; which as soon as he had done, he ordered fifteen crowns to be counted out for the boy, and so dismissed me. I tell you this that you may understand how much weight and influence your letter had with this personage; and that a letter is required from you in return, in which you should express your grateful acknowledgment of this his kindness to us. We shall always be diligent and attentive in our respectful observance of you both.

As to the rest, though I doubt not but that, as heretofore on my account, so now for the sake of your own consistency you will continue in the same favourable disposition towards me; yet, my master, I earnestly entreat you again and again, that the kindness which you shewed me at first, and which you afterwards continued, may be increased and extended by you to the end. You are the only one of us all, who have any favour with the great, and who likewise were the first to determine upon aiding and defending us by your counsel and protection. I therefore earnestly implore you to persevere in your inclination to love me. If you intend to present any book to the earl of Warwick, send it together with the rest to me; I shall do nothing without the sanction and concurrence of Traheron. Only let them be given in charge to some confidential person at Frankfort. The Byrchmans are careless, and by no means to be depended upon; therefore beware of them. The safest way will be for them to be brought hither by Cellarius, a kinsman of master Gualter, who, I have no doubt, will take charge of them either for yours or the Lord's sake. I hope you will send a copy to the daughter of the marquis, and take my word for it, you will never repent your having done so. Let this be the form of address: "To Jane Grey, daughter of the marquis of Dorset, &c." and you will elicit from her a most learned and courteous letter. She has herself rendered into Greek a good part of that book "On marriage," which I translated into Latin, and presented it to her father on the last day of December for a new year's gift.

Every thing here is in a state of the greatest quietness and tranquillity. In Ireland, they say, the archbishop of Dublin[1], who so long opposed the king in religion, has now, of his own accord, come over to our side, and altogether taken leave of the Roman pontiff. Walter the Scotsman, who was formerly here with me, and afterwards went to Ireland, is reported to be dead. All these things I have ascertained from an Irishman to be really true. Farewell, most excellent and learned sir. Stumphius and Alexander desire their warmest salutations. Remember me to Zuingle, your father-in-law, and to my brother Ziegler: I would write to him, were I not prevented by illness.

Oxford, Dec. 31, 1551.

Your reverence's most attached scholar,

JOHN AB ULMIS.

LETTER CCII.

JOHN AB ULMIS TO HENRY BULLINGER.

Dated at LONDON, [about *March*, 1551].

FOUR vessels left Antwerp at the same time, of which one was wrecked; your books alone arrived safe in Abel's ship. One of them I gave to Cox; and took care that another should be delivered by [sir John] Cheke to [the earl of] Warwick. The rest, namely, the one for Peter [Martyr] and those for the marquis [of Dorset] and his daughter, I have determined to take with me down to Oxford. The marquis is gone into Scotland, with three hundred cavalry and some good preachers; with the view, principally, of faithfully instructing and enlightening in religion that part of the country which has been subdued during the last few years. I think

[1 George Brown, D.D. late provincial of the order of Friars Augustine in London, was archbishop of Dublin at this time. But as he was the head of the reforming party in Ireland, it is probable that he was mistaken by John ab Ulmis for his great antagonist, George Dowdall, archbishop of Armagh, who "laid a curse upon those, whosoever they were, that should own the king's supremacy." See Strype, Cranmer, 53, &c.]

of joining him there in a few weeks, and shall probably send you a letter from thence, if I can meet with a trustworthy messenger. I will give both to Wullock and Skinner a copy of the Decade in your name, at which I think you will not be displeased. The earl of Ireland ordered me to return to him this morning; but when I arrived at his lodgings, he was said to have been summoned to the king: your salutation was indeed very gratifying to him. I will certainly take care to send his letter to you at Zurich, together with my next. I am now setting off on my journey to the marquis. To you, most honoured father in Christ, do I offer again and again my lasting thanks for the exceeding favours you have conferred upon me; I will write to you respecting each particular, and very distinctly, on my return. The brother of the marquis, and Skinner, with both of whom I dined yesterday most sumptuously, salute you very much. London, in haste.

Your worship's most affectionate scholar,

JOHN AB ULMIS.

LETTER CCIII.[2]

JOHN AB ULMIS TO HENRY BULLINGER.

Dated at BRADGATE[3], *May* 29, 1551.

I RETURNED from Scotland on the 29th May to the marchioness, the marquis's wife, where I have been passing these two days very agreeably with Jane, my lord's daughter, and those excellent and holy persons Aylmer and Haddon. Your book, believe me, was most acceptable to the marquis, and long and anxiously expected by him. I presented it to his lordship in a numerous assemblage of persons; for at that time many of the Scottish nobility, with the bishop of [Argyle] and the lord Maxwell, had resorted to him at Berwick, with the view of making peace between both kingdoms. I under-

[2 The original of this letter is printed in Fueslin, p. 289.]

[3 Bradgate is about five miles from Leicester. The ruins of the mansion once belonging to the Greys of Groby, and in which lady Jane Grey was born in 1537, are yet remaining.]

stand it was much approved by all, especially by the bishop of Norwich[1], an Englishman, very learned, and on the most intimate terms with our marquis. I wish you therefore to be thoroughly assured, that this your courtesy has been honourably and deservedly bestowed upon this great and illustrious nobleman. He would most willingly have written to you, had he not been entirely occupied by very important business of the king's majesty, and by public affairs; and he most anxiously begs you to excuse him, as well by my letter, as by that of his daughter. At that time much inquiry was made of me respecting yourself, your habits of life, your children, and, in fine, all your household; but most especially as to what gift or present I thought would afford you most pleasure. But I constantly made answer to the marquis, that your only desire was that the doctrine of the Son of God might be advanced, the ruined house of God restored, and the tyranny of the pope condemned; and that you neither required any thing else from the king's majesty, nor indeed expected any other recompense from the marquis. I have given you only a summary of what I said, but I spoke more fully and expressly to the marquis, as the occasion then seemed to demand; for I had considered beforehand what it might be necessary for me to say. To his other inquiries I replied as I judged most expedient.

You will easily perceive the veneration and esteem which the marquis's daughter entertains towards you, from the very learned letter which she has written to you. For my own part, I do not think there ever lived any one more deserving of respect than this young lady, if you regard her family; more learned, if you consider her age; or more happy, if you consider both. A report has prevailed, and has begun to be talked of by persons of consequence, that this most noble virgin is to be betrothed and given in marriage to the king's majesty. Oh, if that event should take place, how happy would be the union, and how beneficial to the church! But the supremely great and good God will preside in this matter; who alone causes to prosper, and cares for, and remembers, and foresees, and disposes of all things according to his good pleasure.

[[1] Thomas Thirlby, who had been translated from Westminster in 1550.]

Haddon, a minister of the word, and Aylmer, the tutor of the young lady, respect and reverence you with much duty and affection. It will be a mark of courtesy to write to them all as soon as possible. Skinner is at court with the king. Wullock is preaching the word of God with much labour on the borders of Scotland. Traheron has retired from court to the country, and very much enjoys more recondite literature, that is, Greek. My last desire is that you may be well, and, should you write any letter to the marquis, take care that it be first of all delivered to me. But this as you please; I most earnestly request it of you. I wish you would salute for me very dutifully master Gualter, and, if convenient, especially master Pellican. Again and again, most learned sir, farewell. Bradgate, May 28, 1551. I am thinking about my return to Oxford.

Your most loving and constant son in Christ,

JOHN AB ULMIS.

LETTER CCIV.

JOHN AB ULMIS TO CONRAD PELLICAN.

Dated at [BRADGATE], *May* 29, 1551.

THAT I have not yet sent you a letter, most excellent sir, has not arisen from want of a subject to write about, for in that I abounded; but because I have not hitherto ventured to address a man of your gravity, and eminence, and learning, with my dull and illiterate correspondence. But now, as you have repeatedly sent me your friendly salutation, and as I have ever looked up to you with especial respect, I cannot do otherwise than prove and declare my grateful remembrance of you by a letter, though I do not think that you have any doubt of my regard for you; for I should be very unlike myself, were I not to admire your exceeding probity and learning, and to acknowledge with a grateful recollection your innumerable kind offices to me. Only therefore bear in mind that I am bound to you by the perpetual remembrance of your kindness. I am more bold in writing to you by reason of the daughter of the most noble the marquis of Dorset, a lady who is well versed both in Greek and Latin, and who is now especially desirous of studying Hebrew. I have been staying with her these two days: she is inquiring of me the best method of acquiring that language, and cannot easily discover the path which she may pursue with credit and advantage. She has written to Bullinger upon this subject; but, if I guess right, he will be very willing to transfer the office to you, both because he is always overwhelmed with affairs of greater importance, and because all the world is aware of your perfect knowledge of that language. If therefore you are willing to oblige a powerful and eminent nobleman with honour to yourself, you will by no means refuse this office and duty to his daughter. It is an important and honourable employment, and one too of great use. The young lady is the daughter of the marquis, and is to be married, as I hear, to the king. By your acceding to my request, she will be more easily kept in her distinguished course of learning: the marquis also will be made more stedfast in religion, and I shall appear to be neither unmindful of, nor ungrateful for, the favours conferred by them upon myself.

You will perhaps say, "I shall seem to have but very little modesty, in writing to a young lady, the daughter of a nobleman, and one too not even personally known to me." But believe me, you need not entertain any fears of this kind: for I well know how great is the reputation of your name in this country; how influential the weight of your character, how venerated is your old age; and I wish you too to remember this, namely, that bashfulness is considered by philosophers as a defect in old men. Put away, therefore, all awkward excuses, and take in hand the business itself. I promise you, indeed, and solemnly pledge myself, that I will bear all the blame, if you ever repent of this deed, or if the marquis's daughter do not most willingly acknowledge your courtesy. Write therefore a letter to her as soon as possible, in which you will briefly point out a method of learning the sacred language, and then honourably consecrate to her name your Latin translation of the Jewish Talmud. You will easily understand the extent of her attainments by the letter which she wrote to Bullinger. In truth, I do not think that among all the English nobility for many ages past there has arisen a single individual, who, to the highest excellences of talent and judgment has united so much diligence and assiduity in the cultivation of every liberal pursuit. For she is not only conversant with the more polite accomplishments, and with ordinary acquirements, but has also so exercised herself in the practice of speaking and arguing with propriety both in Greek and Latin, that it is incredible how far she has advanced already, and to what perfection she will advance in a few years; for I well know that she will complete what she has begun, unless perhaps she be diverted from her pursuits by some calamity of the times[1]. But I have said too much upon this subject. Do you, reverend father, I pray you, only take my request in such part as my extreme respect for you or your kindness towards me requires; and I doubt not but that you will accomplish by your learning and diligence at the very first opportunity whatever shall seem most proper to be done. If you write a letter to her, take care, I pray you, that it be first delivered to me.

There is no news of any kind: every thing is settled and quiet, except that a terrible earthquake has taken place near Croydon. It is now stated that our Frenchman has renounced the pope. With respect to the Irish, Welsh, Manksmen, and those of Jersey and Holy Isle, you must have the same persuasion of them as of the English, namely, that all these islands entertain right opinions as to religion. My marquis is still in Scotland. I was with him on the first of May; he is safe and well. Farewell, most excellent sir. Dated May 29, 1551. In the house of the daughter of the marquis.

Your reverence's most attached,

JOHN AB ULMIS.

As soon as you determine upon any mode of procedure upon this subject, pray let me know by the earliest opportunity.

[1 This anticipation proved to be painfully correct.]

LETTER CCV.

JOHN AB ULMIS TO RODOLPH GUALTER.

Dated at BRADGATE, *May* 29, 1551.

GREETING. I should have sooner replied to your letter, most excellent and learned sir, had I been anywise able to do so by reason of the duties that were then imposed upon me. Now, however, when I have almost reached the end of my journey, and have met with a trustworthy messenger, I cannot do otherwise than write you something of a letter: though I hardly know what to write about, unless you would, perhaps, wish me to give you an account of my visit to Scotland; which if you do, you shall have the whole story in few words. Bullinger dedicated at my request the fifth decade[1] of his sermons to the marquis of Dorset, and wished me to present it to him as soon as published. The marquis, however, had gone to Berwick, a Scotch town, a little before the copies arrived in England: wherefore I thought it best for me to hasten to the utmost extremity of Britain, both for the sake of presenting the book to the marquis, and also from a desire of seeing Scotland. Nor, indeed, do I repent me of a journey now almost completed; for not only was my visit very gratifying to the marquis, but in the mean time I acquired a knowledge of those things, an opportunity of observing which could scarcely be obtained for many years to come. There appears to be great firmness and no little religion among the people of Scotland: but in the chiefs of that nation one can see little else than cruelty and ignorance; for they resist and oppose the truth in every possible way. As to the commonalty, however, it is the general opinion, that greater numbers of them are rightly persuaded as to true religion than here among us in England. This seems to be a strange state of things, that among the English the ruling powers are virtuous and godly, but the people have for a long time been most contumacious; while in Scotland, on the contrary, the rulers are most ferocious, but the nation at large

[[1] The title of this book is as follows: Sermonum Decas quinta ad illustrissimum principem Heinrychum Grayum marchionem Dorcestriæ, &c. authore Heinrycho Bullingero.]

is virtuous and exceedingly well disposed towards our most holy religion. I have no hesitation in writing this to you; for both what I say is true, and I perceive that this circumstance is frequently and seriously deplored by the English themselves. I saw, moreover, an island, which they commonly call Holy Island[2]: the land is of small extent, and surrounded by that sea which they call the [German] ocean. It is not far from the town of Berwick, and abounds in all kinds of fish, and also in much gold. The inhabitants there are rightly instructed in religion, and obedient to all the laws and ordinances of the English. May the almighty God, the chief governor of all things, grant that our life and actions may sometime correspond to the word and doctrine of his Son, which is at this time gloriously proclaimed both by land and sea! All persons are beginning to speak well about Christ, but there are yet very few who live agreeably to christian principle. But why γλαῦκας εἰς 'Αθήνας[3],' since men of this description are wont to rise up in our country also?

The horrible and severe and shameful calamity, that has befallen the city of Constance[4], still grievously distresses my mind, and torments me night and day. For I am very distrustful, and almost in despair, that those men will ever be restored to their former liberty. I am well assured that God is able to effect this, but am greatly in doubt whether he is willing to do so. But I only increase my distress by dwelling upon the subject, and will therefore bring my letter to a conclusion. Farewell, most learned sir. Bradgate, May 29.

Your most attached scholar,

JOHN AB ULMIS.

[[2] Holy Island, or Lindisfarn, is situated in the German ocean, a mile and a half from the coast of Northumberland, and about ten miles from Berwick.]

[[3] *Send owls to Athens;* a proverb answering to the English one of "carrying coals to Newcastle."]

[[4] See above, p. 385, *n.* 4.]

LETTER CCVI.[1]

JOHN AB ULMIS TO HENRY BULLINGER.

Dated at BRADGATE, *July* 12, 1551.

GREETING. As soon as I returned from Scotland, I diligently acquainted you by letter with all that I had done and intended to do in matters relating to your excellence. I will now only recapitulate them in a short and summary manner, from the fear that, should my former letter have been intercepted by any chance, those things, in which I think you take much interest, may seem to have been neglected by me. And first of all, you must know that your sermons are very much approved by the marquis; and for my own part, as one out of many, I am fully persuaded that you have transferred into that book whatever discernment you possessed in sacred literature. May Almighty God, the supreme governor of all things, grant that our life and actions may sometime correspond to the word and doctrine of his Son, which is now gloriously proclaimed both by land and sea! The marquis assures me that he will write[2] to you as soon as he returns to London or Bradgate: he now desires you to excuse him on account of numerous and important engagements, by which he is occupied more than I can express. He earnestly entreats you in the mean time not to be offended at his silence. The letter of Jane Grey, my Lord's daughter, has, I suppose, reached you, in which she endeavours to give you a proof both of her gratitude and respect: but as letters are always in danger of miscarrying, I have thought it best for your sake to have a copy made of this, lest it should either be intercepted, or lost altogether. It is verbatim as follows[3].

[1 The original of this letter is printed in Fueslin, p. 292.]
[2 The marquis's letter is given above, Letter III. p. 3.]
[3 Lady Jane Grey's letter is given above, Letter IV. p. 4.]

LETTER CCVII.

JOHN AB ULMIS TO HENRY BULLINGER.

Dated *Nov.* 7, 1551.

I WILL now write to you very briefly, and more fully when I have more leisure. Our marquis is created duke of Suffolk: he most positively assured me yesterday, that both he himself and his daughter would write to you within a month. I called to-day upon Cheke, the king's tutor; but as I could not fully converse with him upon your affairs, I am directed to call again to-morrow. But, Stumphius and Andrew[4] being now on the point of embarking, I also am prevented from writing to you at this time. I entreat you to excuse my brevity. I will make amends for it in future by especial diligence and attention. Nov. 7, 1551.

Your excellency's most devoted,

JOHN AB ULMIS.

I ought particularly to remind you respecting the sister of the king of England. But you will learn every thing both better and more correctly from my friend Andrew: you must therefore make inquiry of him.

LETTER CCVIII.

JOHN AB ULMIS TO HENRY BULLINGER.

Dated at OXFORD, *Dec.* 4, 1551.

PERPETUAL health in Christ our Saviour! I wrote to you very briefly, most excellent sir, when I was lately in London, partly because I was then prevented by want of time, and partly because I thought you would be more fully informed by Stumphius of every thing which it might concern your dignity to be acquainted with. Now, however,

[[4] Andrew Croariensis. See Harding's letter above, p. 311.]

since I have both obtained more leisure, and also a more interesting subject is supplied me for writing about, I cannot do otherwise than inform your excellency, at the earliest opportunity, of what I am assured will be most gratifying and acceptable to you. A few days therefore, after Rodolph[1] and Andrew had departed, I called twice upon sir John Cheke, knight[2], the king's tutor, a man, believe me, who is a very great admirer of yours; and I courteously inquired whether your book was acceptable to the duke of Northumberland. He gave me an answer to this effect: "I am very sure, John, of that present having been most acceptable to the duke; for he had always a regard for illustrious men, and before this time he very much loved and reverenced the writings of Bullinger: but that you may more certainly know this to be the case, I would have you either call with me upon the duke, or else carefully write to him such a letter as you may think proper, and which I may be able to present to him, as from yourself, at night when he retires into his chamber: for he is then alone, and less encumbered by his public duties; and I also am then released from attendance upon the king." We sought therefore, an opportunity of convenient access to the duke; but as a free access is never permitted, I wrote him a letter on the subject I was requested: which as soon as the duke had read, he declared that your zeal and labour met with his entire approbation, and that he, for his part, would discharge the duty of a most kind and active friend; in which light he wishes you to consider him as having ever been hitherto, and to believe that he ever will be. Moreover, that it was not through forgetfulness or neglect that he had not yet written to you, but partly through expectation of your performance of that promise which you courteously made to his grace two years since, and partly through the administration of the affairs of the state, by which he desires you to believe that he is wonderfully occupied and distracted; especially in this dangerous and turbulent crisis of the state, than which I know not whether any more troublesome or dangerous ever before

[1 Namely, Stumphius. See the preceding letter.]

[2 Sir John Cheke was knighted Oct. 10, 1551, on the same day that the marquis of Dorset and earl of Warwick were respectively made dukes of Suffolk and Northumberland.]

existed. Cheke, indeed, had intended to write you to this same effect; but when on that account I had waited four whole days in London, news was suddenly brought him of his wife's confinement, and that she was anxiously expecting the return of her husband. As he went away in great haste to his wife early in the morning, he left a note at the palace addressed to myself, but which contained nothing besides the title of Warwick, and an apology for not having written. From this you will consider, as your prudence may suggest, what will be most expedient for you to do. For my part, I think it will be best, and most agreeable to the duke, if you will take the earliest opportunity of fulfilling your promise, that is, of honourably dedicating to his grace some of your lucubrations. Your courtesy will not allow you to deny this to so exalted a personage; besides that you will by no means allow any promises made by you to be broken.

The noble personage in question is most eminent for renown, most influential in authority, most deserving as to religion: he is praised by many, and by the king he is regarded in the place of a father. Why should I say more? He almost alone, with the duke of Suffolk, governs the state, and supports and upholds it on his own shoulders. He is manifestly the thunderbolt and terror of the papists. When the duke of Somerset last year, at the urgent entreaty of the king's sister, had given her licence still to attend mass and have access to her sacrificing knaves, and was unwilling to restrain her in any respect; Warwick is reported to have been very angry with him, and to have said, "The mass is either of God or of the devil: if of God, it is but right that all our people should be allowed to go to it; but if it is not of God, as we are all taught out of the scriptures, why then should not the voice of this fury be equally proscribed to all?" Scarce a year had elapsed from this expostulation, when, lo! the wretched and calamitous fall of the duke of Somerset, by which he is hurled headlong from the highest pinnacle of his power; and doubtless for this especial reason, that he was of a more gentle and pliant nature in religious matters, than was befitting a nobleman possessed of so much authority. Warwick therefore, as soon as he had succeeded into his office, immediately took care that the mass-priests of Mary should be thrown into prison, while to herself he entirely interdicted the use of the mass and of popish books.

You may use this form of dedication: "To the most illustrious prince and lord, lord John Dudley, the most mighty duke of Northumberland, earl of Warwick, &c., president and first lord of the council of the king of the kingdoms of England, Ireland, and France." Our friend Hilles of London, in whose house I left Cheke's note to me, will inclose it in this parcel. It will, I am sure, be pleasant and agreeable to both of you, if you should by this correspondence form a mutual friendship for each other. You are superior to him in age and judgment; he, from his learning and good qualities, has great influence with the king. I am nobly recommended by you, and by him in many ways befriended and benefited. Let this then be the ground of your writing to Cheke, if no better occur to you. He twice entertained my cousins very courteously for your sake in the king's palace, when they arrived here some months since; and making affectionate inquiries respecting yourself and master Pellican, he repeatedly expressed his desire to see one or the other of you in these parts. In the next place, he was almost the only cause of my admission into the king's college, no one making interest for me except Traheron, who stated that I was recommended to him by yourself. Last of all, he has faithfully promised for your sake, to settle with Warwick the cause of Alexander, which Hooper had already entered upon. But this excellent young man cannot expect to derive any advantage from your recommendation, till you have performed your promise to the duke: for then the affair can be arranged of itself, without any compromise of your dignity, and also with due regard to the feelings of Alexander. Do not make any request to Cheke, but only give him to understand that we are not unmindful of, or ungrateful to, either of you. You may in your letter to him make honourable mention of Alexander's father, and say how gratifying it is to you, that for your sake he shewed such attention and kindness to the son of a most honourable and excellent man.

Just as I was writing this, a general and undoubted report has gone abroad, that the duke of Somerset was four[1] days since brought from prison to the house of parliament, and examined before a crowd of people. There were twelve

[[1] He was brought to trial Dec. 1, 1551. For an account of the proceedings see Burnet, II. 286, and Soames, III. 671.]

judges, of whom the duke of Suffolk was the chief. He is said to have been accused, first of high treason, and then of murder, which he had plotted against the duke of Northumberland, and the other members of the council. The first charge, they say, was ably repelled by him; but they state that he was found guilty on the second, and condemned to be hanged according to law. Warwick, observing the grave and sorrowful aspect of the entire audience upon this occasion, exclaims from his seat in the midst of the assembly, "O duke of Somerset, you see yourself brought into the utmost danger, and that nothing but death awaits you. I have once before delivered you from a similar hazard of your life; and I will not now desist from serving you, how little soever you may expect it. I desire you therefore to appeal to the royal clemency, which I doubt not will be extended to you. As far as regards myself, I shall willingly forgive you every thing, and will use every exertion in my power that your life may be spared." Somerset therefore appealed to the king, and implored him to remember the dangers and toils which he had so often undergone in behalf of his country. The most excellent and pious king is said to have shewn himself, with his usual kindness, easy to be entreated[2] by his uncle, and to have restored him to his former friendship with Warwick. And thus every one is happy and rejoicing at this reconciliation of these noblemen. He is not, however, as yet altogether at liberty, but again committed to custody for a fixed and definite period.

Thus much of these things. You will learn many things from Stumphius respecting Hooper, and these few particulars from myself. When he was lately accused by certain persons of acting with severity in the discharge of his function towards tradespeople and those of the lower orders, but lax and indulgent towards those of higher rank, "My brethren," he says, "I wish you would bring before me any of the chief nobility, whom you can prove by positive evidence to have been guilty either of fornication or adultery, and you

[2 The duke was condemned on the 1st of December, but not executed till the 22nd of January, which delay Burnet supposes to have arisen from the management of the duke of Northumberland, who thus seemed to act in his favour, that he might be covered from the popular odium which he saw his death was likely to bring upon him. Burnet, III. 314.]

may punish me with death if I fail to convince you of the impartiality of my proceedings towards all alike." It happened some days after that sir Antony Kingston[1], a man of great influence, was accused of adultery before Hooper. Hooper cited him into his court, but the knight at first refused to make his appearance: induced however at length, as I suppose, by the hope of impunity, he waited on the bishop; and, being severely rebuked by him, gave him a blow on the cheek before all the people, and loaded him with abuse. Hooper laid the whole matter before the government; the council summoned the man forthwith, and treated him so severely that it would have been better for him to have endured anything rather than the punishment inflicted on him by the government: for he was both mulcted in the penalty of five hundred pounds, and handed over to Hooper to be dealt with according to law and custom, to do penance, which kind of punishment is the most shameful and disgraceful of any.

My last words shall be to remind you to perform your promise to Warwick as soon as possible, and then to write to sir John Cheke. You may inclose in mine the letters last written to them.

I will send you more news, and, as I hope, more agreeable, in my next letter. Peter Martyr will do every thing according to your wish. He earnestly bade me to salute in his name both yourself and the other ministers of the church. Oxford. Dec. 4, 1551.

Your excellency's most devoted,

JOHN AB ULMIS.

The books of Peter Martyr have not yet arrived, nor is there any expectation of soon recovering them.

[[1] Sir Antony Kingston was one of the council for the marches of Wales, and afterwards knight marshal. He was subsequently one of the commissioners at Hooper's cremation, when he endeavoured to persuade him to recant, and save his life; failing in which, he said, "Well, my lord, then I perceive there is no remedy, and therefore I will take my leave of you: and I thank God that ever I knew you: for God did appoint you to call me, being a lost child; and by your good instructions, whereas before I was both an adulterer and a fornicator, God hath brought me to the forsaking and detesting of the same." See Foxe, Acts and Mon. VI. 654.]

LETTER CCIX.

JOHN AB ULMIS TO HENRY BULLINGER.

Dated at OXFORD, *Jan.* 10, 1552.

As soon as I received the letter addressed to your excellency by our duke[2], I thought it best to interpose no delay, but that you should, as early as possible, enjoy the greatest gratification, namely, the correspondence of these most noble and exalted personages. I cannot express how much it has delighted me, partly, because I knew that it would be most gratifying to your excellent and honourable self, and partly because I was at the same time informed by Skinner of the exceeding liberality of the duke towards me, by which I shall be able for the future to carry on and pursue my studies with much greater facility. For, induced by your recommendation, he presented Alexander with six pounds, and myself with five; having generously presented me with ten marks not long before. But I do not feel so much gratified by this munificence, as I rejoice and triumph in the extreme kindness and good-will of the duke towards us: for which indeed I can readily understand, and indeed willingly acknowledge, that I am most deeply indebted to your excellency; for unless you had by your kind recommendation placed us in such favour with this nobleman, we should not only have felt the want of the duke's liberality, but also have been unable to pursue with success any kind of learning whatsoever. And that I may at once come to that which you seem to have a right to expect from me, I beg you to be assured and to take for granted, that you have not only secured my lasting respect, which indeed, though it is not of any importance to yourself, yet certainly very much concerns me; but that I will also do my endeavour, that you may never have reason to repent your kind inclination and desire to love me and to do me service. I should make this promise at greater length did I not bear in mind that I must approve myself to you not by words but by actions, and by my diligence in the discharge of my duty exceed even your very thoughts. And lest you should suppose that I have written this without due

[2 The duke's letter is given above, p. 3.]

consideration, I desire that this my writing may have the force of a bond, and not be considered as a mere letter; so that you may quote my own hand and seal against me, if I do not most scrupulously observe every thing, as I have here undertaken, and surpass your expectation by my endeavours to advance and defend your dignity.

Thus much then upon this subject. As to any news that I can write to you, there is not even a rumour of any; for the clamour of all the disaffected is appeased and put down, and this island is now brought by an excellent and religious government into a state of the greatest peaceableness and tranquillity. The duke of Suffolk lately stated it to Skinner as a fact, that, unless Warwick had suppliantly interceded for the life and honour of the duke of Somerset, an executioner from Calais would have carried into effect ere now the sentence that has been already publicly pronounced against that nobleman. You may hence perceive how various and changing is the condition of human life, how fickle and inconstant is fortune, how lamentable is the unfaithfulness of friends, how time-serving is the dissimulation of the great, how wretched and miserable is the life of courtiers!

The convocation began to be held by command of the king's majesty, on the 12th of December, by most excellent and learned men, who are to deliberate and consult about a proper moral discipline and the purity of doctrine. The archbishop of Canterbury and Peter Martyr, the archbishop of York, and the bishop of London, together with the newly appointed chancellor of England, who was previously bishop of Ely[1], and our friend Skinner (who is almost the only acknowledged manager and leader in all controversial matters concerning religion), are to form a select committee upon these points. The affairs will then be submitted to the approbation of every member of parliament, that is, to the judgment both of high and low. It is uncertain what will be the issue. I wish they may be able to provide for the safety of the now wretched and deplorable state of Christen-

[1 Thomas Goodrick received the seals Dec. 22, 1551, to be keeper thereof during the lord Rich's sickness. He was made chancellor Jan. 19, 1552, "because as *custos sigilli* he could execute nothing in the parliament that should be done, but only to seal ordinary things." K. Edward's Journal. Burnet, IV. 226.]

dom. Cox, who is a great admirer of yours, kindly tells me, that as soon as any thing is determined upon, he will let you know by letter.

I wish you would at this time, with your wonted fidelity and discretion, and for the sake of my not newly begun, but long cherished regard for you, endeavour to accomplish what you promised of your own accord to the duke of Northumberland, and dedicate one of your books to his grace as honourably and as speedily as possible. That you should stand by your promises is of great importance to the credit of us both; but most of all for the sake of religion and therefore of godliness itself, which I am fully persuaded will by this means be greatly promoted and maintained. I am induced therefore both by your past favours, and by my love for religion, to advise you to persevere in those exertions, whether of a public or private character, to which you have been encouraged by God himself, with all care and diligence, and never to swerve from that kindness and consistency, which I have always admired and always held up to commendation, through the influence or authority of any individual whatsoever. The opinion of mankind respecting you is great, their praise of your learning great, the reputation of your writings great. He too, of whom I speak, is of the highest rank and most illustrious reputation, and will readily permit the lasting eulogy of his actions to be recorded by yourself: nor will it appear only as a commendation bestowed upon him, but also as a weighty testimony rendered by a great and illustrious man. You will, I hope, let me know as soon as possible both what you are doing and what you intend to do. I am continually expecting a letter from you, and such an one too as I most desire. And I make it an especial request that you will inclose in your letter to me, having carefully sealed them, the letters which you purpose to write both to our duke, and to sir John Cheke, the king's tutor. Respecting this I earnestly wrote to you in my last letter, that is, on December 4th. He is, believe me, a most learned man, one who loves you much, and who deserves well of me. Being induced by your recommendation to Hooper, he kindly promises that he will manage with Warwick the affair of Alexander Schmutz. I should wish him therefore to understand from yourself, that this circumstance will be both gratifying to you, and most convenient for our studies. The matter, indeed, might have been properly settled ere now, when I was last in London: for the duke voluntarily and of his own accord inquired respecting the youth, who had been recommended to him by yourself; and not only promised to forward the studies of this young man at his own charge, but also to make application to the king himself upon this subject. This I had from Cheke. For my own part I was not very anxious about the fulfilment of this promise, because I perceived that the affair would some time or other turn out well of itself, when both you had performed your promises, and we probably should stand most in need of patronage. Farewell, most learned sir.

Your scholar and son in Christ,

JOHN AB ULMIS.

Oxford, Jan. 10, 1552.

LETTER CCX.

JOHN AB ULMIS TO HENRY BULLINGER.

Dated at OXFORD, *Feb* 5, 1552.

IF you are well, I rejoice; I am well myself, as is also the duke. His letter to you I gave to the courier on the 4th of January, to be forwarded to Zurich. I do not know whether it has been delivered, but I am very doubtful of it, not only because winter voyages are in themselves so tedious, but because it is the general fault of men of this class, that they are either careless, or altogether faithless: on this account therefore I have caused the letter to be copied over again for your convenience. You will receive much information from the letters, three in number, which I have written to you since Stumphius left us. I do not doubt, my very dear sir, but that the accounts communicated by me, respecting the favourable disposition of noble personages towards you, are very gratifying and delightful; and I will use every exertion in my power that this friendship may daily be increased and maintained between you. You are indeed more dear to me every day, and your eminent merits constantly quicken my anxiety lest I should lose any portion of your love or favourable opinion. There has been a confident report for some days past, that sir John Cheke, the king's majesty's tutor, is to be made lord chancellor of England in this session: the bishop of Ely is only holding that office for a time, until some one else shall be permanently appointed to that honour by parliament. I would have you write to him without fail; for he greatly loves and esteems you, and is a man, too, of the most distinguished reputation and dignity: so that you cannot in any wise be in want of a subject. It is he principally, and almost solely with Traheron, who has always been the promoter of my welfare. Induced too by your recommendation of them to Cox, he very kindly and courteously entertained my kinsmen[1] in the king's palace. Last of all, he promises of his own accord to take care that the interests of Alexander shall be provided for and promoted by the earl of Warwick. You have already received Warwick's title at full length: he only now requires you to perform your promise, which that you will endeavour to do, or rather that you will do, (for I am well aware of your ability,) I earnestly and repeatedly entreat you. It is a matter of great weight and importance, as with your great discernment you will easily imagine for yourself. Believe me, you will act most judiciously, if you will make a point of writing to him at this next fair, presenting to him your especial respect and service, and thanking his grace for his favourable disposition towards you; but in all this you must carefully interweave whatever may seem to make for the dignity of so distinguished a nobleman.

Peter Martyr is still in London, taking his part in framing ecclesiastical laws. His book has not yet reached us; the Byrkmans are not at all to be trusted. The duke's daughter has recovered from a severe and dangerous illness. She is now engaged in some extraordinary production, which will very soon be brought to light, accompanied with the commendation of yourself. There has lately been discovered a great treasure of most valuable books: Basil on Isaiah and the Psalms in Greek, together with some other writings, or rather fragments, of the same author; Chrysostom on the gospels, in Greek; the whole of Proclus; the Platonists, Porphyry and Plotinus. I have myself seen all these books this

[[1] These were Henry and Conrad ab Ulmis, who came over to England in 1551.]

very day. It now only remains for me, most reverend father in Christ, to bid you farewell, and to entreat you to pardon the rusticity of my letter; for I have written it in haste, and amidst many interruptions. Oxford, Feb. 5, 1552.

Your disciple, and son in Christ,

JOHN AB ULMIS.

Send all your letters, and especially that to Cheke, under cover to me. If I do not procure you a letter from Warwick, never trust me more.

The form of address suitable to the rank of Warwick: "To the most illustrious prince and lord, the lord John Dudley, most potent duke of Northumberland, (or of the people of Northumberland,) earl of Warwick, lord Lisle, first lord of the council to the king of the kingdoms of England, Ireland and France."

The duke of Suffolk, his daughter, Haddon, Aylmer, and Skinner, have all written to you. I have forwarded you all their letters as above stated.

Dr Oglethorpe, the vice-chancellor of this university, is now anxiously expecting a letter from you, as is also Harding, a man of exquisite learning.

LETTER CCXI.

JOHN AB ULMIS TO HENRY BULLINGER.

Dated at Oxford, *Feb.* 8, 1552.

This is the fifth letter that I have written to you since the departure of Stumphius; chiefly for this reason, that, having no confidence in the fidelity of the couriers, I was very unwilling that the letter, addressed to your excellency by the most noble duke, should be lost in its way, as I have no doubt but that it would be most gratifying to you. I rely upon your friendship and kindness to let me know as early as possible whether all the letters have been faithfully delivered to you, and I entreat you not to keep me long in suspense about this matter. Every thing here is in a quiet and settled state, except that in London yesterday, at eight o'clock in the morning, the duke of Somerset[1] was beheaded by an executioner from Calais. Cox was his confessor, as they call it, and doubtless to his exceeding grief and distress; for they had always been upon the most intimate and friendly terms. Plots of an altogether strange and novel character are said to have been contrived by him against Warwick. These circumstances of the times are truly wretched and deplorable. The fall and ruin of this distinguished nobleman is most deeply and universally lamented. It seemed indeed to have been destined long before, that such a death should, some time or other, be the harbour of his unhappy and long harassed fortunes. What farther is to be expected he alone knows, who is at once the immortal sovereign and most righteous judge of the whole world.

Do you, in conclusion, cause some one of your books to be dedicated to the duke of Northumberland as soon as possible; and write also a letter to sir John Cheke, the king's tutor, which may convey your especial acknowledgment of the favours conferred upon me chiefly for your sake; making particular mention of the business of my, or rather of your, friend Alexander: for Cheke[2] promises that he will manage this matter effectually with Warwick. You will not in this case do any thing but what is worthy of you, and at the same time most gratifying and agreeable to our wishes. I entreat you, most accomplished sir, with all the earnestness in my power, to comply with this request. Send all the letters to me, and especially the one for Cheke. Again farewell. Oxford, Feb. 8, 1552, late at night.

Your pupil, and son in Christ,

JOHN AB ULMIS.

[[1] The duke of Somerset was beheaded on Tower Hill, Jan. 22, 1552. For an account of his execution see Foxe, VI. 293; Burnet, II. 294; Strype, Mem. II. 1. 537; Soames, III. 679. The date of this letter appears to have been incorrectly copied, or else wrongly given in the original autograph.]

[[2] Both sir John Cheke and bishop Hooper solicited the duke in behalf of Alexander, who, on the return of John ab Ulmis to Switzerland, was elected into the fellowship vacated by him at St John's, Oxford. See Strype, Mem. II. 1. 534.]

LETTER CCXII.

JOHN AB ULMIS TO HENRY BULLINGER.

Dated at OXFORD, *March* 1, 1552.

HEALTH in Christ, and the joy of the Holy Ghost! Such, most excellent sir, is the state of our affairs, that I have really nothing to acquaint you with by letter, unless perhaps you may wish to know what has been decreed in convocation respecting ecclesiastical matters, and in what condition are the affairs of our duke. But as I am aware that you will learn all these matters both from the letter of [lady] Jane, the duke's daughter, and from Traheron, I deem it superfluous to write more concerning them at this present time. I am daily in anxious expectation of letters from you, and such too as I most desire. You will find Cheke to be a most learned man and a very faithful friend, and Warwick himself a most accomplished and generous nobleman. If the letters are delivered through my hands, I dare pledge my word that you will soon receive answers to them all. As soon therefore as I have received them, you shall know what steps I have taken. I have no news to communicate respecting myself, except that, at the desire of Cox, and with the concurrence of Martyr, I have assumed the dignity of a master of arts[1]. I shall at the same time lay aside these trifles and my longing for home, and will endeavour to attain by singular assiduity and application the object for which I left it. May you, most learned sir, my very dear Bullinger, live long and happily! Oxford. In haste. March 1, 1552.

Your excellency's most devoted son in the Lord,

JOHN AB ULMIS.

[1 See above, p. 389, *n*. 1.]

LETTER CCXIII.

JOHN AB ULMIS TO CONRAD PELLICAN.

Dated at OXFORD, [before *June* 19][2], 1552.

PERPETUAL health in Christ! I received your letter, reverend father, on the 20th of February, though it was dated on the 5th of August last year; and it was acceptable to me in proportion to my long and anxious expectation of it. It was indeed most delightful, though, to confess the truth, I was beginning to suspect that I had lost all hope concerning it, because, when I received numerous letters from Zurich, I never found any addressed to me from yourself; which circumstance as it kept me in long and grievous suspense through anxiety and expectation, so a single perusal of your letter most powerfully restored my spirits. But you must know in the first place, and take my word for the fact, that this mark of your respect to the most godly daughter of the duke of Suffolk has been very gratifying and acceptable to her. For I delivered your letter to her in person, and easily perceived the great veneration that is both entertained and expressed for you by the whole of the duke's household. Your reputation here is very great, as is the commendation of your well-spent life, and the remembrance of your writings: I could wish you therefore, my very dear father in Christ, to continue to assist and advance the studies of the daughter of a most valued nobleman, and one too who has deserved so much at my hands; and as you find her well prepared, and making a steady progress, do not cease to exhort her, that she may daily more and more excel herself in learning and in the cultivation of her mind. Persons do not usually disregard the commendations of distinguished men, especially when they do not seem to be offered lightly, or without sufficient ground; but are rather more vehemently excited by such exhortations to the pursuit of excellence. And that this is the case with this noble and excellent young lady, you will perceive, to her great

[2 Pellican states, in a MS. journal preserved at Zurich, "On June 19, 1552, I received a Latin letter written with admirable elegance and learning from the noble virgin, Jane Grey, of the illustrious house of Suffolk." This letter is not now extant.]

credit, from the letter addressed to your excellency, in which she endeavours to manifest and let you know the gratitude and courtesy she feels towards you. Do you therefore take her kindness in good part, and continue to esteem her as you have begun.

We are all well here, and improving every day: I have a most liberal patron, a most favourable opportunity, and certainly such an especial commendation from Bullinger, that I only fear lest I should seem wanting to myself. I will guard against this, as far as God shall enable me, and will endeavour by my own assiduity, and the blessing of God, to attain the object for which I left home. Whatever news there may be here, you will shortly learn from Froschover. I saluted in your name, as dutifully as I could, Peter Martyr and à Lasco. They are both of them safe and well, and desire to salute you much in return. The convocation respecting ecclesiastical affairs begun to be held three[1] months since: as soon as any thing has been determined, I will let you know. I will, moreover, studiously and diligently see to whatever I think you may require, and which will conduce to your interests. Affectionately salute for me your son Samuel. Again and again, most reverend Pellican, and my very dear father in Christ, I bid you farewell. Oxford, from the king's college, 1552.

Your son in the Lord,

JOHN AB ULMIS.

LETTER CCXIV.

JOHN AB ULMIS TO HENRY BULLINGER.

Dated at OXFORD, *July* 7, 1552.

HAVING been informed by John Byrkman of the intended departure of the courier for Zurich, I have just been scribbling I know not what. In the first place, I cannot in the least make out what feeling has rendered you averse from the duty of writing to the duke, and so far made you forgetful of

[[1] Namely, on Dec. 12, as stated above, p. 444. This letter, therefore, was probably written about the middle of March.]

persons who are so well disposed towards you. For how can I persuade myself that the letter from the palace of our duke has never reached you? when I know, that I transcribed it not once or twice only, but six times over, and that I delivered no copy of it but to persons to whom your name was well known; besides which, the profit and payment of the couriers arises from the carriage of letters. But you may possibly have returned an answer, which has been either lost, or opened, or intercepted on the road. Should this be the case, your excellency, I hope, will make inquiry to whom you entrusted it to be forwarded to me. So far from having received any letter from you, I certainly have not, for the last six months, heard a word about you. Wherefore I am wretchedly anxious, and full of complaint; yet at the same time I can hardly tell what to complain about, since your constant regard for me, and your acute judgment in every thing prevents my supposing you to have acted either rashly or unkindly. Then again, this so unusual and prolonged silence, when you have so many motives for writing to these noble personages, acutely goads and harasses my mind, lest either some severe calamity should have happened either to you, so that you cannot write, or else, relating to my affairs, so that you will not. The duke of Northumberland desires the fulfilment and satisfaction of his expectation respecting yourself and your promise. But my duke[2] has long since begun to express his surprise at not having received any answer from you, so eloquent as you are, and at other times such an excellent correspondent. Wherefore, both for the sake of your own honour and of my credit, I hope you will write as soon and as carefully as possible to both these noblemen. For these good men will by no means receive your apology from me. I ask you therefore, as earnestly as I can, to comply with my request. Peter [Martyr] desires me to send his salutations. Farewell, most learned and very dear Bullinger. Oxford. July 7, 1552.

Your scholar and most constant son in Christ,

JOHN AB ULMIS.

[2 Namely, the Duke of Suffolk.]

LETTER CCXV.

JOHN AB ULMIS TO HENRY BULLINGER.

Dated at OXFORD, *July* 27, 1552.

I AM tormented with waiting for your letters, which, I believe, are by this time written, but I am sadly afraid of their being lost. I entreat you therefore to write them over again, especially those to the dukes. Warwick[1] proceeded at the beginning of May, with a great retinue, to Berwick, and is daily expected on his return. But our duke has been staying these last few days at an estate here in the neighbourhood of Oxford, which has come to him by inheritance from the late duke of Suffolk[2]. I waited upon him, and paid my respects, according to the custom of the university. At my request he made a present of three bucks to our society. Respecting yourself, I assure you, he very kindly inquired about what you are doing, and how you are. I made such answer as I thought expedient. It is now your part, and I must say your duty, to write to him in return as soon as possible. Give me, I pray, to understand that you are interested in me and mine, which will prove to be the case, provided only in your letter to Warwick you will mention Alexander in the way I wish. Skinner salutes you. Martyr is absent. Oxford, in haste. July 27. The gloves shall be faithfully delivered to your wife. Farewell, my very dear and much esteemed Bullinger.

Your excellency's most attached,

JOHN AB ULMIS.

[1 The earl of Warwick was ordered to go into the north as warden general, May 11, 1552. Strype, Mem. II. 1. 498.]

[2 Henry, duke of Suffolk, and his brother, lord Charles Brandon, died of the sweating sickness, July 16, 1551. The marquis of Dorset, who married their half-sister, was invested with the title of the dukedom, and succeeded to part of the estates. Strype, Mem. II. 1. 491.]

LETTER CCXVI.

JOHN AB ULMIS TO HENRY BULLINGER.

Dated at OXFORD, *Aug.* 9, [1552].

HEALTH in the Son of God! I could never have believed it possible, that either you would have so long forborne writing, or that I should be so greatly tormented by the expectation of a letter from you. I suppose that the disturbances which we hear have lately arisen in Germany, have hitherto prevented your writing to me. But still I can hardly imagine that you have been unable to meet with another mode of conveyance through France, since I have already twice received letters from Zurich by this route. It sometimes comes into my mind to suspect that the duke's letter, of which I have sent you from hence about ten copies, has not been faithfully delivered; which indeed I should readily believe, did I not know for certain, that the original was conveyed as far as Basle by a most confidential messenger. On the whole, I am at a loss what to do, or what excuse to make to the duke. I must therefore, as a last resource, tell you what I think. If you love me, if you desire the good opinion of the duke, do make me happy by a letter as soon as possible. And I wish too, that you would honourably perform the remainder of your promise and duty to the duke of Northumberland. Commend Alexander to Cheke as earnestly as you can, since, induced by your recommendation, he has taken the entire management of his affairs upon himself. I entreat and implore you to do this, again and again, and with all the vehemence and earnestness in my power. Though I expect every thing from you, there is nothing, most learned and very dear Bullinger, by which you can afford me greater pleasure. And as for myself, I thus call God to witness, while I promise and declare that, as the only means afforded me, as a grateful man, of making any return, I will undertake any duties and labours whatsoever for your excellency, so as even to go beyond your opinion of me; which though I feel to be a matter of difficulty, yet I trust to be able to prove it to you by the result. Not however to be too tedious, I bid you farewell, and entreat you to love me as you do.

I send you, inclosed in mine, a letter from lady Jane, the duke's daughter. I had intended indeed to return home this summer, as you will perceive from the letter of Augustine, with whom I have lived in the greatest intimacy, as a fellow-student. But as I understand that every thing yonder is in a state of disorder[1] and confusion, I think it best to remain in these parts, until I hear how those disturbances will end; so that the gloves, which the daughter of the duke desired me to present to your wife as an especial token of her regard, cannot be conveniently sent to you before the autumn fair. Again and again, most excellent sir, farewell. Affectionately salute in my name masters Pellican, Gualter, and Wolfius. Peter Martyr desires his respects. Every thing here is settled and quiet. Cheke[2] has recovered from a most dangerous illness. Oxford. Aug. 9, [1552.]
Your excellency's most attached,

and constant son in Christ,

JOHN AB ULMIS.

As I was about to inclose lady Jane's letter in this, it occurred to me that I had inclosed it together with the others in the parcel that I sent you from hence, I think, on the 10th of July; so that I suppose you will have received it before this time.

[1 The taking of Augsburg and other places by duke Maurice of Saxony, and of Metz by the French king, are the disorders here referred to. They were ended by the treaty of Passau, concluded August 2, 1552.]

[2 The king was extraordinarily concerned for him, and not only recommended his schoolmaster to the care of his physicians, but also to the heavenly physician, whom in his devotions he earnestly implored to spare his life: and upon his prayers such a strange assurance was impressed in his mind that Cheke would recover, that when the doctors (as was said) despaired of him, the king made this surprising reply to them: "Ho," said he, "Cheke will not die this time; for this morning I begged his life in my prayer, and obtained it;" and so it came to pass, for towards the latter end of the month of May he recovered. Fuller's Church History, B. VII. Cent. xvi. 19, 20. Strype, Cheke, 88.]

LETTER CCXVII.

JOHN AB ULMIS TO HENRY BULLINGER.

Dated at OXFORD, *Aug.* 16, 1552.

I WILL write more when I have more leisure; I am now writing to you in great haste. I have not received a single letter from you for ten months, at which I cannot sufficiently express my astonishment. I do not think that you have forgotten me, for I have given you no reason to do so: yet on the other hand this long and painful silence of yours most wonderfully harasses and torments me, lest any evil should have befallen our common affairs. The daughter of the duke has now written to you twice, and the duke himself once; and I have taken care that their letters should be conveyed to you by confidential messengers. Wherefore, if you love me, if you value your reputation, write back to these noble personages as diligently and as quickly as possible. In your letter to Warwick make especial mention of Alexander, and at the same time return him your thanks for the extreme kindness that he offered and has now manifested towards me. I wish you would also do the same to the duke of Suffolk. I entreat you most earnestly to do this. The gloves, which the daughter of the duke had given me to be sent over yonder to your wife, cannot conveniently be forwarded before the fair. She wished also to send her a beautiful gold ring, but I did not receive it for certain reasons, which would be too long to enumerate in this letter. Farewell, most learned sir, and take in good part this letter, witten as it is in so rude and careless a manner. Oxford, Aug. 16, 1552.

Salute, I pray you, our common friends.

Yours entirely,

JOHN AB ULMIS.

P.S. Cheke[3] is now quite well again. Cox will be no longer chancellor of this university. We shall, I understand, have an election within these two hours. There is good hope,

[[3] See above, p. 456, n. 2.]

nay, the very best, that the duke of Suffolk will take upon himself this dignity, and the patronage of our city. It is currently reported that Cox will very soon be made a bishop. Write, I pray you, as promptly as you can to Cheke. This is written to you in the greatest haste.

LETTER CCXVIII.

CONRAD AB ULMIS TO RODOLPH GUALTER.

Dated at OXFORD, *Aug.* 10, 1551.

GREETING. That I have not yet written to you, most learned sir, you must not impute to neglect, than which nothing can be farther from my thoughts; nor to any forgetfulness of your deserts, the remembrance of which no time shall ever efface: but partly, because in the short period of my residence here, I could neither give you any information respecting the affairs of England or my own; and partly, because I waited to see the result of your letter of commendation. Wherefore, if my silence has displeased you, I earnestly request you, by your love for me, and by my respect for you, to pardon me this once. And now, as things are in such a state as that I have something certain to write to you about, I cannot any longer defer my letter. You must know then that your letter to master doctor Peter Martyr on our behalf had very great weight and influence with him, so much so indeed, that he has promised to be ready at all times to afford us his services and assistance for your sake. It shall be my endeavour that you may not seem to have been mistaken in your opinion of me, and that I may not have enjoyed in vain the commendation of so great a man. I therefore offer you my lasting thanks for your commendatory letter, and will give you occasion to understand, some time or other, that you have conferred an obligation upon one who is neither unmindful nor ungrateful; and though I am sensible it may be difficult to effect this, yet I trust that in the issue I shall be able to accomplish it. Continue to love me as you have begun, and farewell, and let us be commended to you again and again.

John our friend and my very dear brother sends his salutations. Oxford, Aug. 10, 1551.

Your worship's most devoted,

JOHN CONRAD AB ULMIS.

LETTER CCXIX.

CONRAD AB ULMIS TO JOHN WOLFIUS.

Dated at Oxford, *March* 1, 1552.

Greeting. As I never entertained a doubt but that it was my duty to write to you, as my preceptor, some account of my studies; though I wrote last month at the house of Joshua Maler, my dear friend, and one too who has a great respect for you; yet as I have at this time changed my course of study, I have thought fit to write to you again. Receive therefore a brief account of my studies. I devote the hour from six to seven in the morning to Aristotle's politics, from which I seem to derive a twofold advantage, both a knowledge of Greek and an acquaintance with moral philosophy. The seventh hour I employ upon the first book of the Digests or Pandects of the Roman law, and the eighth in the reconsideration of this lecture. At nine I attend the lecture of that most eminent and learned divine, master doctor Peter Martyr. The tenth hour I devote to the rules of Dialectics of Philip Melancthon *de locis argumentorum*. Immediately after dinner I read Cicero's Offices, a truly golden book, from which I derive no less than a twofold enjoyment, both from the purity of the language and the knowledge of philosophy. From one to three I exercise my pen, chiefly in writing letters, wherein, as far as possible, I imitate Cicero, who is considered to have abundantly supplied us with all instructions relating to purity of style. At three I learn the institutes of civil law, which I so read aloud as to commit them to memory. At four are read privately, in a certain hall in which we live, the rules of law, which I hear, and learn by rote as I do the institutes. After supper the time is spent in various discourse; for either sitting in our chamber, or walking up and down some part of the college, we exercise ourselves in dialectical questions. You have now a brief account of my studies, with which I think you will be pleased. Do you take care, in the first place, to preserve your health, and in the next place, to address me occasionally by your letters; for you can hardly conceive how much pleasure I shall derive both from their elegance and agreeableness. Salute for me those most honourable ladies, your wife and mother. Farewell. Oxford, March 1, 1552.

Your pupil,

JOHN CONRAD AB ULMIS.

LETTER CCXX.

JOHN STUMPHIUS TO HENRY BULLINGER.

Dated at OXFORD, [about the end of *May*], 1549.

YOUR exceeding kindness and long approved fidelity not only towards me, but towards my very dear parents, have manifested themselves in every possible way, both by the numberless other favours with which you have loaded us, and especially by your last valedictory conversation with me, so full of courtesy, friendship, attachment and devotedness. Encouraged therefore, and relying upon these, I have no hesitation in intruding upon you by this my letter, wherein I shall first acquaint you with my present condition, and then add, in a few words, my present wants. After I left home, and had accomplished a long journey[1] attended with labour, expense, peril and trouble, I at length reached London, the wished for goal, on the 16th of May; where having left master Hooper with his dear family, on the 25th of the same month I proceeded to Oxford. I was received there by all the learned men with the greatest kindness: they all began upon the first interview to inquire and converse about you, and to promise me all their services and friendly offices for your sake. But your sincere friend master doctor Peter Martyr, and also master Sidall, a man of great influence, con-

[1 An account of this journey is given by Hooper, whom Stumphius accompanied to England, in letters XXVI—XXXI. above.]

siderable erudition, exceeding uprightness, and a courteous and friendly person, are my especial patrons, partly through the advantage of master Traheron's commendation, and partly out of regard to you. To these things must be added the remarkable liberality of master Cox towards me and my studies: for by the especial assistance of that individual, I am admitted into the college which they call the king's college, upon these terms; namely, upon payment of a moderate sum for a year, I shall be enabled to live most comfortably among the king's scholars, who are the most eminent both for learning and authority in the whole university. For this beneficence therefore of persons so distinguished I think it an incumbent duty to shew my grateful remembrance in every possible way, whenever an opportunity shall occur. And I perceive that this can nowise be more conveniently or properly effected than, if I can only obtain from you so great a favour, by the occasional assistance of a letter from you. For whatever has been done in this matter, no one can doubt but that it has been done out of respect to yourself. For these persons have a very high opinion of you, a great reverence for your learning, a perfect acquaintance with your writings, and, in fine, a great value for and hope of your friendship. And you perceive how much more lively and evident will be these sentiments, if some little commendation should occasionally be afforded by your kindness. Since this, therefore, is the case, I earnestly request and entreat and beseech you to be pleased to aid and assist me by your kind offices, and to take care that my studies be commended to these distinguished individuals, and thus testify your wish that my interests and usefulness should be protected and augmented by your means. I have no doubt but that you have no less ability than inclination, and that whatever may be most easy for you to do, will be most gratifying to them, and advantageous to me; for I am quite sure that I shall obtain much more in this place by an assiduous acknowledgement of favours, than by an importunate solicitation of them. If therefore you shall think proper to do this, I promise and warrant you from my own experience, that you will confirm all worthy persons in their regard for you, and will add them to your list of friends: and I would have you address in your letter the courteous and grave, yet gentle, master Sidall, the zealous preacher of Christ, and your most attached friend, no less than doctor Cox, that he may understand my acknowledgement of the favours he has bestowed upon me to have been of no common kind; for I cannot but bear testimony to his exceeding regard and respect for yourself. For very frequently is he wont to converse with me about you, not only when any occasion is afforded him on my part, but also of his own accord, entertaining as he evidently does a very exalted opinion of you. Wherefore I pray you to regard me in this matter, now I am absent from you; which if you will do, I shall think you have rendered me every possible service.

I have always held such familiarity and friendly intercourse with master Hooper, as that nothing can exceed it; for I am quite unable sufficiently to express the benefit I have received from his aid and counsel. He is a true friend of the liberties of the church and commonwealth of Zurich, and their defender from every calumny. I am on the most intimate terms with John ab Ulmis; for we were old acquaintance, and your letter, in which you commended him to Cox, made us better acquainted than before. All friends in England are well. Dated at Oxford, in the year after the birth of Christ, 1549.

Your worship's most devoted,

JOHN RODOLPH STUMPHIUS.

LETTER CCXXI.

JOHN STUMPHIUS TO HENRY BULLINGER.

Dated at Oxford, *Jan.* 29, 1550.

Your letter, most excellent sir, written at the end of October last, in the year 1549, I received on the 27th of January of this present year: nothing was ever more agreeable or acceptable to me, and that for many reasons. And first of all, because you have so courteously accepted those humble services of mine, and have honoured me in return by your recommendation to that most celebrated man, master doctor Peter Martyr. You have also informed me of the tranquil state of my country, and added some wholesome and truly paternal advice, which I most gratefully accept. And whereas you recommend me to decline receiving any pecuniary assistance either from the king or any other noble personages, I acknowledge your friendship and regard for my welfare; but I would not have either you, or my very dear parent, to be uneasy on this account. For though the way and method of making interest for appointments of this kind has long since been pointed out to me, yet that law[1] of my own country has always been written in my remembrance. You must not however find fault with me from the circumstance of my being permitted to live with the king's scholars; for this permission is not given gratuitously, but I have to pay for my board five English crowns, more or less, at the end of every term. And if you will not believe this, I have the royal mandate to prove it; for it is provided therein that no foreigner shall be admitted into a fellowship at any college. Besides, I can call to witness masters Hooper, Martyr, and Richard Hilles, who well know how much I pay, and how much I have spent in the present year. I pray you therefore, by your great kindness and friendship, that should this matter be mentioned among you, you will be pleased to defend me by your approbation. There is very little news at present: the chief is the report that a peace is now meditated between the kings of England and France; and there are not wanting those who assert that the English have paid due regard to your interests in this matter, so that the gospel and the church may be preserved in Switzerland; but I cannot positively affirm whether this be the case or not. You will hear every thing else from our friend John ab Ulmis, who has taken upon himself this office. Masters Hooper and Martyr are well. Francis Dryander, whom you saluted in your letter to me, is lately gone to Basle. Farewell, ornament of your country. Dated at Oxford, Jan. 29, 1550.

Your worship's most devoted,

JOHN RODOLPH STUMPHIUS.

[[1] It appears that the citizens of Zurich were prohibited by the regulations of that canton from receiving any pecuniary emoluments from foreign states.]

LETTER CCXXII.

JOHN STUMPHIUS TO HENRY BULLINGER.

Dated at OXFORD, *Feb.* 28, 1550.

THOUGH we have each of us replied to that last letter of yours which so much delighted us, I shall nevertheless begin my present writing by a reference to it. For among other things which you most kindly mentioned to us, you exhorted us to communicate to you any new intelligence we might have to offer; and this I am now endeavouring to do to the best of my power. For I am now able to write with greater freedom and more fully, inasmuch as the sixth of February[1] of this present year has proved a truly joyful and most prosperous day to us. For it put an end to the London council, and delivered from prison the duke of Somerset, who, entangled in the snares of the papists, and wrongfully accused of many and grievous crimes, was not only removed from the protectorate of the whole realm, which he had held in charge since the death of Henry the eighth, but was also placed in very severe confinement, insomuch that there remained very little or no hope of deliverance during his life. The distress which this most grievous calamity of the duke occasioned to the gospellers, and to all good men, is wonderful to relate; for those cruel beasts the Romanists, with which Oxford abounds, were now beginning to triumph over the downfall of our duke, the overthrow of our gospel now at its last gasp, and the restoration of their darling the mass, as though they had already obtained a complete victory. They had begun to revive the celebration of their abominable mass in their conventicles, to practise their ancient mummeries at funerals and other offices of that kind, and to inundate themselves with wine, as became the champions of such a religion as theirs. And their furious rage had gone so far, as to threaten, in their

[1 On the sixth of February the duke of Somerset was set at liberty, giving bond of £10,000 for his good behaviour; and being limited that he should stay at the king's house of Sheen, or his own of Sion, and should not go four miles from them, nor come to the king or council, unless he were called; he had his pardon on the 16th of February. Burnet, II. 226; Soames, III. 539.]

most shameless discourses, the faithful servants of Christ with exile, fire, and sword, and all kinds of evil, unless they should gain wisdom by the extreme danger of this nobleman, and come back to their party. But oh! the audacious and insane act! For all the wisdom they had, they wasted when they had nothing to oppose them, and completely betrayed to every one their malicious disposition. For, contrary to all expectation, the duke was set at liberty, and religion established by the common consent of the whole council. Hence it happens, that though I have not hitherto dared to write you any news, I hope for the future to have the means of doing so with greater safety. On the breaking up of the council, master Cox betook himself to Oxford, where he is still residing: we hope also that means have been discovered by which such rotten members of antichrist may be altogether cut off, and driven away from the university; and certain regulations laid down by master Cox upon his arrival have confirmed this hope. But more of this at some future time; I now turn to other matters. They say that a bishoprick has been offered to Latimer, the king's preacher, whose place is now occupied by our friend master Hooper. Master Cheke and master Traheron have entered upon the duties committed to them by the council: the one, that of tutor to the king; the other, that of tutor to the duke of Suffolk, who is of the same age with the king.

These are the circumstances, reverend father in Christ, with which I wished you to be acquainted at this present time, in the hope that they would not be unacceptable to you, unless perhaps you have already heard them more fully related by others; in which case I think there is no occasion for my troubling you with a longer letter. This only I most earnestly request of you, that you will continue to regard me with the same benevolence and kindness that I have hitherto experienced. You have no reason to be afraid of my accepting any presents or salary, as you have already been sufficiently informed by my last letter in reply to yours, if indeed it has reached you. Farewell in Christ, ornament of your country! Salute, I pray you, in my name your son-in-law, master Huldrick Zuinglius, my dear friend, to whom, if I thought he would have been pleased by it, I would have written even now. Masters Peter Martyr and

Oglethorpe are alive and well, and affectionately salute you. Dated at Oxford, Feb. 28, 1550.

Your reverence's most attached,

JOHN RODOLPH STUMPHIUS.

LETTER CCXXIII.

JOHN STUMPHIUS TO HENRY BULLINGER.

Dated *June* 1, 1550.

[EXTRACT.]

THUS much of my own affairs[1]. With respect however to the English government, every thing is now upon a right footing; and there is also the greatest hope as to religion, for the archbishop of Canterbury has lately married a wife[2]. The bishop of London too has cast down, throughout all the churches committed to his charge, the altars, which had hitherto been retained for the administration of the holy eucharist. Our friend master Hooper likewise, who on the feast of the Ascension was made bishop of Gloucester, has committed such havoc with the pontificial ceremonies, that, should there follow such another, it will be all over with them. For he nobly stood forth in the king's council against those bishops who strenuously supported the vestments and such-like triflings; and the reverend fathers were at last brought to confess that these things were merely matters of indifference. This being conceded, the council forthwith nominate Hooper to be a bishop, adding this resolution, that

[1 The greater part of this and the following letter relates to the private affairs of the writer. Copies therefore have not been sent from Zurich.]

[2 *Nuper uxorem duxit.* Orig. This however must mean that "in the time of king Edward, when the marriage of the clergy was allowed, he brought her forth, and lived openly with her. He had previously married her, when he was ambassador in Germany, in the preceding reign, during which he kept her secret; and upon the act of the Six Articles he sent her away into Germany, that he might give no offence, nor draw any danger upon himself." See Strype, Cranmer, 600.]

since they have determined these things to be indifferent, they must regard each other with mutual kindness, and acknowledge Hooper in his vestments as a brother and companion in the ministry; and that he on the other hand must do the same to them. But with regard to the cardinal points of faith, the majority of the bishops, and most of the council, are on our side: and as to the others, if there be such, they dare no longer mutter a single word.

I will conclude my letter with the mention of a circumstance that occurred among us at Oxford during these holidays. A certain sacrilegious mass-priest, the head of the papists, of whom a great number still remain, the enemy of God and of all faithful people, having often acted the fable of the mass in the popish conventicles, was at last caught in the fact during these holidays, and thrown into prison, upon these terms, that for ....[3] entire months he should be fattened and .... upon dry bread and pure water, even should no severer punishment follow. And each of his hearers has to pay for such excellent instruction ten English pounds, that is, ... florins of our money, to the king, that they may at length learn by experience, that the mass is not rashly to be despised, upon which the king sets so great a value. Farewell.

Your worship's most attached,

JOHN ROD. STUMPHIUS.

LETTER CCXXIV.

JOHN STUMPHIUS TO HENRY BULLINGER.

Dated at OXFORD, *Nov.* 12, 1550.

[EXTRACT.][4]

As to what is going on at Oxford, though it is hardly worth a letter, yet I think I ought to make you acquainted with it. The Oxford men, who have been hitherto accus-

[3 The omission in this and other passages is occasioned by the original MS. having been torn at the edge.]

[4 See the preceding page, note 1.]

tomed to do so, are still pertinaciously sticking in the mud of popery; and master Cox, in his opposition to them, seems to be rather too fond of the Fabian tactics: for he has begun to act with greater laxity, for the purpose, I suppose, of wearing them out by delay. Master Hooper is planning great and noble designs, especially against the power and luxury and ceremonies of the priests and bishops, nor have his godly endeavours hitherto been without success; for you will soon, perhaps, hear from himself the great progress that he has made. As I am at a great distance from London, I have been unable to procure any farther intelligence.

Sidall was exceedingly gratified by your letter; but as he could not reply to it at this time, by reason of his government of the king's college, over which he presides during the absence of Cox, he desired our friend John and myself to make his excuse, and to salute you very respectfully for him in our letter. Farewell. Dated at Oxford, the day after the feast of St Martin. 1550.

Your worship's much attached,

JOHN RODOLPH STUMPHIUS.

LETTER CCXXV.

PETER MARTYR TO MARTIN BUCER.

Dated at OXFORD, *Dec.* 26, 1548.

I HAD intended to have written to you long since; and nothing has prevented my doing so, but that I have been awaiting the result of this parliament[1]: but as its proceedings are not yet made known, I am unable to tell you any thing respecting religion; concerning which if I neglect to inform you, I do not see what weight or authority my letter would have as to other matters; inasmuch as to us, to whom to live is Christ, every thing that does not relate to the administration of his kingdom is altogether futile. Up

[[1] Parliament assembled for business this year on the 15th of October. A bill was passed to legalise the marriage of the clergy; and another to authorise the new book of Common Prayer. See Burnet, II. 141.; Soames, III. 400.]

to this time this subject has been one of doubt and uncertainty; for many persons have been afraid, that by reason of the unhappy events in Germany this kingdom would be yet more tardy, and employ new delays in fully taking up the cause of religion. But things are going on far otherwise, because diligent exertions are now making for this sole object, and there is generally entertained the best hope of success. There are two things, however, which alarm me exceedingly. The one is, the most obstinate pertinacity of the friends of popery. If you knew by what fury, impudence and perverseness they are actuated, you would be astonished: and then they argue with such cunning and artful sophistry, that I cannot but think that they are speaking in opposition to their own private convictions; and indeed all men of this stamp seem to have agreed upon this one point, that they will say any thing rather than bring their minds to entertain the clear and open truth. May it please God some time to deliver his church from this plague! Nor are there a few persons only of this mischievous and unhappy temper, but they are very numerous, and consisting of bishops, doctors, and men of that class; who are so cunning as to draw a multitude of ignorant persons along with them, and so bold, that, perceiving the supreme power of this kingdom, which is commonly called a parliament, is shortly about to make some regulations respecting religion, and feeling that the result will not be in their favour, they are consoling themselves with expectations from the emperor, and muttering every where that he will not long allow of such proceedings.

The other matter which distresses me not a little is this, that there is so much contention among our people about the eucharist, that every corner is full of it. And even in the supreme council of the state, in which matters relating to religion are daily brought forward, there is so much disputing of the bishops among themselves and with others, as I think was never heard before. Whence those who are in the lower house, as it is called, that is, men of inferior rank, go up every day into the higher court of parliament, not indeed for the purpose of voting, (for that they do in the lower house,) but only that they may be able to hear these sharp and fervent disputations. Hitherto the popish party has been defeated, and the palm rests with our friends, but especially with the archbishop of Canterbury, whom they till now were wont to traduce as a man ignorant of theology, and as being only conversant with matters of government; but now, believe me, he has shewn himself so mighty a theologian against them as they would rather not have proof of, and they are compelled, against their inclination, to acknowledge his learning, and power and dexterity in debate. Transubstantiation, I think, is now exploded, and the difficulty respecting the presence is at this time the most prominent point of dispute: but the parties engage with so much vehemence and energy as to occasion very great doubt as to the result; for the victory has hitherto been fluctuating between them. May the Holy Spirit grant that nothing may be determined upon but what may be for the advantage and welfare of the church! With respect to a change of religion, they can no longer retrace their steps; for such great innovations have every where taken place, and all things are so changed and removed from their former state, that if they were long suffered to remain so, wonderful disorder would ensue. Wherefore I have no doubt but that something must be decided upon; and I hope it may be under good auspices, and with the favour of Christ: and when this shall be the case, we must also entreat the Lord that the powers of hell, which are every where in arms, may not prevail against the truth of his word.

But I will lay aside these things for a while, and commit them, as it is right I should do, to the care of our Almighty Father. I cannot, however, be quite easy respecting you; for I am always afraid lest you should so long rashly expose yourself to danger[1], until there be no longer any way of escape. I am well aware that the pastoral office, which is committed to your charge, weighs much with you, and that you have determined not to quit your post till you are driven away by force. I do not blame your deter-

[[1] For an account of the danger incurred by the people of Strasburgh, for their noble stand against the Interim, see Sleidan, B. xxi. pp. 471, 473, 4, 479. Bucer, who had rejected it, writes in a letter to Calvin, dated Feb. 7. 1549: Jam episcopo promissum est hic non permittendum prædicari contra Interim. Vel hodie itaque, vel intra perpaucos dies, obsignabitur meum et præcipuorum collegarum ministerium. Calv. Epp. p. 372.]

mination, but I do not understand what kind of expulsion you are waiting for: if, as we hear from London, the mass[2] is universally received among you, the monks restored, and not a single church left to our friends, in which they may both preach Christ sincerely, and legitimately teach him to their flocks, what, think you, is to be expected? Beware of being fed by a deceitful and dangerous hope. We have cherished many hopes heretofore; but we now clearly perceive how things have turned out by the most righteous judgment of God. He is at all times willing to protect his people, but by such methods as he himself thinks best, and not as we do. At one time he would have his servants absent themselves for a season from the churches committed to them, either that they may after a while be restored to their friends, or benefit the people of God elsewhere; lest they should refrain from doing that good in other quarters which they were unable to do at home. As long as you were allowed to preach and teach in those parts, I never recommended you to quit your post; but now, when, as we hear, our harps are hung upon the willows, what else can you do there but weep and lament? The sheep, I admit, are not to be given up to wolves; but when a man is unable through the predominant power of the wolves to render help to a particular flock, ought he not to listen to others who implore his aid, and who may be benefited by him; and who, though not entirely destitute of lawful pastors, are nevertheless labouring under a most grievous want of them?

You have, I know, been invited hither more than once, and I will not deny that the reason of your hesitation has hitherto been excusable; but now, if you do not undertake the charge to which you are called, you will, I am afraid, be actuated by too excessive zeal. You would, beyond all doubt, lecture here with great advantage to the church, and whatever leisure time you had remaining, might be employed in publishing commentaries on holy scripture. Even in this

[2 This report was premature. The senate of Strasburgh sent James Sturmius, and others, in Sept. 1548, as deputies to the emperor, to deprecate the enforcement of the Interim. After some time, the affair was settled by a compromise, the senate allowing the bishop three churches for the exercise of their popish religion, and retaining the college of St Thomas for a public school, together with the rest of the churches. See Sleidan, B. xxi. p. 485.]

one particular, of what exceeding use might you be to the flock of Christ! We have already had a specimen, and that too given by you when overwhelmed with business: what would those be, I pray you, which you would write when more at leisure? Yonder, it may be that in the midst of so many dangers you may lose your life, which God forbid; but what you would lay up in store here among us, could hardly be lost. It will live, believe me, for many generations; and if you do not preach in your own person, you must not doubt but that you will preach in those of others; for he who supplies materials for the preaching of others, may be said to preach in them. There is, you know, a time for all things: as therefore there is a time for teaching the flock of Christ publicly in the churches, so also is there a time for teaching them in the schools, and for illustrating by your writings the word of God. There is also a time for a pastor to cheer by his presence the flock entrusted to him; and there is a time for preserving himself in safety for them by a temporary absence. If you knew how great is the scarcity in this country of those who are conversant with ecclesiastical order and government, you would, I am sure, take compassion upon the Lord's flock. Those who possess any share of learning, are either wholly opposed to religion; or if they are actuated by any feeling of it, are either not engaged in the sacred office, or are so cold as altogether to shrink from the endurance of any labours or perils.

Why then, you will say, do you so strongly urge me to come? for if the case is so bad, it is far better for me to be away. But it is not so, and therefore I advise and press your coming, because the harvest is plenteous and the labourers are few; because the magistracy, like yours, is altogether disposed to the reformation of the church, but, with very few exceptions, does not possess the proper instruments for that object. Then, there are no dangers in this country, (provided that the present state of things, which God forbid! be not overthrown,) except those of an ordinary character, and which you and I, and others of our stamp, would never shrink from; partly from our being foreigners, partly from having become callous, and especially because we know that the kingdom of Christ is advanced by the cross. In addition to this, such is the splendour of your name in this country, both from report and from your writings, that you cannot but be most honourably received, and this not only by ordinary persons, but by men of rank, and who possess much influence by their piety and learning as well as by their civil authority. I will not use many words to tell you, in the last place, how delightful it will be to myself, and to all my friends, to welcome one whom I dearly love in Christ, uniting with me beyond the reach of danger in the same employment of cultivating this fallow ground. For God knows that I scarce promise myself that I shall be able to live without you. May God so influence your mind, that those things which I am fully persuaded are right, may evidently commend themselves to you! And I do not say this, as not desiring every success and happiness to that city[1], its school, and our college of St Thomas: for I could wish that they would retain Christ among them, which can nowise be the case, unless they will protect his ministers and doctrine. But if the authority of the better part is overthrown in the city, I do not consider it to be your duty to surrender without any benefit a life, which might in many other ways advance the glory of Christ.

Farewell. Salute your wife and all your family in the name of my wife and Julius: I also wish much health in the Lord to all our fellow-ministers and brother professors, especially to master Conrad Hubert, your assistant, and my very dear brother in Christ. I next congratulate our friend Christopher on account of his wife Verity, and I hope that as the marriage is under good auspices, it will be a happy one. I do indeed perceive it necessary, that whoever is the friend of Christ must ever bear his *verity* along with him. Oxford, Dec. 26, 1548.

Yours from my heart,

PETER MARTYR.

[1 Strasburgh.]

LETTER CCXXVI.

PETER MARTYR TO MARTIN BUCER.

Dated at Oxford, *Jan.* 22, 1549.

Greeting. I have received the letter that you sent me the day before Christmas, and am of opinion that I ought not on any account to defer an immediate reply. A far more grievous account of your affairs than I can gather from your own letter had been brought hither many days before: as far, however, as I can conjecture from it, those events are only in immediate prospect, which I was grieving over as having already occurred[1]. Would that I had any solid comfort wherewith to refresh your mind, distressed as it is, and not without cause, by reason of the desolation of the church of Christ! But though I have not expressed it so fully as yourself, but yet, believe me, deeply bewail this great anger of God; such comfort as I can, I tender from my heart. Among those who planted that church you have distinguished yourself by your labour and exertion; yet, as I think, not you, but the grace of God which was with you more than with others: and though I was absent at the beginning, yet I have had the best means of knowing, both from the report of others, and from what I have myself witnessed, the perils you have endured, and the difficulties you have undergone for the advancement of the gospel. Wherefore I must now be either a stock or a stone, not to be sensible of the groans and tears and sighs that must burst forth from you, when you were expecting the sweetest grapes and fruit, which you might offer as a sweet-smelling savour to the Lord, and lo! there are brought forth sour and ill-savoured wild grapes. You wish that there were granted you the tears of Jeremiah, the groans of David, and the weeping of Christ; and wearied with lamentation you seek for a comforter. But I, who did not long labour in that quarter, but was rather refreshed myself by the food of doctrine and every office of christian love; who endured no perils, but rather escaped from them by coming to you; who was not weighed down by any trouble, but rather unburdened of

[1 See above, p. 471, *n.* 2.]

great anxiety; when I now hear of this dreadful destruction, I fear the impending overthrow, and shudder at the devastation of so well cultivated a vineyard. I dare not put my grief upon a level with yours; but yet be assured it is so severe, that I am altogether unable to afford you any comfort. Strasburgh [Argentina, the silver city,] has hitherto been flourishing, and its church especially had been so distinguished among others by reason of the gospel and of its school, as to be called Aurentina [the golden city] by some persons: but now, alas! it is to be feared, lest, should it give place to antichrist, it should be changed into an iron city [Ferrentina,] and instead of a faithful city become a tower of unfaithfulness; for what was before the sweetest wine always makes the sourest vinegar. O God! look down at length with a serene look and an eye of compassion, from thy lofty and holy habitation in heaven, upon our present condition! We are suddenly fallen from the highest happiness to the most extreme misery. O spare, Lord, spare thy people! We have deserved far heavier punishment, but regard the glory of thy name.

But whither am I carried away? Is this the way to write a letter? Is this the way to console an incomparable friend in his distress? I feel it is not; but when calamities exceed all bounds, neither can language flow in its proper order. The only comfort that we can derive from evils of this kind, is to bewail them together before the Lord. This is the only comfort now remaining to us, that we have many who mourn together with us. This alone is some mitigation of our grief, when we perceive that there are many persons who seriously feel the present evils. May the Lord at least vouchsafe (as I do not doubt he will) to preserve a remnant out of this overthrow, which will not bow the knee to Baal; for when the anger of the Lord hath passed by, a little spark may produce a great flame. But though I have been unable to give you comfort, I would nevertheless advise you, as you now perceive the case to be hopeless, not to linger too long in that quarter, or wait there till the very last moment. If you do, I fear lest the opportunity of escape will slip from you. You know what I mean. The antichrists are athirst, athirst (I say) for your life, and that of those who are like you: you must take care, therefore, if you love the church of Christ, to withdraw yourself for its benefit in time. Ezekiel was of great use as an exile, and Daniel very greatly benefited the elect of God at a distance from Jerusalem. But you will say; they did not flee away of themselves, but were forcibly led into that captivity. I admit this to be the case, but I do not think that it makes any difference, whether any of us be torn away from his church by the violence of a tyrant, or be compelled to leave it, because no further opportunity is afforded him for his work, and he is in danger of losing his life without any hope of doing good. I have no need to teach you. You have your fellow-ministers and mine, who ought in no wise to be left behind, and I will make suitable arrangements for them as soon as I possibly can.

I am at present, as you know, at Oxford, and cannot communicate with [the archbishop of Canterbury[1]] except by letter, which I do not consider adviseable. Meanwhile you and Paul Fagius, who are invited, ought to come over; and how welcome and acceptable you will be, there is no occasion for me to tell you: for besides that he is most earnestly wishing for you both, you are very much wanted in these universities; and when you are settled here yourselves, I doubt not but that it will be very easy to make provision for the other three persons whom you mentioned, and who, as I confidently expect, will be invited forthwith. I must go to London during this Lent, and shall abide some days, as I am wont to do, with my lord of Canterbury; at which time I will arrange such matters for our brethren as I may think necessary, and will take care that you shall not have recommended them to me in vain. Do you only take care to get away in safety from your present position. Greater perils await you than you are aware of. You are indeed in the midst of difficulties, but you do not see them so clearly as I do, who am a great way off. The case, I think, is just the same as when a pestilence is prevailing in any quarter; it is more dreaded by those who are dwelling in safety at a distance, than by those who are living where it rages most. What I am now telling you is not from the report of others, but from my own experience. You will therefore do well and wisely, if you judge that you have now satisfied the duties of your calling, when you perceive yourself no longer able to be useful in it in that quarter.

[[1] These words are written between brackets in the Latin copy.]

You must know that many things have been determined in our parliament respecting religion, but with such obstinate opposition from certain bishops, as no one ever expected would be the case. The acts, however, are not yet made public. My lord of Canterbury told Julius that he had forwarded them to me, but I have not yet received them. An event however has taken place, to the great distress of many persons. The brother of the protector of the king, the lord admiral[2], as they call him, was committed to prison four days ago, together with many other persons of rank. Whatever the cause may be, it cannot be a light one. It is not however considered of such consequence as to delay the progress of religion: yet it is a grief to us that a man who was in other respects a great friend to religion, should have fallen into this misfortune. He is the uncle of the king, and married the queen [dowager] lately deceased. The devil is using every endeavour to drive away Christ: wherefore we must all of us be most earnest in prayer. My wife and Julius affectionately salute you and all your household, especially your wife; and we all wish for your happiness in the Lord, and your immediate deliverance from the dangers that are hanging over you. Oxford, Jan 22, 1549.

Yours,

PETER MARTYR.

LETTER CCXXVII.

PETER MARTYR TO HENRY BULLINGER.

Dated at OXFORD, *Jan.* 27, 1550.

GREETING. If I have appeared, most excellent as well as learned sir, to have replied to your letter more tardily than I ought to have done, I cannot justly be charged with neglect, inasmuch as though it was written by you on the 30th of October, it did not reach me till the 24th of January. I truly regret that the pleasure and profit I have received from

[2 The admiral was sent to the Tower, Jan. 19. For an account of the proceedings against him, see Burnet, II. 155; Soames, III. 410, &c.]

the perusal of it have been so long withheld from me. Scarcely any thing could have been more gratifying to me than to have received and read your letter, so full of kindness and courtesy to myself. You congratulate me upon the happy result of the disputations[1], which however is rather to be attributed to you than to me, since you have for so many years both taught and maintained that doctrine which I there undertook to defend: but if you knew what numerous and powerful enemies the devil has stirred up against me on this account, you would be surprised. There are, nevertheless, many things which afford me no little comfort: in the first place, nothing has happened to me which I had not foreseen long before; in the next place, I perceive it to be so ordered, that in proportion as any doctrine of faith is true and tends to the more firm establishment of the church, the devil is attacked by that doctrine with greater vehemence, and it is in turn more vehemently attacked by him. Add to this, that although there are many adversaries, I have, on the other hand, many supporters, and such, if I am not mistaken, as I have no reason to be ashamed of. But above all others I look to God himself, who is the author of all truth: as long as he is on my side, which I hope will always be the case, he will be a sufficient spear and shield against all the power of Satan. I possess therefore a firm and resolute mind, though I have not yet obtained a complete victory in this contest; for I hear, and it is considered as certain, that my opponents are presently about to renew the battle. They have prepared something, I know not what, to publish in answer to a book[2] already set forth by me; as thinking perhaps that they will

[1 For an account of these disputations, which took place at Oxford on May 28, 1549, and the three following days, see Strype, Cranmer, 283, &c.; Burnet, II. 168, &c.; Foxe, Acts and Mon. VI. 298, &c.; Soames, III. 507, &c. The propositions maintained by Peter Martyr were the following: 1. In the Eucharist there is no transubstantiation. 2. Nor are the body and blood of Christ present under the species of bread and wine. 3. This body and blood are united to the elements sacramentally. The entire disputation is published with Martyr's Common Places, Ed. 1574.]

[2 Richard Smith, who preceded Peter Martyr as regius professor of divinity, published his book, *De cœlibatu sacerdotum et votis monasticis contra Petrum Martyrem*, shortly after the disputation at Oxford, and also his *Diatribe de hominis justificatione, ædita Oxoniæ in*

succeed better when the contest shall be carried on, not with the energy of a verbal dispute, but by a paper warfare. But I hope that by the blessing of God, and the aid of the Holy Spirit, the truth, which could not be resisted by verbal argument, will in no wise yield to paper and ink.

I am writing thus freely to you, not as confiding in my own strength, as I am well aware how dull and heavy I am both in speaking and writing; but the gospel hope which maketh not ashamed, and the goodness of the cause, make me courageous. I trust also that I shall be so aided by your prayers, that my want of knowledge and skill, both in materials and expression, may be rather injurious to me in any private affairs of my own, than in any way detrimental to celestial truth. When, therefore, I consider with myself the vast importance of this controversy, and how great is the vehemence, and hatred, and knavery of my adversaries, and lastly, how utterly insufficient are my own powers, I am proportionally the more anxious for the benefit of your prayers.

I congratulate also your churches upon the agreement[3] among your ministers; and I beg and implore God to make it perpetual, whereby we may at length see one spirit, one faith, one baptism, as there is one Lord, and ought to be one body, the church.

I will not write much respecting the progress of Christ's kingdom in this country; for I suppose there are others by whose care and diligence you are made acquainted with all our affairs. The sum however is this, that many things yet remain to be done, which we have in expectation rather than in reality. The perverseness of the bishops is incredible; they oppose us with all their might: yet some of that order, though very few, are favourable to the undertaking. The labour of the most reverend the archbishop

Anglia 1550 *adversus P. Martyrem, &c.* And about the same time, a book in verse, called *Diacosio-Martyrion,* was written against Martyr by John White, warden of Winchester, though, in consequence of his being imprisoned for writing it, its publication was suppressed till 1553. Before it is an epistle to P. Martyr, full of reproaches for his tenets about the eucharist, his lectures at Oxford, and other matters. The above works are probably referred to in the text. See Strype, Mem. I. i. 419, 423.]

[3 Namely, the *Consensus Tigurinus*, respecting which see above, p. 121, *n.* 2.]

of Canterbury is not to be expressed. For whatever has hitherto been wrested from them, we have acquired solely by the industry, and activity, and importunity of this prelate. And this circumstance gives us encouragement, that some addition is always being made to what we have already obtained; and we are in hopes that at the end of the parliament, which is now sitting, some enactments will come out, which will in no small degree promote the reformation of the church. May the Lord give us quiet times; for whatever tumult, or disturbance, or sedition breaks forth in this country is altogether, both by the enemy and the people at large, imputed to the reviving gospel. And the devil is not idle, but by the most subtle contrivances and deceitful arts occasions impediments of this kind. A peace[1] between this country and France has just begun to be treated of, and envoys are dispatched on both sides. I wish it may be favourably concluded. The king's uncle, who was also his protector, will shortly be released from prison[2]; and not only will his life be granted him, but likewise his estates and fortune, whereby he may keep up his rank and dignity. These things are very pleasing to godly persons, because they know him by experience to have been a most firm supporter of religion. I have nothing more to write upon public affairs. But I thank you all for regarding me, as you say you do, with sincere affection, and I congratulate myself not a little upon hearing that I possess in your country both candid friends and faithful brethren in Christ. I pray you to salute all of them affectionately in my name. Your countrymen, whom you commend to me, I will aid in any way to the best of my power. I implore the great and gracious God to preserve you long in safety to his church. Farewell. Oxford, Jan. 27, 1550. If you think that I can be of any use to you here, it will be sufficient for you to let me know.

Yours heartily,

PETER MARTYR.

[[1] This peace was proclaimed in London on the 29th of March. The terms are given in Burnet, II. 236.]

[[2] The duke of Somerset was set at liberty Feb. 6th, giving bond of £10,000 for his good behaviour, and being limited to the king's house of Sheen, or his own of Sion, that he should not go four miles from them. See Burnet, II. 226.]

LETTER CCXXVIII.

PETER MARTYR TO HENRY BULLINGER.

Dated at OXFORD, *June* 1, 1550.

GREETING. Most excellent sir, and very dear friend in Christ, I ought to have replied to your letter long since; and was strongly impelled to do so, not only by the accustomed duty of friendship, but also because your letter itself was so delightful, and so agreeably accompanied by most gratifying letters from my other brethren in the ministry. But when it was put into my hands, I was in some measure suffering from ill health; and as soon as I recovered, I was overwhelmed with such a mass of business, that I was unable to accomplish what I so greatly desired. I will explain to you in few words the kind of employment in which I have been engaged. In addition to my daily expositions of St Paul, which of themselves would almost entirely occupy the time of any one who should employ himself upon them as they deserve, a new burden has been imposed upon this university by laws lately enacted by the king's majesty. For it is decreed that public disputations upon theological subjects should be held frequently, that is, every alternate week, at which I am required to be present and to preside. Then, in the king's college, wherein I reside, theological disputations are held every week, which, inasmuch as all persons are freely admitted to hear them, may in like manner be called public; and over these I am appointed moderator, as over the others. I have therefore a continual struggle with my adversaries, who are indeed most obstinate; so that I am easily compelled, whether I will or not, often to lay aside other matters, and devote the whole time allowed me to the vocation to which I am bound. But I well know you will take my silence in good part, and according to your wonted kindness not be offended with that which you perceive has not arisen from neglect. I am very glad that you received with so much pleasure and satisfaction the letter I wrote, and I give you no ordinary thanks for having so readily and cheerfully offered your services, if you can anywise be useful to me. May God reward your kindness, as I accept it with sincere affection!

You must know, that the business of religion is making

progress in this country, not indeed with the success and ardour that I could wish, but yet far more than our sins deserve, and somewhat more favourably than I dared to promise myself four months since. There are certainly very many obstacles; especially the number of our adversaries, the lack of preachers, and the gross vices of those who profess the gospel; besides the worldly prudence of some parties who think it quite right that religion should be purified, but are willing only to make as few alterations as possible; for, feeling as they do, and thinking as civilians, they consider that any great changes would be dangerous to the state. But you perceive yourself, that when innumerable corruptions, infinite abuses, and excessive superstitions have grown every where into use in the church of Christ, it is impossible that a proper reform can be effected, unless those things which have been perverted to abuse, be restored to their true origin, their most pure sources, and unadulterated beginnings. Satan is very subtle in his attacks upon all godly exertions: for under this pretext he would have the most numerous relics of popery remain undisturbed; partly that men might not readily forget it, and partly that the return to it may be made more easy.

But, on the other hand, we derive no little comfort from having a king who is truly holy, and who is inflamed with so much zeal for godliness. He is endued with so much erudition for his age, and already expresses himself with so much prudence and gravity, as to fill all his hearers with admiration and astonishment: wherefore we must entreat God with most fervent prayers very long to preserve him to the kingdom and to the church. There are also very many of the nobility and men of rank who entertain right views; and we have some bishops who are not ill-inclined, among whom the archbishop of Canterbury is as a standard-bearer. And then, Hooper is enrolled among them, to the exceeding joy of all good men, and, as I hear, a people not ill-disposed has fallen to his lot. I hope to see him when he visits his diocese; for if he goes to Gloucester, where his cathedral is, he will pass this way. By what means he was induced to accept a bishoprick, I would relate at large, were I not wholly assured that from his respect towards you he would write you a most full account of the entire proceedings[1]. There is likewise another

[[1] See above, Letter XXXIX., p. 86.]

excellent man, Michael Coverdale, who some few years since had charge of a parish[2] in Germany. He is actively engaged in Devonshire, both in preaching and interpreting scripture. You are, I think, well acquainted with him. He is to be made bishop[3] of Exeter; and nothing can be more convenient and conducive to the reformation of religion, than the advancement of such men to the government of the church. Master a Lasco[4] too has come over hither on account of his country Friesland having received the imperial Interim; and I expect he will preside over the German church in London, which event will gratify me exceedingly. He is now residing with the archbishop of Canterbury.

You have now heard the state of our affairs in England, which this peace made with the French king, and which seems daily to be consolidated, will in some measure tend to improve. Only some persons are afraid lest, as they are beginning to boast, a council should be held by the pope for the destruction of the godly: but if we are wise, we shall cast all this kind of care upon God. The sermons you have published have been useful monitors at this period, which, as they are strengthened by quotations from the holy scriptures, were both agreeable, and will I hope be read with advantage.

To John ab Ulmis and Stumphius, whom you commended to me, I shew every kindness in my power; and they, on their part, treat me with attention and respect. They frequently pay me a visit, and if there is any writing or other business to be done on my account, they do not hesitate to undertake it, but perform it with a willing and ready mind; for which reason I am not a little indebted to them. I hear however, that Stumphius has been accused among you of having acted

[2 Bergzabern. See above, Letter CXIV., p. 247.]

[3 Miles Coverdale was first made coadjutor to Veysey in the see of Exeter, whom he succeeded in August 1551. See his Remains, Parker Soc. Ed. p. xiii.]

[4 A Lasco's first visit to England was in September 1548. He then resided six months at Lambeth with abp. Cranmer, and returned to Embden in the spring of 1549. The introduction of the Interim into Friesland accelerated his departure from that country, and he reached England for the second time in the spring of 1550, and was nominated the superintendent of the foreign protestant congregation in London, by Edw. VI., on the 24th of July. See Krasinski's Reform. in Poland, I. 257.]

contrary to your laws by accepting I know not what stipend from the English. You may be assured that this is not the fact: he lived some time in our college, but at his own charge; and that he may not be subject to this prejudice in future, and may abstain from any appearance of evil, he has left his rooms, and is now lodging with a bookseller in the town.

It only remains for me to entreat your prayers, and those of your friends, with all the earnestness in my power, that the work of the Lord may make progress in this kingdom, and that the hearts of the fathers may at length by our ministry be turned towards the children, and the hearts of the children towards the fathers. Oxford, June 1, 1550. Farewell in the Lord, and continue your affection for me.

Salute, I pray you, in my name all our worthy brethren in Christ who are with you, and especially master Bibliander and doctor Gesner.

Yours heartily,

PETER MARTYR.

LETTER CCXXIX.

PETER MARTYR TO RODOLPH GUALTER.

Dated at Oxford, *June* 1, 1550.

Greeting. Though you have hitherto, my Gualter, very dear brother in Christ, been dear to me on many accounts, yet I have now derived the greatest pleasure from your having written me a letter full of kindness and christian benevolence. The friendly and loving conversation we held together, when I travelled through your city, had previously recommended you to me in no ordinary manner, and, to say the truth, it can never be forgotten by me. But you have now acquired no small accession of regard by your late letter, breathing as it does kindness and sincerity in every part of it. You congratulate me upon having undertaken the office of teaching in the church of this island, and that the result of my labours is not altogether unsuccessful; for which kind feeling and exceeding goodwill towards me I return my best acknowledgments. Never, indeed, can I suppose that you do not very much approve my endeavours, since you are yourself engaged in the same field, and exerting yourself there to the utmost of your power. The healthy state of this kingdom is certainly a matter of exceeding joyfulness and very just congratulation, if only it can be brought to completion. There are many things in this business of religion which we have already attempted, but, believe me, very little or nothing has hitherto been accomplished. The pertinacity of the adversaries is very great, while of those who are either able or willing to instruct the people, the number is very small; nor can this inconvenience be remedied by the aid of foreigners, by reason of their want of acquaintance with the English language. There is no lack of preachers in London, but throughout the whole kingdom they are very rare: wherefore every godly person mourns over and deplores this great calamity of the church. The sheep of the divine pasture, the sheep of God's hand, the sheep redeemed by the blood of Christ, are defrauded of their proper nourishment of the divine word; and unless the people be taught, the change of religion will certainly avail them but little.

We have, thank God, a king of such a disposition, that nothing can increase his inclination and love for religion: and very many too of the nobles of the kingdom are very favourably disposed. The people in most places are still opposing us, owing to their want of instruction, and they are secretly confirmed in their errors by the subtle artifices of the papists. The tender age, too, of our Josiah is no slight hinderance to the business; but we have placed our hope in God, and are daily looking for no less progress than was made at first: but when we compare the church of Christ at its earliest infancy with that which is now reformed, we cannot but sigh most deeply, and weep with the Jews on their return from captivity, that the appearance of this second temple is not to be compared with the glory of the first, unless perhaps Christ may glorify it sooner than we expect with the presence of his second coming. Do you, I pray you, aid the work of the Lord by your prayers, and continue to love me. Farewell in the Lord. June 1, 1550. Oxford.

Yours heartily,

PETER MARTYR.

LETTER CCXXX.

PETER MARTYR TO HENRY BULLINGER.

Dated at OXFORD, *Jan.* 28, 1551.

GREETING. As nothing is more desirable or delightful to me than to hold frequent intercourse and correspondence with godly brethren in Christ, I am not a little grieved, and in no common way, that by reason of my engagements I so seldom have it in my power to write to you. Your letter, which you had written long before, I received only in the month of November; and I am heartily glad to hear that you are in good health, and that every thing yonder is in a state of peace and tranquillity. As to ourselves here, though we are not yet in possession of those things which are requisite for the proper regulation of the church, yet we do not despair but that matters will improve every day. Success, alas! is but tardy: O that abundance of fruit may some time or other make up for its delay! I think you were informed respecting doctor Hooper, how he fell into a dispute, and indeed a very grievous one, with the bishop of London[1], a most learned man, and in other respects a valiant defender of the gospel; which circumstance, as it has much distressed us all, so it has turned out most acceptable to the papists, inasmuch as they now suppose us to be quarrelling with each other: but I feel assured that the goodness of God will ultimately suffice for the settlement of this controversy. And though there were at first very many points on which they appeared to disagree with each other, I believe that all other

[1 Nicholas Ridley, who wrote to Hooper, when they were both in prison in queen Mary's time a letter, in which is the following passage, as translated in his works, Parker Soc. Ed. p. 355. "But now, my dear brother, forasmuch as I understand by your works, which I have yet but superficially seen, that we thoroughly agree and wholly consent together in those things which are the grounds and substantial points of our religion, against the which the world so furiously rageth in these our days; howsoever in time past, in smaller matters and circumstances of religion, your wisdom and my simplicity (I confess) have in some points varied; now, I say, be you assured, that even with my whole heart, God is my witness, in the bowels of Christ, I love you, &c." The original Latin is given in p. 357.]

things will easily be settled, if only they can come to an agreement about the vestiarian[2] controversy. The bishops wished the ministers of the church in the performance of their sacred function to be distinguished from other persons by a peculiar dress: Hooper denies the lawfulness of such distinction, as being ungodly and contrary to holy scripture. And as nearly two years have elapsed since the mass was abrogated by the general parliament (as they call it) of this realm, and a certain administration of the Lord's supper appointed, in which some vestments are assigned to the ministers of the church; it is very offensive to the king's councillors, and to very many others, both among the nobility and commonalty, that a decree publicly received, and confirmed by the authority of the kingdom, should be found fault with as ungodly, and condemned as though it were at variance with the sacred writings. There are also on the other side very many persons who are attached to Hooper, and who wonderfully take his part. The bishops indeed admit (I speak of our own friends), that this use of vestments is a matter of indifference, so that it may either be adopted or done away with; but they altogether deny it to be ungodly, and contrary to holy scripture, and will by no means suffer such a notion to be taught the people. And, what distresses me most, this dispute has become so vehement, that Hooper is not yet in possession of the bishoprick to which he was appointed, and is excluded from the office of preaching, in which he was employed not without success. God grant that some tranquillity not to be repented of may at length succeed to this turbulent tempest: and this I entreat you to ask again and again from the Lord in believing prayer.

When it was demanded of me, some days since, what I thought upon this question, I replied, that I was a very great advocate for simplicity in the sacred ministry, and would therefore recommend the distinctions of dress to be done away with, and that too, as soon as it could be decreed by public authority; but that I could not, meanwhile, admit that the use of them was ungodly, or that it was condemned in the sacred writings: yet, since that diversity of apparel possesses

[2 For a statement of the particulars relative to this controversy, see Strype, Mem. II. i. 350; Cranmer, 302; Burnet, II. 242; Soames, III. 560; Foxe, VI. 640. See also above, p. 87.]

little or no edification, and very many persons superstitiously abuse it, I therefore considered that it ought to be removed[1]. Bucer made very nearly the same answer; so that in fact we all of us agree that this use of ecclesiastical vestments should be abolished, though we do not all of us allege the same reasons. And though we may not obtain all we wish, I am nevertheless easily led to believe that we shall obtain greater simplicity than has hitherto been allowed. All things cannot be done in a moment, and there must be labour and time for this misshapen embryo to attain its proper symmetry and shape. There is only one thing in this matter which distresses me greatly, namely, that the dispute should have taken place with those bishops, by whose labour and instrumentality, and with no little danger to themselves, the gospel has gained a footing in this country.

You are now acquainted with the whole business: as soon as any favourable result shall take place, I will by no means delay letting you know. Meanwhile, I am going on, with all the diligence in my power, in the discharge of the duty, severe as it is, imposed upon me at Oxford: on account of which, in proportion as I have to deal with minds hardened against the truth, so much the more earnestly do I implore the benefit of your prayers. Next, my excellent and very dear friend in Christ, I entreat you, that with the authority you rightly and deservedly possess, you will be pleased to assist me in a certain affair of mine, or, rather, one which publicly concerns the church and school. I gave my commentaries on the first epistle to the Corinthians to Byrchman the bookseller, that he might get them printed. And as he has determined, according to my wish, that they should be printed in your city, and (as I hear) is now resident among you, I could desire one of the brethren there, at your bidding, to take some little pains that the book may be published more correctly than it otherwise would be. For I was wonderfully pressed by want of time, and had therefore no leisure to make every correction with such care as the matter required, and as I could have wished. For which reason I would have that repaired by the diligence of an-

[1 The letters of Martyr and Bucer upon this controversy are published in "A brief examination for the time," &c. n. d., but said to be in 1566. See also P. Martyr's Epistles, p. 116.]

other, which I was unable to effect myself: and as the subject is a theological one, and quotations are frequently made both from the Greek and the Hebrew, it will be requisite to employ a learned and godly corrector of the press; for as by reason of his learning he will not wander from the sense, so his piety will induce him, from motives of kindness, whereever he may discover any passage to be corrupt, to supply a better in its place. It is indeed no small favour that I require from you, but fruit may possibly be produced that we shall have no reason to repent of: for this work is importunately and continually called for in this kingdom; and though I do not consider myself to have written anything very valuable, or what has not been said by other godly men, I am nevertheless aware that the desire and earnest expectation of the works of certain writers frequently renders them so popular, that they are read by many persons with the utmost avidity, not for their merit, but from the hopes conceived respecting them. Whence it is that the diligent and apposite writings of the most learned men are often slighted, while the same things published by others of far inferior acquirements are most readily attended to. I would therefore that our friends should be diligent in writing, and that they would inculcate the same truths in various and different forms; for sometimes it happens that what does not produce much effect in one way, is successful when treated in another.

But I will cease to converse with you more at length; for as you have correctly written much, and diligently read much, you must be well aware of the great importance of having all books well revised and corrected on their issue from the press. And if I seem bold in making this request, I pray you not to blame my confidence, but rather impute it to the kindness of yourself and all your friends, who have so frequently and so kindly in your letters offered me your services. And as I have been told that Wolfius is both well qualified for this task, and that he will perhaps be willing to undertake the office, you can, if you are so inclined, recommend him to do so. I will take care that the epistle dedicatory, which is wanting in the book, shall be sent over in a few days. I wish you every happiness in the Lord. Salute in my name all your fellow-ministers from the least to the greatest; and though I do not now write to them, I will not be wanting in that duty, as soon as I shall obtain leisure. January 28, 1551. Oxford in England.

Yours heartily,

PETER MARTYR.

LETTER CCXXXI.

PETER MARTYR TO CONRAD HUBERT.

Dated at OXFORD, *March* 8, 1551.

GREETING. You will probably suppose, Hubert, my very dear brother in Christ, and reverend colleague, that as I have not yet written to you, I have entirely effaced the remembrance of you from my mind. But if there are any remains of christian charity in you, as I am persuaded there are, and believe too that no change has taken place in your singular kindness towards me, you must beware of entertaining such a supposition. I have not, indeed, written before, because our mutual friend Bucer was then living, who I am fully assured was never wanting in that duty, and was continually writing both to yourself in the first place, and to our other brethren in Christ at Strasburgh; and he communicated to me by letter from time to time, as a most loving colleague, whatever passed between you. Wherefore, as this kind of duty was so diligently discharged by him, I did not consider that there was any occasion for my services. But he has now departed in peace to our God and to Christ Jesus, to the universal regret of all good men, and to my incredible sorrow. I am so broken and dismayed by his death, as to seem mutilated of more than half of myself, and that the better half; so that I am almost worn out by anxieties and tears, and seem scarcely to retain my senses by reason of the bitterness of my grief. He died on the last day of February, having been a valiant conqueror in many of the battles of the Lord. God called him to himself in peace, and would not suffer him to fall into the hands of his enemies: he indeed is now happy, but we are to be lamented who are still exposed to the most grievous calamities and woes innumerable. This most estimable doctor and father was lent to us by God for a time, to be recalled at his good pleasure. It is our duty not to find fault with his judgments, but to appeal to his compassion, and diligently entreat him by earnest and persevering prayer, that in the room of those soldiers who have finished their warfare, and whom he is from time to time continuing to discharge by death, he would again supply the now empty ranks with valiant warriors. O wretched me! as long as Bucer was in England, or while we lived together in Germany, I never felt myself to be in exile. But now I plainly seem to myself to be alone and desolate. Hitherto I have had a faithful companion in that road in which we were both of us so unitedly walking. I am now torn asunder from a man of the same mind with myself, and who was truly after my own heart, by this most bitter death which has taken him off. Truly the hand of the Lord has touched me. He still lives, and is in the enjoyment of the most delightful fruits of his labours; he is transplanted by God into a better state of existence; he has left those dear to him, but he is received by those still more dear into everlasting habitations. He has cast away that which was corrupt and perishable, and has put on the robe of an everlasting immortality. Oh, how continually had he on his lips the church of Strasburgh! what anxieties he underwent for her! Though he was far off, and as to his body seemed altogether disunited from her, yet in spirit, believe me, he was always present with you. Last summer he came to visit me here at Oxford, and staid in my house eleven days. What discourses, what conversations took place between us respecting all of you, our worthy brethren in Christ! When we were talking together, we seemed to be conversing in the midst of you all at Strasburgh: we were thinking of our return, but he has outstripped me, and betaken himself not to our Argentine [silver] church, but to the golden one of heaven. God has now assigned him an eternal abode and a blessed habitation, from whence no violence can drive him away, nor any inducement make him willing to depart. I pray God, that as I was so thoroughly united to him in life, he will not long suffer me to be separated from him by death.

There are many other things that I could wish to write to you, but my mind is so depressed by this load of grief, that even my hand is heavy; and since my strength is not sufficient for me to write any more, I pray you to bear me in your remembrance, and as you can no longer write to master Bucer, sometimes to cheer and refresh me by your letters. Deliver in my name to our venerable chapter of St Thomas the inclosed letter[1]; and salute all our brethren in the Lord, together with masters Hedio and Theobald, and likewise John Garner, the worthy pastor of our church of strangers. My wife and Julius salute you and your family in the Lord. I wish you every happiness in Christ, and that you may bear the loss of master Bucer with greater fortitude than I am able to do. March 8, 1551. Oxford.

Yours heartily,

PETER MARTYR.

His reverend corpse was honourably interred. For three doctors delivered funeral orations at his burial with great eloquence and much feeling, and the whole body both of scholars and townsmen attended his obsequies[2].

[[1] A translation of the letter here mentioned is printed in P. Martyr's Epistles, at the end of his Common Places, p. 81.]

[[2] For an account of Bucer's funeral see Strype, Cheke, 56, &c. It is thus mentioned in K. Edward's journal: "Feb. 28, the learned man Bucerus died at Cambridge, who was two days after buried in St Mary's church at Cambridge, all the whole university, with the whole town, bringing him to the grave, to the number of three thousand persons. Also there was an oration of Mr Haddon made very elegantly at his death: and a sermon of [Dr Parker.] After that Mr Redman made a third sermon [on the following day.] Which three sermons made all the people wonderfully to lament his death. Last of all, all the learned men of the university made their epitaphs in his praise, laying them on his grave." See Strype, Mem. II. i. 382. Burnet, IV. 214, and especially Historia vera de vita, obitu, sepultura, &c. D. Martini Buceri et Pauli Fagii. Argent. 1561. The oration is also given in Haddoni Lucubrationes, Lond. 1567.]

LETTER CCXXXII.

PETER MARTYR TO HENRY BULLINGER.

Dated at OXFORD, *April* 25, 1551[3].

GREETING. I received your two letters, most excellent and learned sir, nearly at the same time; and as they greatly refreshed me, so they have rendered me more and more beholden to you. For you have not only recommended my work to the printer, but have also selected that individual to superintend the printing, upon whose thorough integrity, eminent learning, and extraordinary regard for me I place full reliance. May God himself abundantly recompense you, as I am unable to do so! I thank you likewise, that though the manuscript is confused and difficult to make out, and there may occasionally, perhaps, be detected an error in the writing, so that your undertaking will be more laborious than I contemplated, you have nevertheless not declined to take upon yourselves so troublesome an office. I therefore again implore God to bestow upon you a recompence for such great labours, since I myself cannot even sufficiently express my gratitude.

You have moreover sent me a present, I mean the fifth decade of your godly sermons, and the agreement between yourself and Calvin upon the sacramentarian controversy. The Decade I have not yet received, so that, as I have been unable to read it, I can express no definite opinion respecting it; but I cannot promise myself any thing else but that it will be godly, learned, erudite, and tend greatly to edification. What you have mutually agreed upon respecting the sacrament of the eucharist is very gratifying to me; and I desire nothing more than that a plain and perspicuous statement upon that subject may be set forth in the churches of Christ: as far as my own opinion[4] is concerned, I go along with you altogether, and scarcely deliver any other sentiments in this place, when any conversation or disputation takes place respecting the Lord's supper. You would not, however, believe with what bitterness, obstinacy, perverseness and inflexibility

[3 There is a letter to Gualter of the same date in Peter Martyr's Epistles, p. 84.]

[4 P. Martyr's opinion respecting the Eucharist is given in his Common Places, part 4, ch. 10.]

of mind we are resisted by our adversaries, and especially on this very subject. The devil cannot endure that these seals of the promises of God should be purified; for he plainly perceives that when they are restored to their native integrity and simplicity, the chief part of superstition will be overthrown. I shrink from no dangers or exertions in the defence of this sound doctrine; and unless God himself had been present to support me, I sometimes do not know how I could have survived: but as I have great confidence in your prayers, so I doubt not but that I am greatly benefited by them.

You have, I believe, been informed by other correspondents respecting the case of our common friend, the bishop of Gloucester[1]. I made use of whatever arguments I could, and was never wanting to him at that time, as he himself felt and perceived; so that he is now out of all difficulty, and is gone to his bishoprick. I foresaw that this would be the result, and therefore in my letter to you I expressed great hopes of his being set at liberty. He is now actively engaged in preaching to the flock committed to him by the Lord, and this, it is hoped, not without effect, as he has a numerous and attentive and earnest congregation. You may therefore be delivered from all fear respecting him, and aid him with your prayers, as I believe you do. He was here with me at Oxford three days before Easter, together with Michael Coverdale, a most effective preacher, and one who deserves well of the gospel. Both of them preached to our people at Oxford, and attended my public exposition of the epistle to the Romans: we mutually exhorted each other very lovingly in the Lord, and regard each other with the greatest cordiality and affection.

You are, I believe, aware, that a certain brawling Oxford doctor[2], who has left England, because he refused to make a recantation of his superstitions, has now written against the most reverend the archbishop of Canterbury[3], on the sacrament of the eucharist; and likewise against me, respecting

[1 See above, p. 486.]

[2 This was Richard Smith, who preceded P. Martyr as regius professor of divinity. He fled to Louvain, where he printed his book for the celibacy of priests and monastic vows against Peter Martyr. Strype, Mem. II. i. 64. See above, p. 478, *n.* 2.]

[3 Dr Smith's book was set forth under this title: "A confutation of the true and catholic doctrine." Strype, Cranmer, II. 1089. See Cranmer's Early Writings, Parker Soc. Ed. p. 368.]

the celibacy of the clergy, and justification[4]. The lord archbishop is now replying to him, and I shall write my defence[5] on both the above subjects during the next autumn vacation. I mention this that you may understand the reason, why I have not now leisure to reply to that bold writer upon traditions: otherwise I should have wished to have done so immediately, as you so kindly recommended.

I will aid the young men whom you have sent over to us, with all the favour and good-will in my power, and I pray God that their progress may be answerable to your expectation and my wishes. Master Cox has conferred with me about them, and will see that they be properly provided for. I say nothing respecting your other townsmen who were here previously, as I suppose they will have much to write about themselves. They are good young men, and are doing well, and my services are always at their disposal.

You have heard, I think, long ere this of the death of master Bucer, who departed on the last day of February to God, whom he had long valiantly served. Thus the church is deprived of her most learned ministers and veteran soldiers, as is easily made apparent from the raw recruits who now supply their places. Nothing grieves me more, than that the church should suffer so great a dearth of ministers. There are very few who are willing to endure dangers, and to undertake the defence of the cause of Christ. The university of Cambridge must speedily be succoured; but I cannot as yet perceive this to be a matter of easy accomplishment. I wish they might be permitted to obtain from you what they are seeking for. May God long preserve you in safety to his church! I salute all your fellow-ministers in the Lord. Farewell, and love me as you do. Oxford, Apr. 25, 1551.

Yours heartily,

PETER MARTYR.

[4 The full title of the latter work is Diatribe de Hominis justificatione ædita Oxoniæ in Anglia, anno a nativitate Domini nostri Jesu Christi 1550. Mense Februario adversus Petrum Martyrē Vermelinū, olim Cartusianū Lucensem in Italia, nunc apostatam in Anglia Oxoniæ, acerrimum improborum dogmatum assertorem, sed imperitum et impudentem cum primis. Per Ricardum Smythæum Anglum Mygorniensem. Louvanii 1550. Mense Octobri.]

[5 This defence was printed at Zurich in 1551. Strype, Cranmer, 378.]

LETTER CCXXXIII.

PETER MARTYR TO HENRY BULLINGER.

Dated at OXFORD, *Aug.* 6, 1551.

GREETING. As your young townsmen[1], most excellent sir, are now leaving us on their return home, I could by no means allow them to depart without a letter from me to you. You must know, therefore, that I am in good health, which is at this time an especial favour of God to me; for the English sweating-sickness[2] has been prevalent throughout the kingdom. And, what is grievously to be deplored, we have lost some distinguished men[3]; among whom was that most noble youth, the duke of Suffolk[4], the king's most intimate friend and contemporary, and brought up together with him. He was a youth of such hopes, that he was considered to have no equal for his age, the king's majesty alone excepted; and he had made such progress in learning, godliness, and piety, as to be the admiration of every one, and he would shortly have been a great support both to the state and the church. And, that nothing might be wanting to this calamity, his younger brother died with him: so that this summer has been by no means a happy one to the people of England. God grant that this woe may not be the precursor of other calamities: and I mention this because I see the gospel of Christ to be of such a nature, that it is most dangerous to treat it in a light and perfunctory manner; and as there is no end or measure to our sins, the more ripe knowledge of divine things frequently calls down a severer punishment. I do not write thus, as perceiving by my own sagacity any

[1 Namely, Stumphius and Andrew Croariensis. See above, p. 437.]

[2 In London, in one day, viz. July 10, died an hundred people; and the next an hundred and twenty. Strype, Mem. II. i. 491. See above, p. 94, *n.* 1.]

[3 Strype mentions the lords Cromwell and Powis; Sirs John Luttrel, Thomas Speke, John Wallop, K.G., and Peryn Negroo, who all died in July, within a few days one of another.]

[4 Henry, duke of Suffolk, and the lord Charles Brandon his brother, died in one bed, July 16, at the bishop of Lincoln's house at Buckden: they were admitted of King's college, Cambridge, under Dr Walter Haddon. See a full account of them in Strype, Mem. II. i. 491, &c. Also Haddoni Poemata, Lond. 1567, pp. 89, 90, and a long and interesting oration in his Lucubrationes, pp. 89-108.]

immediately impending dangers; but I know that the treasures of God's wrath and of his wisdom are alike unsearchable, and therefore I can never think that we are safe, till, having cast away all else, we cling solely and entirely to Christ, and him crucified.

With respect to civil affairs, tokens of the greatest friendship between the king of the French and our own sovereign are exhibited on both sides. Our ambassadors[5], from among the principal councillors and nobility, are gone over into France, and have been received there by the king with greater splendour and magnificence than any former embassy. And the like entertainment, and in no wise inferior, was given to the French deputies[6] when they came hither. Many reports, moreover, are in general circulation as to the mind of the French king[7] being irritated against the pope. I wish the Phrygians would come to their senses, however late. I shall write nothing about the affairs of Italy, because as you are in the neighbourhood, you can obtain more accurate information respecting them than we can. Master Hooper is ministering in his episcopacy with great diligence and success, and is well reported of by all godly persons, as I always expected would be the case. God grant that we may at length have many other bishops who shall bestow the like diligence and labour on the church!

I am expecting my book in print at the next Frankfort fair; and I greatly desire, if it can be managed, to have five or six copies before the booksellers' parcels arrive here from Frankfort, that I may be able to present them to my friends before the books are generally exposed to sale. For there is great delay in that conveyance, and many persons are frequently teasing me, from their overweening desire to obtain the exposition. Your little book on the sacraments was printed here four months since; for which I am much

[5 The embassy consisted of Par, marquis of Northampton, Sir Philip Hoby, Goodrick, bishop of Ely, Sir Thomas Smith, and others. They arrived in France in June. Strype, Mem. II. i. 474.]

[6 The French ambassador was monsieur le Mareschal St Andre, who landed at Rye, in Sussex, in July. For an account of his reception see Strype, as above.]

[7 For the French king's protestation against the council of Trent, in September, 1551, followed by his edict against the pope, see Sleidan, B. XXII. p. 518, &c. Robertson, Charles V. IV. 33.]

obliged to you, as it is greatly approved of by all godly persons, and especially by myself. I have moreover received and read the fifth decade of your sermons, that you sent me as a present; and it has so commended itself to me, that I am anxiously desirous for you to proceed, as far as possible, in that department of labour; for you are by this means providing most useful materials for ecclesiastical preachers, which if they will always have, as they ought, ready and at hand, they will be able both abundantly and profitably to instruct the people. I shall only make this one observation in regard to the Zurich young men who are residing here, that they are conducting themselves with regularity, sobriety, and godliness, and, if I am not mistaken, are making no small progress in their studies. Farewell in the Lord, and love me as you do. I much wish you would salute all your fellow-ministers individually in my name, especially my friend Gualter, who has employed himself so laboriously in the revision of my book. Oxford, Aug. 6, 1551.

I will thank you to take care that the letters addressed to Geneva, which I have folded up with this, may be carefully forwarded thither. The great admirer of your piety and learning,

PETER MARTYR.

LETTER CCXXXIV.

PETER MARTYR TO HENRY BULLINGER.

Dated at Oxford, *Oct.* 26, 1551.

Greeting. As I am unable, most distinguished sir, and much beloved in Christ, to express the gratification I have derived from your letter, I shall leave it to your kind partiality to picture it to yourself. Though I have before offered you my thanks for the pains you have taken that my book might be accurately printed, yet, as I understand the work is now completed, I must again repeat them; and I feel myself so great a debtor both to you and to our excellent friend Gualter, that I despair of ever being able to discharge the obligation. I will therefore pray God that he may be pleased to repay you in my stead, what it is quite out of my power to accomplish. The book has not yet reached me, but I am expecting it every day. Your approbation of it, as you state, cannot but be most gratifying to me, because, though I am well aware that no praise is due to me on account of it, yet when it is commended by so distinguished a personage, I abundantly congratulate myself on this my agreement with you in matters of religion; and I pray God, through Jesus Christ our Lord, that he may daily increase and confirm it more and more. And as you give me such encouragement, I shall now prepare my commentary on the Romans, that it may be sent over to you as soon as possible. I would not, however, have you in future bring so heavy a charge against your young men[1], as though it were through their fault that so many errors have crept into my book. They were indeed of great assistance to me in copying, and I am very much indebted to their kindness, and am grieved that the favour they have conferred upon me should be met by such a requital. From henceforth, therefore, you must lay upon me the charge of negligence in writing, and I will endeavour to be more careful in future. As to those other commentaries of mine which you inquire after, I do not see how they can possibly be published in so short a time: for what I have written upon Genesis, Exodus, Leviticus, and the minor prophets, are brief and hasty annotations; so that there needs leisure for revising, and copying over again, what I at first wrote out for my own sole use, and not for that of others. But if it please God to spare my life, and I should obtain a little leisure, I shall not object to publish them; not that I consider any work of mine as of any value, but that I may not seem arrogantly to disregard the wishes of my friends.

The affair of the bishop Vergerio[2], which you commended

[1 Probably Stumphius and John ab Ulmis are here intended.]

[2 Peter Paul Vergerio, bishop of Capo d'Istria, wrote a book "Against the apostates of Germany," to vindicate himself from the charge of Lutheranism, which, it was said, prevented his being made a cardinal. On studying the arguments of his adversaries, with a view to their confutation, he yielded, and became a protestant. Whereupon he left his bishoprick, and went and preached the gospel among the Grisons, where, in 1551, he published a book to dissuade the Switzers from repairing to the council of Trent. His brother, John Baptista, bishop of the neighbouring city of Pola, also yielded to conto me, cannot now be undertaken or promoted by me; partly because I am now a long way from court, and from persons in power: for I am residing, as you know, at Oxford, where I have no intercourse with any but students. In the next place, some great commotions have been raised in the state, which though they have no reference whatever to religion, nevertheless occupy the minds even of the common people, so that they will not pay any regard or consideration to these matters: but when an occasion shall be afforded, I will not be unmindful of this duty. Do you, in the mean time, I pray you, and all your fellow-ministers, earnestly implore God to grant us a season of tranquillity, in which the gospel of Christ may be enabled to strike its roots more deeply.

With respect to the bishop of Gloucester, you must know that he is admirably conducting himself in his ministry, and that his vocation hitherto has not been without fruit. He cannot however do all that he would for the glory of the Lord, forasmuch as nothing can be obtruded upon the superstitious against their will, unless what has been previously enacted by the laws of the realm. We were in hopes that many things would have been established in this parliament, as they call it; but it is prorogued[1], I know not for what reason, till the month of January. But the probity of this bishop, and his zeal for religion, together with the long intimacy that has existed between us, and, lastly, your especial commendation of him, (which has very great weight with me, as it ought to have,) render him an object of my peculiar regard: wherefore you need not doubt but that I shall exert myself in his favour to the utmost of my power. Your young countrymen here, thank God, are in good health, and lead me to hope that their studies will be attended with success. Two of them, Andrew Croarius[2] of Constance, and Stumphius, your townsman, are now leaving us: they are indeed excellent youths, and if they so conduct themselves with you, as they have done here, you will have no reason, I think, for regret. But

viction, and concluded the popish doctrine to be false. See Sleidan, 476, 527. Bayle, art. *Vergerio.*]

[1 The parliament that should have met November 4, whether the cause were the remainder of the sweating-sickness, or something else, was put off till the first of Hilary term. See Strype, Mem. II. i. 505.]

[2 See above, p. 437.]

as I do not think there is any necessity for me to commend them to you, I will not write respecting them more fully: I only pray you to manifest the same kindness towards them when present, as you have already shewn them when absent, for they are by no means unworthy of your favour and good-will.

As to myself, I am in good health, and have been so hitherto; and though my domestics have been very dangerously ill of the English sweating-sickness, I have not suffered in the slightest degree. That you were so deeply afflicted by the false report of my death, is a most certain token of your regard for me. I therefore return you all the thanks in my power for this benevolent and friendly feeling; and if you think I can be in any way useful to you here, only let me know, and you shall find me prompt and ready to serve you. Salute Gualter affectionately in my name, as also your fellow-ministers, to all of whom, together with yourself, I wish every happiness in the Lord. Oxford, Oct. 26, 1551.

Your most attached,

PETER MARTYR.

LETTER CCXXXV.

PETER MARTYR TO RODOLPH GUALTER[3].

Dated at LAMBETH, *March* 6, 1552.

GREETING. Were I not to thank you, most learned sir, for the pains you have taken in the revision and correction of my book when it was in printing, I should both seem very ungrateful, and undeserving of having any favour conferred upon me by any one in future. I plainly perceive that you have bestowed no small labour upon this matter; for in copying out the book which I sent you, there was not such care taken as there ought to have been. But I will endeavour that greater accuracy shall be observed, when I next forward anything to you to be printed. I therefore pray Almighty God to recompense your exertions on my behalf; for through your careful superintendence it has come to pass, that the

[3 A translation of this letter is given in P. Martyr's Divine Epistles at the end of his Common Places, p. 85.]

work has made its appearance with tolerable correctness. But as much as you have aided in the printing, so much hath fortune failed us in the carriage of the books; for up to this day only thirty copies have found their way hither, so that they are in vain inquired after by many persons, as they are not on sale anywhere in this kingdom. Byrchman, who promised me twenty copies, has not sent one; which however I would not ascribe to any ill will, but rather believe it to have happened through some mischance.

With respect to our affairs I am not able to give you much more information than this our carrier (I mean your townsman Froschover) is able to communicate: he is certainly an honest and godly young man, and has conducted himself soberly and religiously during the whole of his residence among us; whence it appears that he was not unadvisedly recommended by you at first. May God increase his godliness, and grant you to proceed as you do in the instruction of your boys and young men!

Great rumours from Germany are spread about here, but so various and uncertain, that we cannot easily ascertain what we ought to believe. We wish much to know whether any of the Swiss[1] who profess the gospel, have determined upon sending any of the ministers of their churches to the council of Trent. But it may perhaps seem out of place to make much inquiry upon this subject, inasmuch as the cause of Christ must be especially committed to Christ himself. Nevertheless, as the members of Christ's body, which is the church, are naturally joined together by the most firm bond of the Spirit, it is but right that they should be mutually solicitous about each other. I wish you every happiness in the Lord. Salute in my name masters Pellican and Bibliander, with the rest of our fellow-ministers. Dated from the house of my lord of Canterbury, March 6, 1552.

Your most attached,

PETER MARTYR.

[[1] See above, p. 23, where it appears, that archbishop Cranmer recommended to Bullinger, Melancthon, and Calvin, that a council of protestant reformers should be held in England or elsewhere, in lieu of sending delegates to the council of Trent.]

LETTER CCXXXVI.

PETER MARTYR TO HENRY BULLINGER.

Dated at [LAMBETH], *March* 8, 1552.

GREETING. Since, most noble sir, and much esteemed in the Lord, our mutual friend Froschover has determined upon returning to you, I would on no account allow him to depart without a letter from myself, whereby you may know that I am in good health, and that I do not forget you.

I came to London some time since, on account of the holding of the assembly commonly called a parliament. For the king's majesty has ordained, that, as the gospel is received in his kingdom, and the bishop of Rome is driven out, the church of England shall be no longer ruled by pontifical decrees, and decretals, Sixtine, Clementine, and other popish ordinances of the same kind: for the administration of these laws has for the most part prevailed up to this time in the ecclesiastical court, under the tacit authority of the pope; though many other laws were enacted by which the external polity of the church might be regulated. To the intent therefore, that so powerful a kingdom should not be deprived of this, as it appears, necessary advantage, the king has appointed two and thirty persons[2] to frame ecclesiastical laws for this realm, namely, eight bishops, eight divines, eight civil lawyers, and eight common lawyers; the majority of whom are equally distinguished by profound erudition and solid piety; and we also, I mean Hooper, a Lasco, and myself, are enrolled among them. May God therefore grant that such laws may be enacted by us, as by their godliness and holy justice may banish the Tridentine canons from the churches of Christ! But as I am conscious we have need of the prayers of yourself and your colleagues in furtherance of so great an undertaking, I implore them with all the sincerity and earnestness in my power. For it is not only necessary to entreat God

[[2] For an account of this commission, and the names of the commissioners, see Strype, Cranmer, 388. Burnet, II. 313. Soames, III. 706, &c. The result of their labours, though never sanctioned by authority, was published in Queen Elizabeth's reign, under the title of Reformatio Legum.]

that pious and holy laws may be framed, but that they may obtain the sanction of parliament, or else they will not possess any force or authority whatsoever.

With respect to other matters, we are now tolerably quiet. It is true indeed that disturbances took place in the state some months ago, but they now seem to be composed. May God bestow tranquillity both upon the kingdom and on the church, though I am well aware that a full and perfect rest is to be looked for elsewhere; for while we live here below, it is rather to be wished than really hoped for.

I have at length seen my commentaries on the epistle to the Corinthians, some copies of which arrived here about the 15th of January, but so few in number that there are not any now remaining for sale. I know not by what mishap it has occurred, that Byrchman's books have not yet been able to be brought over to us: in fact, he owed me some copies, of which I have not received even one. Yet I cannot but commend the diligence of the printer; which however I ascribe not to him alone, but to your authority, and the exertions of our friend Gualter. I therefore thank you all, and am not a little grieved at my inability to return the obligation. But as to my other commentaries on Genesis and Exodus, I promise you, that as soon as I shall have had leisure to revise them, I will forward them to you to be printed; but I am now pressed by so much business as to be almost overwhelmed. I am also anxious to complete my commentaries on the epistle to the Romans, that they may be printed by you. I cannot but bear a favourable testimony to this Froschover, to whom I have given in charge this letter to you. He has conducted himself well at Oxford, and resided there without having given any cause of complaint. John [ab Ulmis] also, and the young men of your town, are living soberly, and studying diligently. I wish you every happiness in the Lord, and desire your colleagues, every one of them, to be saluted in my name. March 8, 1552. From the house of the archbishop of Canterbury.

Your very affectionate,

PETER MARTYR.

LETTER CCXXXVII.

PETER MARTYR TO HENRY BULLINGER.

Dated at STRASBURGH, *Nov.* 3, 1553.

GREETING. I have at length, my excellent friend, arrived here, at Strasburgh, on the 29th of October: but what perils I have undergone, both in England and during my journey, it would be too long to relate; and, wearied as I still am with travelling, I am unable to write them. This only I would not have you ignorant of, that the most reverend the archbishop of Canterbury is imprisoned, and together with him are the bishops of Worcester, (Hooper,) Exeter, (Miles Coverdale), London, the archbishop of York, Latimer, and several godly and learned preachers, for whom I earnestly entreat the abundant prayers of your church, forasmuch as they are in the most extreme danger. I thought that I too was on the point of perishing[1] in this great overthrow; but our good and gracious God has preserved me by his secret counsel and wonderful providence. I did not flee away from thence by stealth, lest my enemies should report that I had withdrawn myself because I was unwilling to defend the doctrines that I had delivered. Nay, when they were boasting every where that disputations upon religion were to take place instead of preaching, the archbishop of Canterbury[2] posted up notices throughout all London, stating that he was ready, together with myself and some others, to defend in public disputations everything that we have taught and asserted respecting religion: by which means they were so confounded, that they now declared in their discourses that it was not safe to dispute upon such matters; and that it was not to be allowed that any doubt should be entertained respecting those things which had been received by the uni-

[1 See above, Letter CLXXXII. p. 369.]

[2 See above, p. 371. n. 1. and the references there quoted; to which add Jenkyns' Cranmer, I. CXI. IV. 1. It will be observed that Peter Martyr's account agrees with that of Terentianus, which, as Dr Jenkyns remarks, differs from the ordinary accounts, in stating that the placarding of the *Declaration against the Mass* throughout London, was not only designed, but actually executed by the archbishop.]

versal consent of the church. They therefore cast the archbishop of Canterbury[1] into prison, but have dismissed me[2], with licence to depart, under the queen's sign manual. Hence it is that I am now here, but I do not yet know whether I shall again be received in this church and school; for, as I suspect, the sacramentary controversy will occasion some difficulties: however, I am not very anxious about it. Nay, I derive no small advantage from this, in that I clearly perceive that the better and more learned part are most desirous of retaining me. May God ordain what may most conduce to his glory, and the edification of the church! I pray you not to be offended at my not having replied to your letter which I received in June; for I was then suffering from illness: the king's death then took place, and such grievous calamities distracted me, that I was scarcely ever able to attend to my private affairs. And then, you must know, after I left England, some letters of yours to me, as I heard at Antwerp, had been forwarded to Oxford, and I have not yet received them. As soon, therefore, as they are brought back hither, I shall read them with great pleasure, and, as I hope, derive that comfort from them which I have been accustomed to do.

But whereas I recollect that in a former letter you wrote me somewhat upon predestination, I will now content myself with replying, that in the treatment of that subject[3] I have been especially on my guard, lest men should cast all their faults and sins upon God, or derive from the will of God an excuse for their wickedness: and for the rest, I so treat it, as to follow the holy scriptures as closely as possible. But I have now neither room nor opportunity to

[1 He was removed from Lambeth, and sent a prisoner to the Tower, "as well for the treason committed by him against the queen's majesty (in signing, with other privy councillors, king Edward the sixth's will for settling the crown on the lady Jane Grey), as for the aggravating the same his offence by spreading about seditious bills, moving tumults to the disquietness of the present state." Jenkyns, as above.]

[2 "When some zealous Catholics urged the imprisonment of Peter Martyr, Gardiner, to his honour, pleaded that he had come over by an invitation from a former government, and furnished him with supplies to return to his own country in safety." Lord Campbell, Lives of the Chancellors, II. 56.]

[3 For Peter Martyr's opinion respecting predestination, see his Common Places, Part III. ch. 1.]

dwell longer upon the subject. You will perceive the nature of what I have taught, as soon as I shall have published my commentaries on the Romans, which I shall do this year. I must however candidly confess, that I cannot but lament that our churches are agitated from time to time by new controversies: we have had, I think, quite disputing enough. May God of his goodness grant us all so to feel respecting predestination, that what ought to be the greatest consolation to believers, may not become the painful subject of pernicious contention! As far as I am concerned, I am not of such an obstinate opinion in these matters, as that if an opinion differing from my own were pointed out to me from the sacred writings, I should refuse to yield to the truth. I hope however that, through the goodness and mercy of God, we shall all of us at last come to feel and express the same sentiments. I beseech you to entreat God for me, and to salute all your fellow-ministers in my name. I pray the immortal God long to preserve you to us in safety. If you wish me to do any thing for you here, only let me know, and I will execute your wishes to the best of my power. Farewell. Strasburgh, Nov. 3, 1553.

Yours heartily,

PETER MARTYR.

LETTER CCXXXVIII.

PETER MARTYR TO HENRY BULLINGER.

Dated at STRASBURGH, *Dec.* 15, 1553.

GREETING. As soon as I arrived at Strasburgh, most illustrious and much esteemed sir, I wrote you a letter, in which I not only informed you of my own affairs, but also of the state of things in England. I now think fit to write to you again, that you may not be ignorant of what has since occurred in England, and of the existing situation of my own affairs in this place. On the 14th of November the archbishop of Canterbury, together with the late queen Jane, and the sons[4]

[[4] Lords Guilford and Ambrose Dudley. The four individuals above named were arraigned in Guildhall on Nov. 13th, and pleaded guilty. Soames, IV. 91.]

of the duke of Northumberland, were brought to trial, and condemned to death; and to the archbishop is assigned a most cruel kind of punishment, namely, that of being hanged and quartered: and though they in reality act thus on account of religion, they are unwilling to allege this, as being a more honourable accusation, and only charge him with the crime of treason; whereas they have pardoned other noblemen who were implicated in the same offence, because they have either apostatized from the religion heretofore received, or else never heartily embraced it. They have moreover decreed in parliament[1], that the mass shall every where be admitted, and have fixed the 20th of December as the time of its introduction. They have also established the doctrine of transubstantiation[2], which was no difficult matter for them to do, since they would not admit learned and godly men to those deliberations and conferences[3]; but at the very time they were treating of these matters, they either kept them shut up in prison, or excluded them from their assembly of evil-doers. Still, however, they were unable, with all their contrivances, to prevent great opposition to the doctrine of transubstantiation: but the opponents could do no good, inasmuch as they were overwhelmed by numbers, though not convinced by arguments, which are of no value. These things indicate to us what may be expected from the convocations of the bishops; for either good men are not admitted, or should they be summoned inadvertently, they are of no avail, since they are overpowered by a crowd of unlearned and ungodly men: whence our

[1 The parliament assembled at Westminster Oct. 5, and was prorogued for three days on the 21st of that month; after which it was enacted, after a vigorous opposition of six days' continuance, that after the 20th day of December next ensuing no other service should be allowed than that in use at the death of king Henry. Soames, IV. 88; Burnet, II. 395.]

[2 The convocation assembled in October. A full account of the proceedings is given in Soames, IV. 99, &c.; Burnet, II. 407, &c.; Strype, Mem. IV. 65, &c.; Cranmer, 461, &c.; Foxe, Acts and Mon. VI. 395, &c, and Philpot's writings, Parker Soc. Edition, 165, &c.]

[3 No individuals were present, favourable to the Reformation, who were not either deans or archdeacons, dignitaries entitled to seats in the lower house. From this it has been inferred, that pains were taken to prevent the return (by the election of the clergy) of any delegates adverse to Romanism. Soames, IV. 103.]

modern bishops, and the fathers and councils of our own times, lead us to regard the ancient councils with suspicion, so that we rightly withhold our confidence in them, without the authority of the word.

Thus much respecting the church of England. It is reported of the queen, that she is preparing for a journey to Calais, whither the other Mary[4], the emperor's sister, is about to proceed: they will there hold a conference, and it is generally thought that a marriage will take place between the queen of England and Philip, king of Spain; which, should it be the case, will deprive the English not only of their religion, but of their kingdom. They must therefore be aided by most effectual prayer to the Lord on their behalf.

My own affairs are in this condition. Our friend Sturmius[5], and the principal professors, with the greater portion of the clergy, have made strenuous exertions for my remaining here; and they had the governors of the school sufficiently favourable to this arrangement. But two or three of the ministers, who possess some influence, object to it on account of my opinions respecting the sacrament, and have raised such an opposition that the matter cannot yet be concluded. Since therefore I am loth to be with persons unwilling to receive me, I implore you, by our friendship and affection in Christ, to look about for some situation or other, in which I may be able to exercise my calling with honour and advantage. As I am well assured that you have no need of a more lengthened exhortation from me, I will say no more upon this subject,

[[4] See above, p. 343.]

[[5] At Strasburgh Peter Martyr's old friends, excellent and learned men, [John] Sturmius, Sleidan, Zanchius, Herlinus, Dasipodius, Sapidus, Hubertus, and the rest, did receive him with great joy. Also the senate, since they very well knew his virtue and doctrine, commanded that straightway should be restored unto him his ancient place which he had before his departure into England. But in the mean time, some which wished him not well, spread sinister rumours of him, namely, that in the doctrine of the Lord's supper he was gone from the opinion of the confession of Augsburg, and that therefore it was to be feared, lest he would make some troubles in the church. Hereof he being admonished by his friends, purged himself by a writing presented to the senate; the result of which was, that he was restored to his former office, which he held till July 1556, when he was appointed to succeed Conrad Pellican at Zurich. See the life of Martyr, at the end of his Common Places.]

but shall very anxiously and also speedily expect your answer. The Lord grant that you may not bestow your labour and exertions on my behalf to no purpose! You see how freely I treat you. But there is nothing that I dare not promise myself from your kindness, and I greatly desire that you would act in the same manner towards myself. May God preserve you very long to us in safety! Salute all your fellow-ministers in my name. Strasburgh, Dec. 15, 1553.

Yours wholly in Christ,

PETER MARTYR.

LETTER CCXXXIX.

PETER MARTYR TO HENRY BULLINGER.

Dated at STRASBURGH, *Jan.* 22, 1554.

GREETING. I will afford you, most excellent sir, in few words, according to your request, such information as I possess touching the affairs of England. A marriage is now projected between Philip, king of Spain, and the queen of England; and, as is reported, upon these conditions: the king is to enter England with a very small Spanish retinue; no Spaniard is to have the government of any port, or citadel, or fortified place; the principality of the Netherlands is united to England, whereby any son that may be born of this marriage will be king of England and prince of Lower Germany. Moreover, should the former son[1] of Philip, who is now educated in Spain, chance to die, the king of England will also succeed to the throne of Spain. England will be governed, as heretofore, by her own laws and parliaments, as they call them, and no Spaniard is to be admitted among the privy councillors. The queen is not to be compelled, upon any pretext, to go out of England, and is to receive yearly from Spain thirty thousand ducats. The people of England are not to be bound to undertake any war on account of king Philip. The emperor has agreed to all these conditions, by

[[1] Don Carlos, son of Philip II. and Mary of Portugal.]

which, as you may easily perceive how greatly he desired this match, so you may likewise conjecture with what fidelity he is likely to keep his promises. A fleet is on the point of being dispatched from England, to bring over Philip to the queen in the month of April. The deputies who accompany it, are the bishop of London, the lord high Treasurer, and Sir [Philip] Hoby. It is rumoured that the duke of Suffolk is dead, but the fact is not certain, nor do I feel inclined to believe it.

As to religion, every thing is in a most calamitous condition, nor, as far as I can see, is there any remedy: nay, it is rather to be feared, that should this Spanish alliance go on, things will daily become worse and worse. I do not know how you can address any letters thither: I am myself in the same predicament, and there is only, I think, one way left, namely, to send them to Antwerp; for if you have any friends there, they will be able to forward your letters, whithersoever you wish, without much trouble: otherwise it is very difficult to find out whereabouts our good friends are living in England; since they are compelled to lie in concealment, or wander about, unless they choose to give their sanction to ungodliness. And those who are more wealthy, are in alarm for their property, and are therefore unwilling to take upon themselves the charge of our letters, for fear of being suspected.

Your congratulation on my being restored to my former office in this place, which business however was only concluded to-day, is in accordance with your friendly and benevolent disposition. May the Lord grant that I may some time reap the desired fruit of my labour! And as you know that he that planteth and he that watereth is nothing, it remains for you to aid me with your prayers, that God, who giveth the increase, may be pleased to open the way.

I have had some conversation with your son[2] respecting his studies; and if things are as he states them to be, he does not appear to employ his time unprofitably: but when I have

[2 Bullinger's son was at this time studying at Strasburgh, and living in Burcher's house. There are many letters from Bullinger to him, preserved at Zurich. In one of them he gives the following advice: Frequenter legito, Deum timeto, creberrime orato, diligentissime studeto, cave ne quid tibi pereat temporis. Frugi et parcus esto: cogita te mox revocandum. Volat sagittæ in morem tempus. *Fronte capillata, post est occasio calva.*]

obtained farther information, I will not fail to let you know; meanwhile I would have you be of good hope, for you shall daily be informed by me of his proceedings, according as I may have the means and opportunity of writing.

The young man who is the bearer of this letter, is a countryman of yours, and has resided some years in England; and as he is a youth of excellent morals and piety, and as I am assured of his diligence in his studies, I recommend him to your notice; for should you befriend him, I do not think that your services, whatever they may be, will be ill bestowed. Farewell, and love me as you do. Master Zanchy salutes you. Do you in turn salute all your fellow-ministers in my name. Strasburgh, January 22, 1554.

Your most attached,

PETER MARTYR.

LETTER CCXL.

PETER MARTYR TO HENRY BULLINGER.

Dated at STRASBURGH, *Feb.* 24, 1554.

GREETING. You have now, excellent sir, requested of me in two letters to communicate to you forthwith whatever information I might possess respecting that distinguished man, and very dear brother in Christ, master à Lasco; and also to acquaint you with the tidings brought over to us respecting the state of affairs in England. Wherefore, since I have some intelligence to impart concerning the latter, I do not think it well to defer writing to you upon the former subject. Our friend à Lasco, as I have informed you before, had gone into Denmark[1] with his [congregation of] foreigners, but was

[[1] A Lasco embarked Sept. 15, 1553, at Gravesend, with 175 individuals, who resolved to follow their pastor and to share his fate. The ship in which he was embarked entered the port of Elsinore, in Denmark. The king granted him a favourable audience; but Noviomagus, his chaplain, a zealous Lutheran, succeeded in changing the mind of the monarch. The congregation of à Lasco were told that the king would rather suffer papists than them in his dominions, and received there with much harshness, not to say, barbarity: not indeed, as I suppose, through the fault of the king, but of the doctors and ministers of the church, by whose preaching and attacks[2] he and his friends were at length driven away from that kingdom. You need not doubt but that those men, by reason of the controversy respecting the eucharist, regard us as worse than papists. But God, who never forsakes his people, provided that this man of God should be most honourably entertained, with all his congregation, in Friesland; where the princess[3] went out to meet them, supplied them with most liberal alms, and gave them permission to have two churches of foreigners at Embden, namely, the one English, and the other French. But the errors of Schwenckfeldt[4] are most cruelly prevalent in almost all those parts. Thus much of our brother à Lasco.

We now come to the affairs of England. The people are so greatly displeased with the queen, chiefly on account of the Spanish marriage, that they have broken out into a formidable insurrection[5]. An army of twenty thousand men has been gathered together, besides cavalry: they have taken possession of the whole of Kent, together with the harbours of that district, and have robbed the ships of their ordnance, which they now make use of in their camp. They have moreover chosen not only a vigorous leader, but one who is well skilled in military affairs, and have now advanced as far as London. They have taken possession of the house of the

they were obliged to re-embark, notwithstanding the inclemency of the season. See Krasinski, Reform. in Poland, I. 264.]

[2 Westphalus, a Lutheran divine, called the wandering church of à Lasco the martyrs of the devil; and Bugenhagius declared they should not be considered as Christians. Krasinski, as above.]

[3 Anna of Oldenberg, sister and successor of Enno, count of East Friesland.]

[4 *Suencheldii,* Orig. Caspar Schwenckfeldt is probably intended. He was a Silesian knight, and councillor to the duke of Lignitz. He differed from Luther in the doctrine of the eucharist, in the hypothesis relating to the efficacy of the divine word, and also concerning the human nature of Christ. An account of his confession of faith is given in Kocheri Bibliotheca Theologiæ symbolicæ, p. 457.]

[5 For an account of sir Thomas Wyat's rebellion, see Holingshed, p. 1094; Stowe, p. 619.; Strype, Mem. III. i. 132; Burnet, II. 416, &c.; Soames, IV. 119, &c.]

bishop of Winchester[1]; and are not far from the palace of the archbishop of Canterbury at Lambeth. When they came to the bridge, they found the gates[2] of London shut against them: not indeed that the Londoners were hostile to their cause, but they were afraid of being plundered, either by the queen or by the rebel army. The army in encampment make three demands of the queen: 1. that a king shall be chosen of English blood; 2. that the religion that flourished under Edward shall continue to be in force; and, 3. that all the pasture lands which had been forcibly seized by persons in power shall be restored. And they require the bishop of Winchester and the lord Paget as hostages for the fulfilment of these demands. During this expedition of theirs they have hung a large number of mass-priests[3]. The city of London is in great danger: should it be pillaged, (which God forbid!) the merchants there cannot suffer loss without involving very many others in the same calamity. The emperor, moreover, is reported to have prohibited all the goods of the English merchants at Antwerp from being either sold or exported. English youths have come over to us in great numbers within these few days, partly from Oxford, and partly from Cambridge; whom many godly merchants are bringing up to learning, that, should it please God to restore religion to its former state in that kingdom, they may be of some benefit to the church of England. Thus much have I had to write to you. May God very long preserve you in safety! Master Zanchy salutes you; and I desire all your fellow-ministers to be saluted in my name. Strasburgh, Feb. 24, 1554.

Yours in the Lord,

PETER MARTYR.

[1 On Feb. 2, sir Thomas Wyat fell into Southwark. Some of his company had a mind to have broken into Winchester-house, and robbed it; but he threatened to hang any that should do it. Burnet, as above. Stowe, however, p. 619, states that the house was pillaged, and the books in the library destroyed.]

[2 Five hundred men, chiefly foreigners, were posted on the Surrey side of London-bridge. These troops prevented Wyat's entrance into the city. Soames, as above.]

[3 This statement appears to be unsupported by any other authority.]

We have since received farther information respecting English affairs; but I do not think it necessary to write it, as you may learn every thing from the worthy person who is to deliver this my letter. You must know that he is an Englishman, and a great favourer of our doctrine; and one, too, who by his preaching has defended and maintained it with great labour and assiduity. But now, as such dangerous times have arisen, he is travelling, as you see, with a view to relieve his anxiety of mind by visiting those churches which he considers to be peculiarly well ordered: wherefore I commend him to you again and again.

LETTER CCXLI.

PETER MARTYR TO HENRY BULLINGER.

Dated at STRASBURGH, *April* 3, 1554.

GREETING. Together with your very delightful letter, most excellent sir, I received some days since the book that you have now published, for which I return you abundant thanks, which will, I doubt not, be yet more abundant, when I have read it through, which I have not yet had it in my power to do. For such is the diligence of our bookbinders, that, although I put it into their hands the moment I received it, I have not yet been able to get it bound. I hear nothing else from England, except that every thing is getting worse and worse. Jane, who was formerly queen, conducted herself at her execution with the greatest fortitude and godliness, as did also her father and her husband. God be thanked that they persevered in the confession of the true faith! It is indeed a most distressing and remarkable fact, that we perceive those very persons in that kingdom, whom you would have considered the most resolute, now wavering, and even yielding. May God have pity upon his people, and at least preserve a remnant to that church. The archbishop of Canterbury, with the late bishop of London [Ridley], and Latimer, have been carried down to Oxford[4], where a parliament, as they call it, is shortly to be held;

[[4] It is stated above, p. 154, n. 2, upon Foxe's authority, that Cranmer and his companions were sent to Oxford about the 10th of

for it is proclaimed to meet there, unless they change their purpose. According to the general opinion, the pope will be restored by an act of this parliament, and these holy men will be put to death. May God bestow upon them constancy and boldness in the faith of Christ, as I doubt not but that he will do; for he has hitherto perpetually strengthened them under the most grievous trials. Do you, meanwhile, as you do, aid them with the prayers of the holy church; for those who do not feel themselves smitten by the swords of the ungodly in their brethren, are not to be regarded as members of the body of Christ. I have scarce been able to write this through grief, and I can hardly write a word more. May God bless you and your fellow-ministers, and your holy church! Strasburgh, April 3, 1554.

Yours,

PETER MARTYR.

LETTER CCXLII.

PETER MARTYR TO HENRY BULLINGER.

Dated at STRASBURGH, *Dec.* 31, 1555.

GREETING. I was intending, most excellent and much esteemed sir, to write to you last week, but by reason of my various engagements have put it off till now. For I have received a letter from that distinguished man, master à Lasco, who, alas! is dangerously ill at Frankfort: he desired my opinion upon a question relative to marriage, and requested

April. The date of this letter of Peter Martyr, and that of Lever (Lett. LXXVII.), must lead us to suppose that this is a mistake for the 10th of March. The order for their departure from the Tower, according to Foxe, (VI. 439,) was sent to the lieutenant of the Tower on the 10th of March, or the 8th according to the council-book. Bishop Ridley (Works, p. 390. Park. Soc.) says that they were sent to Oxford "a little before Easter," which was March 27th. Two documents in Strype's Cranmer, Appendix, No. 77, 78, dated Cambridge, April 10, speak of the three martyrs as then at Oxford. And see Cranmer, II. (Park. Soc.) p. xi. n.]

me to consult you also upon the same subject in his name. I received his letter very late, for it was not delivered to me more than eight or ten days since. Wherefore, not to place before you the whole history, or case, as the lawyers say, I wish you to learn it all from the same letter of master à Lasco, and will therefore add it to my own. As far as my opinion goes, I think that he has answered properly and according to law. But I could wish, as it is an evangelical government under which the individual is placed, whose cause is brought forward, that the consent and authority of the magistrate should be interposed; for marriage is not only a divine institution, but has also something of the nature of a civil contract: wherefore I could desire the decision of the civil power to prevent either such a connection in the state from being regarded as fornication, or the offspring arising therefrom from being counted as illegitimate.

It happened, moreover, some days since, that a certain pastor of the Grisons, who has a church in the Valteline, gave me to understand that an individual of some note, who wishes to seem to favour our religion, had given out at some entertainment, that I had written upon the sacrament of the eucharist contrary to my real sentiments, and that it was declared to him at Zurich that this was positively the case. This assertion, most excellent sir, and much beloved in Christ, exceedingly disturbs my mind, and that for two reasons: first, because in those places where my name and character, however undeservedly, are in a certain degree of estimation, the progress of pure doctrine might in some measure be impeded, if rumours of this kind should extend further; in the next place, because I should be grievously distressed, if (which God forbid!) I were to labour under such a suspicion in your church. Those indeed who either speak or think thus do me a most manifest injury: for I have ever taken the greatest possible care not to blow hot and cold out of my mouth; and as I have done this upon every occasion, how much the more should I exercise this caution when so great a mystery is concerned! You have, reverend sir, a copy of the writing which I gave to the magistracy here, when I again took upon myself the office of teaching; you have also other letters of mine, and you will have this. Produce them all, if you deem it necessary; for I do not care wherever they are read, and would endure any thing rather than be regarded as given to change in matters of religion. I continue, thank God, and by his blessing will continue, in the same opinion as I have recorded in writing, and which I have so often defended in controversies however sharp and dangerous. Wherefore, as I have never spoken a word in opposition to those sentiments either in public or private, those parties certainly deserve very ill at my hands who thus positively affirm what they are entirely ignorant of. No man has a right to consider any person as having either changed his belief, or recanted, who has not written or taught, either publicly or in private, differently from what he had previously written. I have thus, O man of God, written to you at length, both because I am so closely united to you in spirit and in Christ; and also that you may vindicate me from these calumnies in the manner you think best, which I do not doubt but that you will do, as you have ever been eminently attached to truth and justice.

As to other matters, I have nothing else to write, except that the emperor, as it is reported, has given up his intention of going into Spain. The English have dissolved their parliament without having installed Philip in the possession of the kingdom. The church is grievously suffering under popery. As to myself, I am living, and teaching, and enjoying my health as usual[1]. I have an English friend yonder, of the name of Parkhurst, an excellent, godly, and not unlearned man. Should you have it in your power to be of any service to him, you will greatly oblige me. Farewell, and love me in the Lord as you do, and do not forget me in your prayers. Salute, I pray you, all your fellow-ministers in my name. Strasburgh, Dec. 31, 1555.

Your most attached,

PETER MARTYR.

[[1] Peter Martyr remained at Strasburgh till July 13th, 1556, on which day he removed to Zurich, by the senate of which city he was appointed to succeed Conrad Pellican as professor of divinity.]

LETTER CCXLIII.

PETER MARTYR TO JOHN WOLFIUS.

Dated at STRASBURGH, *Feb.* 18, 1556.

GREETING. Your letter, most learned and much esteemed sir, has afforded me no ordinary satisfaction; for I most clearly perceived therein the candid and sincere friendship towards me, which God knows how greatly I have always appreciated, both of yourself and your fellow-ministers, whom I love as very dear brethren in Christ. You have removed, believe me, from my mind all suspicion under which, to say the truth, I did not so labour as to be led to believe that any one from among the ministers of your holy church had detracted from my reputation: but yet I was afraid that something of the kind had been said yonder by some one else, which, when afterwards carried into the Grisons, (as was the boast of that individual who said that he heard it in your city,) might so offend your ears, as to occasion some surmises respecting me, whereby that kindness and brotherly love, which I desire always to be increased between us, might in some measure be diminished. Now, however, by the testimony of Bullinger and yourself, I am entirely relieved, and am altogether persuaded that the individual, whoever he might be, had invented a falsehood, to which he himself gave currency; and therefore said that he had heard this falsehood at Zurich, with the view of diminishing my influence with our Italian churches in those parts. But, my worthy and candid friend, you must not wonder that this has happened to me; for even holy love has a certain emulation, or, to express it in Greek, *ζηλοτυπίαν*, [jealousy.] I entertain such a regard for you and for your church, that I congratulate myself not a little upon my belonging to it, as I trust I do; though I am well aware that Satan will endeavour, with all his might, to separate brethren in the church of Christ from each other[2]. Wherefore, I thank you, as I ought to do, for your christian and delightful consolation; and I pray God, the Father of our Lord Jesus Christ, perpetually to comfort you with his Spirit,

[[2] The meaning of this sentence is uncertain, owing to erasures in the original letter.]

as I doubt not but that he does. Live to Christ, and love me in him, as you do. Strasburgh, Feb. 18, 1556.

Yours in the Lord,

PETER MARTYR.

LETTER CCXLIV.

MARTIN BUCER TO THE ARCHBISHOP OF CANTERBURY.

Dated at STRASBURGH, *Oct.* 23, 1538.

I PRAY for your reverend fatherhood grace and peace in our Lord Jesus Christ, and most dutifully offer my respects. The letter of your reverence, without any date, but, as I learn from my truly noble friend Thomas[1], written a year ago, and given me by the said Thomas within these few days, I have read, together with those you wrote to Capito[2] and Grynæus; each of them having sent me his letter for my perusal. By these letters, and by the conversation of Thomas and others, I have been much refreshed in the Lord, because I perceive that our Lord Jesus Christ has graciously vouchsafed remarkable success, and such too as we have hitherto hardly ventured to expect, to your most godly designs, [ ][3] endeavours, and exertions, not only unwearied, but also, if you take into consideration the world and the flesh, most difficult of accomplishment. For inasmuch as the Lord has united with you (not as Theseuses, but as Barnabases,) the Latimers, the Foxes[4], and others endued

[1 Probably Thomas Tybald, mentioned above, p. 16, and who is stated in one of Cranmer's letters to Crumwell, dated July 22, 1537, to be on his return to Germany. See Cranmer, II. p. 340. (Park. Soc.) where will be found also the letter conveyed by Tybald to Capito, in which Foxe, bishop of Hereford, is mentioned.]

[2 This letter is given above, p. 15.]

[3 A word is illegible in the original.]

[4 Edward Foxe, bishop of Hereford, had been ambassador to Smalcald in the winter of 1535, for the double purpose of concluding a treaty of alliance with the German Protestants, and of drawing up a joint confession of the faith. On this occasion he incurred the suspicion of duplicity, being charged with representing Henry VIII.'s inclination to Lutheranism to be greater than was the fact. See Jenkyns, Cranmer, I. 179. His speech at Smalcald is given in Sleidan, IX. 188.]

with so much courage, so much activity, and, in fine, with so much zeal; what else can be inferred from this, but that he favours your purpose and undertaking, and that he will enable you to produce abundant fruit unto Christ throughout the whole kingdom? Truly, therefore, are you happy, in whom Christ so lives and reigns; and woe, I will not say to that sluggishness, but to that senselessness and all but treason of ours, who in a place and time so convenient and desirable have not aided you by the slightest exertions. Such is our understanding, such our consideration, of what we daily address in prayer to our Father which is in heaven: *Hallowed be thy name, thy kingdom come.* O Lord Jesus! make us to perceive and feel that we are only thy disciples, when we bring forth much fruit, and neglect no opportunity whatever of advancing thy cause, and of benefiting mankind. But how it shames and grieves both our senators here, and us ministers of the word, that besides all those betrayals (let me call it by its right name) of the kingdom of Christ among you, the letter of our Smalcaldic[5] council was sent in so disgraceful a manner! For what could be more disgraceful, or more shameful, what could be done so unworthy of us, as thus to send the letter of a council so eminent, as it seems to me, on a matter of such importance, to so illustrious a king, and one too who had before so honoured us beyond all expectation even of those who hoped the best, and offered us of his own accord in a more than royal embassy those things which, if we really desired to advance the kingdom of Christ, it would have behoved us to obtain at the expense of all we have? But how piously in your letter to Grynæus do you withdraw yourself altogether from these sins and calamities to the consideration and handling of such things as there is some hope of considering and handling with success! May Christ therefore grant you so to forgive this rudeness of ours, although (to give glory to God,) it amount to an impiety, as that you may forget it altogether. If it rested with us ministers and our senate, you would doubtless perceive our earnest desire to make amends to

[5 For an account of the negotiations of Henry VIII. with the protestant princes at Smalcald, see Burnet, III. 170; IV. 471, &c.; Seckendorf, III. § 66.]

you for the very grievous sin of which our people have hitherto been guilty.

And now, with respect to my copious and unmethodical commentaries[1], dedicated to yourself, I earnestly entreat your reverence to admit me into the place of a true client and son in the Lord, and at some future time, if your good-will towards us should predominate over those numberless engagements by which it is distracted in defence of the kingdom of Christ, that you would again condescend to write to us, and instruct and correct me as a client and a son. I am not of so ingenuous a disposition as to be amended by praise, but require rather to be disciplined by plain and severe chastisement. Besides, the commendation I read in your letter is so excessive, as to grieve me exceedingly. I attribute, however, that writing to your troublesome engagements, which are all but killing you, not to say that they sometimes cause you to forget yourself: otherwise I should be very sorry that you did not exercise towards me paternal *severity*, I will not say *verity*. I am well aware of the defects that are to be found in my writings; and unless I thought that some of the more unlearned might perhaps be benefited by them, by accustoming themselves to handle the scriptures with somewhat greater accuracy, I am aware that it would have been intolerable presumption in me to have published a single page, and especially at a period so abounding in learning. I was moreover in circumstances of the greatest disquiet, and obliged to hurry every thing most prodigiously while I was writing my commentary on the Romans: wherefore I am well aware that there are innumerable defects in that work which even the most indulgent partiality must necessarily condemn. You have stated, however, the plan which you desire to lay down for these writings; and in this I acknowledge your paternal admonition, for which also I offer my best thanks. And I wish that I may be able to follow the method which you point out, since I am sensible it will be of the greatest benefit to the churches. I will endeavour, however, in some measure to attain it in the remaining epistles, if perhaps I may stir up some one of those, to whom the Lord has granted the ability, to pursue the same

[[1] On the Epistle to the Romans.]

method hereafter. I have been harassed by so many journeyings since the publication of the first edition, and have been so struggling with a painful disease which has very much weakened my brain for these two years past, that I have been unable in the meantime to write any thing upon the apostle. This winter I hope to be allowed to return to this work, although there are some things still pressing upon me which must previously be finished for the church at Augsburg, and which will take up a certain portion of time.

I have before thanked your reverence for your very liberal present sent by Reyner[2], and I now repeat my acknowledgments as warmly as possible. Christ knows, that when I dedicated my lucubrations to you I had this object in view, to set forth your faith to the godly as far as was in my power, and thereby to encourage our hopes, and also to procure some kind of access from us to you, and some communion in the Lord. We know also, that your truly excessive liberality towards those, whom you consider in any way to labour for the church of Christ, does not permit them to discharge the debt which you have contracted in the cause of Christ: wherefore you must not send any thing more. For our friend Thomas informs me that you desired an additional sum of thirty crowns to be presented to me. I have never yet received a farthing from any one for dedicating my works: so that if your reverence will treat me with such liberality, there will be some danger of my growing covetous. For the love of money increases in proportion as the money itself does. Thank God, I have always lived very frugally and sparingly during the whole time of my ministry; and it is for my advantage to persevere in this frugality.

As to the letter of Grynæus to your reverence, it is well that you should know the candid frankness of this individual. He is a theoretical, and not a practical divine. He conceives a form of a church, and of the process by which a church

[2 Reyner, or Reginald, Wolfe is probably intended. He was a native of Switzerland, and a very famous and skilful printer, at the sign of the Brasen Serpent, in St Paul's church yard. He was much in favour with Henry VIII., Cromwell, Cranmer, and queen Elizabeth. He died in 1574. See Strype, Ann. II. i. 530. Nichols's Literary Anecdotes, III. 549. Herbert's Ames, i. 595.]

ought to be reformed; but since he is not himself an agent in the work, he does not know by experience what difficulties arise, when the tyranny of antichrist is really to be destroyed, and the kingdom of Christ restored. Whatever he sees founded upon the word of God, and therefore beneficial to men, he thinks at the same time will be very easy of accomplishment; for that no one will be disposed to resist God, and reject the things which make for his own salvation. In fact, he judges every one else by his own disposition. We, namely, Capito, Grynæus, another a native of Basle, and myself, were in September last at Berne in Switzerland for the purpose of commending to them a form of agreement respecting the eucharist; in which matter the Lord was wonderfully present with us. In the course of that journey he most vehemently accused both myself and others, whom he charged with I know not what indolence, in not having long since caused all Germany to unite together in restoring the churches, and preserving their liberty: for that there were many commonwealths and princes, whom, if we were duly to call them together, we should be able without any difficulty to draw over into an alliance with Christ. Every one indeed has perceived long since, that nothing else is to be expected from the pseudo-ecclesiastics but the destruction both of things present and eternal; and also how much the liberty of Germany is endangered both from this cause, and the treachery of those who are seeking their own ends with the emperor to the ruin of their country. This worthy man reasons on the subject in this way. These things are true, excellent, and also necessary; and therefore every one would approve them, and be ready to embrace them, if only those, whose interest it is, understood them. Now it can be most clearly shewn that this is the case. This and that person therefore, who have any authority with the princes, and are qualified by their talents clearly to point out these things to any one, are idle and betrayers of their country. These assertions he considers as proofs, admitting of no contradiction[1]. For he has never experienced how easy it is to imagine such things, and how difficult to accomplish them. And as he supposed that your reverence possessed unbounded authority with your most serene and wise sove-

[1 Some words here are unintelligible.]

reign, so he judges in like manner respecting myself; and if a man is once allowed to have an interview with any prince, he immediately supposes that he can obtain from such prince whatever he desires. And when any persons condemn some things among the papists, and in any measure approve of any thing in us, he forthwith concludes that such persons can be brought over by a word to give themselves entirely to the cause of Christ. For he has not yet found out by experience, with what difficulty even persons of no common attainments, and who are by no means ill-disposed to what is true and right, are persuaded to embrace things which are really good. I say nothing of those who, though they excellently set forth the doctrine of Christ in their preaching, yet will not undergo in the cause of Christ the slightest peril or exertion. When I have brought him into some kind of practical acquaintance with church matters at Basle, he will learn a lesson that he little thought of. In the meantime, as your reverence is aware, nothing can be more sincere, or candid, or friendly, than this man. But because he so entirely looks up to, and reverences you as in every respect an apostolic character, it is for this reason that he takes such a liberty with you; and not only demands of you a courage and zeal worthy of an apostle, but requires that, according to the apostle's wish, which however was never granted to any of the apostles, you should become all things to all men.

We all of us acknowledge how graciously England is dealt with, to whom alone it is given so far to recover itself in the midst of so many impediments. And we count you altogether happy in the Lord, from whose labours has resulted such fruit. I am anxious to write these things that you might know that all the godly men, who have experience in ecclesiastical matters, consider the progress of the kingdom of Christ among you as most extensive, and your exertions to promote it exceedingly successful: on which account they most joyfully praise and extol the mercy and goodness of our Lord Jesus Christ towards all of us, whom we pray both in your country and in ours to restore and establish every thing that is yet to be desired. For there are too many things still wanting to us, unless it be enough to have shaken off the yoke of the pope, and to be unwilling to take upon us the yoke of Christ. The agreement of our churches (thanks to Christ!) is making fair progress. My fellow-ministers are very anxious respecting the proper government of the churches. Meanwhile, however, we are grievously infested by epicureans within, and papists without, by whom we are surrounded on all sides. And those who are wonderfully strengthening themselves with duke William[1] of Bavaria, have collected a great quantity of money; while those who are able and willing to make a campaign, or are any way inclined to or qualified for a military life, engage either infantry or cavalry. But if God be for us, who can be against us? And christianity is a warfare. Only let us earnestly beseech him to extend his kingdom, both among ourselves, and every where else. I pray him (that I may cease at length from intruding upon your most holy affairs, or rather those of Christ in you) to vouchsafe evermore to accomplish the wishes of yourself and all your colleagues, to his glory, and the welfare not only of your kingdom but of his whole church. I entreat your reverence to number me among your true sons and clients, and admonish me as a father and a patron should do. I will endeavour on my part not to be wanting in the duty of a son and a real client. Strasburgh, Oct. 23, [1538.]

Your reverence's most devoted client and son,

M. BUCER.

LETTER CCXLV.

MARTIN BUCER TO ARCHBISHOP CRANMER.

Dated at STRASBURGH, *Oct.* 29, 1539.

GRACE and peace from the Lord, most excellent prelate! My friend Grynæus has sent this his letter to you for my inspection, that, should I not consider it too harsh, I should forward it, but if otherwise, retain it. It appears indeed to be harsh and vehement beyond measure: but as I believe that you really love Christ, I do not doubt but that you will read with benefit to yourself this reproof, however severe,

[1 William and Lewis, dukes of Bavaria, joined the Holy League for the support of the Catholic religion in 1538. See Sleidan, VII. 245.]

which is administered to you for the glory of Christ, and by one too, who is especially desirous both of his glory and your salvation. I pray you therefore to take in good part the design both of the writer and of the sender. Grynæus wished me to add a letter from myself; but I would rather consult with you as to the remedies for this mischief, if any can be hoped for.

We are all of us amazed more than I can express, at the sight of those decrees[2], and at the previous rejection of the terms of alliance between his serene majesty and ourselves, since they were the very same which the bishop of Hereford[3], a most cautious man, and one best acquainted with, and most observant of, the royal sentiments, at the beginning declared would be most satisfactory. We have altogether perceived a great change, and one too, the result of deep counsels. We suspected therefore, that something had blown over from France, inasmuch as you no longer appeared to have any necessity for our alliance, or even our friendship. For it would have been too idle to suppose that we should not have been offended by those most severe decrees. For not to enlarge upon the others, in what light we should view even that alone, stating "that it is contrary to the law of God that duly appointed ministers of churches should have wives," might easily be ascertained by those who have now been in communication with us nearly five years, and who are well aware that the principle maintained in this our most difficult and dangerous struggle is, that salvation is obtained for us by Christ alone, and therefore that nothing is to be imposed upon men beyond what Christ himself has imposed; nothing is to be regarded as holy, nothing as useful, which is devised without the sanction of his word; likewise, that nothing whatever is to be allowed, even in respect to things indifferent, of which it is not the aim and tendency that he should be most fully acknowledged and devoutly worshipped as the only Saviour. It was believed therefore that the king had been so far acted upon, as to wish to take leave of us altogether; and it appeared that antichrist had evidently gained the victory; for whatever may yet remain of christian doctrine, those

[2 Namely, The Act of the Six Articles, which passed June 28, 1539. See Burnet, II. 416, 588.]

[3 See above, p. 520, n. 4.]

decrees seemed so likely to empty the kingdom of all duly qualified ministers of Christ, as that all the churches would be for the future entirely in the hands of the followers of antichrist, who had thus found their opportunity for restoring the Roman pontiff without any great difficulty.

These were the thoughts that we were revolving in our minds. But as the present ruler of France is altogether on the side of the pope, and it is so greatly opposed to the consistency of the king [of England] to admit the pope, because the king is said to have read and acquired so much information on the subject, we could not entirely lay aside the hope of bringing him back into the right way. This hope, however, was entertained solely by those of our friends who are residing here; for the other princes and states regard us as all but mad, for entertaining any hope on the subject. Our people, however, sent both to the elector and the landgrave, and used their utmost endeavours that ambassadors should even now be sent to the king under the common authority of the allies, who should endeavour to obtain, if not a suspension of the decrees, at least a deferring of the punishment denounced against those who should refuse obedience. For we trust that there are many persons still remaining in your kingdom, who are earnestly looking for the kingdom of Christ; in behalf of which persons if our legates could obtain even the shortest respite, we willingly persuade ourselves that, in the result, the falsehoods of antichrist being detected, the king would at length receive the truth of Christ. For we suspect that this change of purpose has chiefly been extorted from him by antichrist, by raising his fears as to the state of things both at home and abroad beyond the truth, and by depreciating our assistance below the truth. But such tricks even by the lapse of time betray themselves and come to nothing. And the high spirit of the king cannot but be very indignant against those who are detected in thus seeking to deceive him for the sake of their own interests.

But even now our hope respecting the king is a little revived, on our having seen what he has announced to our princes through Christopher Mont, that he should still persist in his opposition to the pope; and that though he disagrees with us on some points, yet he will nevertheless continue our friend; and also, that if we ourselves should wish to inform him of any matters, he will readily attend to them: besides which, he endeavours to throw the blame upon ourselves, that a treaty of alliance has not been made between us. These things, I say, in some measure revive our spirits, for he still appears to make some account of our friendship; which is an evidence that there is not yet so much succour afforded by France, as that the king will altogether betake himself to that quarter. Now, if he persevere in his opposition to the pope, he will find out that not one of those who still continue to worship the beast will prove a faithful friend or ally to himself. Wherefore we shall be yet more urgent that an embassy may be sent over to you. On the 19th of November our friends will assemble at Arnstadt[1], which is not far from Erdfurt, to consult upon affairs of importance; among which yours also will be considered, and I hope with greater prospect of success, as we hear that a matrimonial alliance has been formed with the duke of Cleves. The elector[2] will judge more favourably respecting his kinsman; for he was, as Christopher [Mont] perceived, exceedingly disturbed by those decrees.

I am writing to you of these things, that you may see that we are anxious about you all; and if we could only discover by what means we might be able to help you, it would be our greatest delight to afford such assistance as is due from brethren and members of the same body. The Lord grant in the mean time, that you may faithfully retain and rightly explain that chief head of christian doctrine, namely, the article of justification. For as long as that is retained in the churches, even in any degree, the kingdom of Christ will yet remain amongst you. Albeit we admit that the church of Christ existed in the times of Gregory, during which a great portion of your decrees was in force; and we trust also that the church of Christ will continue among you,

[1 The Protestants appointed a convention on the 19th of November, at Arnstadt, a town in Thuringia. Here they consulted about strengthening their league with new alliances, and had to prepare for a necessary defence, in case the emperor would not allow the treaty of Frankfort. They agreed to meet at Smalcald on the 1st of March following. Sleidan, XII. 251.]

[2 The elector sent John Dulcius, and Francis Burcart, his vice-chancellor, into England, to be present at the solemnity of the King's marriage with Ann of Cleves, whose sister Sibill was his own duchess. The marriage took place Jan. 6, 1540. Sleidan, XII. 252.]

and that some time or other it will aspire to a purer dispensation of religion. Nay, we know that in this terrible scattering by the Roman antichrist the churches of Christ yet survive, though their government is almost entirely antichristian; and we hope that they will recover themselves, and restore a legitimate discipline. Nothing grieves me more, than that private masses are so approved of, and the marriage of the clergy condemned: for the one will perpetuate superstition among the people, while the other will perpetuate impurity and ungodliness in the ministers. For a wounded conscience cannot sustain the faithful discharge of ministerial duties; and those persons who can really conform themselves to a life of celibacy, are very rarely to be met with. It appears also from those two decrees, that neither the authority of the primitive church, nor the word of God, nor even reason itself, had any influence in that council of yours. For if the authority of the primitive church had prevailed, you would neither have approved of retaining the mass, nor of transubstantiation; and you would have framed regulations entirely different as to the life and government of the bishops and clergy. If the word of God and reason had prevailed, you would not have made so much esteem of monkery and celibacy. Truly then your regulations respecting them are monstrous. They are partly popish, partly evangelical, and are partly intended to appear in conformity with the ancient government of the church.

Grant, Lord Jesus, that it may be acknowledged that thou hast all power in heaven and in earth; that all thy commands are salutary, and that all things will turn out to the good of those who trust themselves to thee. So shall we easily come to an agreement with respect to doctrine and the entire administration of thy kingdom.

May he preserve and bless both yourself and all the saints who are with you! Amen. I am anxious about that excellent man, master Nicolas Heath[1]. May the Lord preserve him! Strasburgh, Oct. 29, 1539.

Your reverence's most devoted,

MARTIN BUCER.

[[1] "Nicolas Heth, the archdeacon, alone excels in humanity and learning among our guests." Melancthon to Camerarius, cited by Strype, Mem. I. i. 351. He was afterwards archbishop of York, and deprived in 1559. See Zur. Lett. Series II. p. 182, n. 1.]

LETTER CCXLVI.

MARTIN BUCER TO ARCHBISHOP CRANMER.

Dated at [STRASBURGH, *Sept.* 3, 1548.][2]

MAY our Lord Jesus Christ, who is charity itself, and the most gracious recompenser of all charity, repay, most reverend father, with the abundant consolation and mighty strengthening of his Spirit, your abundant charity and compassion towards the afflicted members of Christ, by which also you have condescended to refresh me with another letter, though you are yourself involved not only in exceeding care and anxiety, but engaged also in most severe contests and struggles for the kingdom of Christ. As to ourselves, we are daily suffering more and more severely the punishment for our ingratitude, and are flowing away like water poured out, after having persisted for so many years in embracing with so much coldness, and to so little purpose, the abundant mercy of God towards us. There are indeed still remaining in all parts of Germany numberless souls truly devoted to Christ the Lord; and who are unceasingly calling to him, Lord, continue with us! But they are unable to be of any service except by their prayers and most bitter groanings, but which the good Shepherd is prevented from regarding by reason of the wickedness of the majority, not of the people only, but of those especially who ought to be their examples; by which means some persons are most shamefully falling away from our only Saviour, and others are even beginning to assault his kingdom. It has therefore come to pass, that those to whom the Lord now commits the reins of government, have declared that they can proceed no farther in the public administration of the Christian religion, than as they shall obtain permission from the emperor; to whom they yesterday sent a second deputation[3] to request some connivance, though but a very

[2 This letter was written the day after the senate of Strasburgh sent a second deputation to the Emperor, which took place on the 2nd of September, 1548. Sleidan, XXI. 473.]

[3 This deputation consisted of James Sturmius and others. The letter they brought to the Emperor from the senate is given in Sleidan, XXI. 473.]

doubtful one, at the preaching of the gospel. For they offer to use every exertion in their power, that nothing shall be decreed here in opposition to his ordinance respecting religion, which they call the Interim. They have long been treating with a pious bishop, wishing him to use the same dissimulation as themselves, and desiring to divide the churches with him. But he shews himself much more faithful to his Roman master than we have done to our heavenly one: for he will not admit any persons to the ministry of the churches unless they are ordained, and lawfully called and confirmed; that is, sworn and devoted to antichrist.

But I thank the Lord our Saviour, and the faithful Bishop of our souls, that he has so preserved to himself my colleagues, in number twenty-three, that none of them has hitherto been inclined to agree to any change of doctrine, although most of them are broken down by years and infirmities, and as to external circumstances, not so rich in any thing else as in the number of their children. The senate however, though so far bound by the religion of Christ as not to endure our being altogether silenced, or deprived of our ministry; yet, forasmuch as it has so humbled itself through fear of men, as to promise both to the emperor and the bishop a lowering of doctrine which we are not able to admit; it is not without cause very solicitous on our behalf, and for those especially, in regard to whom it is well aware what favour is already provided for them with the higher powers by the servants of antichrist. Wherefore we are daily expecting, some of us more especially, the termination of our ministry. And as we would prefer to undergo any suffering rather than to dwell in the tents of Kedar, how very acceptably does your reverend fatherhood offer yourself to our relief. For though we must acknowledge how little we are able to contribute in any quarter to the restoration of the things of Christ, seeing that our labours and endeavours have thus fallen to the ground; yet we neither can nor ought to do otherwise than receive gratefully this mercy of Christ our Saviour, offered by your reverence, and embrace it with our whole heart. As soon therefore as the Lord shall have clearly dismissed us from hence, and we have administered to the Lord's remnant, which he has here, and one indeed which is by no means to be despised, that service and support which he himself requires of us; we will pray him that, should he still be pleased to make use of our ministry, he will bring us over to you as soon as possible. For there appears no reason for us to doubt, that we hear from your reverence the voice of Christ. In the mean while, and at all times, we shall earnestly implore him to supply, as he has hitherto done in so wonderful a manner, such strength to your reverence, that you may be enabled successfully to sustain the weight of the ministry imposed upon you, most difficult indeed, but yet most blessed and glorious; and also to bring the work you have begun to the desired termination, to the eternal glory of the Lord our Saviour, and to the abundant salvation of your countrymen, and also to the comfort and preservation of ours, who are all but worn out with sorrow and anxiety under this overthrow of our churches. May the same Lord our Saviour cast down Satan shortly under the feet of his people, both in England and every where else, and enrich with every blessing both your reverence, the most serene king, and all his council and kingdom! Amen.

[M. BUCER.]

LETTER CCXLVII.

MARTIN BUCER TO ARCHBISHOP CRANMER.

Dated at STRASBURGH, *Dec.* 23, 1548.

THOSE persons, most reverend lord and father, who profess to be the physicians of this state, are deferring indeed its destruction, but do not apply those remedies by which alone its death can be prevented, and its health restored; I mean, solid repentance, and the re-establishment of all things agreeably to the laws of Christ; by which remedies the affairs of God's people have in former times been snatched out of the very jaws of death, and happily recovered. The vital power of this our body is in consequence decreasing every day. But since Christ, our life, has here no small number of those who will never die, we ought not to deprive them of such consolation as we can afford, so long as it is permitted us to do so: and we must also to the very last testify to others both of the compassion and the severity of God. Thus is protracted also the time of our death, most bitter as it truly is, which we suffer by observing so illustrious a state, regardless of such faithful and repeated warnings, daily hastening to its ruin. For which cause most assuredly, as far as we are concerned, there is nothing that I should more delight in, than in rendering assistance to a church which is so nobly recovering itself as yours is, and making such happy progress in Christ our Lord. And it is a great consolation to us in the midst of so great anxieties, that your reverence has called us from death to life. For I trust, as I have also written before, that the wish of your reverence concerning me, and with which you acquainted me by letter, proceeded from the Spirit of the Lord; to which therefore by the Lord's help I shall gladly yield myself, and will faithfully adhere to and obey it. May the Lord Jesus so grant his kingdom yonder to be established, and to strike root, that that tempest, by which we are now oppressed by reason of our own deservings, may never fall upon you! And may the same Saviour ever preserve your reverence, with your colleagues and all ministers, and evermore prosper his work in your hands. Amen! Dec. 23, 1548.

LETTER CCXLVIII.

MARTIN BUCER AND PAUL FAGIUS[1] TO THE MINISTERS AT STRASBURGH.

Dated at LAMBETH, *April* 26, 1549.

To the eminent servants of Christ, our very dear masters and fellow-ministers, masters Hedio, Theobald, Jos. Lenglin, Marpach, Lewis, and the other ministers of the church of Strasburgh.

May our Lord Jesus Christ preserve you to himself, together with your whole church, and again bestow upon you, when delivered from your present affliction, the desired peace! Amen.

[1 See Fagius's letter to his son-in-law, of the same date, above, p. 332.]

We pray you in the Lord to thank the Lord on our behalf, who of his wonderful mercy has conducted us hither. For as our journey by land was altogether undisturbed by enemies, so he bestowed upon us a quiet passage, and free from wind, across the channel, in which we were not detained more than five hours. We yesterday waited upon the archbishop of Canterbury, that most benevolent and kind father of the churches and of godly men; who received and entertains us as brethren, not as dependents. We found at his house, what was most gratifying to us, our most dear friend doctor Peter Martyr, with his wife and his attendant Julius, master Immanuel [Tremellius] with his wife; and also Dryander, and some other godly Frenchmen whom we had sent before us. All these are entertained by the archbishop of Canterbury.

The cause of religion, as far as appertains to the establishment of doctrines and the definition of rites, is pretty near what could be wished. Efforts must now be made to obtain suitable ministers, who will carry these wholesome doctrines into practice, and deliver them to the people. For as is the case in France or Italy, so it is also in this country, that the pastors of the churches have hitherto confined their duties chiefly to ceremonies, and have very rarely preached, and never catechised. Hence the people are labouring under a very great scarcity of teachers. But if the Lord be pleased to continue, as he has begun, the manifestations of his mercy in that kingdom, this lack of persons to instruct the Lord's flock will shortly be supplied. For there are numerous and liberal stipends assigned to students in theology; for which reason very many young men apply themselves to sacred learning. As soon as the description of the ceremonies now in use shall have been translated into Latin, we will send it to you. We hear that some concessions have been made both to a respect for antiquity, and to the infirmity of the present age; such, for instance, as the vestments commonly used in the sacrament of the eucharist, and the use of candles: so also in regard to the commemoration of the dead, and the use of chrism; for we know not to what extent or in what sort it prevails. They affirm that there is no superstition in these things, and that they are only to be retained for a time, lest the people, not having yet learned

Christ, should be deterred by too extensive innovations from embracing his religion, and that rather they may be won over. This circumstance however greatly refreshed us, that all the services in the churches are read and sung in the vernacular tongue, that the doctrine of justification is purely and soundly taught, and the eucharist administered according to Christ's ordinance, private masses having been abolished.

We foreigners, as far as we can learn, are to be incorporated in the university, and probably in that of Cambridge, since Peter Martyr is at Oxford. God grant that the result may be for his glory! The work of the Lord and the building of his church is carried on as is usually the case at first, when the strong man armed stoutly keepeth his palace. In proportion therefore as those are few in number who fight the Lord's battles, upon those few presses more severely the weight of the contest. The Lord grant that we may hence more effectually repent of our sins, and of our negligence in our respective ministries. For we have deserved on this account, that whereas, considering the length of our ministry and our time of life, we ought to have reaped the fruit of our labours at home, (where we have laboured in some measure for so many years,) and that in the desired advancement of all ranks and ages of the church in all knowledge of the Son of God and of the discipline of his kingdom,—we are led forth, not to say driven, at this time and age, to stir up the fallow ground, and that too among a nation which, though itself enriched with many gifts of the Lord, yet so greatly differs from us both in language and customs; and which, like all others, has its own peculiar impediments to the right reception of God's word. We must however acknowledge in the meantime this greatest benefit of the divine indulgence to us, that the Lord will have us to contend and labour in a country where it is permitted to explain all his commands with the utmost freedom, and where there are not wanting persons who are inclined both to comfort and assist us in these contests and labours. Let that then be the time of our rest, when the Lord shall translate us to himself. Only let him be present with us, so long as he chooses us to remain in this our pilgrimage; and do you diligently unite with us in thus entreating him, that we may shew ourselves faithful to him, and useful ministers to his church, in whatever place and with whatever temporal convenience or inconvenience he may choose.

We are in anxious expectation of a letter from you, that we may learn how the Son of God is overcoming antichrist among you, which may he entirely and speedily accomplish! Let us mutually commend ourselves to the Lord in constant prayer. Farewell, all of you, most happily in the Lord, with all your wives and children, friends, and your whole church and school. As soon as we have more certain information both respecting ourselves and the kingdom of Christ in this country, we will let you know. The blessing of the Lord be increasingly with you at all times! Amen. April 26, [1549]. At Lambeth, from the house of the archbishop of Canterbury, near London.

Yours wholly in the Lord,

M. BUCER and P. FAGIUS.

LETTER CCXLIX.

MARTIN BUCER TO JAMES STURMIUS.

Dated at [LAMBETH], Ascension Day, [*May* 30], 1549.

GREETING. It is now eight weeks since I left Strasburgh, and I have not received a single thing or letter in all this period; so that I fear our letters have been intercepted in their way to the individual to whom we agreed to direct them. That this may not be the case with those I am now sending, I have inclosed them in this that I have written to you. Take this, I pray you, in good part, and order the letters to be forwarded to their respective addresses. The most reverend archbishop of Canterbury still retains us at his house, and treats us in a brotherly manner. After the vacation, if the Lord permit, we are to begin our lectures at Cambridge. May the Lord be with us! There is a deep silence here respecting the government and all foreign affairs; which would be very agreeable, if only we might be permitted to hear any tolerable news respecting our church and school yonder, our anxiety on account of which greatly distresses us: for during the whole of these two months we have not heard a word either from thence, or from any part of Germany. May the Lord be present with his people, lest they so wretchedly turn aside from him who is the only giver of life, by reason of the empty dreams of present things! I send my best wishes to your brothers, sisters, and my colleagues in the school. On the day of the ascension of our Lord, 1549.

[MARTIN BUCER.]

LETTER CCL.

MARTIN BUCER TO ALBERT HARDENBERG[1].

Dated at LONDON, *Aug.* 14, 1549.

GREETING. I have several times written to you, most faithful servant of the Saviour, and also to our friend Peter Medman; but I have received no letter from you in return. I am aware, however, of the wickedness of the times, and the malice of our enemies; for I am convinced that you have relaxed nothing of your love and esteem for me in the Lord, since you so earnestly and constantly set forth the kingdom of Christ, the kingdom of everlasting love, not only of the love of God towards us by his Son, but also of ourselves towards each other.

As I and my very dear friend Fagius could not give up the privilege of preaching the whole of Christ's kingdom, our authorities sent us away on the first of March, as being, it was said, considered in the court of the emperor more criminal than the rest. The remainder of our colleagues staid till the 18th July, on which day was written to me the last letter from home; and the majority retained their former liberty of teaching. The bishop, however, is very urgent for their removal. The Lord preserve that

[1 Albert Hardenberg, the friend and correspondent of John à Lasco, was educated at the university of Louvaine. He commenced his ministerial labours at a monastery in Groningen; from whence he moved to Cologne on the invitation of archbishop Herman. He presided over the reformed church at Bremen, from 1547 to 1561, when he retired to Embden, to avoid the troubles of the Ubiquitarian controversy, and died there in 1574.—See Jenkyns, Cranmer, I. 331, note; and Cranmer's Remains, Park. Soc. Ed. p. 422.]

church, in which there are indeed very many who are true children of God. When we were dismissed, we had received no public invitation but to this place, whither we were so invited as that there seemed to be no doubt but that the calling was of the Lord. So we came hither in April, where the most reverend the archbishop of Canterbury received us, and treats us with the greatest kindness and familiarity. We are to go to Cambridge at Michaelmas, and there to begin to lecture somewhat in theology, if the Lord permit. We are waiting therefore the Lord's will respecting this matter, and we pray him to afford us his Spirit, that we may faithfully and ably discharge our office, and that the accession of our ministry may be salutary to the church. It is fallow ground here, such as the devastation of antichrist is wont to leave: for, as in Italy, very few sermons have been preached here, nor are they even now very frequent, neither is there any catechetical instruction whatever. For those who preside over the parishes are for the most part neither very learned nor zealous in matters appertaining to Christ's kingdom. Among the nobility and persons of rank there are many individuals endued with singular godliness and learning, but these are unable so speedily to supply the want of teachers. Meanwhile Satan is raising much disturbance, both from the common people, and from France. Yet the Lord has much people in this country. The harvest is very plenteous: let us pray the Lord to thrust forth suitable labourers into his harvest. There are, for instance, from six to eight hundred Germans, all godly men, and most anxious for the word of God. They requested me and my friend Fagius to provide for them some faithful preacher in the language of Brabant, to which country they most of them belong. We have indeed at home Martin Faber, a most approved brother, as you know, and with a very small, and, as things now are, uncertain income. I had thought of inviting him over, but his voice is so weak, that I dare not hope he would be able to suit this situation. I have therefore had recourse to you, if perchance you should know of any one to whom you can safely entrust this office. You are aware, my brother, that the gospel can never produce its proper fruit without christian discipline; you are aware too, how few there are, even in our profession, who are willing to submit to it. Wherefore, should you be able to meet with any one who is soundly instructed in the kingdom of Christ, and who entertains a right zeal for it, and who is willing to take upon himself the entire ministry of the cure of souls, send him hither, I pray you, as soon as possible. The brethren will pay the expenses of his journey, and afford him a comfortable means of subsistence. You must send him, however, to those persons whose names will be written with this letter, and inform us, if you can, by the earliest opportunity, what we may expect from you in this matter. You will receive information, together with this letter, to whom you should forward your letters at Antwerp. But send us word about the kingdom of Christ, in what state it is among you in your present straitened circumstances; though difficulties are of no consequence in that kingdom, wherever it is vigorously flourishing. Our ingratitude, and most pernicious contentions, and the banishment of christian discipline, have deserved yet far heavier punishments. Yet so many among the churches throughout Germany, oppressed as they are, and scarcely able to support themselves, are every where turning to the Lord, and seriously repenting, and exercising discipline, and are instant in prayer, that I entertain great hope that God in mercy will speedily assuage these storms and tempests. We needed to be tried. Our worthy old man[1] of Cologne still stands out most manfully for the Lord, as do also many private individuals: but there remains not one single state, or sovereign, or count, or nobleman in upper Germany, who has not bowed his knees to the *Interim;* though every one adopts as few of its provisions as possible, and the bishops have no persons whom they can substitute in the place of our ministers. Our friends, after having for a long time deprecated that ferment, at length offered to receive such portions of the *Interim* as they could with a good conscience; and that they would leave the rest to be arranged by the bishop[2].

[1 Herman de Wied, archbishop of Cologne, who was deprived and excommunicated by Pope Paul III. in 1546, for favouring the reformation, died in 1552, aged 80 years.—See Sleidan, 310, 374, 573; and his character, in Strype, Cranmer, 410; see also Mem. II. i. 41.]

[2 Namely, of Strasburgh. The letter of the deputies of Strasburgh to the Emperor is given in Sleidan, 473, and confirms the statement in the text.]

But as he attempted to enforce beyond what the *Interim* requires, the time has so far been protracted, that nothing, I hope, belonging to antichrist is as yet re-established. I fear, however, that our friends will not be able to make any longer delay. May the Lord be present with so many excellent persons in those parts! The servants of mammon have there prevailed by their votes and decrees over the servants of the Lord. Timidity, too, and a worldly prudence unworthy of Christians, has overthrown some. The Lord preserve and restore those who are yet curable! I wish every happiness to yourself, your colleagues, and the whole church, and that you may some time, and that speedily, see Satan cast down under your feet. London, Aug. 14, 1549.

MARTIN BUCER.

LETTER CCLI.

MARTIN BUCER TO EDMUND ALLEN.

Dated at LAMBETH, *Aug.* 27, 1549.

GREETING. I was advised by master Bernardine Ochin[3] to recommend a certain excellent and godly youth to the most serene princess your mistress[4]; but he is not able to perform the duties which I understand to be required of him, and I believe he will obtain a situation with master Bernardine. The person, however, whom I now introduce, is a scholar of my friend master Philip Melancthon, and, as it seems, one of whom he need not be ashamed. He is living here without any employment, which is very irksome to young men of good dispositions; and is competent to the performance of those duties which were required of the other. He came over some weeks since strongly recommended by a most grave and learned man to the most reverend the archbishop of Canterbury, with a letter of commendation also from master Philip, that by

[3 Bernardine Ochin came over to England in 1547 with Peter Martyr. A curious bill of the expenses of their journey from Basle, as submitted by John Abel to the privy council for payment, is printed in the Archæologia, Vol. XXI. p. 471. The whole sum disbursed amounted to £126. 7*s.* 6*d.*, a large proportion of which was for wearing apparel and books.]

[4 Edmund Allen was at this time one of the chaplains of the princess Elizabeth. He was afterwards an exile in Q. Mary's time, and died in 1559.]

the assistance of the said archbishop he might obtain some employment as a teacher; and he is especially commended in that letter both for his skill in teaching, and also his solid piety, modesty, and purity of life. With the advice therefore of master Bernardine, I have commended him to her most serene highness in a letter, wherein you will perceive upon what grounds and for what reason I have done so. For I see that affairs are now in so disturbed a state, and the archbishop is so engaged, as not to be able to provide for him. And I am also doubtful, in the next place, whether a situation can be procured for him in your universities, abounding, as they do, in teachers of languages and sciences. If therefore it should please you, and you should think him capable of discharging in a proper manner the duties which you require, I pray you to afford your help so far as at least to make trial of such talents as the Lord has given him, that he may be usefully employed in your service. I am much interested about him, and deservedly so, when I perceive that to a fair degree of learning is united a love for Christ's kingdom, which must ever be accompanied by integrity of morals and sincere love to man. This statement, I hope, will be sufficient and more than sufficient in commendation of this person to you, who are a preacher of the loving-kindness of the Son of God towards man, and who are wont so abundantly to illustrate it. My best wishes attend you and your wife, and I pray you to excuse my boldness in recommending this man to your most serene mistress. Lambeth, Aug. 27, 1549.

Yours heartily,

M. BUCER.

LETTER CCLII.

MARTIN BUCER TO BRENTIUS.

Dated at CAMBRIDGE, *May* 15, 1550.

GRACE and peace from the Lord! I have received two letters from you since I have been here, for which service I am very much obliged to you: for I am greatly in need of comfort, and the greatest comfort is afforded me by the letters of my friends[1]; especially when they inform me of the zeal of

[[1] *Anglicorum*, MS. Probably a mistake for *amicorum*.]

some persons for the kingdom of Christ continuing yet unsubdued. May the Lord preserve your Obadiah[2], especially if the schoolmaster should now come, whom however they state to be so worn out by disease, and engaged upon his own affairs, that most persons are in hopes that he will not henceforth give so much trouble to the godly as their enemies desire. Others however, who take an unfavourable view of things, suppose that he will hurry onwards, and perhaps beyond the Mediterranean, but yet that he will previously arrange with the father of fathers about a council. But he, who has received from his Father all power in heaven and earth, will not leave his children comfortless.

Affairs in this country are in a very feeble state: the people are in want of teachers. Things are for the most part carried on by the means of ordinances, which the majority obey very grudgingly, and by the removal of the instruments of the ancient superstition: and some persons have been, and still continue to be, very docile pupils of our countrymen, with carnal liberty and spiritual bondage. The king, however, is godly and learned to a miracle: he is well acquainted with Latin, and has a fair knowledge of Greek; he speaks Italian, and is learning French. He is now studying moral philosophy from Cicero and Aristotle: but no study delights him more than that of the holy scriptures, of which he daily reads about ten chapters with the greatest attention. Some youths from among the principal nobility follow his example in these studies, and with good success. Of those devoted to the service of religion but a very small number have as yet entirely addicted themselves to the kingdom of Christ. In the universities the Balthazars[3] for the most part have the direction of affairs; though there are not wanting very many, even among the heads, who are sound in godliness and well instructed to the kingdom of God.

It is a very great alleviation of my anxiety, that I am permitted to set forth the kingdom of Christ with the most entire freedom, in my lectures, disputations, and Latin sermons. But ever since August it has pleased God to chasten me by severe illness, the remains of which still confine me, namely,

[2 Ulric, duke of Wurtemberg, with whom Brentius took refuge, when driven from Halle in the troubles about the Interim. The "schoolmaster" here mentioned is no doubt the emperor Charles V.]

[3 i.e. Belshazzars; meaning probably men given to feasting.]

excessive weakness in my legs, arms, and hands. In my left hand one, and in my right hand two fingers, still refuse their office; so that I am not yet able to write. The Lord gave me some respite about Christmas, so that from that time until the middle of March I was enabled tolerably to perform my office; but since that time my most painful disorders returned, from which the Lord began to relieve me a little more than a month ago, so that I have since then returned to my duty. My disorder consisted of incredibly cold and slow humours in all my muscles and joints; colic pains, gravel; severe pains at first in all my limbs, succeeded afterwards by the greatest weakness and prostration of strength; together with a constant obstruction of the bowels. The Lord spared me to my fifty-ninth year without afflicting me with any grievous disease: it is therefore time for me to feel something of what I have deserved by my sins.

I am as sorry for master Martyr's book as any one can be; but that disputation took place, and the propositions[1] were agreed upon, before I arrived in England. At my advice he has inserted many things in the preface whereby to express more fully his belief in the presence of Christ. Among the nobility of the kingdom those are very powerful, who would reduce the whole of the sacred ministry into a narrow compass, and who are altogether unconcerned about the restoration of church discipline.[...][2] While they seek to provide against our bringing down Christ the Lord from heaven and confining him in the bread, and offering him to the communicants to be fed upon without faith, a thing that none of our party ever thought of; they themselves go so far as, without any warrant of holy scripture, to confine him to a certain limited place in heaven; and talk so vapidly about his exhibition and presence in the supper, (nay, some of them cannot even endure these words,) that they appear to believe that nothing else but the bread and wine is there distributed. No one has as yet found fault with me for my

[1 These propositions are given above, p. 478, n. 1. Peter Martyr and Melancthon thought it convenient, in speaking of the Eucharist, to express themselves with perspicuity and distinctness. Bucer, on the contrary, for the sake of peace, recommended the use of more dark and ambiguous forms of speech, that might be taken in a larger acceptation. See Strype, Cranmer, 586.; Mem. II. i. 190.]

[2 A sentence is here defective in the original MS.]

simple view of the subject; nor have I ever heard of any one who has been able to confute it from any solid passage of scripture, nor indeed has any one yet ventured to make the attempt. Their principal argument is, that the mysteries of Christ can be well and intelligibly explained; (which would be true, if they would add, "to faith, but not to reason"). They now assume, that it cannot with reason be supposed of Christ, that he is in heaven without being circumscribed by physical space; and since he is thus in heaven, as they take for granted, they insist, not only upon what no one will allow them, but also without any solid reason, that it cannot be understood that the same body of Christ is in heaven and in the supper: and when we reply, that no one supposes a local presence of Christ in the supper, they again say that the body of Christ cannot be understood to be present any where without being locally circumscribed. The sum therefore of their argument is to this effect. Reason does not comprehend what you teach respecting the exhibition and presence of Christ in the supper; therefore they are not true, and the scriptures which seem to prove them must be otherwise interpreted. Let us pray for these persons. I have as yet met with no real Christians who were not entirely satisfied with our simple view of the subject, as soon as it had been properly explained to them. I wish you and all yours every happiness in the Lord. Cambridge, May 15, 1550.

Yours wholly,

M. BUCER.

LETTER CCLIII.

MARTIN BUCER TO JOHN CALVIN.

Dated at CAMBRIDGE, Whitsunday, 1550.

I GREATLY stand in need of the consolation of your letters. For though there are not wanting to me in this country faithful friends and brethren in the Lord, yet I know not how it is, but I am most anxiously desirous to learn what my old friends and long tried colleagues are doing, how the work of the Lord is making progress among them, and also that they may advise, comfort, and exhort me. Accounts are from time to time sent me from my native place and other parts of Germany, which greatly distress my mind;

and the cause of Christ too is likewise so conducted in this country, that unless the Lord look upon our most innocent and religious king and some other godly individuals with his especial mercy, it is greatly to be feared that the dreadful wrath of God will very shortly blaze forth against this kingdom also. The bishops have not yet been able to come to an agreement as to christian doctrine, much less as to discipline, and very few parishes have pastors qualified for their office. Most of them are sold to the nobility; and there are persons, even among the ecclesiastical order, and those too who wish to be regarded as gospellers, who hold three or four parishes and even more, without ministering in any one of them; but they appoint such substitutes as will be satisfied with the least stipend, and who for the most part cannot even read English, and who are in heart mere papists. The nobility too have, in many parishes, preferred those who have been in monasteries, who are most unlearned and altogether unfit for the sacred office; and this, merely for the sake of getting rid of the payment of their yearly pension. Hence you may find parishes in which there has not been a sermon for some years. And you are well aware how little can be effected for the restoration of the kingdom of Christ by mere ordinances, and the removal of instruments of superstition.

Each of the universities in this country has many excellent colleges, furnished with such large endowments and useful statutes, as are possessed by no university in the world. For not only are very many persons exceedingly well educated in these colleges, in most of which there are above a hundred students, but they afford also honourable exhibitions for clothes and books. It is from these colleges that the swarms of faithful ministers ought to have been sent forth from time to time; for all masters of arts are required to become students in theology, with the exception only of four in each college, two of whom are expected to study medicine, and two law. But such connivance has so long existed, and is especially so prevalent at this time, that by far the greater part of the fellows are either most bitter papists, or profligate epicureans, who, as far as they are able, draw over the young men to their way of thinking, and imbue them with an abhorrence of sound christian doctrine and discipline. And even our friends are so sparing of their sermons, that during the whole of Lent, which nevertheless they still seem to wish to observe, with the exception of one or two Sundays, they have not once preached to the people, not even on the day of the commemoration of Christ's death or of his resurrection, or on this day[1]. Sometimes, too, many of the parochial clergy so recite and administer the service, that the people have no more understanding of the mysteries of Christ, than if the Latin instead of the vulgar tongue were still in use. And when complaints respecting these shocking abuses of the church are laid by godly men before the rulers of the kingdom, they say it is the business of the bishops to remedy the evil: when they are laid before the bishops, those, namely, who have long since made a profession of the gospel, their reply is, that they cannot rectify them without an act of parliament for that purpose. And though the great council of the nation is assembled every year, so many secular matters are forced upon their attention, that the cause of Christ can find no room for admission. Then they commit the consideration of these matters to so many individuals, and those too of such discordant sentiments, that they cannot even be got together and assembled, much less come to any right and solid decision upon affairs of such importance. In which procrastinating of the cause of Christ the bishops, to whom the idleness and luxury of antichrist is more agreeable than the cross of Christ, are aided by the activity of many noblemen, enriched by the possessions of the church, and who themselves consider that the present desolation of the churches will be more to their interest, than the godly reformation of them.

We must observe in addition to these evils, that not a few persons, laying aside all desire after true repentance, faith, good works, the communion and discipline of the church, do nothing but dispute and contend, and often very profanely, how they may seclude Christ our Saviour from our sacraments and holy assemblies, and confine him to his place in heaven. And these chiefly follow those teachers who dare to write and assert publicly, that it is a fanatical attempt to construct any system of ecclesiastical and penitential discipline, whereby those who have openly offended should be compelled to do penance, and, when that is performed, to be absolved of such offence, and receive absolution of the church for their particular sins. Thus they allow themselves to put such interpretations upon any part of God's word, however clear it

[1 Namely, Whitsunday, on which day this letter was written.]

may be, which their own wisdom, or even dislike, not to say hatred of those who teach more correctly, or perhaps both of these motives, may suggest.

I have written to you, most excellent Calvin, thus freely, that you may be more earnest in your prayers for these churches, and that, when you write to the duke of Somerset, you may most seriously admonish him respecting this desolation and betrayal of the churches, which with very few exceptions are entrusted to those who neither know, nor care to know, any thing about Christ. I request moreover that no one, except Farell and Viret, read this letter; for you are aware of the inexpediency of these things being made public, and especially by our means. Redouble your prayers for the most serene king, who is making wonderful progress both in piety and learning. For you may easily perceive the danger in which he is placed, humanly speaking, when the papists are every where so furious, and when they see and know that the king is exerting all his power for the restoration of Christ's kingdom. But they see his elder sister most pertinaciously defend and maintain popery, either because her disposition leads her to do so, or because she places so much confidence in her cousin[1]. But indeed the coldness of our exertions in behalf of Christ's kingdom deserves these dangers and oppositions.

Thank the Lord with me, that he has in great measure relieved me from the diseases which had a second time attacked me most severely till the middle of March. For I am again able after a manner to perform my duty, though great weakness still remains in my legs, arms and hands, which I am not yet able to use in writing. My stomach too is easily put out of order, and my bowels are in an obstinate state. Pray ye the Lord for me, that, if possible, he may either deliver me from hence, or make me in some way useful to his church; yea, that he sanctify his name in me in whatever way seemeth him best. Farewell with all your friends, the worthy Farell, Viret, and your other associates of the same stamp. Cambridge, Whitsunday, 1550.

Yours,

M. BUCER.

[[1] Namely Charles V., whose mother was sister to Catherine of Arragon.]

LETTER CCLIV.

MARTIN BUCER TO THE MINISTERS OF STRASBURGH.

Dated at CAMBRIDGE, *Dec.* 26, 1550.

HEALTH in the Lord. Most esteemed and very dear colleagues and brethren, considering by how many ties the Lord has bound me to you, and you to me, whom he has permitted for twenty-six years to serve your church and school, certainly with all fidelity, and not without labour, whatever the success may have been; I have thought it my duty once more to write to you, though you have not yet replied to some of my letters; and especially as I have so sad an occasion for doing so. For that worthy and most faithful minister of Christ, Paul Fagius, departed to the Lord on the 13th of November, after having suffered most severely from a quartan fever since the 28th of August. For he was burned up with dark bile, which rendered him delirious, so that he drank things that were injurious to him; and at first he was in a room without a fire, where he was severely affected by the cold; at last inflammation came on, and ulceration of the throat, which, together with the fever, put an end to his life. He was continually breathing forth his prayers to Christ, as soon as he perceived that his disorder was making progress, and he bore the greatest pain with much patience; and when he felt his end approach, he commended his wife and wards to your fidelity, and wished me to bid you farewell in his name: and he begged, that whatever he had said or done in this country, either respecting the maintenance of the kingdom of Christ in all its integrity, or the restoration of discipline, you would not ascribe to any other motive than to his conscientious regard to God's word; that he had been very unwilling to offend any one, and had often proposed to himself great caution in speaking, lest he should thereby afford any cause of offence. But when he came into the pulpit, and considered the majesty of that almighty Being whose words it was his duty to declare, and thoroughly weighed the meaning of the subject proposed, he was unable, he said, to speak otherwise than as he had done: and he did not remember that he had spoken to any other effect, than that full reliance must be placed in God's protection, the purity of Christ's doctrine must be retained in all its integrity, and christian discipline must be established; and when these things were secured, we must obey and shew compliance in every thing else: that therefore he was with a good conscience willing to depart to God, and entreated him long to preserve you in your respective ministries, and to bestow upon you his blessing. I promised him that I would write you this account, which I pray you to take in good part, and communicate to those who deservedly loved him. We shall send his widow to you at the beginning of the spring. She most faithfully attended upon her husband.

My own health is still in a very doubtful and unsatisfactory state. Pray the Lord, that he may be pleased either to make me useful to his flock, or else to take me to himself. As far as the king, and the chief administration of the kingdom, and the public laws are concerned, every thing is favourable to the kingdom of Christ. But the people are still without pastors. The Lord however is raising up from among the younger many godly and learned men, well fitted for this office. But not a little of the old leaven is yet remaining. Oh, how greatly would the excellent Paul [Fagius] have profited them by his facility of teaching! Besides, too, he had his lectures then in hand. The event is most happy for him; but we must grieve most sincerely at the loss which the church of Christ experiences by his decease. But who knows what times are yet to be endured by the churches? The Lord preserve you, and never suffer your regard for me so speedily to vanish from your breasts. I have several times written to you, but you have not once thought fit to favour me with an answer. And so when I took leave of you, and commended myself to you, no one uttered a word in reply, the French preacher alone excepted. Yet I laboured among you with all fidelity, and there are few of you to whom I have not endeavoured also to make myself useful in my private capacity. If you knew what I have suffered since I left you, you would, I am sure, be moved with much compassion for me. For think what it must be for this frail body of mine, which has been from my childhood utterly unable to bear the cold, to be without a stove during the winter, which is occasionally most severe, and at all times injurious; and also to be without my usual wine and diet. May the Lord preserve you in your nests, but with a sincere confession of his name; and so I bid you farewell, with all your families, and all who belong to Christ. Salute our common fathers in Christ in my name. Cambridge, St Stephen's day, 1550.

LETTER CCLV.

ŒCOLAMPADIUS TO ZUINGLIUS.

Dated *Aug.* 20, [1531.]

GREETING. I have read, very dear brother, the opinion[1] you have expressed respecting the affair of the king of England, and I readily subscribe to it, as clearly perceiving with what unbiassed judgment you have weighed all the circumstances of the case; and I have no doubt but that the result of this labour will not be to be repented of. I therefore thank you for it. I shall keep the copy you have written out, which however shall be returned to you if you wish it. My own opinion[2] in no respect differs from yours, except in the manner of expressing it: you shall read it for yourself, as it is not at any great length, but pretty much like a letter. Bucer[3] and Capito have hitherto held views different from ours; but I hope that when they have read your opinion, they will no longer dissent from us, although greatly prejudiced in favour of their own opinions,

[1 Zuingle expressed a decided conviction that Henry VIII.'s marriage with queen Catharine (the affair alluded to in this letter) was unlawful, and ought to be dissolved. See Burnet, I. 151. Soames, I. 265.]

[2 Œcolampadius was of opinion that the law in Leviticus did bind all mankind; and said, "That law of a brother's marrying his sister-in-law was a dispensation given by God to his own law, which belonged only to the Jews; and therefore he thought that the king might, without any scruple, put away the queen." Burnet, I. 150.]

[3 Bucer thought the law in Leviticus did not bind, and could not be moral, because God had dispensed with it in one case, of raising up seed to his brother: therefore he thought these laws belonged only to that dispensation, and did no more bind Christians than the other ceremonial or judiciary precepts; and that to marry in some of these degrees was no more a sin, than it was a sin in the disciples to pluck ears of corn on the Sabbath-day. Burnet, as above.]

especially one of them, a circumstance that occasions no small inconvenience to a church so distinguished. They would allow the king to have two wives: but be it far from us to follow Mahomet in this respect rather than Christ.

And now, with respect to reconciliation with the five cantons[1], I wish I may be mistaken; but though some persons expect it, I have not the slightest hopes of it, unless one of the parties either humble itself or be humbled. I had written the day before yesterday, (and intended to give this letter to your messenger, but I could not find him,) at the urgent desire of those who had sent the answer from the senate to your people. I send the letter, though it is now unseasonable and superfluous; but I wish you to be informed of the anxiety of your friend, even though it be employed to no purpose. Farewell, with your wife and brothers. Aug. 20.

ŒCOLAMPADIUS.

LETTER CCLVI[2].

SIMON GRYNÆUS[3] TO MARTIN BUCER.

Dated *Sept.* [10], 1531.

HEALTH. Whether she [Anne Boleyn] has children by the king, I do not know. She has not any acknowledged as

[1 The cantons of Lucerne, Uri, Schweitz, Zug, and Unterwalden, had made, in 1529, a league with king Ferdinand against the cantons of Zurich and Berne for the suppression of the reformed religion, but a war was then prevented by the interposition of the neighbouring cities. In the summer of 1531 the sore was rubbed up afresh, and the cities of Berne and Zurich, having possessed themselves of all the passages and avenues, would not suffer any provisions to be carried into the five cantons. The king of France, with the cantons of Glarus, Fribourg, Soleure, and Appenzel, in vain offered their mediation, and the five cantons marched towards Zurich on the 9th of October, on the 11th of which month the Zurichers were defeated, and Zuinglius killed in the battle. See Sleidan, VIII. 155.]

[2 The original of this letter is preserved in the Archives of St Thomas, at Strasburgh.]

[3 Simon Grynæus was Greek professor at Basle, where he was employed by king Henry VIII. to collect the opinions of the Reformed in Switzerland respecting the lawfulness of his marriage with his brother's widow. See Burnet, Hist. Ref. I. 150.]

such[4]: they may probably be brought up in private, (which, if I am not mistaken, I have heard more than once,) though there are those who positively deny that the king has any intercourse with her, which in my opinion is not at all likely. But she is young, good looking, of a rather dark complexion, and likely enough to have children; and he himself is in the vigour of his age: indeed you never saw a taller or more noble looking personage. Your first letter to Zuinglius I sent; the last two I return you. You will employ some one, whom I will recompense for his trouble, to procure an elegant volume, in which he will forthwith copy out either both letters, or the latter only, which is the most strong in argument, and manifestly expresses your judgment twice over. I would have had them transcribed, if I had a suitable copyist at hand, or if we could accomplish every thing by merely reading them over: and as both letters are to go to the king, you will suppress whatever seems to be irrelevant to the subject. But as far as I can see, you need not alter any thing. The others too will send their last letters. Capito[5] will make no alteration, neither will Matthew. Hedio[6] will make some slight alterations, which he well understands. You will make a single packet of all the letters in such a manner, that they may be distinguished by a certain mark as they follow each other; so that the first written may be first in order. This you can do immediately; for you can tell of your own knowledge when you received the two letters of Œcolampadius, the two of Zuinglius, your own two, together with those last sent by Capito and Hedio and Matthew. So the king will perceive, as I have stated to be the case, that you are still occupied in this business[7], and also the feeling of each party at the present moment. But let the

[4 These slanderous imputations upon Anne Boleyn's character have been fully and effectually refuted by Sharon Turner, Hist. of Henry VIII. Vol. II. p. 200—206. Ed. 1828. See also Burnet, I. 66, &c.; Soames, I. 380. The report in the text seems to have been utterly false, and was never in any way authenticated or confirmed.]

[5 Wolfgang Fabricius Capito was professor of divinity at Basle. He died in 1541.]

[6 Caspar Hedio was minister at Strasburgh. He died in 1552, and was succeeded by Zanchy.]

[7 Namely, of the king's divorce from queen Catharine, to which the letters mentioned in the postscript refer.]

letters be copied on the evening that the bearer reaches you; for there will be time, unless he intends to go on foot as far as Cologne. The fair will be over. If you wish him to go on to Wittemberg, you will act just as you think best.

Yours,

SIMON.

The order will be as follows. The long letter of Zuinglius, then the first of Œcolampadius. The former of your last two letters. The shorter letter of Zuinglius, and the other of Œcolampadius which you still have by you, and the two replies of Phrygio[1]. The last reply of Phrygio. Your last letter, together with those three letters of Capito, Hedio, and Matthew. You will oblige me too by inserting mine, giving the name and date, which you may ascertain with sufficient accuracy. You will insert this also in its proper order, as also the replies of Phrygio which you have not yet sent. It is necessary however that your letters should all be copied by the same person, lest they should seem to be in divers handwritings. I will take care that they shall be copied in London by the king's secretary, and in the same order, before they are presented to himself. For they adopt the French character, and the king could not read our writing. You will place first, that is, before the rest in the packet, the letter which I intend to write[2] to the king. I send you my signet ring, that you may seal all the letters, having fairly transcribed them in the order in which they are to be placed. It will only be an hour's trouble, which I beg of you not to refuse me.

LETTER CCLVII.

SIMON GRYNÆUS TO KING HENRY VIII.

Dated *Sept.* [10], 1531.

I SEND your majesty, most illustrious sovereign, all that I have by any means been able to obtain from men of the

[1 Paul Constantine Phrygio was minister of St Peter's at Basle in 1529, and afterwards at Tubingen, where he died in 1543.]

[2 See the next Letter.]

greatest learning, by reason of the public employments in which they are now very much engaged. What reply they have made to my inquiries, and what has been their mutual correspondence with each other, and how far the business has proceeded, and how far completed, and what difference of opinion yet exists, your majesty will be able to see from these presents, which I have sent, though still incomplete, for this reason, both because in the midst of such busy occupations greater progress could not be made, and also that your majesty might understand both that the business is going on, and is one of the deepest interest to all of us; and that all good men are anxious, with truth for their guide, to gratify your majesty and the most serene queen in every possible way. For in a short time, as soon as the meetings they are now engaged in shall allow them leisure, and when all circumstances shall have been duly considered, a decisive answer shall be given to your majesty: but certainly, in the present lack of time nothing can be determined in a matter of so much importance, and especially in the midst of so many and weighty engagements by which most of them have been for a long time kept away from their own homes. In the meantime, if I am not mistaken, both your majesty and the queen will derive the greatest comfort from these letters, since in these replies the most sacred regard has been paid to the conscience and honour and reputation of both parties, and also to the wish and desire of your majesty. I have applied more than once to other states, wherein are some learned men; from whom however I have as yet obtained no answer, by reason of their important engagements with their respective governments.

The replies, if you choose to collect them, are of this kind. Some consider a marriage with a brother's wife to be altogether unlawful, as being ranked among abominations[3], and that for this reason it cannot be made valid by any prescription of time: they therefore allow of a divorce. Others, though they admit the unlawfulness of the marriage, yet think it may be permitted, if any one has such strength and firmness of conscience, as to be able to use after a godly manner what is forbidden by law; of which there are many instances. These therefore also allow of a divorce, if only your majesty's conscience has a real aversion from this

[[3] See Levit. xviii. 16, 26.]

marriage; and they permit you to relieve your conscience by marrying another. These opinions come to the same thing; and the only question is this, whether christian liberty can be so extended, as that without the especial command of God we may do with a safe conscience what is abominable to nature, or at least to be eschewed by the general consent of all nations, and of nature itself. And this question I hope will shortly be solved, and forwarded to your majesty with the replies of some other divines. And I now bid your excellent majesty farewell.

LETTER CCLVIII[1].

MELANCTHON TO MARTIN BUCER.

Dated *Nov.* 8, 1531.

I HAVE received your letter upon the English controversy, respecting which I have written my sentiments to Simon [Grynæus], and see no reason to change them. I cannot recommend a divorce, where a marriage is not repugnant to the law of God. Those who think differently, terribly exaggerate the divine law, and carry it to an unwarrantable extent. I, on the contrary, would magnify, in political matters, the authority of the magistrate, which indeed is of no little weight; and there are many things which are made lawful by reason of such authority, the lawfulness of which might otherwise be doubted. If the king were sufficiently instructed upon this point, his conscience, I think, might be satisfied. As to myself, I will have nothing to do with the business: if any one recommends a divorce, he shall perform his part without me.

I had heard of the death of Zuinglius[2] before your letter reached me, but have learned all the circumstances from your letter. I lament his loss both upon public and private grounds. The war, we see, is begun; it now remains for us to entreat Christ to end it to the advantage of both state and church. Farewell, and believe that I heartily desire your welfare. I

[1 The original of this Letter is preserved at Zofingen.]

[2 Zuinglius was killed in battle Oct. 11, 1531. For an account of his death, see Sleidan, VIII. 155, and above, p. 552, n. 1.]

have replied to Simon, and request you to forward him the letter. Again farewell. Nov. 8, 1531.

PHILIP [MELANCTHON].

LETTER CCLIX.

MARTIN MICRONIUS TO HENRY BULLINGER.

Dated at LONDON, *Sept.* 30, 1549.

MUCH health. As I am aware of your great anxiety to know the state of master Hooper's affairs, and those of all his family; and perceiving too that Hooper has not sufficient leisure to allow of his writing, and that the messenger can wait no longer by reason of the importunities of the sailors; I think it my duty to send you a brief statement of our present condition. In the first place, Hooper is imposing upon himself a severe and constant labour in instructing the people, who are most numerous and attentive. He lectures at least once every day; more frequently two or three times. The archbishop of Canterbury has become somewhat more favourably disposed to him. The bishop of London preached on the first of September at St Paul's to a most numerous congregation, and maintained with all his might the corporal presence in the Lord's supper, which Hooper had strenuously opposed in that day's lecture. The same bishop was ordered in his sermon to inform the people, that our king is no less to be obeyed as a boy, than if he were an old man, and that his decrees possess the same authority. The bishop omitted to do this[3]. He was therefore summoned before the tribunal, where he behaved with so much effrontery[4] and stubbornness, (for I was present, and saw every thing that took place,) that you

[3 See Latimer's Sermons, Parker Soc. Ed., p. 118, where the preacher alludes to Bonner, bishop of London, and Gardiner, and the popish party generally, who to excuse their opposition to the Reformation, during Edward the Sixth's reign, invented the theory that laws made during the minority of a king were invalid. See Strype, Cranmer, 272. See also Burnet, II. 194—202.]

[4 Bonner's conduct before the commissioners is thus described: "He entered the room in which they sate with his cap upon his head, as if he did not see them. He turned the witnesses against him into ridicule, saying, one of them speaks like a goose, the other like a woodcock." See the whole account in Soames, III. 470, &c.]

would rather call him a buffoon than a bishop. He is put in prison for this obstinate disobedience, until there shall be an end of the controversy: but what kind of an end it will be, we do not know, especially as he has many persons on his side.

The disturbances[1] of the English peasantry are quieted, through the divine blessing, by the punishment of some of the rebels. Many of them are still kept in confinement. There is no certain news respecting the Scots. Mistress Anna, Hooper's wife, is not in very good health. The rest of us are well. Master Paul Fagius is very dangerously ill. Bucer has not yet recovered from the disorder under which he has been suffering for a month or more. Their wives have come over to them. Farewell, most vigilant pastor. God grant that you may ever have the people obedient! We are much grieved and surprised that the gospellers could have been drawn over into that sanguinary alliance with the French. May God strengthen you! Amen.

Written in much haste at London, Sept. 30, 1549. You will commend me to my preceptors, masters Bibliander, Pellican, and Gesner.

Your most obedient servant,

MARTIN MICRONIUS.

LETTER CCLX.

MARTIN MICRONIUS TO HENRY BULLINGER.

Dated at London, *May* 20, 1550.

All that is going on here, most excellent and right worshipful prelate, I have fully related in another letter, not so much to yourself as to my preceptor master Bibliander. And though I have not yet received any answer, yet as I gave my letter in charge to trustworthy persons, I cannot doubt but that it has reached you. I shall therefore resume my account of all that has occurred among us from the point where I broke off in my last letter; and shall speak of public affairs in the first place. The long wished for peace[2]

[1 For an account of these disturbances see Burnet, II. 181—190; Soames, III. 434, &c.; above, p. 391, n. 3.]

[2 For the articles of this treaty see Burnet, II. 236. The French were to pay 400,000 crowns for the surrender of Boulogne, which took place on St Mark's day, April 25 See above, p. 410.]

between France, Scotland, and England, was proclaimed in London on the 29th of March. Boulogne was restored about the 24th of April. The French have paid a moiety of the sum agreed upon. Three French hostages[3] remain with us in the mean time, some of whom are converted to Christ. Some French noblemen are expected to come over for the purpose of ratifying the peace: God grant it may be a lasting one! There is a great change here in our affairs; but praised be God, it is for the better as far as religion is concerned. The duke of Somerset was most honourably received into the council about the 9th of April[4]. We are expecting a more complete reformation of the church in the ensuing parliament, which is put off till October.

Master Hooper is diligently and usefully labouring in the church of Christ: you would learn from him, if he had leisure to write, its entire condition. But the messenger is urgent, and he himself is not at home. I will therefore write about these matters, as far as I am acquainted with them. His Lent sermons[5] before the king were preached with the greatest freedom, and attended with great advantage. Only he stirred up some lazy noblemen and bishops against himself, especially because he exhorted the king and council to a more complete reformation of the church. But the king took every thing most kindly, as he shewed afterwards; for he offered him by the chancellor on the 7th of April the bishoprick of Gloucester. Hooper however refused to accept it, unless the bishoprick were granted him without any superstitious ceremonies. He had some difficulty in obtaining this, owing to the great opposition of the bishops, who sought to defend the vestments, and the oath by created beings[6].

[3 The duke d'Enghien, the marquis du Main, and Mons. Montmorency were to remain here on the French part for surety of the first payment. Strype, Mem. II. i. 358.]

[4 He was called, April 10, to the privy council. Strype, Mem. II. i. 363.]

[5 These were the sermons on the prophet Jonah, reprinted in the early writings of Hooper, Parker Soc. Ed. p. 443.]

[6 Namely, the oath of supremacy, the ending of which, "So help me God, all saints, and the holy Evangelists" in the prayer book of 1549, was altered in that of 1552, to "So help me God through Jesus Christ." See Liturgies of Edw. VI. Parker Soc. Ed. pp. 169, 339. See also below, p. 567.]

But, contrary to all expectation, on the 15th of May he gained the victory. He is at this time, therefore, bishop of Gloucester, and will shortly go down to his bishoprick. He intends, however, to visit his parents during these next holidays; from whence he will return hither, and, the Lord willing, proceed to Gloucester. I pray the Lord that he may root up and plant for the benefit of the church of Christ. He has finished Daniel[1], and has lately been lecturing upon the prophet Nahum; on finishing which he began the prophet Zechariah, on the 5th of May. He received your letter and Decades on the Kings, on the 22nd of April. He presented to the king your book[2] splendidly bound on the 25th of April: how acceptable it was to his majesty, you will learn better from Hooper himself at some future time. As far as I can understand, your name is beginning to be in favour with the archbishop of Canterbury.

Master John à Lasco[3] arrived in England on the 13th of May. His coming was greatly to the delight of all godly persons. He has determined to remain in London, and establish a German church, of which he is appointed the superintendent. And indeed it is a matter of the first importance that the word of God should be preached here in German, to guard against the heresies which are introduced by our countrymen. There are Arians, Marcionists, Libertines, Danists, and the like monstrosities, in great numbers. A few days since, namely, on the 2nd of May, a certain woman[4] was burnt alive for denying the incarnation of Christ. The

[1 See above, Letter XXXVI. p. 73.]

[2 Bullinger dedicated, in a long epistle to king Edward, his third, and part of his fourth decade; being many learned discourses upon the chief heads of religion. This epistle and book was presented to the king by the hands of Hooper, bishop of Gloucester, personally acquainted with Bullinger: to whom the king declared his good acceptance thereof, and the respect and esteem he had for the reverend author. Strype, Mem. II. i. 390, 394.]

[3 John à Lasco was a nobleman of Poland, and abandoned his own country and honours to dwell in exile in other parts, for the freer acknowledgment of the gospel; but not without the Polish king's good leave, by whom he was well known and beloved. See Strype, Mem. II. i. 376, and more fully in Cranmer, 336.]

[4 This was Joan Bocher, or Joan of Kent, for an account of whom see Strype, Mem. II. i. 334; Cranm. 258; Burnet, II. 177; IV. 208; Soames, III. 543; Hutchinson's works, Parker Soc. Edit. pp. 2, 145.]

churches of Bremen and the rest are strengthening themselves; but are far more injured by their private disagreements in matters of religion, than by any external violence. They are disputing about the descent of Christ into hell, and about the allowance or prohibition of things indifferent. Marvellous is the subtlety of antichrist in weakening the churches of Christ. Our king is a youth of such godliness as to be a wonder to the whole world. He orders all things for the advancement of God's glory. He has on every Lord's day a sermon such as he used to have during Lent. I wish the bishops and nobility were inflamed with the like zeal. The English translation of Peter Martyr's book[5] on the Lord's supper could not be printed, owing to the bishops, and those too gospellers. Master Cox is no longer the king's tutor. He is dean of the church of Westminster; and should he recover, (for he has been dangerously ill within these few days,) it is reported that he is to be made bishop of Winchester. Thus godly men are substituted in the place of the ungodly bishops. Nothing however, as far as I know, is yet finally determined respecting this appointment.

I wrote in another letter about a certain Zuricher here, who is imprisoned, and condemned to death, as I understand, for a trifling theft. We used every exertion in his behalf, and have obtained his discharge from the king, which will cost four pounds. This sum is being scraped together by some worthy persons by way of an eleemosynary contribution. The man's name is Valentine Werdmuller[6]. If you are acquainted with his parents, and they are persons of ability, I should wish that sum to be remitted to the Flemish church which is assembled here, and which has paid it for him. He will still remain in prison for some days. He promises every thing that is good. We shall send him back to you; he seems to be a person well-born. John Stumphius is a very worthy and studious youth. I greatly commend him to you for his godly character. Whatever money may be expended upon him will not be lost, but return to the church with

[5 This work was entitled *Tractatio de Sacramento Eucharistiæ; habita publice Oxonii, per D. Petrum Martyrem Vermilium Florentinum, in ea Academia sacræ Theologiæ publicum et regium Professorem*, &c. A notice of it is given in Strype, Mem. II. i. 306, &c.]

[6 See above, p. 85, where this person is called by his name in Latin.]

abundant interest. Master Utenhovius is residing with master Hooper, and is in good health: he is too much engaged to write, but meanwhile desires to be commended to you. Mistress Anna, the wife of Hooper, is not at home. She has gone to the mansion of a certain noble lady in the neighbourhood of the city, for change of air. I have nothing particular to state concerning her, except that both she and her little daughter are in good health; but I have no time to go and call upon her by reason of the importunity of the messenger. Dryander's wife is now in London, on her way to her husband in upper Germany[1].

Be pleased to commend me to the lady your wife, to my honoured preceptors masters Pellican, Bibliander, and Gesner; and likewise to Froschover, masters John Frisius and Sebastian, and the rest of our friends. Joanna requests you to pay the widow of master Zinkius a crown in her name: she will take care that it shall be repaid you by master Hooper. She commends herself to you and to your family. Farewell. London, May 20. 1550. The messenger is so urgent that I have no time to read over my letter.

Your devoted servant,

MARTIN MICRONIUS.

LETTER CCLXI[2].

MARTIN MICRONIUS TO HENRY BULLINGER.

Dated at LONDON, *May* 28, 1550.

MUCH health. Though I have been, most worthy sir, more negligent in writing to you than I ought to have been, I am nevertheless unwilling to repeat what I wrote on the 20th of May, lest I should be troublesome to you, who are already more than sufficiently occupied by important public and private engagements. The cause of Christ remains, by the blessing of God, in the same favourable state: meanwhile, however, the old serpent ceaseth not his stealthy attacks upon the heel

[1 See above, p. 77.]

[2 The original of this letter is given in Fueslin, p. 286.]

of Christ; notwithstanding his head is often bruised by the power and help of God. We are apprehensive of mischief from that Flandro-Spanish machination. He has, I hear, a well equipped fleet; but what he intends to do, God knows. The illustrious lord à Lasco told me, four days since, that he had learned for certain, that the Spanish fleet had been dispersed and destroyed by a storm; and that this circumstance has detained the emperor in Lower Germany. A firm peace is expected to take place between England and France. A French nobleman, by name the Lord Châtillon, came over on the 23rd of May, and publicly confirmed the peace[3] by oath on the 25th of the same month. God grant it may be a sure and lasting one!

Master Hooper is overwhelmed by so much business arising from his new bishoprick, that he has no time for lecturing in public, much less for writing letters. Wherefore he deserves every excuse, if he seldom or never writes them. Some of the council lately proposed certain articles for him to subscribe to, but he excepted against three of them. One is, that the sacraments confer grace. He wished the word *confer* to be changed into "*seal* or *testify to*." The second is, that the book set forth by the bishops must be diligently observed in every particular, without any alteration whatever. The last is, wherein he is required to approve the book of ordination of ministers of the church. What will be the result, I do not know. Within these three or four days he is about to take a journey to his native place. His most excellent wife and little girl are in good health, as is also Joanna; and they send their best respects to you, and all your family.

I wrote in a former letter about a certain Zuricher, of the name of Valentine Werdmuller, who was in prison, and under sentence of death; but who is now discharged by the beneficence of the king. We are surprised at not having received any answer respecting him; for we are afraid of some deception. Meanwhile, we have been scraping together, as far as we can, charitable contributions for his ransom. But the amount is too great for us Flemish foreigners to collect without inconvenience; since, beyond my expectation,

[[3] For the terms of this peace see Burnet, II. 235. The French king acknowledged the king's styles of supreme Head of the Church of England, and king of Ireland. Strype, Mem. II. i. 360.]

we shall have to pay about six pounds, that is, nineteen crowns, and we are few in number, and for the most part poor. If his parents are able, we hope they will send a sum of money that he may soon be set at liberty, as one of their kinsmen has told me will be the case. Master John Ullenson, who is now living with Master Hooper, salutes you.

Just as I am about to close this letter, a man worthy of credit has come to me, and states that the king has this day given orders for six of the largest ships[1] to be furnished with all munitions of war. But what is to be their destination, no one as yet knows. Entreat God on behalf of his church, now sold by the Spanish antichrist. Salute, if you please, in my name, my most reverend preceptors, masters Theodore Bibliander, Conrad Pellican, Gesner, and the other worthy persons. London. May 28, 1550.

Your much attached,

MARTIN MICRONIUS.

LETTER CCLXII.

MARTIN MICRONIUS TO HENRY BULLINGER.

Dated at London, *June* 4, 1550.

Much health. As I know you are very anxious to hear about our affairs, I am unwilling to be negligent, but shall continue so to write to your reverence, that you may be as accurately acquainted with what is going on here, as if you were yourself present. I should not take upon me this office, if master Hooper had leisure to write; for he could afford you more abundant and certain information. I only write what I know undoubtedly to be facts. As to those six men of

[1 In king Edward's journal it is stated, under the date of July 1, 1550, that "whereas certain Flemish ships, twelve sail in all, six tall men-of-war, looking for eighteen more men-of-war, went to Dieppe, as it was thought, to take M. le Mareschal by the way; order was given that *six ships being before prepared*, with four pinnaces and a brigantine, should go both to conduct him, and also to defend, if any thing should be attempted against England, by carrying over the lady Mary. See also under June 20. Burnet, IV. 217, and below, p. 568, n. 2.]

war that I wrote about in my last letter of May 28, I understand there is no apprehension whatever. The lord Châtillon, the French ambassador, having ratified the peace, will leave this country on the 2nd of June. Master Hooper has obtained from the king's councillors all he wished for: he is gone to his native place, whence he will return in about ten days, and shortly after go to his bishoprick, where master John Utenhovius is in expectation of meeting him. I shall remain in London, to undertake the ministry of the word in the Flemish church that has been established here by master John à Lasco. I am not quite certain that such a church[2] will be granted; nevertheless we are in great hopes of it. Should I be appointed minister to that church, I shall not be able with a good conscience to go down to master Hooper. May God do what seemeth him good, provided only I labour for his glory! Joanna, the attendant of mistress Hooper, was married on the 2nd of June to the French preacher[3], a worthy and learned man. I wish them every happiness. On the third of this month, too, was celebrated a marriage[4] between the daughter of the duke of Somerset, and the son of the earl of Warwick, at which the king himself was present. This event, I hope, will wonderfully unite and conciliate the friendship of those noblemen. Master John Utenhovius, a man illustrious by piety and descent, desired me to commend him to you. Farewell, most noble sir, and salute all our godly friends in my name.

[2 The date of king Edward's grant of this church, which is in Austin Friars, and still used by Foreign Protestants, is set down in that king's book of sales, in these words: "The king, *de speciali gratia*, of his especial grace, granted the superintendent and ministers of the church of the Germans and other strangers, *totum illud templum sive ecclesiam nuper fratrum Augustinens. in civitat. Lond. ac totam terram, fundum et solum ejusdem ecclesiæ.*" Strype, Mem. II. i. 376. The letters patent are given in Burnet, IV. 308.]

[3 Richard Vauville, of whom see above, p. 339, n. 2.]

[4 "June 3. The king came to Shene, where was a marriage made between the lord Lisle, the earl of Warwick's son, and the lady Ann, daughter to the duke of Somerset; which done, and a fair dinner made, and dancing finished, the king and the ladies went into two ante-chambers made of boughs, where first he saw six gentlemen of one side, and six of another, run the course of the field twice over." King Edward's journal, in Burnet, IV. 209.]

What I principally intended to write had almost slipped my memory, namely, that master John à Lasco will shortly go to Cambridge, for the sake of having a conference with Bucer. I pray God that some godly way may be discovered of reconciling the points on which they differ. London, 1550. June 4.

Yours from my heart,

MARTIN MICRONIUS.

LETTER CCLXIII.

MARTIN MICRONIUS TO HENRY BULLINGER.

Dated at LONDON, *Aug.* 28, 1550.

MUCH health. Master Hooper, most vigilant prelate, received your letter on the 22nd of this month; but whenever I exhorted him to send an answer, he replied, that he had determined to be silent until the settlement of this business of his about the bishoprick. But as I know that from your especial affection to the king, the church of England, and to Hooper himself, you are exceedingly anxious to know what is going on here, though you might obtain fuller information from others, yet I have thought it my duty to relate it, while Hooper is in the mean time settling his own affairs, which are of great importance, and, as it appears, of doubtful issue. The king, as you know, has nominated him to the bishoprick of Gloucester, which however he refused to accept, unless he could be altogether relieved from all appearance of popish superstition. Here then a question immediately arises as to the form of the oath, which the bishops have ordered to be taken in the name of God, the saints, and the gospels; which impious oath Hooper positively refused to take. So when he appeared before the king in the presence of the council, Hooper convinced the king by many arguments that the oath should be taken in the name of God alone, who knoweth the heart. This took place[1] on the 20th of July. It was so agreeable to the godly king, that with his own pen he erased the

[[1] "July 20. Hooper was made bishop of Gloucester." King Edward's journal; Burnet, IV. 211. See above, p. 81, n. 3, and p. 416.]

clause of the oath which sanctioned swearing by any creatures. Nothing could be more godly than this act, or more worthy of a christian king. When this was done, there remained the form of episcopal consecration, which, as lately prescribed by the bishops in parliament, differs but little from the popish one. Hooper therefore obtained a letter from the king to the archbishop of Canterbury, that he might be consecrated without superstition. But he gained nothing by this, as he was referred from the archbishop of Canterbury to the bishop of London, who refused to use any other form of consecration than that which had been prescribed by parliament. Thus the bishops mutually endeavour that none of their glory shall depart. A few days after, on the 30th of July, Hooper obtained leave from the king and his council to be consecrated by the bishop of London without any superstition. He replied that he would shortly send an answer either to the council or to Hooper. While, therefore, Hooper was expecting the bishop's answer, the latter went to court, and alienated the minds of the council from Hooper, making light of the use of the vestments and the like in the church, and calling them mere matters of indifference. Many were so convinced by him that they would hardly listen to Hooper's defence, when he came into court shortly after. He therefore requested them, that if they would not hear him speak, they would at least think proper to hear and read his written apology. His request was granted: wherefore he delivered to the king's councillors, in writing, his opinion respecting the discontinuance of the use of the vestments and the like puerilities. And if the bishop cannot satisfy the king with other reasons, Hooper will gain the victory. We are daily expecting the termination of this controversy, which is only conducted between individuals, either by conference or by letter, for fear of any tumult being excited among the ignorant. You see in what a state the affairs of the church would be, if they were left to the bishops, even to the best of them.

Blessed be God, who has bestowed upon England a discreet and godly king, who most diligently purifies and gathers together the church of Christ. By his favour the church that was formerly the Augustines' has been made over to the German and French foreigners, that they may have the pure ministry of the word and sacraments, according to the apostolic form. We are altogether exempted, by the letters patent of the king and council, from the jurisdiction of the bishops. To each church (I mean the German and French) are assigned by the king two ministers of the word, (among whom is my unworthy self,) over whom has been appointed superintendent the most illustrious John à Lasco; by whose aid alone, under God, we foreigners have arrived at our present state of pure religion. Some of the bishops, and especially the bishop of London, with certain others, are opposed to our design; but I hope their opposition will be ineffectual. The archbishop of Canterbury, the especial patron of the foreigners, has been the chief support and promoter of our church, to the great astonishment of some; but God can make use of all persons to the advancement of his glory. He has lately published a large volume[1] upon the Lord's supper, in which he strenuously opposes the corporal presence of Christ. Bucer was advised, some little time since, by our superintendent, master à Lasco, not to raise any disturbance respecting the sacramentary controversy; and modestly replied, that he had no intention of the kind, but that he hoped that, were he present, he should easily agree with him. Wherefore the superintendent is shortly about to visit him for the sake of a conference.

The emperor privately sent to England in July a certain Scepper[2], one of his principal councillors, for the purpose of carrying away the king's eldest sister, Mary; but, by God's blessing, the thing was discovered and prevented. Unless God had watched over his people, it would have been all over with them. The same Spanish tyrant is harassing the Low Countries with the most cruel persecutions. He has establised the most sanguinary Spanish inquisition, which drives our countrymen to seek refuge in England. May God preserve his church! We commend our English church and that of the foreigners to your united prayers. The book you sent to the king was

[1 See Cranmer's Works, Vol. I. Parker Society edition.]

[2 The lady Mary was privately to be conveyed out of England from some creek in Essex by Shipperius, admiral of the navy, belonging to the emperor. And then an open war was to be begun, and an intestine conspiracy to be at home, as sir Thomas Chamberlain, ambassador with the queen of Hungary in the Low Countries, had learned at that court. Strype, Mem. II. i. 344.]

very acceptable. Master John Utenhovius salutes all of you who are ministers of the church, to whom also I commend myself. London, Aug. 28, 1550.

Your servant to command,

MARTIN MICRONIUS.

While these worthy men are waiting for a favourable wind to cross over, something has occurred respecting our foreigners' church. The church assigned to us by the king is being carefully repaired at the royal expense, through the instrumentality of the lord treasurer, to whom the choir of the said church belonged. But as the repairs went on slowly, master à Lasco requested the key of the church to be given us, that we might be able to have a sermon there at least every Lord's day. But this was refused by the lord treasurer on the plea that the church was the king's gift, and could not therefore be given up to us until it had been handsomely decorated. Speaking also upon our liberty in respect to ceremonies, he inquired why we chose to have them different from the English, since the English ones are not repugnant to the word of God. At last, when they had talked a good deal about ceremonies, the treasurer concluded by stating, that we foreigners must either adopt the English ceremonies, or disprove them by the word of God. All this mischief is stirred up against us by the bishops, and especially by the bishop of London, who does us the more harm, in proportion as he seems more actively to support the word of God. The lord treasurer is the mouth-piece of the bishops in this business. You know what a difficult work it is to build up the nation of Christ. We need the prayers of all godly persons; for it is "not by might, nor by power, but by my Spirit," saith the Lord. Again, farewell. Aug. 31, 1550.

The same as above.

We are much surprised at not having received any answer respecting Valentine Werdmuller; whether he is of the family of the treasurer of Zurich, as he would have us believe, or not. We have certainly incurred considerable expense in getting him out of danger. If his parents are the persons whom he states them to be, I hope that the sum we have expended on him will be repaid for the benefit of our poor.

LETTER CCLXIV.

MARTIN MICRONIUS TO HENRY BULLINGER.

Dated at LONDON, *Oct.* 13, 1550.

MUCH health. I have received, most vigilant pastor, your very kind letter, in which among other things you complain of not having received all that I have written to you. If the couriers had not deceived me, you would have learned my great anxiety to make you acquainted with the state of the church of England. Though I have no doubt but that every thing which occurs here is reported to you by others of great authority and credit, it is nevertheless a pleasure to me to testify in some measure my gratitude to you and to your church; which I cannot do by any other means than by faithfully laying before you the condition of our own, as you are doubtless exceedingly anxious for its welfare. It is, thank God, in a better condition than ever: God grant it may last! We have obtained, through the activity of our superintendent, master à Lasco, the church of the foreigners, (which is divided into a French and a German church,) free from all superstition. The church which was assigned to foreigners by the king and his council is cleansed and repaired. But as the reparation of the church was being protracted day after day to a lengthened period; by the special blessing of God a church has been made over to us Germans by the favour of some citizens of London, in which we are allowed to preach till the other is completed. At the desire of the brethren I have been appointed preacher, and have unwillingly taken upon myself that most difficult office. But the call of God must not rashly be resisted. I began to preach in this church on the 21st of September, and the German congregation is now so numerous that the place will not hold them. When we perceived this happy condition of our church, a consultation took place among our countrymen as to the establishment of a regular plan of government. Therefore, on the 5th of this month, we appointed four elders according to the apostolic ordinance, to assist the minister, not indeed in the ministry of the word, but in the conservation of doctrine and morals in the church. The most illustrious master John Utenhovius is one of the number. They were inaugurated with public prayer and imposition of hands. On the twelfth of this month we in like manner ordained four deacons, to take the charge of the poor and exiled for Christ's sake. The same ceremony was altogether adopted which the apostles observed with their deacons. The multitude of believers (praised be God!) is increasing every day. Should we be permitted, by God's blessing, to go on in this way for some years, we shall attack our Flanders with fiery darts, and, I hope, take it by storm, that, antichrist being put to flight or at least weakened, our Saviour may reign there.

I need not write very fully upon master Hooper's business; for you will get more certain information from the letter which he tells me he is about to send you. I will only add thus much, that the other bishops are giving him much trouble. Master Hooper is indeed elected bishop of Gloucester, and sworn into the office, but not yet consecrated, as they call it. For the bishops will not depart a nail's breadth from their prescribed form of consecration, which is manifestly superstitious. And as they are all of them intent upon subjecting Hooper to their ceremonies, so he opposes them with all his might, and refers every thing to the apostolic ceremonies. Hence there has arisen a most grievous controversy respecting the use of vestments in the church. The bishops defend the use of peculiar vestments in the church upon two grounds; first, that they are matters of indifference, and, secondly, that they are prescribed by the king's majesty, with whom rests the removal or appointment in the church of things indifferent. Hooper denies, on the other hand, that they are matters of indifference, inasmuch as they obscure the dignity of the priesthood of Christ, and nurture hypocrisy, superstition, &c. Hooper has written very fully upon this subject to the earl of Warwick, but he replies that the king must be obeyed in matters of indifference; that we must avoid placing a stumbling-block in the way of the weak, as Paul did when he made a vow, and was shorn, and when he circumcised Timothy. Hooper has written him a reply, but I do not yet perceive with what effect: nay, on the third of this month he wrote another letter on the same subject to the whole council, which they have not yet answered. We are suspended between hope and fear: the nobility seem inclined to take part with the bishops. God grant that I may prove a false prophet in this matter! The bishops are struggling for their own credit, which they prefer to Christ.

Master à Lasco, a man of such integrity, courtesy, piety and erudition, as cannot easily be expressed or described, sent you, some months since, his opinion respecting your alliance with the Genevese. He paid a visit to master Bucer last month. They came to an agreement on every subject except only that of the corporal presence in the supper. Bucer wrote down the heads of his opinion respecting the Lord's supper, which he left for master à Lasco to examine: this learned and excellent man is writing some annotations upon them, and most strenuously confutes Bucer's opinion. When he has finished them, he will send back to Bucer his heads with the annotations annexed. I pray that God may see fit to open his mind. We are exceedingly grieved at that rascal Valentine having so imposed upon us. He went away without taking leave of us, nor do we know whither he is gone. May the Lord recall him into the right way!

The Πρόσκαιρος[1] of Musculus is published in French; to which have been added the opinions of many worthy men upon the same subject; as of Œcolampadius, Zuinglius, the church of Zurich, master à Lasco, Calvin, and others, all of them carefully drawn up here. If master Froschover will send me the Chronicles of your country, I will faithfully provide for the payment of it, in whatever place he may point out. I wish he would also have the kindness to send me, at the next fair, if he cannot do so before, one or two copies of all your sermons. I have hitherto been living with master Hooper, but my present vocation has now separated me from him. The most illustrious master Utenhovius is about to board with me; for, having been elected one of the elders of the church, he is unable to accompany master Hooper to Gloucester. We shall however be present with master Hooper by our correspondence with him, as far as may lie in our power. I return you my sincere thanks for your kind wishes respecting the marriage in my family; and pray the same blessings in

[1 This book, entitled Proscerus, or "Temporizer," was published in 1549, upon the question, whether it be allowable for a protestant to take part in any external superstitions of popery. See Bayle.]

return to your daughters married in the Lord. Farewell, most excellent sir, and, though I am undeserving of such honour, be pleased to enrol me among your friends, and those of your church, which is the church of Christ. Be pleased also to salute for me my reverend preceptors, masters Bibliander, Pellican, Gesner, and master Sebastian. I have written in haste by reason of the magnitude of the affairs by which I am now daily overwhelmed. October 13, 1550. London.

Your most devoted and obedient,

MARTIN MICRONIUS.

I did not seal this letter, written a week since, because I was not aware at what time master Burcher intended to set off; and I easily conjectured that circumstances might take place in the mean time, of which it would be worth while to inform you. And so indeed it has turned out. For we have discovered that the whole of the king's council are inclined to side with the bishops in this controversy about the vestments, against master Hooper. In addition to this, the privileges of our German church are in the greatest danger. By canvassing and persuasion the bishops have procured from the king's council, that we are not to enjoy the free use of the sacraments, but must be fettered by the English ceremonies, which are intolerable to all godly persons. This circumstance occasions the greatest distress to our superintendent, John à Lasco, and to all the godly. I have thought fit to acquaint you with it, that you may be pleased to commend to God the cause of our church.

Master Hooper has just called upon me as I am writing, on his return from court. He tells me that yesterday the bishop of London was most violent against him before the council, and that he impugned his doctrine, and loaded him with the greatest insults. A copy of his letter is refused him, for the bishop demanded this from the council. But Hooper remains stedfast in his opposition to all the relics of popery. Farewell. Oct. 20. Masters John à Lasco and John Utenhovius commend themselves entirely to your church.

The same as above.

LETTER CCLXV.

MARTIN MICRONIUS TO HENRY BULLINGER.

Dated at [London], *Aug.* 14, 1551.

Much health. Though I am distracted by various engagements, and especially in making provision for this infant state of our church, yet I cannot pass over this offered opportunity of writing to you, lest you should think me forgetful of you, whereas you are deeply seated in my regard, both by reason of the most christian sermons that I have heard you preach, and also of your lately published Decades, from which we derive no ordinary assistance in edifying the church of Christ. We have need of help in the present difficulty of our affairs. We, who are desirous to hand down to the churches the sincere doctrine of God, are attacked on every side. We have not only to contend with the papists, who are almost every where ashamed of their errors, but much more with the sectaries and Epicureans and pseudo-evangelicals. In addition to the ancient errors respecting pædobaptism, the incarnation of Christ, the authority of the magistrate, the [lawfulness of an] oath, the property and community of goods, and the like, new ones are rising up every day, with which we have to contend. The chief opponents, however, of Christ's divinity are the Arians, who are now beginning to shake our churches with greater violence than ever, as they deny the conception of Christ by the Virgin. Their principal arguments may be reduced under three heads: The first is respecting the unity of God, as declared throughout all the scriptures both of the old and new Testament; and that the doctrine, as well as the name, of the Trinity is a novel invention, as not being mentioned in any part of scripture. Their next argument is this: the scripture, they say, which every where acknowledges one God, admits and professes that this one God is the Father alone, (Joh. xvii. 3,) who is also called one God by Paul, (1 Cor. viii. 6.) Lastly, they so pervert the passages which seem to establish the divinity of Christ, as to say that none of them refer intrinsically to Christ himself, but that he has received all from another, namely, from the Father; (Joh. v. Matt. xxviii.): and they say that God cannot receive from God; and that Christ was only in this respect superior to any of mankind, that he received more gifts from God the Father.

I have replied to these things as God has enabled me, and (thank the Lord!) master à Lasco, who is, next to God, the principal defender of our church, affords me his assistance. I was desirous, however, to lay these things before your reverence, that, should you have leisure, you may be pleased to write me word what may most fitly be replied to these three arguments of the enemies of Christ; for from your decade, wherein you most solidly establish his divinity upon other grounds, I have been able to elicit little or nothing which may be satisfactorily brought against them. You, who are our fathers, teachers, and guides in the reformation of the churches, will not grudge affording us your advice and instruction, that we may rightly direct the church of God, and fortify it against all heresies. We are using every exertion to that effect; and especially, we have established in our church a collation of scripture in the German language, in which are discussed the sermons of the preceding week, to preserve the purity of doctrine; and this arrangement, in some measure, represses the heretical, and confirms the ignorant in the christian doctrine. We have, besides, in our German church, two other lectures in Latin; one by master à Lasco, the other by master Walter Delvin; after which there takes place a comparison of scriptures on the subject of the lectures last delivered, to the great advantage of the churches. Thus we have three collations of scripture every week, whereas at first we had only determined to have two. One thing in particular is still wanting in our church, namely, the administration of baptism and of the Lord's supper. Liberty is granted us by the royal licence, but we are prevented by the malevolence of certain individuals from the enjoyment of so great a benefit. Master à Lasco is indeed diligently exerting himself with the bishops, as his duty requires him to do, that we may be permitted to enjoy the liberty that has been conceded to us; but all his exhortations are without any effect. I fear we shall have to wait till the meeting of parliament, and I know not when that will take place.

The sweating sickness[1] made sad havoc in London in

[[1] In one day, viz. July 10, died an hundred people; and the next an hundred and twenty. And it came even into the king's family

July, and master à Lasco, who was seized with it, was in so much danger, that we altogether despaired of his life. But he has now recovered, for the Lord had compassion upon us; for had he been taken away, the churches of the foreigners, there is reason to fear, would have perished with him. The Lord is the only defender of his church! In what state are the affairs of master Hooper, the bishop of Gloucester, you will best learn from his own letter. As far as I can understand, he is faithfully employing his talent. I pray you to exert your influence in recommending to him meekness and gentleness. Exhort mistress Anna, his wife, not to entangle herself with the cares of this life. Let her beware of the thorns, by which the word of God is choked. It is a most dangerous thing for one who is in the service of Christ to hunt after riches and honours. Your admonitions will have much weight with them both. The bishop of Lincoln[1], a favourer of evangelical doctrine, departed this life not long since. The sweating sickness has carried off two most noble youths[2], the duke of Suffolk and his brother Charles. The kingdom, thank God, is this summer in a state of tranquillity; for the rising of some of the peasantry, at the beginning of the summer, was very speedily put an end to by the authority and activity of the magistrates.

Farewell, my master, and take my freedom in good part. Be pleased, I pray you, to salute in my name my reverend preceptors, masters Bibliander, Pellican, Gesner, and Frisius. May the Lord deliver your church from all evil! Amen. 1551. Aug. 14. Master à Lasco is in the country with the archbishop of Canterbury: he would otherwise have written

about this time, which caused him to retire to Hampton court. Letters from the council, dated July 18, were sent to all the bishops, to persuade the people to prayer, and to see God better served. Strype, Mem. II. i. 491; Cranm. 388.]

[1 Henry Holbech, or Henry Rands, of Holbech in Lincolnshire, was a true favourer of the gospel, and made much use of in the reforming and settling of the church. He had been lord prior of Worcester, of which he was made the first dean, and was translated from Rochester to Lincoln in 1547. See Strype, Mem. II. ii. 167.]

[2 These young noblemen had been educated by bishop Holbech, and retired from King's college, Cambridge, of which they were members, to his house at Buckden, to avoid the sickness. They died both in one bed, July 16. Strype, Mem. II. i. 491. See p. 454, n. 2.]

to you, as far as I could gather from what he said before he went.

Yours wholly,

MARTIN MICRONIUS.

LETTER CCLXVI.

MARTIN MICRONIUS TO HENRY BULLINGER.

Dated at LONDON, *Nov.* 7, 1551.

MUCH health. I do not think there is at this time any occasion for me to write at length concerning the state of this kingdom, and the condition of both the English and foreign churches; for you will learn every thing from these worthy young men, and from the letters of others, far more accurately than it would be safe and easy for me now to communicate. The disturbance which suddenly took place here on the second imprisonment[3] of the duke of Somerset, his wife, and other noble persons[4], greatly distressed our minds; and the rather, because various and uncertain reasons were commonly assigned for his arrest. But the Lord will doubtless order every thing for the welfare of his church. Master Hooper is most vigilant in his ministry. I grieve that so little help is afforded him by others. Wherefore he must especially be aided and encouraged by your letters: and let him be exhorted to unite prudence and christian lenity to the severity of discipline.

The affairs of the strangers' church are, thank God, in a flourishing condition: they daily make great progress in doctrine, consolation, exhortation, public comparing of the scriptures both in Latin and German; and also in the diligent exercise of ecclesiastical discipline. We feel indeed that we are sometimes assailed by Satan through those enemies of Christ, the hypocritical and heretical bishops; but the Lord protects us, to whom it belongs to build up the church, and to defend

[3 This imprisonment took place Oct. 15 or 16, according to king Edward's journal. See Strype, Mem. II. i. 497, Burnet, II. 283, who mentions the 17th of October as the date of the duke's committal.]

[4 Among these were the lord Grey, sirs Ralph Vane, Thomas Palmer, and Thomas Arundel. Burnet, as above, and IV. 222.]

and preserve it when so built up. Master à Lasco, our superintendent, a man (to speak it in one word) almost divine, is not only of the greatest use to the foreigners' churches, but also to the English, by teaching, exhorting, counselling, and writing. I could wish this man to be especially noticed with commendation by all the learned men who are dedicating any work to the king or his council; by which means some accession might be made to his influence (which is great in the country,) to the advantage of his churches in this realm. He will shortly publish a most learned work[1], in my opinion, upon the sacramentarian controversy, of which he has given me a certain portion to read. On the 17th of last month a certain godly brother[2], and sincere in the christian religion, was burnt at Antwerp on account of the dispute about the sacraments, and yielded his holy soul to Christ the Lord. London, Nov. 7, 1551.

Deign to salute in my name my worthy preceptors, masters Bibliander, Pellican and Gesner. Utenhovius would have written to you, had he not been prevented by ill health; for which reason he begs me to make his excuse, and promises to atone for this long silence by a most copious letter at another time.

Yours wholly,

MARTIN MICRONIUS.

LETTER CCLXVII.

MARTIN MICRONIUS TO HENRY BULLINGER.

Dated at LONDON, *March* 9, 1552.

MUCH health. Master John à Lasco, our superintendent, would have written to you, my most honoured master, respecting

[1 The treatise here mentioned was printed in 1552, and bore this title: *Brevis et dilucida de Sacramentis ecclesiæ Christi tractatio. In qua et fons ipse et ratio totius sacramentariæ nostri temporis controversiæ paucis exponitur, naturaque ac vis sacramentorum compendiò et perspicue explicatur; per Joannem à Lasco, Baronem Poloniæ, superintendentem ecclesiæ peregrinorum Londini, anno* 1552. In 8vo. See Strype, Mem. II. ii. 33.]

[2 The name of this individual was John Van Ostend. See Brandt's Hist. of Reformation in the Low Countries, B. III.]

every thing that is going on here, had he not been prevented by the mass of business in which he is involved. He has desired me therefore to write to you, in his name, a full statement of every event; which duty I have promised, as it became me, diligently to perform. You have doubtless heard of the imprisonment of the duke of Somerset, his wife, and many others of the nobility. Various grounds have been assigned for this procedure. The real cause, however, as I understand from persons worthy of credit, was his having formed a conspiracy against some of the council, which is a capital offence. For the king's council, after the first imprisonment of the duke of Somerset, with the view of uniting them more closely to each other, passed a law to this effect, that any one of the king's council, who should plot in secret against another of that body, should suffer death by hanging, as a felon. And as Somerset was said to have offended against this law, he was arrested on the 16th of October[3], and on the following day his wife, together with many other of the nobility who were thought to have been privy to this conspiracy. The trial of the duke of Somerset took place in Westminster hall on the first of December, and lasted from an early hour in the morning till the evening. He could not be charged with any treason against the king, and is said to have defended himself against all the charges with boldness and discretion. But as he was unable to clear himself of the charge of conspiracy against some of the council, he was condemned to be hanged, according to a law which he himself had framed. He was, however, beheaded on the 22nd of January, to the great grief of the people. Afterwards, on the 26th of February, two knights were hanged, and two others beheaded for the same offence[4]. I am afraid of a similar end to the wife of Somerset, who is said to bear a principal part in all this mischief. We must pray God, that all things may turn out to his glory, and that in the midst of these disorders he will preserve his church.

[3 See above, p. 577, n. 3.]

[4 A warrant was issued to the lord chancellor to make forth writs of execution of sirs Rafe Vane, Miles Partridge, Thomas Arundel, and Michael Stanhope, knights, that is to say, for heading of Thomas Arundel and Michael Stanhope, and hanging the rest. Strype, Mem. II. ii. 248.]

We have great hopes of a reformation both in church and state during this parliament. For there are appointed[1] to the reformation of the church eight godly bishops, among whom is Hooper; eight doctors in divinity, among whom is master John à Lasco, a man fearless in the cause of godliness, and master Peter Martyr. The business has turned out well enough hitherto; and if the bishops of London and Ely[2] would not stand in the way with their worldly policy, it would, I think, have made yet farther progress. But I hope that their opposition will be ineffectual. For the king is most anxious for purity, and is urgent for a serious reformation; and those who possess the greatest influence in the council are seeking the same. The authority of master Hooper in the council is daily increasing, whence the greatest benefit, I hope, will accrue to the church. Our foreign churches, thank the Lord, are in a most flourishing condition, through the exertions of our superintendent, master à Lasco. We must pray the Lord to perfect what he has begun; and that he will be pleased to defend all his churches, which Satan does not cease to attack with his marvellous devices. But it is well that he is conquered and bound by Christ the Lord, whom I pray to deliver you from the midst of the tumults of war, and that you may receive no evil yourselves from the evil that surrounds you. Farewell, my master, and may God continue to enlighten you with his Spirit! Amen. Be pleased to salute in my name all my honoured preceptors, masters Pellican, Bibliander, and Gesner. London, March 9, 1552.

Yours,

MARTIN MICRONIUS.

[1 A commission was issued, Oct. 6, 1551, to eight bishops, eight divines, eight civil, and eight common lawyers, authorising them to reform the canon laws. Their names are given in Strype, Cranm. 388. The result of their labours was published in queen Elizabeth's reign, under the title of *Reformatio Legum.*]

[2 Namely, Ridley and Goodrick. The character here given of the latter is confirmed in Strype, Mem. II. i. 516.]

LETTER CCLXVIII.

MARTIN MICRONIUS TO HENRY BULLINGER.

Dated at LONDON, *Feb.* 13, 1553.

MUCH health. I know how greatly your piety is delighted by the letters of your friends, in which is set forth the state of the churches: and not without reason, since all the churches, dispersed throughout the world, are only one family of God; and we see that the apostle Paul willingly learned from others, and most diligently declared to others in his turn, the condition of the churches. This consideration has compelled me to write to you, though I am more than enough occupied upon other matters; that you may know that the church of England, and our foreign churches here in London, viz. the German and French, are, by the great blessing of God, in a flourishing condition. Our foreign churches are frequently attacked by the pseudo-bishops, and with wonderful arts and stratagems: but Christ has conquered hitherto, and has turned every thing to the advancement of the church; so that no foreigner is now eligible to the rights of an English citizen, without having previously made a confession of his faith to the ministers of the foreign churches. Should this regulation last some years, this kingdom will be delivered from great and various errors, which are usually introduced by foreign sectaries. Parliament is to meet on the first of March: God grant that it may bring forth some advantage to the church! Certainly I cannot as yet augur any mischief. The Latin lectures in our churches have been suspended since the decease of the wife[3] of master à Lasco, nor will he be able to resume them before Easter, by reason of his various engagements, or rather those of the church; though both he himself and his new wife, whom he married on the 29th of January, are in tolerable health. I hope, however, that this interruption of his lectures will be counterbalanced by some great benefit to the church. We are expecting master Hooper

[[3] This lady died in August 1552. A Lasco's second marriage was commended by Peter Martyr in a letter to Utenhovius. Strype, Mem. II. i. 377.]

in London within these three days: he is to preach, as I hear, before the king's majesty on the 26th of this month. I never could have expected him to be so faithful and diligent in his bishoprick; for when dainty meat is put into the mouths of others, it is apt to make them dumb and inactive. The wife[1] of Peter Martyr departed this life four days since. Master John Utenhovius, who was so ill two months since that his life was despaired of, is now, thank God, convalescent.

I wish you would publish the heads you have collected for your discourses on Isaiah, the books of Samuel and Kings, the Acts of the Apostles, the Epistle to the Romans, and whatever else you may have by you. Far greater assistance, in my opinion, can hence be derived towards a solid knowledge of scripture, than from the bulky commentaries of numerous writers. If I dared recommend this to you, I would endeavour to persuade you: but as I am not in your counsels, and as I doubt not but that you are anxious for nothing but the edification of the church, I dare not advise any thing rashly, but only state my opinion; and I should not even do this, were it not that I hoped to derive some benefit from it.

As to public matters, we are in the enjoyment of peace in this country: God grant that we may employ it to the promotion of godliness! The emperor Charles went to Brussells on the sixth of this month in ill health. He is oppressing the mass-priests of our nation with severe exactions, so that they are beginning in some measure to fear for their kingdom. May God turn every thing to the advancement of his kingdom! Amen. Be pleased to salute my honoured preceptors, masters Pellican, Bibliander, and Gesner. Masters John à Lasco and John Utenhovius desired me to salute them, and especially yourself. London, Feb. 18, 1553.

Yours wholly,

MARTIN MICRONIUS.

[[1] Catharine Vermilia, of whom an account is given in Strype, Parker, I. 200. In the reign of queen Mary her remains were removed from the grave, and buried in a dunghill, from whence they were taken up on the accession of queen Elizabeth, and honourably reinterred.]

LETTER CCLXIX.

JOHN UTENHOVIUS[2] TO HENRY BULLINGER.

Dated at STRASBURGH, *July* 7, 1549.

GREETING. When immediately on my return to Strasburgh with John à Lasco, whom I mentioned before, I observed a letter, I readily perceived it to be the same as that which you gave me to read when I was with you. In the interval, too, of my absence from this place, I received from master Calvin that treatise of his on the Eucharist, or Lord's supper, which he sent me of his own accord. There will not therefore be any occasion for you to send me another copy. You would, however, greatly oblige me, if you would send me whatever you have of Bucer's on the Lord's supper, written by him before he began to dote. I will repay this favour, whenever your circumstances may require it, by any means in my power. Master Butler promised me that he would endeavour to obtain from Musculus, Vadianus, and some others, their opinion upon the subject I proposed to you, and which you doubtless well remember. Should he seem to require your assistance in this matter, I pray you not to decline it: and I wish we could obtain the united assent of the Bernese church. Should any thing be obtained, so that they write to me from thence, the letter may be forwarded to Frankfort, to one Adrian Eding, who is well known to master Butler, and also to Froschover.

As to any news, we have nothing here but what is of a distressing character. All these churches seem to become weaker and weaker every day, and to be altogether going to ruin. For a general inactivity pervades the minds of those, whose duty it was to have acted in a more manly way. Our adversaries, meanwhile, to whom all religion and godliness is a matter of the greatest ridicule, are laughing at us, as they say, with swollen cheeks. Those who were older and more zealous in the faith, and in the proper administration of affairs, and who deserved well of religion, and so were prophets themselves, have either been called out of this life, or are dispersed every where out of Germany into other parts.

[[2] For a notice of Utenhovius, see above, p. 56.]

Add to this, that we are daily hearing the most execrable blasphemies against God and his word from those, who formerly acknowledged Christ, but have now gone over from us to our adversaries. Lastly, we see the people so far from being acted upon by any feelings of repentance, that they are become more listless and perverse than usual; whence it is evident, that nothing less than the severest punishment is awaiting us for our ingratitude. May God, meanwhile, have compassion on us, for the sake of our Lord Jesus Christ, and increase our faith by his Spirit, that we may stand firm in the confession of his name, even in the midst of every evil.

You will learn other matters from the letters of the rest of us. I had purposed indeed to have gone over to England from Cologne; but by reason of the great dangers which await me in Flanders, in compliance with the advice of my friends, I am meditating a journey through France, which, God willing, I shall commence to-morrow. In the mean time, I earnestly commend myself to your prayers. Farewell, most accomplished sir, and honoured master, and inscribe me in the list of your friends. May God strengthen you by his Spirit, that with a firm and unbroken courage you may defend, even to the latest day of your life, the high post you have gained, to the glory of his name. Again farewell, and do not fail to let me know by the next Frankfort fair, whatever you may think it expedient for me to be acquainted with. Strasburgh, July 7, 1549.

Yours, as he is his own,

J. UTENHOVIUS.

LETTER CCLXX.

JOHN UTENHOVIUS TO HENRY BULLINGER.

Dated at LONDON, *April* 9, 1551.

GREETING. Not a single syllable have I received from you in reply to my last letter. I should, notwithstanding, have written to you before now, if I could have given you any certain information about master Hooper's affairs, respecting which I felt assured that you were very anxious: but as I was unable to do so, I thought it best to delay my letter until this unhappy dispute[1] of his with the bishops should have been settled. As this is now the case, I could not refrain from a brief relation of the affair. You are aware, if I am not mistaken, that master Hooper accepted the bishoprick of Gloucester, voluntarily offered him by the king's majesty about nine months since, with the condition that he should, under no circumstances, be compelled to adopt any superstitious observances, and especially at his inauguration, which they call consecration; and this was readily conceded to him by the king and the royal council. The bishops, however, carried the matter so far, I know not under what pretext, before the council, (being, doubtless, far more solicitous for their own glory than that of the Lord Christ,) that they retracted the liberty they had once allowed him according to the word of God; so that, as far at least as relates to the vestments[2] and the carrying the pastoral staff, Hooper was urged to comply with the popish form of inauguration. He resisted the bishops, however, long and manfully, employing many very powerful arguments, asserting that a christian man who was convinced of the ungodliness of the use of such vestments in the ministry of the church, could not use them in the ministry with a safe conscience, both because they bring along with them an opinion of merit, hypocrisy, a thousand kinds of superstitions and stumbling-blocks, and also because they too truly place in the back ground the priesthood of Christ the Lord. But among those of greater learning, master à Lasco alone advocated this notion, and he did not shrink from subscribing alone to what Hooper wrote. When Bucer, of pious memory, and Peter Martyr were asked their opinion upon this subject, they replied, that it was certainly their wish that vestments of this kind should be altogether removed from the church; but yet that they could not perceive, (inasmuch as to the clean all things are clean,) why godly persons who

[1 See above, Letters CCXXX and CCLXIV.]

[2 The episcopal dress, which caused all this difficulty, consists principally of a rochet and a scarlet chimere, which colour was one ground of objection against it. The rochet is a garment of white linen, which has been worn by bishops from a very early age, and in which the Romish canons bound them to appear whenever they were seen in public. The chimere is a robe worn over the rochet, and furnished with sleeves of white lawn. See Soames, III. 560, and above, p. 271, n. 1.]

were otherwise convinced of the impiety of the use of vestments in the ministry of the church, were yet forbidden to use them. However, after a long struggle, Hooper was committed to prison, and about a fortnight after, overcome by the obstinacy of the bishops, the good man submitted himself and his cause to the judgment of the privy council: the result of which was, that he was inaugurated in the usual manner, about the middle of Lent, yet not without the greatest regret both of myself and of all good men, nor without affording a most grievous stumbling-block to many of our brethren; a circumstance that I am unwilling to conceal from you, though, from my affection for Hooper, I am very unwilling to make the communication: and indeed I should not now do it, were I not aware of your sincere regard for Hooper, and that you look upon him as another self. I would gladly add more upon this subject, were it safe to entrust every thing to writing: but I would rather inform you by word of mouth than by a private letter. Meanwhile, take care not to say a word about me to master Hooper; neither will it be worth while to give him any advice about this business, since what is already done can admit of no remedy. If, however, in your discretion, you should think proper to write and advise him, you are at liberty to do so, and it is chiefly for this reason that I have made you acquainted with the circumstances of the case; but you will do this with greater effect, if, without mentioning my name or that of any other person, you write him word that you have gained your information from a friend. I hope, however, that this event will be of use to Hooper himself, and also to the church. He went to his bishoprick a fortnight before Easter, where, as far as we can understand, he is most diligent in the performance of his ministerial duties; on which account thanks be to the Lord God, to whom I heartily commend both his ministry and your own. If I can possibly obtain leave of absence from our church, I shall visit Hooper for some months; and if I can anywise be useful to him in his ministry, I shall not decline such assistance as the Lord may enable me to afford; and this I promised him when he went away.

Our church, moreover, is going on very favourably, excepting only that the bishops[1] will not yet allow us the

[[1] Bishop Ridley opposed the settling the German church in a different way from the rites of the church of England. Burnet, III. 605.]

pure administration of the sacraments. The word, however, is proclaimed in all its purity, with the greatest benefit to the church, by our friend Martin Micronius, who preaches in a popular manner, like the clergy at Zurich, and is at the same time a cautious interpreter of the word, introducing nothing that is forced or trifling, and which does not tend to entire edification. A system of discipline is now established by us, as far as we have it in our power; as a part of which is to be considered the catechism which we are now preparing, and also prophesying, or a collation of the scriptures, which we shall begin next week together with the English. We shall also undertake it in Latin every Monday, after the lecture of master à Lasco, (who is now expounding the gospel of St John, to the great admiration and advantage of his hearers,) and also in German every Wednesday, and that after the lecture of master Gualter[2], who will expound Genesis in Latin. We shall therefore have two collations every week, in the former of which both the preceding lectures will be modestly sifted, and in the latter the sermons preached during the whole week: which employment cannot be without the greatest advantage, if the Lord, to whom it belongs to give the increase of all good things, will afford his blessing. The wife of master Hooper, who is still in London, has requested me to send you, together with my own, the letter I have inclosed with it.

Salute for me, I pray, your dear and amiable wife, and masters Bibliander, Pellican, Gualter, Zuingle, Wolf, Frisius, and Sebastian. And you must not forget master Gesner, and above all my host master Butler, to whom, together with his wife, and to your whole church, I wish every happiness in the Lord. Farewell, most honoured sir and master, in him who is our life. Amen. London, Apr. 9, 1551.

Yours, truly and heartily,

JOHN UTENHOVIUS.

Master Martin dutifully salutes you. He is now so entirely engaged as the sole minister of the German congregation, that he is unable to write to you at present. But he will make amends at some future opportunity.

[[2] Gualter Deloenus is mentioned in the king's letters patent as one of the ministers of the Strangers' church in London. See Burnet, IV. 308.]

LETTER CCLXXI.

JOHN UTENHOVIUS TO HENRY BULLINGER.

Dated at LONDON, *Aug.* 14, 1551.

GREETING. About four months since, I gave a letter to a certain brother, which he undertook to deliver to you. But after some time, I know not under what pretence, he sent it back to me. I have, however, kept it by me till now, in the hope of having some opportunity of sending it, though it is so out of date, that you might at least receive this testimony of my regard for you, and not altogether consider me to have been unmindful of you during so long a silence. But I now send you the letter[1] itself, that you may know the result of master Hooper's affair. I was long in doubt whether I ought to write these things respecting an individual with whom I am upon such friendly terms. But when I considered that the failings both of the prophets and the apostles are not without reason recorded in scripture as a perpetual warning to mankind, I forthwith shook off all hesitation, in the full assurance that, with your wonted kindness and discretion, you would bear with the infirmity of our brother as a Christian should do, and that, if you deem it worth while, you would use the occasion to admonish him of his duty. Meanwhile I have no doubt but that this affair will eventually turn out to the good of the church. For it is by means of this kind that we are wont to become better acquainted with ourselves, and to humble our souls more before God, and also to become more favourably disposed to, and less prejudiced against, the ministry of our neighbours. And, indeed, master Hooper is now labouring with such faithfulness and diligence in the discharge of his office, as deservedly to cheer the hearts of all godly persons. The rest you will easily learn from the bearer of this letter; for, as I think, he has a more intimate acquaintance with the whole of the circumstances of Hooper than I have, inasmuch as he was himself at Gloucester, and also resided some time at Oxford, which is at no great distance. As you will learn from him the state of this church and king-

[1 Namely, the preceding letter.]

dom, I will now conclude my letter, nothing doubting but that our friend Martin will also make you acquainted with all our affairs.

When I returned from hence to Strasburgh, two years ago, John Burcher gave me to taste a piece of spiced cake, which he said had been sent to him by some friend from Zurich. I should much like some of the same kind to be forwarded to me at the next Easter fair at Frankfort; and I request you to purchase one for me which is not too highly seasoned, and forward it to the house of Adrian Eding, at Frankfort, with a statement of the price, which I will take care shall be paid, either here to Stumphius, or to any one at Frankfort whom you may prefer. You will thereby do me a very great favour, and if I can be of any use to you in my turn, or oblige you in any way here, you will always find me entirely at your service. Salute for me, I pray you, all the brethren whom I have mentioned in the other letter, and farewell, my ever honoured master, in the Lord, to whom I heartily commend your ministry, and all your household. London, August 14, 1551.

Yours as his own,

JO. UTENHOVIUS.

LETTER CCLXXII.

JOHN UTENHOVIUS TO HENRY BULLINGER.

Dated at LONDON, *March* 9, 1552.

GREETING. Your letter of the eighth of November was given to me some time since by master Hooper. I should now write to you at some length touching the state of both our public and private affairs, were they not all of them as well known, or perhaps more so, to the individual who has taken upon himself the charge of the letter, as they are to myself. For this reason you will have at this time a shorter letter from me than you would otherwise have received. This, however, I must tell you, that all godly persons in this country entertain good hopes of the advancement of religion; for the restoration of which those persons who are appointed by the king's majesty for that purpose are labouring with the greatest activity. Among these is Thomas, archbishop of Canterbury, John Hooper, John à Lasco, Peter Martyr, and many other learned and godly men. And although the whole of them (in number thirty-two[1]) may sometimes be unable to agree upon every point, yet I hope that those will prevail who are more sound in doctrine, inasmuch as the king, who has altogether at heart the furtherance of pure religion, will interpose his authority whenever it may be required. Nor is there any doubt but that, with the blessing of Christ our Lord, if any sound and wholesome agreement can be effected among the above-named persons, as we all of us hope will be the case, their acts will subsequently be confirmed without any difficulty by the votes of parliament. Meanwhile, it is our duty, and that too of yourselves yonder, earnestly and importunately to entreat God to be present by his Spirit at the convocation which is now assembled, so that every thing which may be debated therein, and especially the things appertaining to religion, may turn out to the glory of his name, and the advancement of the kingdom of his Son: which that he may do, I most earnestly and heartily implore.

I shall say nothing of the expedition[2] which the king of France is now preparing for the liberation of Germany, as it is rumoured here; for I think that you possess fuller and more certain information upon the subject. Master à Lasco, as you may easily believe, is so much occupied by the reformation now going on, that he has desired me to make his excuses to you for not writing at this time. Salute for me, I pray you, masters Bibliander, Pellican, Gualter, Wolf, and the other brethren, not forgetting master Gesner. Salute for me likewise master Butler and his wife. Master à Lasco salutes you, and master Gualter[3]. Farewell in the Lord, most accomplished

[1 See above, p. 503.]

[2 The king of France added a manifesto to that of duke Maurice, containing his reasons for taking arms against the emperor. In this he assumed the title of protector of the liberties of Germany, and of its captive princes. He took the field early, and marching directly into Lorraine, Toul and Verdun opened their gates before him. He then took possession of Metz by stratagem, and advanced towards Alsace. See Robertson, Charles V. IV. 67, 68; Sleidan, XXIV. 554.]

[3 See above, p. 587, n. 2.]

sir, to whom I heartily commend you and your ministry. London, March 9, 1552.

Yours as his own,
JO. UTENHOVIUS.

LETTER CCLXXIII.

JOHN UTENHOVIUS TO HENRY BULLINGER.

Dated at LONDON, *Oct.* 12, 1552.

GREETING. Though I am now involved in various and important engagements, I cannot forbear writing to you somewhat, by which I may in some measure at least express the inclination of my heart towards you. Besides, I cannot but make you acquainted with the happy progress of our church here, on which account we must offer everlasting thanks to our good and gracious God. It has indeed so turned out in accordance with my wishes, that I can scarcely desire to see it in a better state. Our friend Martin most effectively performs his office, and discharges all his duties with fidelity, prudence, and diligence. Four months since I accompanied master Hooper, the bishop of Worcester, from hence to Worcester, and staid with him nearly seven weeks. I cannot speak in sufficient terms of commendation of his faithfulness and zeal. May the Lord God render his ministry fruitful, that the result may correspond with the desires and exertions of the man!

Some disputes have arisen within these few days among the bishops, in consequence of a sermon of a pious preacher, chaplain to the duke of Northumberland, preached by him before the king and council, in which he inveighed with great freedom against kneeling[4] at the Lord's supper, which is still

[[4] October 27, a letter was sent from the council to the lord chancellor, to cause to be joined to the book of Common Prayer, lately set forth, a declaration, signed by the king, touching the kneeling at the receiving of the communion. Strype, Cranmer, 416. See Liturgies of Edward VI. Parker Soc. Ed. p. 283.—The preacher referred to was probably Knox, though it does not appear that he was "chaplain to the duke of Northumberland:" but possibly this state-retained here by the English. This good man, however, a Scotsman by nation, has so wrought upon the minds of many persons, that we may hope some good to the church will at length arise from it; which I earnestly implore the Lord to grant.

Master à Lasco has just received letters from some Polish and Lithuanian noblemen, and has also received one full of all kindness from the king of Poland himself. The purport of them all is to invite him to go into Poland at the public general assembly of that kingdom, which is appointed by the king for the reformation of religion. But, to avoid all ground of his being suspected by the adversaries of the faith, they especially require that he may be sent thither upon some pretence or other as an ambassador from our king. This proposal was made to-day for the first time to the duke of Northumberland by the archbishop of Canterbury. May the Lord grant that it may turn out to the glory of his name! Master à Lasco, and master Martin, who are now occupied in different ways, desire you to excuse their not writing. Meanwhile they salute you most affectionately. Salute for me, I pray you, master Bibliander, and the other fathers and brethren with whom I am acquainted in those parts, and especially master Butler. Farewell, my master Bullinger, most dear and esteemed by me in the Lord, to whom I commend your ministry from my heart. London, Oct. 12, 1552. From the house of master à Lasco, with whom I am lodging.

Yours truly from my heart,

JO. UTENHOVIUS.

LETTER CCLXXIV.

JOHN UTENHOVIUS TO HENRY BULLINGER.

Dated at LONDON, *June* 7, 1553.

GREETING. Your letter, my excellent friend, of the 9th of March, was first delivered to me by Richard Hilles four

ment may have been a mistake of the writer. There is also some difficulty about the date; as, though Knox was questioned before the council on his objections to kneeling at the Lord's supper, this did not take place till April, 1553. See Mc Crie, Life of Knox, Vol. I. p. 89, &c.]

days since, in which you inform me of your having recovered from that very severe illness under which you were suffering in December: whereupon I greatly rejoice, and I pray the Lord to establish your health, and long to preserve you in safety to his church, to the glory of his name. I was also suffering in the same month from very dangerous illness, insomuch that all the brethren, and also my host, master à Lasco, entirely despaired of my life: but through the mercy of God I am tolerably restored to my former health. The Lord grant that I may employ it, according to my weak abilities, to the advancement of his kingdom! Farther, I am not surprised at your complaining to me, as you do, of the neglect[1] of master Hooper, but I am more surprised at the fact itself. I will however shortly remind him by letter, and that seriously; but what I shall obtain by it I do not know: for he is himself so minded, that he never writes to any one of us, not even to master à Lasco[2], though he is certainly much attached to us; so that those complaints of yours are such as are common to us all. Meanwhile I would have you to be assured that Bullinger will ever be very dear to him, and esteemed by him beyond all others, as I can testify of my own knowledge. As to the money which Hooper lent[3] to the students whom you mention, I will ascertain from Hooper himself how he wishes it to be disposed of; and if I receive any answer from him, I will let you know.

Master à Lasco, who is still here, salutes you: he promised me yesterday that he would write to you; wherefore, as I doubt not but that he will perform his promise, I shall not now write any more about him. We have no news, except that the king, who has lately been in the most imminent danger from a most severe cough, which had already attacked his inside even to the very vitals, is now somewhat better, though it is hardly possible that his health will be entirely restored during the whole of this summer. Meanwhile, however, he has always been most favourably disposed towards religion, and is so at this time more than ever. May God

[1 It appears from Hooper's letter given above, p. 100, that Bullinger's complaint was unfounded.]

[2 A Lasco was Hooper's chief supporter in the controversy respecting the vestments. See above, p. 95.]

[3 See the postscript of Hooper's letter, p. 95.]

preserve him to his church; and I entreat you yonder to commend him to God in your prayers. Articles[1] are now printed in the king's name, to which all persons must subscribe who are to be appointed to any office in the church, as also those who are already appointed, under pain of deprivation.

Once more, I again repeat in the Lord the request that I made to you two years since, namely, that if it is not too much trouble, you will procure to be sent to me from thence, either by yourself or some other person, to the Frankfort fair, a large cake[2], not seasoned with much spice, such as you sent to Burcher four years ago. It might easily be arranged for me to receive it by the hands of Richard Hilles after the Frankfort fair, by which means you would confer upon me a greater obligation than I am able to express. You can tell me what it costs, and I will pay the amount to Hooper towards the liquidation of the debt above mentioned, or in any other way you may prefer. If I can do you any service by way of return, I beg you to make use of me as a friend. Master Martin Micronius desires his best salutations. Salute for me, I pray you, masters Bibliander, Pellican, Gesner, and master Butler, to whom I wish better health in the Lord. Farewell, my excellent friend, and ever esteemed by me in Christ, to whom I heartily commend you and your ministry; and do you love me as you are wont to do. London, June 7, 1553.

Yours as his own,

JO. UTENHOVIUS.

[1 For an account of these articles, see Burnet, II. 265, and IV. 314, where he gives them at length, with marginal notes of the differences between them and those set out by queen Elizabeth in 1562. "They are now generally held to have been agreed to in the convocation of 1552, though previously delivered to the bishops to procure subscriptions, and this by royal authority, before they were publicly set forth and fully sanctioned." Burnet, II. 321, editor's note. See also Strype, Cranmer, 391, and Dr Lamb on the Articles.]

[2 See above, p. 589.]

LETTER CCLXXV.

JOHN UTENHOVIUS TO HENRY BULLINGER.

Dated at BASLE, *March* 1, 1554.

GREETING. As soon as I arrived at Basle, most honoured sir, and much esteemed master in Christ, my first care was to look out for a comfortable lodging. I first called upon master Oporinus[3], to whom I gave your letter, having read which, he made diligent inquiry as to the state of your affairs. I replied that every thing was going on favourably. On our first interview he offered me board and lodging, for which he demanded forty crowns. I thanked him for so prompt a manifestation of his kindness towards me, but thought it best not to do any thing in a hurry, since a matter of this kind brings with it much inconvenience, if it turn out unfortunately, and on the other hand much comfort, if it turn out well and happily: wherefore I thought it my duty first to call upon Cœlius[4], because my father desired me to board with him, whenever I should visit Basle. He promised to use all his endeavours and exertions in my behalf; but said that he could not receive me into his own family for various reasons, of which the principal was, the meanness of their fare and the extreme high price of provisions. At length, by the intervention of some friends, a man of good character and tolerable learning has received me into his family, with whom I am staying until a suitable lodging shall have been provided for me. However that may turn out, I perceive that I shall be much more uncomfortably situated, as far as diet is concerned, than I was, honoured sir, in your family; but, as you well know, I am content with very little. You have now the state of my affairs: by the blessing of God I am in good health, and all things succeed according to my wish.

When I diligently reflect, most honoured sir, upon the great favours I have received from you, I do not seem to myself that I can ever repay them; but I am relieved by that peculiar and almost divine kindness of yours, by

[3 Oporinus was a celebrated printer at Basle. See above, p. 106, and Zur. Lett. Series II. p. 112, n. 2.]

[4 Cœlius Secundus Curio. See above, p. 89, n. 2.]

whom a grateful mind, and one that is anxious by every means to shew its gratitude, is regarded as equivalent to a rich present: this I pray you, sir, to accept, and be assured that I am most devoted to you. Farewell, most excellent sir, in Christ Jesus. If it be not too much trouble, respectfully salute your wife in my name, with your daughters Alethea and Dorothy, and most worthy sons-in-law masters Lavater and Simler. Again and again, most honoured master, farewell in Christ. In haste, March 1, 1554. Basle.

Your most devoted,

JOHN UTENHOVIUS.

LETTER CCLXXVI.

JOHN UTENHOVIUS TO H. BULLINGER AND P. MARTYR.

Dated at WLADISLAW[1], *June* 23, 1557.

GREETING. That you may have, most excellent sirs, some information respecting our affairs in these parts, you must know that on the 23rd of February last we set off from Cracow to Wilna, (the metropolis of great Lithuania,) to the king[2], and arrived there, by God's blessing, on the 17th of March. We waited upon the king two days after, who, to the surprise of many persons present, received the noble John à Lasco with the greatest kindness. He held out his right hand to each of us; and while à Lasco, as is the custom, wished every happiness both to himself and his kingdom, and congratulated him on the light of evangelical doctrine which had shone forth, under his government, upon the whole kingdom, and openly declared the reason of his return to his own country, and the object he had in view, the king listened to him with kindness and attention, and pre-

[1 Wladislaw is a town in Poland, on the Vistula, 98 miles from Warsaw.]

[2 Sigismund Augustus. Krasinski states, in his sketch of the reformation in Poland, that à Lasco resolved on going to Wilna to confer with the king, but that the journey did not take place, for reasons he is unable to explain. This letter affords decisive evidence to the contrary.]

sently replied from his own mouth, that his return was very gratifying to him. But the vice-chancellor, a churchman forsooth, and laden with innumerable preferments, the coadjutor of the archbishop of Gresna[3], and the anxious expectant, moreover, of the first vacant bishoprick, that he might satisfy his duty and respect to the pope, replied afterwards on the 22nd, in the king's name, and in his presence, saying among other things, that his majesty acknowledged no other light of the gospel, than that which had been acknowledged by his ancestors, and which Poland had now recognised for near six hundred years; and that this was the true doctrine, and that his majesty, after the example of his forefathers, desired to persevere in it. He added, that it was the prerogative of the king alone to invite any persons to reform the churches here, and that consequently he (à Lasco) could not be invited by the nobles of Poland. The king had, before this, made known to master à Lasco by means of the lord palatine of Wilna[4], that the vice-chancellor was very urgent upon the subject, and was preparing a reply to his address; in the course of which reply, he said, there would be two things (meaning those I have just mentioned) at which he might justly take offence, and he recommended him to reply as briefly as possible, lest he (the vice-chancellor) should again begin a new tissue of rejoinder in the name of his majesty himself; for that no advantage could arise to religion from these mutual disputes. He added, moreover, that if master à Lasco wished for any thing himself, he should mention it in private, apart from any witnesses; for that he would grant him a private audience, in which he might freely enter upon any subject whatever. As soon, then, as the vice-chancellor had finished his speech, master à Lasco replied very briefly, (that he might in this respect comply with the king's request, and relying moreover upon the promise of a private conference with him,) that indeed he had not without reason congratulated the king and his kingdom upon this light of evangelical doctrine. Meanwhile, said he,

[3 Gresna was the capital of great Poland, 125 miles from Warsaw.]

[4 Namely, Nicholas Radzivil, grand marshal and chancellor of Lithuania. He caused the scriptures to be translated into the language of Poland, and published at his expense in 1563.]

let his majesty see that he approve himself and his faith to God the Father and to the Lord Christ, before whose judgment-seat he must one day stand, and render an account of his royal administration: that nevertheless he himself would not cease to hope, as he had always hoped hitherto, respecting his majesty, that God would some time or other give him grace seriously to embrace his pure religion, and to bear testimony to it by a public profession; and that this might be the case, he had hitherto implored the great and good God with the most ardent entreaties and prayers, and would continue to do so. He added too, that with respect to its being the prerogative of the king alone to issue invitations to any individuals for the purpose of effecting a reformation in the churches of this country, he, for his part, had always sincerely acknowledged, and still continued to acknowledge with reverence, the royal authority, especially if a general reformation of the whole kingdom were about to be attempted: but that this did not prevent his kinsmen and connections, and any others of the nobility (by reason of their peculiar privileges in this country) from inviting either himself or any one else to assist them, within their respective territories, in the advancement of religion; which was the sole object of those who had invited him, and his own also in complying with this holy summons, whatever their enemies might calumniously assert to the contrary.

Two days after, the king, according to his promise, admitted master à Lasco to a private audience, at which there were many persons present, but not within hearing. In this he rebuked the king for his sin in denying the Lord Christ, as he had done two days before, and also for some other serious offences; placing in his hands a certain excellent treatise (which he had composed at Wilna a short time since) concerning the obligation of a king to destroy idolatry and to promote true religion, and also concerning the subtleties of the popish bishops, and the dangers that await the king and the kingdom itself through their means, unless timely precautions be adopted, and concerning the necessary preparations to be made before the meeting of the diet. The king bore the reproof with composure, but said that he could not at present act otherwise, especially when he was so greatly beset by his adversaries[1]; but that when this Livonian[2] war should be ended, which is now being carried on with very great activity, he would set himself to a serious reformation of the churches, as at the last diet of the kingdom he promised all the orders of the nobility that he would do. And he acknowledged master à Lasco not only as his subject, but as in his service, namely, as secretary, and in the office that he formerly held under his majesty's father, Sigismund, of happy memory. He promised also to protect him against all his calumnious adversaries, and gave him permission, not only to hold meetings of the nobility and ministers at his house, but also to assemble with his brethren in the houses of others as often as he chose, provided only that they met together for the advancement of religion, and not with a view of raising any disturbance. The king likewise afforded to master à Lasco many other tokens of his good-will, which I have not now room to mention; and at length, having given his hand to each of us, he went away.

The palatine, too, of Wilna, a most gracious prince, and endued with various gifts of nature and of the Spirit, and who last year set forth in a public document a most lucid confession of his faith, most courteously entertained us at his own house for a whole month, and assigned an honourable yearly pension to master à Lasco, promising to his daughter, whom he has never seen, but who he requested might be placed in his own family, a thousand Polish florins for her marriage portion, and also a husband from among his own connections; besides which, he honoured master à Lasco with numerous presents, and myself also with some. Now, forasmuch as this prince is greatly attached to you yonder, you will, I think, do very right to dedicate to him some book, by way of interesting his mind in the cause of religion. For you are aware that great men, especially of this

[1 Pope Paul IV. wrote a letter to the king full of the most bitter reproaches for his listening to the conversation of heretics, among whom Nicholas Radzivil, John à Lasco, and Vergerio are expressly mentioned. The substance of this letter is given in Krasinski's Reform. in Poland, I. 289.]

[2 The occasion of this war was the seizure by the Russians of part of the dominions of the archbishop of Riga, cousin to king Sigismund, who thereupon marched towards the frontiers of Livonia with an army of 100,000 men. The Russian army consisted of 300,000 men. After mutual desolations and ravages, Livonia submitted to Poland in 1561.]

kind, who are entangled in such various engagements, require some spurs and excitements to make them run with greater alacrity in the path proposed. He is acquainted with Latin, and his authority in Lithuania is so far superior to that of any other person, that "whosoever," they say, "has seen him, has seen every thing in Lithuania." Nor is there any one who possesses greater influence with the king himself. It would therefore be of great importance to confirm so influential a personage more and more to the church of Christ the Lord.

Moreover, master à Lasco has occasionally preached at Wilna, to their great edification, in the presence of many of the king's household, and with the knowledge and permission of his majesty himself. On our return, too, from Lithuania, as often as opportunity offered, he preached with the view of confirming the brethren both as to other points of faith, and also in the doctrine of the sacrament. But in the mean time, while we were at Wilna, there came thither seven monks of the order of St Basil, from Moscow, which belongs to the Greek church, who had fled thither for the sake of true religion. For there is at this time such a persecution against them, that had they not withdrawn in time, they would have been destroyed long since. Master à Lasco examined, by means of an interpreter, the principal of the brethren, who was an influential character among the people of Moscow, and who seemed to be superior to the others, both in authority, years, and knowledge of scripture; and he answered so readily upon all the chief heads of religion, and also upon the doctrine of the eucharist, that nothing could be better: whereupon we recognised them all as our friends, and owned them as brethren. They informed us that, about the time of their leaving Moscow, about seventy noblemen were imprisoned on account of religion; and that they knew of more than five hundred brethren in Muscovy, who were favourably disposed thereunto. Hence we perceive the admirable power of the Divine Spirit in God's elect. For these persons have not in any way derived their knowledge from our friends (for they do not understand their writings), but from those whom God himself has raised up by his Spirit in Muscovy. The Ruthenians[1] too, members of

[[1] Or Little Russians, as distinguished from the Muscovites, or Great Russians. They are inhabitants of the Russian and Polish Ukraines.]

the Greek faith, who live at Wilna, and have their churches there, cannot endure the sight of these brethren; and, when they first arrived, they severely beat them for their departure from their faith; nor could they have dwelt here in safety by reason of the Ruthenians, had not the lord Palatine of Wilna taken them under his protection. Further, the king has now written to the bishops of his kingdom, who not long ago had met together in a synod, requiring them without further delay to set about the reformation of the churches, and that, not only as to matters of discipline, but also in respect to the worship of God; for, as he has lately intimated to the bishop of Rome, he can no longer delay the reformation of the churches without certain danger to his kingdom. May the Lord God grant him by his Holy Spirit to make a successful progress in it, to the glory of his adorable name!

But that the reformation which the king meditates next winter may be happily brought to pass, it will be necessary, at least, in my opinion, to have some trustworthy leader in the whole business, to superintend the rest, both in modelling the reformation itself by the word of God, and, when it is so modelled, in carrying it into execution. For if every one be at liberty to bring forward his own plans, and, whatever they may be, to obtrude them upon others at his pleasure, there can be no doubt but that the work of reformation will be unattended with success. And again, supposing the very best plans were proposed, they would avail very little towards the well-governing of this church of God, unless there be some man of fidelity, and prudence, and experience in ecclesiastical discipline, to carry them into effect. Wherefore, excellent sirs, it would appear well worth your while, especially in the infant state of this church, if (as your influence here is so great in all quarters, and even with the king himself,) you would commend master à Lasco, with whose fidelity and prudence (not to touch upon his other noble qualities) you are well acquainted, both to his majesty himself and to the palatine of Wilna, in letters sent to them for this express object, as master Philip Melancthon did not long since. For otherwise it is to be feared that the reformation will not go on favourably, or at least the practical working of the reformation, however good it may be in other respects. For it is certain that almost all persons here are novices, upon whom this duty cannot be imposed without most obvious danger to the church.

All other matters you will readily learn from our honoured father and brother, doctor Lismanini[1], whose fortune it is (so to speak) to be compelled by the providence of God to estrange himself for some time from this kingdom, which has hitherto been to him as his own country; and this for no fault of his, for he has deserved every possible favour both from the king himself and from this kingdom; but from the exceeding rage of Satan and the enemies of Christ the Lord, against which the king (such is his weakness) has not entirely been able to contend. Meanwhile he has always expressed, and still continues to express, the greatest kindness towards master Lismanini, whom he wishes at this present time to sojourn with your church yonder, in preference to all the churches in any part of Germany. And it cannot be doubted but that this trial is a proof to master Lismanini of the especial goodness of God, who is wont to manifest his mercy towards his elect by tokens and (as it were) badges of this kind. And since all things work together for good to those that love God, I am persuaded in the Lord that this very banishment, which is otherwise so very distressing to us here, will tend both to his

[1 Lismanini was a native of Corfu, and confessor to queen Bona, by which means he acquired great influence over her son Sigismund, which he employed in endeavouring to convert him to the doctrines of the Reformation. He was sent by the king in 1553 to inquire into the state of religion in Germany and other parts of Europe, and became intimate with Bullinger and the other leading divines of Switzerland. At Geneva he publicly embraced Protestantism, and married; in consequence of which the king, who did not wish publicly to declare his religious opinions, withdrew all intercourse with him, and signed an order prohibiting his entrance into Poland. He was invited by some influential persons to assist at the synod of Pinczow in 1555, and remained for some time concealed at Ivanovitzve. Permission to remain in the country was finally granted to him by the king, at the intercession of Bonar, Castellan of Bietz, and Cruciger, superintendent of the reformed churches of little Poland; but he was never restored to favour. He soon afterwards began to betray antitrinitarian opinions, and was impeached before the synod of Cracow, by whom he was excommunicated, and retired to Konigsberg, where he ended his life by suicide in 1563. See Krasinski, Reform. in Poland, I. 275, &c.]

edification and comfort. Were he to live, as David did, in Mesech or Kedar, namely, among a barbarous people and those who are destitute of all knowledge or fear of God, that kind of life would doubtless be very painful. But the agreeable intercourse of most distinguished brethren, and the most holy assemblies and meetings of most learned and godly men, cannot but most exceedingly delight and comfort him, and render him better qualified for the service of the church of God and of our Lord Jesus Christ. And this circumstance of itself, independent of any other consideration, ought abundantly to comfort us and our brethren in this place under this visitation of our brother.

There was here not long since a person[2] not altogether unknown to you yonder, who secretly endeavoured to create a disturbance in these churches, and who is even now circulating dishonourable reports in Germany respecting master à Lasco, one who in every respect deserved well of him; and this he did likewise some little time ago in the greater Poland, whenever he had an opportunity, that is, among those whom he knew not altogether to agree with us on the doctrine of the sacrament; with the view of preparing the minds of some of the nobles here to receive the confession of Augsburgh. While he was here, however, he conformed himself to us, and asserted and pretended that he entirely agreed with us; insomuch that he drew over into that opinion of him, besides many others, master doctor Lismanini, who is reported upon that occasion to have borne honourable testimony of the man to you at Zurich. I have thought it right, consistently with my fidelity to the church of Christ, to acquaint you with these circumstances, that you may not be imposed upon by statements of this kind, but may rather oppose for the glory of God his calumnies and hypocrisy. You will hear more concerning this man from master Lismanini.

[2 This person appears from a letter of Burcher's dated at Cracow, March 1, 1558, and which will be given in a subsequent part of this volume, to have been Peter Paul Vergerio, of whom Calvin wrote to à Lasco in 1556: Nihil mihi displicuit magis quam te consilia cum Vergerio miscere, cujus hominis vanitatem tibi non fuisse citius cognitam miror; mihi certe quicquid ille aggreditur suspectum est. . . . Non dubito quin jam expertus sis quam parum tibi profuerit ventosa hominis ostentatio.—He is the person alluded to by Jewel as "Peter or Paul" in the first series of Zurich Letters, p. 19, or 2nd Ed. p. 31.]

Farewell, most accomplished sirs, and esteemed masters and brethren in Christ the Lord, to whom I most earnestly commend you and your ministry, that you may bring forth abundant fruit unto life eternal. Amen! Salute, I pray you, most dutifully in the Lord masters Bernardine Ochin, and Conrad Gesner, and commend me to the Lord in your prayers. I will requite you in like manner. Wladislaw, June 23, 1557.

Your most devoted,

JO. UTENHOVIUS.

LETTER CCLXXVII.[1]

WILLIAM PETERSON TO CONRAD PULBERT.

[Without place or date.]

WHEN I was about to write to you, my worthy Conrad, I was so greatly afraid lest, through my lack of knowledge, you would not be able to understand my letter, that I had almost given up the thought of writing at all. When, however, I had duly considered your kindness towards me, and the request you made that I should write to you at least a few words, I could not refrain from doing so, however rude and inelegant my letter may appear. As to the news which you desire of me, I have not any, except that the images, which formerly used to work miracles in England, are now, as I hear, broken in pieces, and the imposture of the priests is made known to every one. And to mention to you one idol and imposture in particular; you must know that there was in England an image[2], which at certain times used to move its mouth and eyes, to weep, and to nod in sign of dissent or assent before the bystanders. These things were managed by the ingenuity of the priests standing out of sight; but the imposture is now notorious to every person in England.

I request of you, my worthy Conrad, that should any letters addressed to me, or any thing else come into your

[1 The original of this letter is preserved in the archives of St Thomas, at Strasburgh. Simler considers it to have been written in 1538.]

[2 For an account of this image, see below, pp. 606, 609.]

hands, you will forward them to me by that merchant, through whom, as you know, I have made provision for my letters to be sent to England; or else by John Butler, who is devoting himself to literature in the house of master Sapidus. I am in doubt whether or not some letters have been forwarded to me, which I have not yet received. Furthermore, I am about to return into my own country: wherefore, if there is any thing that I can do to serve you, let me know, and I will readily perform it to the utmost of my power. Salute, I pray you, in my name, your wife and your maid. And if at any time I have either spoken or acted as I ought not to have done, I pray you pardon me, and remember me in your prayers to the Lord. Salute masters Bucer and Capito most lovingly in my name. I would have written to them, had I possessed so much learning as to be able to write even tolerably; but I leave that duty to you. Farewell in Christ our Lord.

Yours wholly,

WM. PETERSON.

LETTER CCLXXVIII.[3]

JOHN FINCH[4] TO CONRAD HUMPARD.

[Without place or date.]

JOHN FINCH wisheth to his host and singular good friend Conrad health and innocence of life. The grace of God, and of our Lord Jesus Christ, be with all those who preach his gospel in purity and sincerity of faith! Amen.

When I had expressed to you, my kind friend, some time since, my intention of removing from you, and of endeavouring, under God's guidance, to return into my own country, you earnestly and anxiously entreated of me this one thing, that I would in some way inform you of the state of our affairs, both here and in England, so far as we can obtain

[3 The original of this letter is preserved in the archives of St Thomas, at Strasburgh. Simler dates it in 1538.]

[4 Strype mentions a John Finch, of Billericay, among the persons ordained by bishop Ridley in June, 1550. Mem. II. i. 403.]

any true account of them from the merchants and booksellers. Which request indeed though it seemed to me to be hard and difficult to comply with, by reason of my never having been conversant with business of this kind; I have not thought it right, my excellent friend, to decline this service, that this testimonial of our mutual friendship might hereafter be a constant memorial for our common use, so long as we shall be confined in this corruptible body. But whereunto does this far-fetched exordium tend? Certainly to this, namely, that I may be able in some measure to satisfy your inexhaustible thirst for learning, at least by my feeble and unadorned style of writing, when a more rich and elegant style is beyond my power. But not to weary your refined ears any longer with my complaints and puerilities, I will come at once to the subject of your inquiry, and relate to you, as concisely as I can, the existing circumstances of the church in England.

A certain German merchant here, who is well acquainted with the English language, told me as a certain fact, that all the images, which used to work miracles by the artifices of the devil and his angels, that is to say, the monks, friars, fish-eaters, and others of that stamp, were conveyed on horseback to London, at the command of the bishops: that a public sermon was preached from the pulpit of St Paul's to the congregation assembled in Christ; after which a certain image brought away from Kent, and called in English "The rood of grace in Kent," was first exhibited. The preacher, the bishop of Rochester[1], explained all the trickery and imposture in the presence of the people. By means of some person pulling a cord, most artfully contrived and ingeniously inserted at the back, the image rolled about its eyes just like a living creature; and on the pulling of other cords it gave a nod of assent or dissent according to the occasion: it never restored health to any sick person, notwithstanding great numbers afflicted with divers diseases were carried to it, and laid prostrate before it, unless some one disguised himself of set purpose, and pretended to be sick; in which case it would give a nod, as though promising the restoration of health, that it might by this means confirm its imposture. Then again, by some other contrivance unknown to me, it opened

[1 See an account of the exposure of the rood of Boxley, at Paul's Cross, by bishop Hilsey, in Soames, II. 264, and below, p. 609.]

and shut its mouth; and, to make an end of my story at once, after all its tricks had been exposed to the people, it was broken into small pieces, and it was a great delight to any one who could obtain a single fragment, either, as I suppose, to put in the fire in their own houses, or else to keep by them by way of reproof to such kind of impostors. After this, bishop Latimer, in the western part [of St Paul's], carried a small image in his hand, which he threw out of the church, though the inhabitants of the country whence it came constantly affirmed that eight oxen would be unable to remove it from its place. There were, after this, exhibited many other tricks of the same kind, by which the simple were imposed upon by the priests; so that the ignorant people now call them mere conjurors, and despise their contrivances, objecting the deceits they practised against them, as long as the tower of Babel was safe, which, being now undermined, is daily threatening an overthrow.

What must I say more, except to pray you diligently to salute in my name the indefatigable master Bucer, and his colleague master Capito, together with master Sturmius, and my no less esteemed friend, master Bedrot[2]? and you will also dutifully salute in my name your wife, and the wife of master Bucer, together with John and the maid. Here, believe me, you will find nothing else but what Lucian speaks of in his treatise on the proper method of writing history, people "turning their thoughts and imaginations upon whatever may chance to come uppermost[3]." Farewell, and love me as you do, and write to me in return as soon as you have leisure. I write to you and yours, but not to every one, lest they should expose me to ridicule for this unpolished letter. Again farewell.

Your most devoted,

[JOHN] FINCH.

[2 This name occurs in Calvin's Epistles, p. 47. Ed. Genev. 1575.]

[3 'Επινοοῦντες καὶ ἀναπλάττοντες, ὅττι κεν ἐπ' ἀκαιρίμαν γλῶτταν, φασὶν, ἔλθῃ. Lucian, Vol. IV. p. 43. § 32. Ed. Amstelod. 1743.]

LETTER CCLXXIX.

NICOLAS PARTRIDGE[1] TO HENRY BULLINGER.

Dated at FRANKFORT, *April* 12, [1538].

GREETING. I have received, most worthy master, from Froschover your most courteous letter written to myself, together with a parcel, as you call it, of letters and books written to the leading men in our kingdom: by which I easily perceive how greatly you endeavour to make those persons who are now most attached to you still more attached. These bonds indeed have for a long time been too firm to admit the supposition of their being broken in this present life; so far are you from believing that we can ever cease to remember you here. We are not however much pleased with that parenthesis of yours, if indeed it is worthy of being called such; for unless we would be considered as unfeeling and impious, we cannot but regard these your benefits as most highly valuable. For (to say nothing of other infinite benefits) who but an impious man would think it a small matter to be rightly instructed in religion? It would be impiety not to attend to such instructions with one's whole heart, much more so not to take them in good part. What you write besides, you write from the dictates of kindness itself. We can with much greater justice entreat the same thing from you, and your most worthy family; and we also most heartily promise the same, that as long as we live we will be wholly yours, and you may always make use of us in that character. We could scarcely read without tears what you wrote to us concerning your little daughter Elizabeth, so dear both to us and to all your friends: we hope that she has recovered. Salute, I pray you, diligently in our name your most amiable wife and pious mother, together with all your family.

We shall always most willingly comply with your injunctions, that we should send you information at every fair, both

[[1] Nicolas Partridge, of Lenham in Kent, accompanied Rodolph Gualter in a journey from Zurich to England, in the spring of 1537. He was afterwards in the family of Barlow, bishop of St David's, and also in that of the mayor of Dover. He died in 1540. See below, Letters CCLXXXVII. and CCXCIV.]

respecting the state of our kingdom and our own individual circumstances. Our friend Rayner[2] did not come to this fair, by reason, as I understand, of the recent death of his wife. He has written to me, and Froschover will give you the letter, which I would not inclose in this, because I wish it to be first read by masters Butler and Traheron, who are now living at Strasburgh with master Sapidus; and especially by master Grynæus, because he particularly desired that I would send him information both respecting the state of our country and our own affairs, and those of other friends. In the letter that Rayner wrote to me, and also in his letter to Froschover, he mentioned a certain Englishman from whom he wished us to gain full intelligence of every thing; but no such person, as far as we know, has arrived here. A certain German, who belongs to one of the merchant companies residing in London, has told us some marvellous stories respecting some [images of] saints, which were formerly fixed and immoveable at some distance from London; namely, that they have now ridden to London, and performed most wonderful miracles in a numerous assembly. Concerning the bearded crucifix of Kent, called in our language "The Rood of grace near Maidstone[3]," he told us, that while the bishop of Rochester was preaching at Paul's cross to a most crowded congregation of nobility and others, in the presence too of many other famous saints of wood and stone, it turned its head about, rolled its eyes, foamed at the mouth, and poured forth tears down its cheeks. The bishop had before thundered forth against these images; the satellite saints of the Kentish image acted in pretty much the same way. It is expected that the virgin of Walsingham[4], and

[2 Most probably Rayner, or Reginald Wolfe, respecting whom see p. 523, n. 2.]

[3 For an account of this imposture, called by Bale "the gaping rode of Boxley," and which it seems was detected by the brother of Nicolas Partridge, the writer of this letter, see Burnet, I. 390. III. 199. Soames, II. 264. Ellis's Original letters, 3rd series, III. 168. Lambard, Perambulation of Kent. Ed. 1596. p. 228. Hilsey, bishop of Rochester, exposed the lying wonder at St Paul's cross.]

[4 The shrine of "our lady of Walsingham," in Norfolk, was constructed of wood, after the model of the Santa Casa at Nazareth, and founded in 1061. The offerings presented at this shrine were said to have equalled those made to "our lady of Loretto." Henry VIII., in

St Thomas of Canterbury[1], and likewise some other images, will soon perform their miracles in the same place which, of what character they are, you may, I think, judge for yourself. For the trickery of the wicked knaves was so publicly exposed in the image of the crucifix, that every one was indignant against the monks and impostors of that kind, and execrated both the idols and those who worshipped them. God grant that we may really banish all idols from our hearts!

Do you always especially remember us to God in your prayers. My companions, Woodrooffe, Peterson, and Finch, who are all about to accompany me to England, salute you and your family. Salute in my name masters Pellican, and Leo, and Theodore. Make my excuse, if necessary, for not having taken leave of him. I certainly cannot do otherwise than wish him every happiness, who has always deserved so well at my hands. Farewell in the Lord, with all yours. Frankfort, Apr. 12, [1538].

Yours,

NICOLAS PARTRIDGE.

LETTER CCLXXX.

NICOLAS PARTRIDGE TO HENRY BULLINGER.

Dated at FRANKFORT, *Sept.* 17, [1538].

MUCH health. Your information, most honoured master, respecting the state of your church was exceedingly gratifying, as were also the salutations which you wrote word were sent by your excellent wife, and mother, and sweet children. I heartily implore our good and gracious God not only to

the 2nd year of his reign, walked hither barefoot from Barsham, a distance of two miles, to present a valuable necklace to the image.]

[1 For an account of Thomas à Becket, see Burnet, I. 392. Soames, II. 270. His shrine was the richest in England. While no man brought his gift to the altar of his Saviour in Canterbury cathedral throughout a whole year, offerings were made at the shrine of St Thomas à Becket in the same place, and during the same period, to the amount of £964. 12*s.* 3*d.*]

preserve you in safety, but to retain the church in this pure and holy religion.

You shall now hear, in few words, about your book[2] dedicated to the king, and what has been done with the copies sent as presents. No sooner had we touched the soil of our country than we made diligent inquiry concerning the state of the realm; and we have ascertained from persons of good credit, that your influence had been much diminished by reason of that unhappy retractation of yours, I know not what[3]. We therefore addressed first of all the archbishop of Canterbury, who most courteously received the copy sent to himself: we offered him likewise, for civility's sake, and that it might be received more favourably, the book intended for the king: at first he refused, and thought it would be much more advantageous if it were placed in the hands of the lord Crumwell, that he might deliver it to the king; but after supper he asked for the king's book of his own accord, and promised to deliver it into his hands, provided we were present, in case the king should wish to ask us any questions. He then set himself to the continued reading of the book, that he might not seem to recommend to the king any thing of which he himself had no knowledge. He ordered us to come again after two days. We then called upon the lord Crumwell: Eliot put into his hands your book addressed to himself; he received it very kindly, together with the letter, which he read through, notwithstanding he was overwhelmed with business. That evening he went to court, having some business with the king, to whom he doubtless shewed the book he had that day received. As soon as [the archbishop of] Canterbury heard of this, he forthwith sent the king his book, at a time when we could not be present. But that the gift was acceptable to the king, we collect from this circumstance, that

[[2] Bullinger wrote two books in 1538, which he addressed to king Henry VIII., viz. De S. Scripturæ authoritate, certitudine, firmitate, et absoluta Perfectione; and also, De Episcoporum institutione et Functione.]

[[3] This refers no doubt to the conferences held at Basle a little before this time, "quibus omnibus Bullingerus interfuit; plurimumque in eo laboravit, ut firma inter Lutherum et Helveticas ecclesias concordia iniretur: adeo ut quidam eum in suspicionem vocarint, quasi defectionem ad Lutherum moliretur."—Melch. Adam, Vitæ Germanorum Theologorum, p. 483, Francof. 1653.]

his majesty expressed a wish to those around him, that it should be translated into English. The archbishop promised to acquaint you with all these circumstances this fair. But I called upon him five days before I was to leave England, and inquired whether he had anything to send you by me; when he replied, that he had not your letter by him, for that he had left it at his house fifty British miles distant from London, where he is now residing. At the next fair you may expect letters from all.

Our friend Eliot, I suppose, in his letter to you has made mention of the lord Crumwell, of Matravers and the Polsteds: bishop Latimer certainly inquired of me whether we intended to return to those parts; for that he would most gladly write in reply. Nothing, believe me, was ever more gratifying to him in the whole course of his life, than the present you sent him. At that time I could make no decided promise, but I know not whether he has written to you; for when I left England, he was more than two hundred miles from London, where I embarked. Sir Edward Wotton received your book with the greatest satisfaction, and is diligently engaged upon it; and requested, that as he cannot write himself, I would let you know that he is wholly at your service, if he can oblige you in any way.

Religion is making favourable progress among us. By the order of the king, persons are sent to preach the truth in all parts of England. You have, I suppose, heard long since respecting the lady of Walsingham[1], and the breaking in pieces of the other idols. The boiling flames of purgatory are now extinguished among us. There is a great dispute about private masses: for the ambassadors[2] of the duke of Saxony and the Landgrave of Hesse are still residing in London, and are almost every day at the archbishop of Canterbury's palace at Lambeth, engaged in disputations touching religion. They

[1 See above, p 609, n. 4.]

[2 These were Francis Burcard, vice-chancellor to the elector of Saxony, George à Boyneburgh, a nobleman of Hesse, and Frederic Myconius, superintendent of the church of Gotha. They came to England at the invitation of Henry VIII., for the purpose of forming a league against the pope, and of drawing up, by consultation with the English divines, a joint confession of faith. See Cranmer's Remains, (Park. Soc.) p. 377, n. 4, and p. 472, &c.]

promise us very favourably[3], and we cannot but hope very favourably for ourselves. You will learn the remainder of the news from master John Butler. Pardon me, that I cannot now write more.

I have sent you some British cloth, which will make you two pair of hose, one white and the other black; and also six pair of Oxford gloves. You will give one pair to master John Butler, and a pair each to your wife, mother, brother and his wife. I wish it were in my power to gratify you in greater matters; but I know, meanwhile, that you will take these things in good part. Salute, I pray you, your wife most dutifully in my name, your mother, children, brother, master John, in a word your whole family. You will receive also from Froschover the Roman coin, which Michael Drumæus, who has now written to you, made me a present of. I wish you would write back to him at the next fair, and send also a letter to master Richard Tracy, the father of our friend Traheron; for he greatly admires you, and by so doing you may, I hope, be of service to Traheron. I send you, as you see, six little books, not by way of a return for those you sent me, but that meanwhile I might testify my remembrance of you by some trifling present. Farewell and happily. Frankfort, September 17th.

Yours wholly,

NICOLAS PARTRIDGE.

P. S. I wish some one would copy out for me your discourses on St John. I would reward him well and faithfully. I think that in England people use to polish their pewter dishes with Flemish chalk.

[3 The divines are known, from a letter by Myconius, given in Strype, Mem. I. App. No. 95, to have brought the first division of their consultations to a happy issue; having decided on a form for declaring the principal points of Christian doctrine. But this concord was broken when they came to examine into the abuses and corruptions alleged to have crept into the church, and chiefly, the denial of the cup to the laity, private masses, and the prohibition of marriage to the clergy, all which practices the king maintained to be good and lawful. See Jenkyns' Cranmer, I. xxi.; Cranmer's Letters, Park. Soc. Ed. p. 379.]

LETTER CCLXXXI.

NICOLAS PARTRIDGE TO HENRY BULLINGER.

Dated [DOVER], *Feb.* 26, [1540].

I RETURN you many thanks, most courteous and deservedly dear master, for your kindness in writing to me, not only respecting your own state, and that of your friends, but also respecting the condition of your highly favoured church. The whole account was most agreeable and gratifying to me; and I wish that I could give you an equally favourable account of ourselves in return. Not but that we are upon a sufficiently sound footing, but that all things do not as yet succeed according to our wish. I doubt not but that you will obtain every information from the merchants. But since you have sent me such excellent tidings respecting your church, I will also relate some circumstances not perhaps to be despised. There does not exist here a single monk, at least in name. Punishment has lately been inflicted upon three principal abbots[1], who had secreted property to a great extent, and had conspired in different ways for the restoration of popery. Good pastors are freely preaching the truth, nor has any notice been taken of any of them on account of the articles you mention. The king, who is exceedingly merciful, would willingly desire the promotion of the truth; and to this end he has desired certain bishops to consult with respect to the selection of twelve monasteries, where boys might be piously and holily brought up in all kinds of useful learning. But this is all we hear of these things at present. The assembly of the peers, or, as we call it, the parliament, is proclaimed for the 8th of April.

As to myself, I am residing with a most honourable and worthy man, master Antony Ancher, the mayor of Dover, as tutor to his children. He has requested me to salute you very much in his name. I should most willingly have sent

[[1] These were all mitred abbots, namely, Richard Whiting of Glastonbury, Hugh Faringdon of Reading, and John Beach of Colchester, who were attainted in the Parliament of 1539, and executed in the following December. The two former were found to have aided the northern insurgents by large supplies of money and plate: of Beach's case no particulars are known to exist. Whiting, of Glastonbury, was hanged, with two monks of his house, from the battlements of the tower which crowns the hill at that place, called the Tor. Soames, Hist. of Reformation, II. 278; Burnet, I. 384.]

the gloves, had not your letter reached me so long after its time: for what you wrote on the 20th of August I did not receive till the 26th of February. I will send them, however, by the first opportunity. You will receive from me at this fair, by the hands of Rayner, a golden angel, for you to pay the boy Christian, as is proper, for his trouble. I am now expecting the annotations of Bibliander on the Proverbs and on Job: I should like also to have your own commentary on St John's gospel, and also what you are now preaching upon his epistle.

Salute from me your most honourable wife, your dear mother, your sons and daughters; also Rodolph Gualter, to whom I would most willingly write at this present, did time permit. I am surprised, however, at his not having written to me this fair, which indeed no one would easily make me believe, but I should rather conclude that his letter has been intercepted by some mischance. Present to him from me an English crown[2], and also one each to your mother and wife, as a token, if you please, of our old and constant friendship. I return you my best thanks for your most agreeable present, namely, the books sent by Froschover: I am expecting them this fair by Rayner, who will give to Froschover for you a pair of Oxford gloves. This, however, is rather my master's present than mine; for he gave them to me for this purpose a little before I wrote this. Farewell, and may you be happy. February 26.

Yours wholly,

NICOLAS PARTRIDGE.

P. S. Salute also, I pray you, in my name that illustrious assembly of learned men, those venerable elders, masters Pellican and Leo, the most erudite Bibliander, master Megander, master Ammian, master Binder, &c. Once more farewell.

[2 The MS., as copied from the original, has *scolerum*. It is suggested that this may be a mistake for *solarem*, a gold coin called crown *soleil*, or "crown of the sun." And "whereas the crown of the sun was a strange coin, the king, with the advice of his council, thought fit that there should be a piece of gold of his own coin of the like fineness, weight, and goodness as the said crown of the sun, to be called the crown of the rose, and to be current in like manner for four shillings and sixpence." Ruding's Annals of the Coinage of Great Britain, Hen. VIII. an. 1526.—This "crown of the rose" therefore would be the *solaris Anglicus*.]

LETTER CCLXXXII.[1]

ROBERT BARNES[2] TO JOHN ÆPINUS[3].

Dated at LONDON, *May* 21, 1540.

You do me injustice, my Æpinus, when you accuse me of pride. I wrote to you in a familiar way as our friendship warranted, but you misunderstood my feeling. You will learn from the bearer of this letter all the circumstances respecting myself more clearly than I can write them. I have explained every thing to him. Write, I entreat you, to Philip [Melancthon] in my name, as soon as possible, that he come not hither before he receives a letter from me[4]; for I would not have him exposed to danger by reason of any hopes he builds upon me. For I have been deceived myself; only you must desire him not to say a word about me. I will send you a person of reputation, in whom you may place your confidence no less than in myself, and I will entrust him with every thing. A fierce controversy is going on between the bishop of London, Gardiner[5], and myself, respecting justification by faith and purgatory. He holds that the blood of Christ cleanseth only from past sins previous to baptism, but that those committed since are blotted out partly by the merits of Christ, and partly by our own satisfactions. He adds too, that voluntary works are more excellent than the

[1 The original of this letter is printed in Wolf, Conspectus Supellectilis suæ. Ed. 1736, p.10.]

[2 For an account of Dr Barnes, see above, p. 207, n. 2, and the authorities there quoted; to which add Luther's works, Vol. VII. p. 422, Seckendorf, III. 110. Barnes's Works were published by Day, in 1573.]

[3 John Æpinus was chief minister of the church at Hamburgh, whence he had been sent envoy to England in 1534, at the request of Henry VIII., to consult on matters of religion. See Seckendorf, III. 88.]

[4 Luther in like manner dissuaded Melancthon from coming to England. In a letter to the elector he says, "From the king nothing is to be hoped for: his ambassadors at Wittemberg acknowledged his fickleness, and Antony Barnes said that religion and the worship of God were altogether disregarded by him." Seckendorf, III. 210. Barnes, when he was abroad, was known by the name of Antonius Anglicus, and Antonius Amerius.]

[5 For an account of this controversy, see Soames, II. 434, &c.]

works of the ten commandments. As to purgatory, he says, that if a woman shall have caused masses to be celebrated, and shall have bestowed alms for the soul of her husband, she may boldly demand his soul in the day of judgment, and say that she has paid the price of his redemption. But I, on the other hand, in opposition to all these things, vindicate the efficacy of the blood of Jesus Christ my Lord[6]; but hitherto I stand alone in doing it. For although many persons approve my statements, yet no one stands forward except Latimer[7]. You shall hear the result of this controversy. Only write to my masters that they pray for me. Salute the minister of St James's, masters Dethlef[8], Geskinbuge, Abelke, Peter Hesterbergh, Herr Jochim the miller, and others. My circumstances are no better than they were. Farewell. London, May 21. From the house of Thomas Parnell[9], to whom you will forward your letters.

Yours from my heart,

R. B.

LETTER CCLXXXIII.

NICOLAS ELIOT TO HENRY BULLINGER.

Dated *Aug.* 21, 1538.

SINCE our friend Partridge is now coming to you, and will give you much more information than I can convey by

[6 This Dr Barnes abundantly urges in his Supplication to King Henry VIII, where, under "the whole disputation between the Bishops and Doctor Barnes," he shews how "only faith justifieth before God." One short extract will suffice: "Wherefore I conclude of these scriptures, and of these doctors, that the faith that we have in Christ Jesus, *and his blessed blood*, doth only and sufficiently justify us before God without the help of any works." Workes of Doctour Barnes. Lond. 1573, p. 235.]

[7 "Dr Barnes, I hear say, preached in London a very good sermon, with great moderation and temperance of himself. I pray God continue with him; for then I know no one man shall do more good." Latimer to Cromwell, July 15, 1537. See Latimer's Remains, Parker Soc. Ed. pp. 378, 389.]

[8 These names appear to be misspelt. They are transcribed literatim from the original MS.]

[9 Barnes was brought to London on a former occasion, by a serjeant at arms, during the life of cardinal Wolsey, and "lay at Master Parnell's house by the stocks." Foxe, v. 416.]

letter; and since you know him to be a man of perfect integrity, who can neither counterfeit nor play the hypocrite, you will not, I trust, take it unkind, if your friend Eliot does not at this time write to you so fully, as under other circumstances his duty would require. I therefore earnestly beg and entreat you willingly to listen to and diligently to question Partridge, who is now supplying the place and discharging the duty of a letter from me. And as he will give you the true state of almost all our affairs here, this one thing you must know as a most certain truth, that your books[1] are wonderfully well received, not only by our king, but equally so by the lord Crumwell, who is keeper of the king's privy seal, and vicar general of the church of England. You would have received a proof of this from themselves before this time, had not, as far as I can understand, this sole obstacle intervened, that in monarchies, where in a manner only one individual is wont to manage all differences and causes whatsoever, they are of necessity compelled, if not altogether to omit many duties, yet certainly to be very dilatory in performing them. But your writings have obtained for you a reputation and honour among the English, to say nothing of other nations, beyond what could possibly be believed. Wherefore I pray Almighty God long to preserve you in safety, and not to suffer you to lack that spirit, by which you may persevere in writing more, not only for the use and benefit of the English alone, but of his whole church. Amen Farewell.

I return you my best thanks for your exceeding kindness, and favour, and good-will to myself, and for the letter of master Matravers, written to the two Polsteds my kinsmen; by which you have not only brought them to regard you with the greatest kindness and respect, but have also made them, from being my friends, now my greatest friends. I beg you to take in good part these gloves, which I have sent by Partridge, both to yourself, and your most worthy and excellent wife and mother, as a slight present from a poor friend; and moreover salute them together with your whole family very much in the name of Eliot. Again farewell. Aug. 21, 1538.

Yours,

N. ELIOT.

[1 For an account of the reception of Bullinger's books, see above, Lett. CCLXXX. p. 611.]

LETTER CCLXXXIV.

NICOLAS ELIOT TO HENRY BULLINGER.

[Without place or date.]

GREETING. Though I am aware, most honoured master, that I am so indebted to the great and singular kindness you have always manifested towards me, as that I am unable to return it by any offices, exertions, labours, or industry of my own; yet reflecting that there is no greater proof of an ungrateful mind, than not to acknowledge an obligation when one is unable to repay it, I have determined to write you something of a letter, wherein I might testify my feelings towards you, declare my good-will, and, lastly, return you my thanks for your many and great favours: although I am well aware that I owe you far greater thanks, and that I entertain much higher sentiments respecting you than I am able to express in words, however copious or magnificent. Wherefore, if I do not now write to you so much as both my inclination and duty require, pardon, I pray you, my want of utterance, and be persuaded, as I hope you will notwithstanding, that whatever I may be, I am entirely yours. For I call him to witness, who inspects most intimately all the recesses of the human heart, that there is no one whom I regard with greater affection than yourself, no one whom I more look up to, esteem, and admire, and to whom I am more united than yourself; and deservedly so in respect of yourself, the remembrance of whom is now my only consolation; as I consider it no trifling portion of my happiness to have seen you, to have conversed with you, to have lived with you in your own house, and to have had one for a master, who has imbued my mind with such lessons of faith and piety, and taught me by such an example of a life so upright as yours, that I ought to wish for nothing more earnestly than that I may prove myself a worthy scholar of so great and excellent a master: which I will certainly strive to do to the utmost of my power, and diligently endeavour that I may never be wanting in any opportunity of time or place, wherein I may consider myself able to perform the duty of a grateful pupil towards his master. Meanwhile, I do not cease to implore Almighty God in constant prayer, that he may very long preserve you in health and safety, not to myself only, but to his church. For the benefit of which church, with your usual desire to promote the glory of Christ, you would, I know, long since have published not only your commentaries on Isaiah, but also your other lucubrations, had there not stood in the way (excuse me if I speak too freely) that injurious persuasion of your mind, by which, though your writings are universally approved, yet they never satisfy yourself; so that if you do not altogether think lightly of them, yet you allow them much less importance, and think far more humbly of yourself, than their worth and the great and rare qualities bestowed upon you by God justly demand. Not only the church of Zurich, but all other churches which are in Christ, bear witness to the skill, and purity, and simplicity of faith, with which you have expounded the whole bible, and especially the epistles of St Paul. And how great weight all persons attribute to your commentaries, how greedily they embrace and admire them, (to pass over numberless other arguments,) the booksellers are most ample witnesses, whom by the sale of your writings alone, from being more destitute than Irus and Codrus, you see suddenly become almost as rich as Crœsus. May God therefore give you the disposition to publish all your writings as speedily as possible, whereby you will not only fill the coffers of the booksellers, but will gain over very many souls to Christ, and adorn his church with most precious jewels. Thus far upon this subject.

I would here let you know how very gratifying was your letter, and with how great kindness we were every where treated for your sake, and what moreover is the present state of our affairs, were I not aware that my companions have long since done this by their letters, so that there is no occasion for me to repeat it. We have certainly every where experienced your kindness, so that we cannot say that we have only had you present with us at Zurich. In short we are living in prosperity, and this among excellent men, studious of godliness, and great admirers of you. Farewell.

I should ask you to receive with kindness this my hurried letter, did I not know you, as I am constantly declaring you, to be the kindest person alive. I pray and entreat you therefore most earnestly to salute very dutifully in my name those illustrious persons, masters Theodore Bibliander, Leo Judæ, Pellican, Batt, Binder, and the other godly men; and let them not regard my not having now written to them as arising either from forgetfulness of their kindness, or of my own duty; but they must ascribe it partly to that excessive difficulty in writing, by which I find myself involved in more than labyrinthine entanglements, and partly to the hasty departure of the bearer. For there is nothing which I would not most willingly do to gratify those, to serve whom is receiving the greatest kindness for one's self. I love them heartily, as they deserve, and wish them every good, and am daily speaking well of them, and sounding their praises, as I do not cease to do also respecting yourself. Once more farewell. Salute for me, I pray, your very dear brother. Our most courteous host, and your great admirer, master Antony Honorius, president of the college at Ripen[1], salutes you much. Now for the third time farewell.

LETTER CCLXXXV.

JOHN BUTLER[2] AND B. TRAHERON TO JOHN CALVIN.

[About 1537.]

We wish you the true joy in Christ. May as much happiness be appointed to us from henceforth, as our going away from you has occasioned us sorrow! For although our absence, as we hope, will not be of very long continuance, yet we cannot but grieve at being deprived even for a few hours of so much suavity of disposition and delightful conversation. And this also distresses us in no small measure, lest there should be any persons who may regard us as resembling flies, which swarm every where in the summer, but dis-

[1 Ripen is a seaport of Denmark, in N. Jutland, about 68 miles from Sleswick.]

[2 John Butler was of a noble family, and lived abroad in great state and plenty: having travelled about Germany, and thence into France, and afterwards into Italy, he seated himself at last in Zurich. Strype, Mem. I. i. 545.]

appear on the approach of winter. You may be assured that, if we had been able to assist you in any way, no pleasure should have called us away from you, nor should any peril have withdrawn us. This distress[1] indeed, which the disordered tempers of certain individuals have brought upon you, is far beyond our power to alleviate. But you have one, Christ Jesus, who can easily dispel by the beams of his consolation whatever cloud may arise upon your mind. He will restore to you a joyful tranquillity; he will scatter and put to flight your enemies; he will make you gloriously to triumph over your conquered adversaries; and we will entreat him, as earnestly as we can, to do this as speedily as possible. We have written these few lines at present, most amiable and most learned master Calvin, that you may receive a memorial of our regard towards you. Salute in our names that individual of a truly heroic spirit, and singular learning and godliness, master Farel[2]. Salute too our sincere friends master Olivetan[3], and your brother Fontaine[4]. Our countrymen send abundant salutations. Farewell, very dear friend.

JOHN BUTLER,

BARTHOL. TRAHERON.

[1 The contentions of Calvin and Farel with the anabaptists, in March 1537, and the charge of Arianism and other heresies brought against them by Peter Caroli, and others, are most probably referred to. Ruchat gives many particulars relative to the disputes which caused these anxieties. Hist. de la Reformation de la Suisse, Liv. xv. xvi.]

[2 William Farel was invited to Geneva in 1534, by the inhabitants, who had then renounced Popery; and he was the great means of fixing Calvin at Geneva in 1536. They were both banished thence in 1538. Farel retired to Neuchâtel, where he died in 1565. Calvin returned to Geneva 13th Sept. 1541.]

[3 Peter Robert Olivetan was a relative of Calvin, and like him a native of Noyon. He was banished from Geneva in 1533, and published at Neuchâtel, in 1535, a French translation of the Bible. Poison was administered to him at Rome, of which he died at Ferrara in 1538.]

[4 Nicolas de la Fontaine was a student of divinity, a near connection of Calvin, and put forward by him as the prosecutor of Servetus.]

LETTER CCLXXXVI.

JOHN BUTLER, NICOLAS PARTRIDGE, NICOLAS ELIOT, AND BARTHOLOMEW TRAHERON TO HENRY BULLINGER.

[Without place or date.]

HEALTH in the Lord! Had we any thing else in our power, we should be ashamed to offer our thanks, and nothing but thanks, since your numerous and ample favours towards us demand the performance on our part of whatever we can promise in words. But since our ability is far more limited than our wishes, we are doing as others do for fear of doing nothing, although perhaps with greater sincerity; namely, we desire to thank you to the uttermost of our power for the singular kindness you manifested towards us both at other times, and especially on our departure. We had a very pleasant journey to Berne, except only that the absence of one so dear to us as yourself sometimes distressed our minds. The friends to whom you so kindly gave us letters of recommendation entertained us with more than common courtesy. A great part of this their kindness we place to your account, who did not think it enough to treat us courteously yourself, without causing the same conduct to be manifested by others. We acknowledge the extent of your kindness, and confess ourselves therefore to be entirely yours, as long as we can be our own. We have here no means of repaying our obligations. All that we have in England consider to be yours as much as any thing that belongs to you. We hope you will not think it a trouble to salute diligently in our name master Leo Judæ[5], master Pellican, and that chief ornament of Switzerland, yea, rather of the whole world, Theodore Bibliander; the kindness of all of whom, as well as their rare learning, we regard with such veneration as that we never can forget them. Farewell, master Bullinger, who are, on so many accounts, so dear to us.

JOHN BUTLER,
NICOLAS PARTRIDGE,
NICOLAS ELIOT,
BARTHOLOMEW TRAHERON.

[5 Leo Judæ was for eighteen years a minister at Zurich. His translation of the Hebrew scriptures, suspended by his death in 1542, was completed by Theodore Bibliander, and revised and printed by Conrad Pellican.]

LETTER CCLXXXVII.

JOHN BUTLER AND OTHERS TO CONRAD PELLICAN AND OTHERS.

Dated at LONDON, *March* 8, [1539.]

To the most excellent and learned men, and their revered masters in Christ, Conrad Pellican, Leo Judæ, Henry Bullinger, and Theodore Bibliander; John Butler, Nicolas Eliot, Nicolas Partridge, and Bartholomew Traheron wish salvation through Jesus Christ.

One cause, most accomplished sirs, of our unitedly addressing you in the same letter, is that we have all of us assembled together at London; but our chief motive is, that you may know us to be so joined together in one mind and one sentiment, that out of many is made as it were one man. And the reasons which have impelled us to write are these; that we might assure you of our retaining a suitable remembrance of your extraordinary kindness, and inform you at the same time both of our own situation as individuals, and of the general condition of this realm. But neither the magnitude of the subject, nor your own courtesy will permit us to use many words in returning our thanks for your singular good offices towards us. Let it suffice to assure you that we will return your kindness, should you ever be in a condition to require it, as far as may lie in our power.

We pass on then to the state of this our kingdom, which is as follows: the ceremonies are still tolerated, but explanations of them are added; so that now the holy water, as it is called, is for no other purpose than to refresh our minds with the remembrance of the sprinkling of the blood of Christ; the bread signifies the breaking of the body of the same; the *pax*, which is wont to be carried about, sets before our eyes the reconciliation of God and man. These things are retained for the sake of preventing any disturbances, and are ordered to be kept up until the king himself shall either remove or alter them. Nothing has yet been settled respecting the marriage of the clergy, although some persons have very freely preached before the king upon this subject. The mass is not asserted to be a sacrifice for the living and the dead, but only a representation of Christ's passion. All images that are objects of worship are removed. We doubt not but that you have heard that the principal supporters of popery among us have been cut off, namely, the marquis of Exeter[1], Montague, earl of Salisbury[2], and that very brave but very profligate man, sir Edward Nevill[3]. Not long since, too, Nicolas Carew[4], who had been the king's master of the horse, was brought to punishment. As he was being led to execution by the king's order, he exhorted all persons to a diligent study of the evangelical books; for that he himself had arrived at so shameful a death by reason of the hatred that he formerly bore to the gospel, as he had been notoriously addicted to the popish religion.

There is a report that we are to have war with the French, the Italians, the Spaniards, and the Scots at one and the same time. When the secret machinations of the persons above mentioned were reported to the king, he said that he should not sleep at all the worse for it; and on the day after he declared to his privy councillors, that he now found himself moved in his conscience to promote the word of God more than he had ever done before. The pope has not only

[1 Henry Courtenay, 17th earl of Devon, was the king's cousin-german, as being son of Catharine, daughter of Edward the 4th. He was created Marquis of Exeter, June 18, 1525; attainted and beheaded, with the other persons mentioned in the text, for having entered into Cardinal Pole's conspiracy, 1538; for an account of which see Burnet, Reformation, I. 575, &c.]

[2 Henry de la Pole, Lord Montacute, or Montague, was the son of Sir Richard Pole, by Margaret Plantagenet, daughter of George, Duke of Clarence, who was created countess of Salisbury, 14 Oct. 1513, whence her son was called earl of Salisbury, as in the text. He was executed on Tower Hill, Jan. 9. 1539. Stow's Ann. p. 575.]

[3 Sir Edward Nevill, brother to the lord Abergavenny. See Cranmer's Remains. Parker Soc. Ed. p. 386, n. 3.]

[4 Sir Nicolas Carew had been master of the horse and a knight of the garter. "He was arraigned for being an adherent of the marquis of Exeter, and for having spoken of his attainder as unjust and cruel: he was also attainted and executed upon the 3rd of March. When he was brought to the scaffold, he openly acknowledged the errors and superstition in which he had formerly lived, and blessed God for his imprisonment; for he then began to relish the life and sweetness of God's holy word, which was brought him by his keeper, one Phillips, who followed the Reformation, and had formerly suffered for it." Burnet, Ref. I. 577.]

procured the burning of three English merchants in Spain, but has granted remission of sins to any one soever who shall kill an English heretic. You will entreat God on our behalf not to suffer these madmen to trample on his servants. We have a king of a noble and magnificent spirit, and skilled in military affairs even to a miracle. We have too a people, as we hope, sufficiently obedient to their sovereign, now that the heads of the rebellion are, as you know, taken off. With the help of your prayers we doubt not but that all will be well.

You shall now hear somewhat concerning ourselves. John Butler would have come to you, had he not been restrained by these warlike tidings. The same cause has kept Nicolas Partridge from the Frankfort fair. The former indeed, if he wished, might have an honourable post about the king; but smitten with the love of the muses, he seems to have an abhorrence of a courtier's life. Nicolas Eliot is studying our municipal law, and is in no small degree aided therein by the munificence of the king. Bartholomew Traheron is in the service of the lord Crumwell, and Nicolas Partridge in that of the pious bishop of St David's in Wales. He will be one of the readers in divinity till better provision can be made for him. We are all of us as yet unmarried. So much for our individual circumstances. The archbishop of Canterbury has promised to write to you, most excellent Bullinger. He is now wholly employed in instructing the people, and in composing some discourses in English, which our clergy are to use instead of those Latin ones which they have hitherto prated in their churches like so many parrots.

The letter of our friend Bibliander has been delivered to the bishop of Worcester, who will, we think, send him an answer. Take, most learned sirs, in good part this unpremeditated statement, and fare ye well. Salute very much in our name your wives and all our friends. March 8, 1539. London.

JOHN BUTLER, wholly yours.
NICOLAS ELIOT, yours.
NICOLAS PARTRIDGE, yours.
BARTHOLOMEW TRAHERON, yours to command.

LETTER CCLXXXVIII.

JOHN BUTLER TO HENRY BULLINGER.

Dated [BASLE], *Feb.* 24, 1540.

PEACE and all blessing through Jesus Christ! On the 12th of January I received letters from our English brethren, Richard Hilles and Peterson, the purport and substance of which I purpose to lay before you in this present writing, inasmuch as it seems necessary for you to be acquainted with them. And, not to weary you with a lengthened letter, I will endeavour to explain every thing in few words. The state and condition of that kingdom is much more sound and healthy since the marriage of the queen[1], than it was before. She is an excellent woman, and one who fears God: great hopes are entertained of a very extensive propagation of the gospel by her influence. There is now no persecution, except of the victuallers, of which sect a certain impostor of the name of Wattis, formerly of the order of wry-necked cattle, is now holding forth (O shame!) in the stocks in Canterbury bridewell, after having been accustomed to mouth it elsewhere in opposition to the gospel. Alas! for the changeable nature of all things; for, as the preacher saith, there is nothing lasting under the sun.

Meanwhile, the word is powerfully preached by an individual named Barnes[2], and his fellow-ministers. Books of every kind may safely be exposed to sale; which fact is so important to my excellent friend Froschover, that I have thought it right to make him acquainted with it. More than all this, wonderful to relate, the monasteries are every one of them destroyed, or else will be before Shrovetide[3]; of the most opulent of which, namely, Glastonbury[4] and Reading, the two abbots have been condemned for treason, and quartered; and each of them is now rotting on a gibbet near the gates of the abbeys over which they respectively presided.

[1 The king's marriage with Ann of Cleves took place Jan. 6, 1540.]

[2 See above, p. 616, n. 2, and the authorities there quoted.]

[3 Lat. Carnisprivium. See Du Cange.]

[4 The revenue of the abbot of Glastonbury was estimated at £3508, and that of the abbot of Reading at £2116. Burnet, I. 384. See above, p. 614, n. 1.]

A worthy recompence for their imposture! I have now performed my promise. Further, these good men[1] affectionately salute you: one of them, as he has pledged himself to me by letter, will ere long be with you in person as a living epistle, for the sake of carrying away the bows for which he bargained with Schentzius and others at Glaris last year. I pray you therefore, most esteemed master Bullinger, for his sake, to make such arrangements with those men, that Peterson may not come to no purpose. Lastly, I entreat you, by the Lord Christ, to have compassion upon this exiled and destitute Scotsman, who is the bearer of a commendatory letter to you; and, if I do not seem to ask any thing improper, to promote and befriend his purpose and cause. I will manage, God willing, by means of the father of the family, the things that you ask of me in your letter. Farewell in the Lord Jesus, and may he preserve you and all your family in safety as long as possible. Dated February 24. Salute, I pray you, in the Lord, all your fellow-ministers.

Yours heartily,

J. BUTLER.

LETTER CCLXXXIX.

JOHN BUTLER TO HENRY BULLINGER.

Dated at BASLE, *March* 29, 1540.

A LETTER from Peterson, written in England on the 31st of January, was brought to me at Basle on the 24th of February. It contained no news whatever. The kingdom continues in the same condition that I described to you in my last letter: there is however great hope that it will ere long be in a much more healthy state; and this every good man is striving for in persevering prayer to God. As to other matters, I will not now mention the loss incurred by W. Peterson in the purchase of his wood; which, God willing, he will soon explain far more clearly when he sees you. But it is chiefly owing to his own fault, for not having taken better

[[1] Richard Hilles and Peterson.]

care to procure sound wood, when he first made his bargain at Glaris. Before he left this place, I told him plainly, upon the very first sight of his bow-staves, that when he arrived in England, he would repent of having undertaken a journey for the purchase of wood of that kind. And I was too true a prophet, for which, upon his account, I am very sorry. But no one must think me for this reason to possess any peculiar sagacity; for the very material of the bows gave the clearest intimation of such a loss before he left Basle. For, whereas each bow-stave ought to be three fingers thick, and squared, and seven feet long, and to be got up well polished, without any knots, scarcely one of them answered to this pattern and description. He therefore most earnestly entreats you, in his letter to me, that you would be kind enough to acquaint those individuals with the damage he has sustained, that they may try all the pieces by the pattern I have just described, (though I am afraid the warning will come too late,) lest he should lose his labour and money a second time as he did before. Do you therefore, I pray you, act in this business according as your kindness towards him shall dictate. Farewell most happily in the Lord! Moreover, salute for me, I entreat you, your amiable wife and all your family. Basle. About 11 o'clock at night, March 29, 1540.

Yours from the bottom of my heart,

JOHN BUTLER.

I have not yet learned whether you have received the Roman coins.

LETTER CCXC.

JOHN BUTLER TO HENRY BULLINGER.

Dated at BASLE, *April* 4, [1540].

PEACE and a tranquil conscience through Christ! Your friends Nicolas Partridge, Bartholomew Traheron, and William Peterson, not so successful as a merchant as he is exemplary as a Christian, salute your reverence, most worthy sir, very earnestly in the letters which I have received from them this last fair by my very excellent friend Froschover; and they return you their warmest thanks for the favours which you have conferred upon them. I have not forwarded to you their letters, because they are written in English: I should otherwise have certainly done so, and most willingly; not so much that you might ascertain for yourself from their own writing what they require, and other things, which for their sakes, unless I would be esteemed most ungrateful, it is necessary for me to mention to you; as that I might disburden myself of the labour of writing, which, to speak candidly, is my greatest plague. I will therefore, if I can, acquaint you in few words with the substance of each of their letters. That of Partridge states that he has sent you, by Reyner, an English piece of money called an angel; but that honest man had given some other money to Froschover, (for what reason I cannot tell,) which I received from him, that he might comply with the wish of Partridge, and gave him in exchange for the German coin an angel, which I happened to have by me: he earnestly entreats you to satisfy, with this money, your scholar Christian for the writings which he presented him with. He expresses a wish, too, that, if it can be done, the lucubrations of master Theodore upon the Proverbs and Job may be forwarded to him by the same person: he states that Christian undertook to do this. Your present, the works of master Zuinglius, of revered memory, upon the four gospels, has not yet reached him; but he is expecting it from Reyner when he arrives. He will send you the Oxford gloves at the earliest opportunity, for he has not yet had it in his power either to write or to ride over thither to procure them, (as your letter was delivered rather late,) he being so intent upon his employment of instructing the children of a gentleman in Kent[1]. As to news, since he writes nothing but uncertain rumours, I shall omit all mention of it, until I see the event. Peterson, whom I expect to arrive about Whitsuntide, will certainly, by God's guidance, give us every information in person. He earnestly requests you in the mean time to charge Schentzius to thoroughly polish and ornament the bow-staves: he must make each of them square, as far as he can, and at least three

[1 This was master Ancher, the mayor of Dover, as appears by a letter of Partridge himself, given above, p. 614.]

fingers wide in every part. He must observe the length of that which he left with him for a pattern.

Bartholomew [Traheron] describes [in his letter] a sermon of the crafty bishop of Winchester[2], which I have sent by Froschover to my preceptor, master Theodore [Bibliander].

Master Grynæus sends the inclosed piece of money as a present to your excellent wife, whom I entreat you to salute in my name, together with her mother and the whole family. Salute, I pray you, most diligently in my name my host master Pellican, together with all your colleagues. Farewell happily in the Lord at all times, and pray him, I entreat you, to have mercy upon me. Basle. Apr. 4.

Yours entirely,

J. BUTLER.

LETTER CCXCI.

JOHN BUTLER TO HENRY BULLINGER.

[Probably in *May*, 1540.]

PEACE and a quiet conscience in Christ! I am in daily expectation of the arrival of Peterson; for in his letter, dated in the month of March, he fully determined to be here about Whitsuntide. Should he not come, it is certain that he has been apprehended in his journey through France. I hope better things, relying upon the mercy of God. But should it be the case, we English, God permitting, will take care that Schentzius shall not suffer any great loss; unless indeed I should be deprived at the same time of all that I possess in England. In that case my service will be of little avail[3], but he will, I doubt not, be aided by other good men. I am writing in this strain, because England is now in a most disturbed state. But I will not write about this, as I am persuaded that Peterson will shortly tell you every thing from his own mouth. Besides, want of time will not now permit

[2 Stephen Gardiner.]

[3 *Ficulnum erit præsidium.* A proverbial expression, taken from the unserviceable nature of the wood of the fig-tree.]

me to write more upon this subject. But you may easily imagine, most excellent Bullinger, according to your discretion, the rest of our misfortunes from this, that three[1] of our best ministers are confined in the prison which they call the castle, or, if you choose, the Tower of London. I shall, moreover, proceed straight to Frankfort for the sake of comforting some brethren who are voluntary exiles from England. As soon as I return, you shall know more, if the Lord will. Farewell most happily in Christ, together with your wife and all your family. Salute, I pray you, all your colleagues in my name in the Lord. Again farewell.

Yours heartily,

J. BUTLER.

P. S. Pray the Lord, I beseech you, that he will deign to pity our condition.

LETTER CCXCII.

JOHN BUTLER TO HENRY BULLINGER.

Dated at BASLE, *Nov.* 10, 1542.

PEACE and every blessing from God our Father through Jesus Christ our Lord!

Our brother, J. Burcher, has lately written a letter in common to my brother Richard Hilles and myself, in which he mentioned your kindness to him, namely, in your active exertions, my very dear master Bullinger, with the magistrates of Zurich, to second his endeavours to procure wood for making bows. He told us that this kind of wood is produced in great abundance in a certain wood belonging to the authorities of Zurich; from whom, relying on the aid of your good offices, he hoped to obtain a licence for selecting trees suited to his purpose. In the first place therefore, most loving master Bullinger, we return you our lasting thanks for this your kindness and active exertions in behalf of our countryman. Furthermore we pray and entreat you in the

[1 Namely, Barnes, Garrard, and Jerome, respecting whom see above, p. 207, n. 2, and the authorities there quoted.]

Lord to continue to help him as you have begun. He seems to be an honest and godly youth, and one who, for the sake of our religion, is extremely attached to yourself. Wherefore we have no doubt but that you would have been ready to serve him of your own accord, even though we had not written to you upon this subject on his behalf. Which indeed we have done more with a view of awakening your remembrance of him amidst the laborious occupations by which we are well aware that from the nature of your office you are constantly overwhelmed, than because we had any doubt of your readiness to notice him of your own free will, whenever your engagements should afford you an opportunity. We will desist therefore from addressing you more at length upon this subject. What need is there of many words? or by what means can we requite your good offices, and those of your colleagues, conferred upon us recently when we were at Zurich? Truly we cannot tell; unless we may seem to have satisfied our obligation in this respect, that our inclination is always ready, and there will be afforded us, God willing, the ability, such as it may be, of requiting your kindness. We request you therefore to return especial thanks to your coadjutors in the name of us all, namely, to masters Megander, Pellican, Erasmus, and all the rest. Further, my brother's wife affectionately salutes all your wives. She also returns her thanks for your wife's letter so kindly written to her in German, and says that she will answer it in the same language as soon as she conveniently can.

You perhaps wish to be informed as well of the disturbances in Germany as of those in England. Every one is aware that the affairs of Germany are distracted on every side by their too great fear of war, far too great indeed, as all persons allow, for the well-being of the state. Nor do I suppose you are ignorant that almost the whole duchy of Juliers[2] (sad to relate) has been ravaged and desolated with fire and plunder by the imperial forces. In Hungary too a standard-

[[2] Because the duke of Longueville and Martin Van Rossem had raised an army in the territories of the duke of Cleve, the imperialists under the command of the prince of Orange invade the country of Juliers, put all to fire and sword, and upon composition take Duren, the chief town in these parts. Sleidan, xv. 303.]

bearer of Strasburgh with his soldiers, and another officer said to be of Ulm, were entirely cut to pieces at the siege of Pest, by which slaughter the rest are said to have been thrown into such consternation that they were compelled to retreat.

The English, moreover, (by what spirit they are actuated I leave you to determine) have proclaimed a deadly war[1] with Scotland, unless she will agree to these conditions of peace, namely, to banish the pope from the kingdom, to raze the monasteries, and to prohibit the worship of saints: all of which things, the monasteries excepted, this Proteus obstinately retains in his own kingdom with more than tyrannical cruelty. In fine, there will be peace with Scotland, if she accept our terms: if not, a terrible war is before us, with the soldiers in arms thirsting for blood. There are, including the forces both by land and sea, a hundred and twenty thousand of English and Irish troops.

As to my own affairs, if you wish to know them, they are in this state. My brother and his wife are both well, and as to myself, to speak candidly, I am much better than I deserve; but I have now for fourteen months been suffering severely enough (unless God deem otherwise) from a quartan fever, to the great detriment of my property. But I have now been recommended by some persons to change the climate; for the air of Strasburgh is very prejudicial to me this winter, by reason of its humidity: reason dictates to me the same thing, forasmuch as a paroxysm does me more mischief there than any where else. On this account I have determined, by God's blessing, to winter at Basle; where if I can be of use to you in any way, you will, I hope, always find me entirely at your service.

I pray you, my good friend, dutifully to salute in my name master Theodore Bibliander, my gossip and preceptor; and I desire my salutations to your wife and all your family.

[[1] The cause of this war is said to have been the offence taken by Henry VIII. at the king of Scotland's refusal to meet him at York. He sent 20,000 men into Scotland, under the command of the duke of Norfolk, who entered the country on the 21st of October, and on the 24th of November was fought the battle of Solway Moss. See Burnet, I. 513; Soames, II. 510, &c. and above, p. 239, n. 1.]

Farewell, and may Christ very long preserve you to us for the advancement of his glory. Basle, Nov. 10, 1542.

Your most devoted,

J. BUTLER, *Anglus*.

LETTER CCXCIII.

JOHN BUTLER TO THOMAS BLAURER[2].

Dated *Feb.* 16, 1550.

GREETING. Although I doubt not, most excellent sir, that you can obtain far more accurate information as to the affairs of England from others than from myself, yet from my ancient regard for you, as well as your good-will towards me, I would not be wanting in this duty, nor omit to represent to you in few words the accounts I have myself received from that country. Receive them therefore as follows. John Hooper, that individual who was so long engaged in the study of divinity at Zurich, and who resided at my house during our most wretched calamity at Constance[3], has lately written to me. The affairs of pure religion are now, through the mercy of God, in a more favourable position, considering the state of infancy and rudeness of our nation. Baptism, for instance, and the Lord's supper are celebrated with sufficient propriety, only that some blemishes in respect to certain ceremonies, such for instance as the splendour of the vestments, have not yet been done away with. The psalms, hymns, and collects, in fine, whatever is done in the churches, is said and sung in our own language. Our friend Hooper (as I learn from another quarter) is lecturing in theology at London twice a day, (for he is a public professor there, though in our own tongue) with the entire approbation of all good men. Besides this he frequently preaches both at court

[2 The original of this letter is preserved in the city library at St Gall.—The date of the place appears to be *Vitoduri*.]

[3 See above, p. 385, n. 4. Thomas Blaurer was probably a son of Ambrose Blaurer, the chief minister of Constance, respecting whom see above, p. 392, n. 1.]

and in other places all over London. He has for some time been lecturing upon the Psalms at the king's palace. Very many of the aldermen of London, who were veteran papists, have embraced Christ. In a word, the truth is especially flourishing in London beyond all other parts of the kingdom. In other places too the harvest is great, but faithful labourers are few; though of hirelings and idlers (as is generally the case) there are more than enough. The late protector too of the kingdom, through the innate compassion of the king towards him, when in the judgment of all persons it was thought he would be beheaded, is by the providence of God released[1] from prison, and not only has his life given him, but is also restored to the greatest portion of his estates, with the condition however of being deprived in future of any share in the government. He lives as a private individual, and chiefly upon his own estates; for even now twenty thousand crowns of yearly income are allowed him, and formerly he had very much more.

It remains for me, most excellent sir, to remind you touching the payment, at the day appointed (namely, the first of March next ensuing), of the money you borrowed from me; which nevertheless, so God love me, I do most unwillingly. But I am now so circumstanced that I cannot any longer do without it: for I am desirous of purchasing a small estate; in which event (which I expect will shortly take place) I shall have occasion for five hundred florins from whatever source I can procure them. I therefore entreat you with all the earnestness in my power, not to disappoint my expectation in this matter. Farewell, and be always valiant in Christ. My wife desires to salute you and your wife, together with your family. A long farewell. Feb. 16, 1550.

Yours wholly,

J. BUTLER.

[[1] See above, p. 77, and 464, n. 1.]

LETTER CCXCIV.

JOHN BURCHER TO RODOLPH GUALTER.

Dated at BASLE, about 1540.

HEALTH in Jesus Christ! Did I not know, my very dear friend Gualter, your exceeding good sense and sobriety of character, I should endeavour at some length to skake off this grief under which you are suffering from the death of your friend Partridge, and altogether to restore you to yourself. But since to offer comfort to one who by reason of his singular strength of mind is well able to be his own comforter, will seem obtrusive and presumptuous; omitting all other considerations, I shall content myself with this single observation, that in a world so corrupt and uncertain it is a far happier thing to die with honour than to survive with shame. For how can it be otherwise than shameful to worship wood and stone, and to count a piece of bread for a God? But this, you will say, was not the case with Partridge. I allow it: and lest at any time he should have acted thus by compulsion and against his inclination, God has prevented him by an early death. Being taken away therefore, he is now living happily and everlastingly, that he might not be forced to experience the extreme malice of his family, and to witness the just retribution that would come upon them on account of this malice. There is reason therefore for you to rejoice.

But you will say, How can I rejoice when I am deprived of the society of so dear a friend? I know indeed that many friends like him are not easily to be met with. And yet, what if you should take to yourself Burcher to supply his place, to whom you have never been less dear than you were to Partridge? True, the like intimacy has not yet existed between you and him; but yet his regard for you may admit of a comparison with that of the other. Come then, my Gualter, and let us strive each of us in the duties of friendship to excel the other. Friendship is a bond; and the various duties of life, united with kindness, diligence, and love, most firmly bind this bond and hold it together. You have done me no small service in making your mother, as it were, a mother to myself; and in providing a father for me (I speak of Myconius and his wife) in the place of my own; to say nothing meanwhile of your most agreeable manners, in which you far excel all the Germans whom I have ever seen. I have no means of recompensing you for so many distinguished marks of your regard, except by endeavouring not to shew myself ungrateful by being silent respecting them. But should you under any circumstances require my services, you shall not find me ungrateful. Do you then, shaking off all sadness, as far as you possibly can, be thinking about new friendships; and, that you may no longer be kept in suspense as to where I am, I have now for some months left Strasburgh, and been living with Myconius (at Basle), where, on my return, I first lived with Oporinus, and afterwards with Michael Falcon, as they call him.

Yours,

BURCHER, *Anglus.*

Salute all your friends in my name, especially Haller.

LETTER CCXCV.

JOHN BURCHER TO HENRY BULLINGER.

Dated at STRASBURGH, *Dec.* 31, 1546.

HEALTH in Christ Jesus! After so great a change has taken place in our prosperous condition, I cannot refrain, my very dear friend and master, Bullinger, from communicating to you the evils that are impending over the church in Germany. A messenger of the king of England has this day arrived at Strasburgh, having yesterday left the camp of the emperor, and the emperor himself at Heilbrunnen, in the territory of Wirtemberg. He brings word that the emperor is exceedingly elated with his success[1], and more than usually cheerful. For having heard those persons who had voluntarily surrendered call themselves rebels, he said, "Though you are rebels, yet I will nevertheless shew you how merciful I am." These were the words of the emperor to the magistracy of some city who had surrendered themselves. He added more-

[[1] Namely, the surrender of Bopfingen, Norlingen, Rotenberg, and other cities. Sleidan, XVIII. 412.]

over, that he said not a word about religion, and that he only imposed upon them a pecuniary fine. This was no doubt his policy, that he might not appear inconsistent with himself. But if he should be allowed to bring the whole of Germany into subjection, he will assuredly shew how subtle he is. Besides, the dread of him has overspread the whole territory round Strasburgh, nor is this city in expectation of any thing but a blockade. The count de Buren too has taken possession of a small town near Frankfort, the name of which, if I am not mistaken, is called Darmstadt[2].

So much respecting Germany. The messenger brings us news from England as agreeable as the above account is distressing. It is to the effect that there was a certain nobleman, commonly called the duke of Norfolk[3], whose authority extended towards the north of England, who was a most bitter enemy to the word of God, and who, with his son and others, made a secret attempt to restore the dominion of the pope and the monks. But their design is discovered, and the duke, together with his son, is thrown into prison; nor is any one wanting but Winchester alone, and unless he also be caught, the evangelical truth cannot be restored. Let us then pray the Lord, that he may defend his church which is oppressed on every side. These things I have thought proper to inform you of. I shall depart from hence, the Lord being my guide, straight towards the sea. Farewell. I have written to my wife, whom I pray you to comfort and advise during my absence. Strasburgh, Dec. 31, 1546.

Yours,

BURCHER, *Anglus.*

P. S. Richard [Hilles] and his wife salute you and your wife affectionately. They have had a daughter born to them about six weeks since, and she has recovered from her confinement.

[2 See Sleidan, XVIII. 414.]

[3 See above, p. 42, n. 1, and p. 256.]

LETTER CCXCVI.

JOHN BURCHER TO HENRY BULLINGER.

Dated at STRASBURGH, *Jan.* 30, 1548.

MUCH health. Although I have but little occasion to write, I cannot refrain, my very dear friend Bullinger, from troubling you with a few lines in this moment of leisure. Shortly after my arrival at Strasburgh I sent you, at the request of master Richard [Hilles], a most worthy man, a certain copy of the answer of a very learned man, and one of great judgment in the scriptures, to the letters of Bucer which had repeatedly been sent to him in order to draw him over to his own opinion concerning the eucharist, and bring him into this error respecting the humanity of Christ. As you have never acknowledged the receipt of this book, master Richard wished me to ask you, that we might know whether you have received it; and this is the principal reason of my writing.

We have no news from England, except that our council, which we call the parliament, is prorogued to the first of April. Bucer[1] has been sent for, as it is thought, by the emperor, and left this place secretly for Augsburg about eight days since. We are surprised at the secrecy of his departure, and some fears are entertained about his return. Such, it is reported, is the firmness of the duke of Saxony, that he will by no means make any agreement with the emperor to the detriment of religion. May the Lord grant unto all the godly perseverance even unto the end! Salute all my brethren at Zurich. Farewell.

Yours,

BURCHER, *Anglo-Tigurinus.*

[1 Joachim, elector of Brandenburg, wrote to the senate of Strasburgh, entreating them that, for the sake of religion, they would send Bucer to him; for that, the pope declining the council, the emperor had taken another course, and that therefore there was great hope of reformation. Bucer was therefore sent, who taking his journey privately, about the end of January, stopped not far from Augsburg, to stay there till the prince should send for him. Sleidan, B. xx. p. 454.]

LETTER CCXCVII.

JOHN BURCHER TO HENRY BULLINGER.

Dated at STRASBURGH, *Aug.* 24, 1548.

MUCH health. On the twenty-second of this month our very excellent and singular good friend master Richard Hilles, with his pious wife and dear children, left Strasburgh on their way to England. Your letter, most excellent sir, was just brought to me yesterday, and I opened and read it according to his request before he left. I have long since both received, and duly forwarded to the archbishop of Canterbury, that book and letter which you sent me by that filthy Jew, Michael Adam, who, however, very much deceived my expectation. He borrowed from me three florins, and from master Richard, in my absence and without my knowledge, eight dollars. He left this place a short time after the fair, but, as I hear, not without previously losing a great sum of money at the gaming-table; so that, if I am not mistaken, the sum we lent him is lost, unless there should possibly be some assets with you, whereby both your countrymen and ourselves may be indemnified. Should there be any thing, I request you to help us. He boasted that Froschover was about to give him a hundred florins for some book which he had translated from the Hebrew. But this perhaps is not true. Pray do for me what you can, if there is any hope of recovering any thing.

We are much distressed at the slaughter of the people of Constance[2]; but much more so that, notwithstanding they are conquerors, they think of falling off. May the Lord Jesus have compassion upon us all! We have not heard any thing for a long time respecting the state of England, neither any tidings of John à Lasco. Should I hear any thing, I will take care to let you know. There is some doubtful report respect-

[2 On the 5th of August, 3000 Spaniards marched to Constance, but were obliged to retreat after a severe engagement, in which the townspeople lost an hundred men. The emperor placed the city under the ban of the empire, whereupon a majority of their council received the Interim. See Sleidan, B. xx. 470, and above, p. 385, n. 4.]

ing the English and Scots: I therefore pass it over till we receive more certain information.

Master Richard and his wife requested me, on their departure, to salute most dutifully yourself, your wife and children, and also all the learned ministers of your church. I will send him the book which I have now received, by the first convenient opportunity. I will also write in my own letters to him the heads of yours; for he requested me to do so, both with respect to yours and those of all others. You are again saluted most dutifully by my wife, together with your wife, children, and household. May the Lord keep you very long stedfast in the confession of our Lord Jesus Christ, and bestow the same grace upon me! Amen. The emperor, I hear, is daily expected at Spires. Farewell.

Yours, whom you know, J. B.

LETTER CCXCVIII.

JOHN BURCHER TO HENRY BULLINGER.

Dated at STRASBURGH, *Oct.* 29, 1548.

PRAISE to God alone! Health and peace in Christ Jesus our Saviour. Your letter, dated the 20th of this month, has partly delighted and partly distressed me. Your own good health, my very dear Bullinger, and that of your family, was not the least cause of my satisfaction; but that Constance[1] has acted so iniquitously against itself and against the great and gracious God, is indeed most depressing.

The condition of our England is such as I can neither much commend or find fault with. A more sincere and pure feeling of religion has begun to flourish with success; but Satan, through his hatred of this, has been endeavouring to throw every thing into confusion by means of dissension. The archbishop of Canterbury, moved, no doubt, by the advice of Peter Martyr and other Lutherans, has ordered a

[1 On the 15th of October, the men of Constance, lately outlawed, (see above, p. 385, n. 4,) surrendered themselves for ever to the house of Austria. See the preceding page, n. 2, and Sleidan, B. XX. 474.]

catechism[2] of some Lutheran opinions to be translated and published in our language. This little book has occasioned no little discord; so that fightings have frequently taken place among the common people, on account of their diversity of opinion, even during the sermons. The government, roused by this contention, have convoked a synod of the bishops to consult about religion. God grant they do not produce some prodigy! So much respecting religion.

The English army, consisting of about thirty thousand men, marched last month into Scotland; on the arrival of whom the French returned into their own country. Some of our ships encountered them in the channel, and took from them a large vessel called a galley, with three hundred troops on board; together with some ships, which they brought into harbour at Calais. It is rumoured here, that the French have carried off the queen of Scotland[3]; but of this I have no certain intelligence from England. The French are threatening a war with the English; it is not known what will be the result. If there is any nation more perfidious than another, it is France, who will some time, I doubt not, receive the reward of her perfidy.

Strasburgh still remains in the same state as heretofore, and is not changed in any respect. If indeed bad morals could be changed into good ones, I doubt not but that we should have our God and Father in heaven favourable to us. The preachers are crying out most vehemently; but though they may cry till they burst, they do but little good. We have however many good and worthy individuals. Strasburgh is certainly most happy in one respect, that the nobles and more wealthy inhabitants have for the most part left it.

[2 For a notice of this Catechism, see Jenkyns' Pref. to Cranmer, p. lxxix. and Soames, Hist. Ref. III. 69, who observes that, instead of regarding the doctrine of the eucharist contained in it as Lutheran, "it would be more accurate to say that this catechism maintains the corporal presence without attempting to define the manner of it, hence leaving a latitude for explaining that doctrine either upon Romish or upon Lutheran principles." See above, p. 381.]

[3 Monsieur de Villegagnon, who commanded four galleys in the harbour of Leith, sailing round the isles, received the queen of Scots at Dumbarton, whence he conveyed her to France, and delivered her to her uncles the princes of Lorraine, in the month of July, 1548. See above, p. 387, n. 1.]

Pray for this our church, that God may be favourable to her: for we have need of your continual prayers and those of your whole church. I will take care that the letter you sent shall be safely conveyed to England. May the Lord preserve you and your city! Labour, as you are wont, for the extirpation of vice, that we may have God the Father of our Lord Jesus Christ favourable to us. My wife very dutifully salutes you and all your family. Tell them I wish them all holiness and happiness. Salute all the faithful. Farewell! Dated as above.

John à Lasco, a man very like yourself, endued with all learning and piety, is now in England.

Yours, J. B.

LETTER CCXCIX.

JOHN BURCHER TO HENRY BULLINGER.

Dated at STRASBURGH, *Jan.* 22, 1549.

HONOUR to God alone! Much health. I cannot sufficiently wonder, my very dear friend and master, Bullinger, at the negligence, not to say the abominable carelessness, of some of your townsmen, who are so neglectful in the delivery of letters. I gave the son of old Binder a letter to my intimate friend John Hooper: I gave also another to one of your townsmen who has lost one of his hands, (and heretofore, if I am not mistaken, a basket-maker by trade, who is now selling cloth in this place,) for the same Hooper, in which, because I was pressed for time, I inclosed a letter in English, sent to me here, and which I wished him to communicate to you. From this place too, about six days since, I wrote a letter to Basle, to a certain inhabitant, Valentine Nussbaum; to which I annexed my letter written to your excellence, and which I earnestly entreated him safely to forward to you. I sent also an English letter in addition, which I gave in charge to master Hooper to interpret to you. If none of these letters have reached you, it will be a misfortune which I will remedy by this present writing; for I will briefly touch upon their contents.

And, first of all, the letter written in English, and sent by the lame man, contains the following intelligence. Our king, about the month of September or October, fitted out some ships for Scotland, to carry provisions to the workmen and soldiers who are employed in the erection of some fortifications for the protection of a certain harbour, (which they have taken possession of by force,) and to prevent an enemy from entering. As soon as the soldiers and sailors had arrived there, they disembarked, and made an attempt upon a town named Dunbar, lying in the immediate neighbourhood. On the first attack, when they were just about to retreat, they were rallied by the bravery of their officers: for about thirty of our countrymen were slain, which was the cause of their running away. They repeated the attack a second time, when the governor of the city was slain, and the rest, both townsmen and soldiers, took to flight, leaving the town empty. Our troops therefore gained possession of it. But when they perceived that it was not sufficiently fortified, and discovered that the entire army of the Scots would come up with them on the following day; having taken all the plunder they could, they pulled down the walls, and, alas! set fire to the city. The affair being thus accomplished with success, they returned in safety to the rest of their party to the ships, with a great quantity both of gold, and silver, and household stuff; and also with a very considerable number of beasts of burden, sheep, and horses. After this defeat, the Scots, it is thought, sent ambassadors, and began to sue for peace.

This was the substance of the first letter. The second related to matters of religion, and the discussion which lasted for three days between four bishops, namely, the archbishop of Canterbury and another, called Doctor Farrar[1], on the part of the gospel, and the bishops of Worcester[2] and Westminster on the side of popery. Nothing, however, is as yet decided, nor is there any public preaching[3]. But, as I hope

[[1] Robert Farrar was consecrated bishop of St David's, Sept. 9, 1548. He was one of the martyrs in queen Mary's reign.]

[[2] Nicolas Heath was now bishop of Worcester, and Thomas Thirlby, of Westminster. The latter had been the king's ambassador to Charles V., and on his return home was succeeded by sir Philip Hoby.]

[[3] The king by a proclamation, Sept. 23, 1548, inhibited all preachers for a time, and gave notice of a public form of divine service ere long to be expected. Strype, Mem. II. i. 183.]

you will receive that letter, I pass over the rest. I will not however omit this truly discreet reply which our young king made to the protector. When the disputation was ended, the protector accosted the king with an expression of his surprise, saying, "How very much the bishop of Westminster has deceived my expectation." "Your expectation," the king replied, "he might deceive, but not mine." When the protector further inquired the reason, "I expected," said the king, "nothing else but that he, who has been so long time with the emperor as ambassador, should smell of the *Interim*." A reply truly becoming the young king, and which I did not think right to omit.

But to pass on to Richard Hilles, he begs that you will excuse his delay, and he will write as soon as he has leisure. His affairs have hitherto prevented him, and also his absence from London. For on his first landing he was afraid to go thither with his wife and children, by reason of the plague, which was exceedingly prevalent in those quarters. And he is now entirely occupied in arranging his house. Commend me, I entreat you, most diligently to masters Hooper and Butler. Our Strasburgh remains in the same state as heretofore. The Lord grant that it may long continue so! John à Lasco was in England, nor have I heard from any of my friends either of his death or that he has left it, which master Richard certainly would not have omitted to mention. Gabriel too, the tanner, tells me that he has not heard any thing of the kind. Farewell.

Yours, J. B.

LETTER CCC.

JOHN BURCHER TO HENRY BULLINGER.

Dated at STRASBURGH, *Jan.* 28, 1549.

MUCH health. My friend Gabriel, most courteous Bullinger, has saluted me from you, and stated at the same time that you were anxiously expecting a letter from me: but since I have hitherto had nothing worth relating, why should I be the means of your wasting your valuable hours in trifles and foolish gossiping? Nevertheless, since an occasion, such as it is, has now presented itself, I cannot be silent. My dear friend and your great admirer, master Richard Hilles, has written me word that he has received your letter, and has desired me to tell you so. He has not had time to answer it; besides which, as you are aware, he does not readily write in Latin. He will, however, answer it shortly. The news he communicates is partly agreeable, and partly very distressing: agreeable, because it is hoped that some improvement at least will take place in religion, although not a perfect and complete one. Yet in the mean time those very persons who wish to be, so to speak, most evangelical, imitate carnal licentiousness, under the pretext of religion and liberty. Every kind of vice, alas! is rife among them, and especially that of adultery[1] and fornication, which, he tells me, they do not consider as a sin. Unless this evil be corrected, we are undone.

I would have written more, but the messenger will not allow me, for he is in great haste. Wherefore you shall hear the rest by the inclosed English letter, which Hooper will translate. I have written to him concerning the victory of the English over the Scots, in what manner they gained possession of the city. I hope he communicated the tidings to you. Our Strasburgh remains just the same as heretofore, and the report respecting it and the bishop is all false. Pray continually for us!

Farewell, and salute all our learned friends. Inform, I pray you, master Butler, that Richard has also received his letters. Again farewell.

Yours, J. B.

LETTER CCCI.

JOHN BURCHER TO HENRY BULLINGER.

Dated at STRASBURGH, *Feb.* 15, 1549.

HEALTH in Christ Jesus our Lord! Amen. Within these few days, my dear friend Bullinger, these letters have

[1 The nation, says Strype, about this time grew infamous for this crime. The council thought fit to recommend to the archbishop to take particular cognizance of it. See Strype, Cranm. 293, and Latimer's Sermons, Parker Soc. Ed. p. 244.]

been brought me by the courier, and together with them my friend Richard has written me most horrible intelligence; which however, I hope, has had a happy result, though it must nevertheless be a distressing and lamentable one.

The uncle of our king (I do not mean him whom we call the protector of the kingdom, but his brother) has attempted, by an unheard of treachery and cruelty, to destroy with his own impious hands, in the deep silence of the night, our innocent king. The tragedy was thus acted. He obtained from one of the king's chamberlains, who was privy to his design, a key, by means of which there is the nearest access by a door to the royal bed-chamber, which he entered in the dead of night, accompanied by the accomplices of his crime. There was a space between the door at which he entered and the king's chamber, where was lying hid a little dog, the most faithful guardian of the youth, having been accidentally shut out of the chamber; and when he perceived the assassin hurry towards the king's chamber-door, he betrayed the murderer by his barking. The enraged assassin first killed the dog, and, had not God prevented, would have killed his master also. A faithful guardian of the royal person, roused by the noise, came out, having awakened some of those who from their office are called body-guards. As soon as he beheld with astonishment the murderer at the door of the royal chamber, he demanded of him what was his business there at the very dead of night. The man replied with trembling, that he wished to know whether the prince was safely guarded. But this excuse did not avail him, and on the next morning[1] he was committed to the Tower of London as a traitor; as was also shortly after the king's chamberlain[2], who had supplied him with the key by which he gained admission. And unless the king had accidentally

[[1] The admiral was committed to the Tower on the 19th of January, and beheaded on Tower-hill the 20th of March following. For an account of his crimes, see Strype, Mem. I. ii. 193, &c. Burnet, II. 155, &c.]

[[2] Burnet gives no account of the circumstances here mentioned. He states, however, that "Fowler, that waited in the privy chamber, with some few others, were sent to the Tower, together with the admiral." Burnet, II. 155.]

bolted the inner door of his chamber, which is done very seldom, it would certainly have been all over with him, before that other person could have run to his assistance. Together with the traitor was seized also a certain knight[3] who was the warden of the king's mint at Bristol, which is the richest sea-port in England. Here then you have the happy issue of this tragedy. They have, I doubt not, suffered at length the due punishment of such wickedness.

Give, I pray you, or send the letters tied up with this to the parties to whom they are addressed. Our Strasburgh is languishing: the bishop is daily expected. Three propositions were made to the preachers by the magistracy; That they should not speak ill of the emperor and the princes in their sermons, to which they agreed; That they should receive the religion proposed by the government, to which they consented, provided it were agreeable to holy scripture; and thirdly, That they should not utter a word against the *Interim*. This they refused to comply with. They are only waiting for an answer, and I am afraid they will have to remove somewhere else. John à Lasco is alive and well in England. And may you also be alive and well!

J. BURCHER.

LETTER CCCII.

JOHN BURCHER TO HENRY BULLINGER.

Dated at STRASBURGH, *March* 12, 1549.

GREETING. A lamentable and distressing circumstance has happened to us at Strasburgh. Bucer, and the more eloquent, as well as in my opinion the more solidly learned Paul Fagius, have been deposed from their office of preachers by the authority of the magistrates; and, unless they prefer being delivered into the hands of the emperor, they will be obliged to quit the city[4]. We still have the other preachers, and no other change has taken place than that we are com-

[3 Sir W. Sharington, vice-treasurer of the Mint at Bristol, was pardoned and restored in blood by the parliament in 1549.]

[4 See above, page 538, and Sleidan, XXI. 479.]

pelled to eat fish during this Lent, and on Fridays and Saturdays throughout the year. The bishop is expected every day: should he make any change, you shall hear of it by a letter from me. I have just received a letter from England, but it does not contain any news. Nothing has yet been published by act of parliament. The son of the emperor is coming to-day to Heidelberg, as it is reported, accompanied by duke Maurice and others. I hear from Saxony that the Saxons are indignant at having been driven from the gospel to the *Interim*. It is rumoured that the sea-port towns have returned for answer to the emperor, that they cannot receive the *Interim*. A truce is said to have been made between the king of Wallachia, Poland, and some duke, of Silesia, if I mistake not, and the sea-port towns. I have written thus much to you, in few words, that you may not accuse me of neglect. My affairs are now calling me elsewhere, and will not allow of any longer delay. Our friend Hooper has written me word, that the Swiss have all come to an agreement: I wish it may be true; but I desire to know the same from yourself. Farewell.

Yours, you know who,

J. B.

LETTER CCCIII.

JOHN BURCHER TO HENRY BULLINGER.

Dated at STRASBURGH, *April* 1, 1549.

GREETING. I have received, my very dear friend Bullinger, your two most friendly letters, the first by Farell's brother, and the other by my friend John Hooper[1], who arrived here with his family, by God's blessing, two days since, safe and sound. And I congratulate, not only you Swiss, that you have so happily come to an agreement among yourselves, but also the whole of Germany; for this event will be of the greatest advantage to all the Germans. May the great and good God grant that the peace now

[1 See above, p. 50.]

entered into may be lasting, firm, and perpetual! Our city is daily declining. Two preachers, Bucer and Fagius, have been dismissed by the authority of the senate: Paul has departed, and the other will depart very shortly. May the Lord preserve our England from both of them! We still have preaching among us, and not massing; yet the bishop is anointed, and has celebrated mass once. The whole clergy too of his district are to meet to-morrow at Saverne[2], to consult about putting down Christ and his gospel. But the Lord will, I doubt not, scatter the counsels of the ungodly.

I have no news from England, except that an engagement between the English and Scots took place last February; and our troops lost by treachery the fortress[3] they had before taken. But the battle took place shortly after, in which many Scots and French were slain, and many taken prisoners; among whom were twelve of the French nobility and the commander of the French forces in Scotland. It is rumoured here that a marriage is about to take place between the widow of the duke of Lorraine and the brother of the king of Hungary. May the Lord give us his grace, and preserve his people! Amen.

Yours entirely,

J. B.

P. S. The traitor who plotted the death of our king was condemned to death on the 12th of March, and there is no doubt but that he will be brought to execution.

LETTER CCCIV.

JOHN BURCHER TO HENRY BULLINGER.

Dated at STRASBURGH, *May* 30, 1549.

MUCH health. Your last letter, my very dear friend and master, Bullinger, I have received by the hands of a Polish

[2 "The bishop of Strasburgh, after eight years, takes at length orders, and says mass; and holding a convocation of his clergy at Saverne, made such decrees as suited their purpose." Sleidan, xx. 479.]

[3 See above, p. 387.]

nobleman; by which I perceive you are surprised at not having received any accounts from England, either from master Richard [Hilles] or Hooper, or any one else. I dare answer for our friend Richard that he is not forgetful of you, but that he will write, as he promised, by the first opportunity. He is prevented however, not only by some affairs of importance, but also by his want of expertness in writing Latin, with which he is wont to charge himself; or rather I should say, his fear of writing incorrectly. Besides this, he is not accustomed to be a retailer of mere rumours and reports, but a relater of truth. And for this reason he very seldom writes to me any news, though what he does write is generally true. I have therefore no doubt but that, as soon as he knows any thing certain and true respecting the state of our England, he will write both to you and to myself upon the subject. A book upon religion has been set forth, and this too with the consent of the nobility and the whole council, which we call the parliament; but it is not yet printed. I doubt not but that he will send it you as soon as it shall be published. Bucer and Paul Fagius have safely arrived in England, and have written to this place from the palace of the archbishop of Canterbury. I wish they may not pervert him, or make him worse. John à Lasco has left England, but intends to return thither. John Hooper with his family arrived safely at Antwerp, and are at length in England. He wrote to me from Antwerp, and desired me to salute you, together with the whole church, in the name of himself and his wife.

There are no tidings of the emperor, except that he is still at Brussels, though it was reported that he had gone to Ghent[1]. It is moreover stated that he is about to visit Spires, and it is certain that the people of that place have prepared apartments for himself and his attendants; but the more prevailing report is that he will not come. The king of France, according to custom, is breaking the treaty and peace with England. For he made a violent attack upon Boulogne seven times in one day, but much to his discomfort: for every time he suffered a repulse, and with no small loss of his troops. The Scots, relying on the promises of the French, are becoming insolent, but to their

[1 See above, p. 60.]

great cost; for two hundred of them have been slain in a second conflict with our troops, and five hundred taken prisoners. The emperor, as I hear, has granted our king ten thousand infantry, and five hundred cavalry, for the defence of Boulogne. I wish it were permitted me to write about peace rather than war. The French king has not acted without due prudence in inviting the Swiss to the defence, or rather the recovery, of Boulogne: but the Swiss will act most imprudently if they accept his invitation; for it is at too great a distance from you. I wish, however, the Swiss would interpose between these two sovereigns, so as to treat about a peace, and that upon certain equitable terms, by which it might be established and placed on a sure footing. For there is reason to fear that, while the mouse and the frog are fighting together, the eagle will devour them both.

I have this to write respecting our Strasburgh, namely, that, contrary to all human expectation, we are still in the same state as heretofore; no change has taken place, except that festivals, the Interim, and fast-days are ordered to be observed. Earnestly entreat the Lord for us, as well in your private as in your public prayers, and render him thanks with us for this his divine benefit. Salute your wife and all our learned friends in my name. Farewell.

Yours,

BURCHER, *Anglus*.

LETTER CCCV.

JOHN BURCHER TO HENRY BULLINGER.

Dated at STRASBURGH, *June* 1, 1549.

GREETING. My very dear friend Bullinger, after I had sealed my former letter, and was anxious about the means of sending it, I accidentally fell in with that nobleman of Ghent[2], who was intending to go into your parts. He is alike distinguished by his birth and manners, as by his faith and piety. He lived some time at Strasburgh, from whence he passed

[[2] Namely, Utenhovius. See above, p. 56, n. 1.]

over into England; and has now come to the Wildbaden here for the sake of bathing. It is his intention, when he leaves the baths, to visit some places which he has not yet seen, and especially Zurich, celebrated above the rest both for its reputation and pure doctrine. He does not disagree with us in point of religion, and is moreover a man of learning and of godly judgment. He will remain with you about a fortnight. He desired an introduction to you from me: I therefore, most courteous Bullinger, commend him in such a manner, that he may not be less welcome to you and to the church, than any Zuricher is, and ever will be, to me. He is a disciple of the French church, the doctrine of which is not different from your own. All that remains, I am sure that you will do of your own accord, when you have seen the man two or three times. Farewell.

Yours wholly,

BURCHER.

LETTER CCCVI.

JOHN BURCHER TO HENRY BULLINGER.

Dated at STRASBURGH, *Aug.* 25, 1549.

GREETING. The report of the evils which have befallen our England, most courteous Bullinger, has doubtless extended even to you. But as such rumour is usually doubtful and uncertain, I have thought fit to give you a correct statement both respecting the demands of the rebels, and the cause of the rebellion; as also respecting the penalty and punishment which they have suffered according to their deserts. In the western part of England, which is divided into Cornwall and Devonshire, these rebels assembled in the months of June and July last, to the number, it is believed, of sixteen thousand armed men. The leaders of the rebels, in the first place, proclaimed deliverance to the people from the injustice and oppression of the nobility, who, partly by force, and partly by fraud, had converted to their own use the pastures which had formerly been common[1]. And for this cause the rebellion extended through all parts of England; insomuch that there was scarcely any place in which there were not some disturbances on account of it. But the peasantry were every where immediately pacified by the king's proclamation and promises, except in the abovementioned counties of Devon and Cornwall. In those parts two Romish priests, who were the authors of the sedition, warned the people that their religion was in danger, and that it was the duty of all Christians to be prepared for its defence and re-establishment. They assembled, therefore, so large a number of papists in the name and authority of Christ and the king. The king wrote[2] to them, admonishing them as a father to desist from the rebellion they had begun. I send the document to Butler, who will translate it for you. They disregarded the admonition, and began openly to declare their intention of setting up another king, another council, and another religion, as appears by their articles turned into Latin. The king, being now compelled to it, attacked them as enemies with a regular force, destroyed three or four thousand of them, and delivered the city of Exeter, which they had besieged; whereupon some of the leaders of the rebellion were taken prisoners, and all the rest dispersed in divers quarters. There still remain some rebels in another part of England, who, relying on the aid of those above mentioned, excited a tumult. Against these the protector of the kingdom advanced in person, with a large body of troops, at the beginning of this month. They have, therefore, I hope, received the punishment of their rebellion. In the mean time, while these things are going on in England, the king, or rather the tyrant[3], of France (for you are aware with what tyranny he raged against the Christians at Paris not long since, when he made a pompous entry into the city, how he ordered five persons most cruelly to be burned for his sport and amusement,) has declared war against our

[1 For an account of this rebellion, see Strype, Mem. II. i. 264, &c. Burnet, II. 181, &c. Soames, III. 434, &c. Foxe, v. 730, &c.]

[2 The articles sent to the king by the Devonshire rebels, as also his answer, are given in Foxe, v. 731, &c. See also Strype, Cranm. 264, 799.]

[3 This was Henry II. A painfully interesting account of these martyrdoms is given by Beza in his Histoire Ecclesiastique, Vol. I. p. 81. Anvers. 1580. See also Foxe, IV. 405.]

king and kingdom; having previously got ready troops at sea, who, as soon as war had been declared, were immediately to invade the west of England, and join the disaffected in those parts. But the Lord prevented this calamity: for when it was told our people that the French had arrived and landed their troops, they hastened to the spot, cut off their retreat, and prepared for battle; and there the whole of the French army was destroyed, so that it is written to me by one worthy of credit, that there was not one left alive. The number of the French, he thinks, was five, or at least four thousand.

Thus much I have to relate to you concerning the present state of our England. There is also a report that all the people of Switzerland had formed an alliance with this cruel tyrant of the French; and when I inquired of my informant whether the people of Zurich had also agreed to that treaty, he answered in the affirmative. But I cannot believe your countrymen are so mad, as to enter upon a treaty with this tyrant, who seeks for nothing else but his own aggrandisement and the establishment of his kingdom. I wish to know the truth of the matter from yourself. Master Richard and his wife very much salute yourself and your wife. My wife also dutifully salutes you both. Pray the Lord for us and for our England! Farewell.

Yours from my heart,

BURCHER.

LETTER CCCVII.

JOHN BURCHER TO HENRY BULLINGER.

Dated at STRASBURGH, *Sept.* 1, 1549.

GREETING. I commended to you, most courteous Bullinger, not long since, a nobleman of Ghent, who was on many accounts deserving of my commendation and of your friendship. I now commend to you by this letter an English gentleman[1], who is in no respect inferior to the other.

[[1] This person appears, from Letter CCCIX. p. 660, to have been Christopher Hales, some of whose correspondence is given in this volume, pp. 184—95.]

He is agreeable and quiet in his demeanour, and in matters of faith agrees with your church. He has lived with me for some time, and I have not found any thing in him to find fault with. He is a valetudinarian, by reason of a consumption with which he has been long afflicted. If, therefore, your climate agrees with him, I request you not to be wanting in your good offices to find him a host, with whom he may be allowed to live somewhat after his own way. He would like to board with master Gesner; I request you, therefore, to introduce him to him. I wrote all the news to you about eight days since: he will tell you all the rest. My engagements will not allow me to write more. I therefore commend you and your family to God.

Yours,

BURCHER, *Anglus.*

LETTER CCCVIII.

JOHN BURCHER TO HENRY BULLINGER.

Dated at STRASBURGH, *Sept.* 25, 1549.

GREETING. Your most courteous letter, my very dear Bullinger, was delivered to me at Frankfort, where my engagements would not allow me to write to you in reply. I consider your very friendly offices in serving my relative, as bestowed upon myself, which I will repay to you and to your friends whenever an opportunity shall be afforded me. He is a youth of an exceedingly gentle disposition, but rather slow, as is generally the case with persons of that character. For in proportion as any one is of a sharper wit, he is generally more rough in his temper; while, on the other hand, a person of a meek disposition is often wanting in ability. This, however, may be remedied by application, as I myself have found to be the case in the present instance. For when I was with you some time since, the stimulus applied by me was of more advantage to him than the more lax management of his master without such incentive. If, therefore, you desire him to become a scholar, an active master must be sought out for him, who may urge and spur him on; and I have thought it right to give you timely notice of this, lest my advice, by coming too late, should disappoint the expectation which you have conceived of the young man.

I have received information from England, that the rebellion is entirely ended, and that the principal perpetrators of the crime are daily brought to punishment; especially those impure mass-priests, who stirred up the people. The French have gained possession by treachery of two fortresses[1] between Boulogne and Calais. There is a report (but I consider it to be a false one) that the emperor will shortly come to Spires. In your last letter you mention some damaged cloth which you had received; but I cannot tell what you mean by this cloth, for, as far as I know, I never sent you any. Farewell, with your dear wife. Master Richard [Hilles] salutes you: he informed me in his last letter but one that his wife was very ill, and he desires you to commend her to the Lord in your prayers. Again farewell. Salute master Butler, and tell him that I have received his letters long since, and forwarded them to England. I have not received any letters for you from England.

Yours entirely,

BURCHER, *Anglus.*

LETTER CCIX.

JOHN BURCHER TO HENRY BULLINGER.

Dated at STRASBURGH, *Oct.* 16, 1549.

PERPETUAL health in Jesus Christ our Lord! Your letter, my dear friend and master, Bullinger, has given me great pleasure on two accounts; both because you and your family were in good health, and not forgetful of me, and also that my kinsman John had been kindly received by all good men. I will not fail to give him such advice, as that he may satisfy your expectation. It is his want of application alone that will do him any harm; and as you are aware of this defect, it will easily be remedied. He lived with me most

[1 These were "the Almain camp, near Ambleteuse, and the main fort of Newhaven." Strype, Mem. II. i. 278.]

creditably some time since, and gave me great hopes of his becoming a good man; and I pray our great and gracious God that he may turn out to be such.

The report respecting a renewed rebellion in England is entirely false: for I received by the courier, about eight days since, a letter from our friend master Richard, dated at London on the 18th of September; and also another, written at Antwerp on the 28th of September, in neither of which was there any mention of any thing of the kind, but quite the contrary; namely, that as affairs were now settled in England, the king had determined upon sending all his forces against the French, to drive them away from Boulogne, and to succour the inhabitants of that place. A rumour has again reached us, that the king has recovered the fortresses, and routed the French forces. I wish it may be true. But as soon as I know the facts, I will communicate them. The report respecting the slaughter of the English, at the taking of the fortresses from the French, was without foundation; for I have been informed by a letter from Antwerp, that the French gained possession of those fortresses by treason. The report in reference to the artillery that was taken was probably a true one.

The rumour of the emperor's coming to us is very general. Nothing however is certain, except that I have heard from a worthy man that James Sturmius was the author of this report. It is not the plague, but a most acute fever, that is prevalent among us. I do not however think of moving my quarters, were the plague to come a thousand times over.

No misfortune, that I am aware of, has happened to master Hooper; but, as I have been informed by a person worthy of credit, he is very busy in confuting Lutheranism, and planting the truth. He is performing the duty of an earnest Christian. He is giving public lectures in London, where he has a numerous auditory, and is praised by all good men.

The wife of master Richard [Hilles] has recovered from a very dangerous illness. For a whole month her life was despaired of. Bucer too has recovered from a fever. But master Richard has written me word, that there was scarcely any hope of Paul Fagius's recovery. Acquaint, I pray you,

Christopher Hales with whatever news you may think proper. I thank you exceedingly on his behalf for having received him so kindly. Salute him from me, together with your whole family and all your learned friends. I pray the Lord long to preserve you in safety!

Yours, BURCHER.

After I had written this letter, and before it was sealed, I received letters both from master Richard and from Antwerp, in which there is no mention of any insurrection. They were dated at London on the 28th of September, and at Antwerp on the 5th of October. Master Richard wrote word that the bishop of London[1] had been committed to prison, because he refused, though commanded by royal authority, to preach against the rebels. Tell this, I pray you, to my countrymen. Master Richard and his wife (whose health is daily improving) salute you and your family. It is reported, by those however who have apostatised from the faith, and who place all their hopes on him, that the emperor is coming to Spires about the first of December. The bishop of London is deposed from his dignity. He was accused by Hooper and another[2] on points of doctrine.

LETTER CCCX.

JOHN BURCHER TO HENRY BULLINGER.

Dated at STRASBURGH, *Dec.* 12, 1549.

HEALTH and peace through Jesus Christ our Lord! The many kind offices you fulfilled towards me, when I was at Zurich, will not allow me to be unmindful of my promise, though in the midst of numerous engagements. You desired me, my dear friend Bullinger, to write frequently, which I

[1 Bonner was required to preach against rebellion, "setting out the heinousness of it: he was also to shew what was true religion, and that external ceremonies were nothing in themselves, but that in the use of them men ought to obey the magistrates, and join true devotion to them." Burnet, II. 194. Soames, III. 466.]

[2 William Latimer. Burnet, as above.]

am now beginning to do, though I have scarcely any thing to write about. Whatever news there may be from England, you will doubtless learn from the letters of our dear friend Richard Hilles. Nor indeed have I received any tidings, except that a certain individual, named Paget, a man excellent in every way, has been made president of Wales. Where Wales is, and who Paget is, Butler and Hales will explain to you. Every thing else remains in the same state and order, as when the protector was committed, respecting whom not a word is mentioned, except that he is still kept in prison.

There is great uncertainty respecting the emperor's coming to us, and it is not thought that he will visit us before the spring. The mass-priests, together with the bishop, are endeavouring to bring back the mass to us at Christmas[3]. We are waiting to see what will be done. May the Lord Jesus Christ for his mercy's sake keep us inviolate from all error. Amen!

I return both you and your wife my lasting thanks for your very great kindness towards me. Salute her in my name and in that of my wife. Send, I pray you, the inclosed letters by trustworthy couriers, the one to Arau, the other to Constance. There is an excellent woman, whose husband has now for a year past been in the service of a widow lady at Constance. He promised to return hither by Christmas, but has now written to the contrary. His wife has written to him in reply, and desires her letter to be safely conveyed to him as soon as possible. Farewell.

Yours,

BURCHER, *Anglus*.

[3. The bishop of Strasburgh had resolved to begin the office in his churches on Christmas-day, and had prescribed a method to be followed by the clergy; but, because they were not then in a sufficient readiness, he put it off till the first of February. And then the priests said vespers in those three churches which the senate had granted the bishop by composition, and the next day mass was performed, which had not been seen there for twenty years before. See the whole account in Sleidan, XXI. 491, &c.]

LETTER CCCXI.

JOHN BURCHER TO HENRY BULLINGER.

Dated at STRASBURGH, *April* 20, 1550.

HEALTH and peace through our Lord Jesus Christ, our only Saviour and our life. Your friend Froschover, my very dear Bullinger, amidst the bustle of the Frankfort fair, has brought me a letter and some books, which he desired me faithfully to convey by a safe hand into England; and your very acceptable letter contained the same request. I have willingly performed this office. There happened to be here a servant of my very faithful friend, master Richard Hilles, whom he had sent to me upon especial business. To this man I entrusted the book and letter to the king, together with all your other letters. The remainder of the books I declined to give into his charge, and not without reason. For in the first place, it is becoming that the king should be preferred to others, and receive his copy before any one else, lest that which might be more acceptable from its rarity should become less so from being made common. The two remaining copies, therefore, which belong to Hooper and another, I inclosed in some goods, which I took care should be forwarded direct from Antwerp. I ordered the servant to give the letter and books to master Richard, to whom I also wrote to forward the same to Hooper. The name of Hooper is celebrated throughout all England. He is appointed a royal preacher, and is an opponent of Lutherans and Bucerians, but a constant defender and promoter of the true faith. His praise is universally proclaimed both on account of his innocency of life and strictness of discipline. May the Lord accomplish what he has begun by him!

Bucer has had a most dangerous relapse into his old disease. Richard writes word that there is little or no hope of his recovery. In case of his death[1], England will be happy, and more favoured than all other countries, in having been delivered in the same year from two men of most

[1 The deaths of Bucer and Fagius were much regretted on account of the services they had rendered and were expected to render to the reformation in England. See above, pp. 19, 329, 492, n. 2. Strype, Cranm. 281.]

pernicious talent, namely, Paul [Fagius] and Bucer. From these sources new sects are daily arising among us, and religion is always assuming a new appearance. I really think that our men of learning delight in novelty and change: moreover they have established a confraternity under the direction of Paul Fagius, and hold their conventicles on stated days, in which, as I hear, much more absurd questions are asked by the silly people than even those of the followers of Thomas or Scotus. A new kind of confession too, or, as they call it, a preparation before the Lord's supper, is instituted by the preachers without the consent either of the magistrates or the people. Nor is any one allowed to approach the holy communion, without having previously presented himself to the priest. And they defend this practice solely from that passage of the holy gospel, "I know my sheep, and am known of mine." Therefore it is not lawful for any one to approach the Lord's table, unless he be known to the preacher. Marbach made this assertion from the pulpit, to whom I was very nearly replying: "'And I call my sheep by name;' therefore it is necessary to call all who come by their proper names." These things are very ridiculous, but really lamentable; and I have written them for no other reason, than that you may understand into what errors the church still recent and infirm is falling. What do you think will take place a hundred years hence, if we are now blundering in open day-light? May God preserve you and your church uncorrupted, and bestow his grace, that our English one may be established and preserved in purity! I have inclosed for your perusal some regulations just established here, and which can be explained to you by master Butler.

We have now with us at St Thomas's a Swiss preacher, who is reported either to have been expelled by you some time since, or else to have absconded, on account of adultery. Having then become your enemy, he fled to Berne, where he endeavoured to raise I know not what riot and disturbance, for which reason, it is said, he was expelled by the magistrates. His reputation is bad enough, and hitherto has created in me no little disgust; but I think it a false report. Should I find it to be true, I shall certainly regard the man in no other light than as a heathen and a publican, unless he become reconciled to your church, and that of Berne:

nor is he a proper person to take the holy testament into his mouth, inasmuch as he despises discipline himself. I wish for information from you upon this matter. As to the rest, the state of the church at Strasburgh is the same as it has been since the defeat of the papists. The magistrates have sent master Cope[1], who is thought to be a good man, ambassador to the emperor. We have certain news of a peace having been agreed upon between the English, French, and Scots. I have not yet learned the conditions; but shall hear them shortly, and will let you know.

I wish for more information about the circumstances and condition of my kinsman John; whether he is pronounced to be qualified for your church or not. Should he not seem to be sufficiently prepared, which I have always feared, and still do fear will be the case, a situation is offered him, by which he can obtain a respectable livelihood. I wish therefore that an examination of him may take place, that we may know what to expect concerning him. For if he neglects the present opportunity, and should afterwards be rejected by you, provision cannot easily be made for him in future. He will be waited for till the next festival of St John. Should he not seem to you to be sufficiently qualified, I should wish to be informed of it before that day, that provision may be made for him. There is a sufficiently creditable means of livelihood at my disposal, and one suited to his abilities; which if he now suffer to escape him, and hereafter prove troublesome to you, we shall assuredly not find it easy to provide for him in future. I desire therefore the expression of your opinion upon this matter. But if you are not willing to have him, let him be sent to me. Farewell with your dear wife and children.

Yours,

BURCHER.

P. S. The letter which master Christopher Hales received from your church, he has lost together with the portmanteau. If therefore there was any thing of importance contained in it, you can repeat it in your next. May God preserve you! I received the inclosed letter the day before yesterday.

[[1] Henry Cope. See Sleidan, XXI. 478. He had been sent in a similar capacity in 1543. Seckendorf, III. p. 425.]

LETTER CCCXII.

JOHN BURCHER TO HENRY BULLINGER.

Dated at STRASBURGH, *June* 8, 1550.

HONOUR to God alone! Much health. Two days since, my very dear Bullinger, was brought me your letter, dated at Zurich on the 17th of May; wherein you express your satisfaction at I know not what diligence and trouble of mine in forwarding your books and letters to England, and you promise to return the obligation. I certainly cannot allow that I have done any service that I do not owe, and a great deal more, to your kindness. Besides, you have authority to command me in matters of this kind. But I inclosed the books, not the letter, for master Hooper, in some goods: the letters both to him and to the king, together with the book dedicated to his majesty, I gave in charge to a servant of master Richard.

The word of God is daily making progress through the labour and ministry of master Hooper, and I pray our great and good God to establish what he has begun. A friend of mine has written to me from England, that the king called Hooper to him after Easter, and wished to reward him with the bishoprick of Gloucester; but he refused it. He was not long since summoned before the council, who urged him to accept it. He made excuse, that he could not allow himself with a good conscience to be consecrated with the vestments and tonsure of the papacy, which is not yet abolished in the case of bishops. They allowed the tonsure to be dispensed with, but he must put on the white linen robe when he goes to parliament. They suppose, however, that this will be done away with by the authority of parliament. So much respecting Hooper. I now come to other matters.

That jolly and impure preacher[2] of ours will be regarded by me no otherwise than as a publican and a heathen, unless he shall be reconciled to your church and to that of Berne.

Bucer is more than licentious on the subject of marriage. I heard him once disputing at table upon this question, when he asserted that a divorce should be allowed for any reason,

[[2] See the preceding Letter.]

however trifling; so that he is considered, not without cause, by our bishop of Winchester as the author of the book published in defence of the Landgrave[1]. I am ignorant as to what the hireling Bucer, who fled from this church before the wolf came in sight, is plotting in England. He is an invalid, and (as report says) is either becoming childish, or is almost in his dotage, which is the usual result of a wandering and inconstant mind[2].

My kinsman came to me unexpectedly a month since. I am glad to hear that he courteously took leave of you. I have taken care to provide him with a situation. I was angry with him for not having before bidden you farewell, and thanked you for your kindness. But you must excuse him, both on account of his time of life, at which men are generally reserved, and also of his early education, which was rude and neglected. There is no certain intelligence about the emperor's coming. It was reported that he was to set off for Brussels towards the end of May; but it is now stated that he did not depart at that time. I sent your last letter by post to Antwerp; it will reach Hooper in less than ten days. There is no other news, except that the papists have

[1 Philip, landgrave of Hesse, in addition to Christina, the daughter of the late duke George, to whom he had been united many years, and by whom he had a large family, married on March 3, 1540, a lady named Margaret de Sala, and this with the consent of the landgravine under her own hand and seal. Previous to this he sought to obtain the sanction of Luther, Melancthon and Bucer, whose want of firmness in this painful case has called forth the most violent invectives from Varillas, and Bossuet bishop of Meaux. A full account of the facts is given in Seckendorf, III. 277—281. Melancthon writes to a friend to advise those who discussed the subject, *ne judicent de re non integre cognita;* and Luther writes, *Ego quæ landgravius sub arcano confessionis per Bucerum mihi exposuit, secretissima tenebo, etiam cum ignominia mea. Præstat spargi Lutherum indulgentia sua desipuisse, quam ut rationes evulgem propter quas landgravio indulsimus.*]

[2 It is but just to Bucer's memory to record the opinion of sir John Cheke respecting him, who thus writes in a letter to archbishop Parker: "Although I doubt not but the king's majesty will provide some grave learned man to maintain God's true learning in his university, yet I think not of all learned men in all points ye shall receive Mr Bucer's like; whether we consider his deepness of knowledge, his earnestness in religion, his fatherliness in life, his authority in knowledge." Strype, Cranm. 895.]

re-established their religion in certain appointed churches, and have many supporters. May the Lord preserve and increase whatever true knowledge is yet remaining! Salute most dutifully from me your wife and all our learned friends. Farewell.

Yours,

BURCHER.

P. S. Hooper has certainly accepted a bishoprick. For the wife of Bucer, who has come over for the purpose of taking her mother and children into England, has brought this intelligence. The emperor is certainly marching towards Spires.

LETTER CCCXIII.

JOHN BURCHER TO HENRY BULLINGER.

Dated at STRASBURGH, *July* 10, 1550.

GREETING. I wrote to you, my very dear Bullinger, not long since, and together with my own letter I forwarded many others received from England and Hooper. I sent them to Valentine Nüssbaum at Basle, that they might be more safely conveyed to you by his means: for a messenger is very rarely to be met with here, except during the fair. I wrote you word in my letter, that our friend Hooper had been appointed to the episcopal office by the king and council of England, which is most certainly the case. I pray God that he may well discharge this office! Our city of Strasburgh, it is rumoured, is receiving the Interim; for three[3] churches are given up to the papists, in which they practise their errors without restraint. The people are divided; part are in favour of popery, but the majority are in opposition to it. Some old men and women adhere to the truth, contrary to the general expectation. Religion still remains free, and the preachers are free. Many persons are doubting what monstrosity the Diet of Augsburg will produce. Every thing is quiet in

[[3] In October 1549, the senate allowed the bishop three churches, that he might therein have the exercise of his religion; and took all the clergy under their care and protection. The bishop, on the other hand, grants the senate the college of St Thomas for a public school, and all the rest of the churches. Sleidan, XXI. 485. See above, p. 661, n. 1.]

England. Religion is making due progress. It has never been reported among us that the emperor is about to invade you; and I suspect the rumour has no other foundation than the opinion of the soldiers, who measure the emperor by their own standard. I am rather inclined to believe that he will make war against the cities[1]. Should I hear any unfavourable news respecting your Switzerland, I will not fail to communicate it. Let us meanwhile pray God to grant us peace! Farewell, my most esteemed friend. My family salute you and yours.

Yours,

BURCHER.

P. S. I have sent by Falckner a large packet of letters directed to master Pellican, whom I pray you to salute in my name. Your books and letters have arrived in England long since. I have received also a letter, which I immediately forwarded by the courier, from master Theodore, to whom I pray you to present my respects, and to inform him of the circumstance. Once more farewell. The bustle of the fair will not permit me to delay any longer. Strasburgh, July 10.

Master Gualter has written to me about some portraits procured for master Hales[2]. I never heard anything from him respecting them. I will write to him, however, and if he requires it, will pay the money. I forwarded, seventeen days since, a parcel sent by master Hooper, and a basket sent by Hales to master Gualter. I hope you have received them.

LETTER CCCXIV.

JOHN BURCHER TO HENRY BULLINGER.

Dated at Strasburgh, *Aug.* 10, 1550.

Greeting. I perceive, my very dear Bullinger, that you are greatly disturbed at not having received a letter from England to announce the arrival there of your books and letters; and you seem to be no less anxious, whether the books have been intercepted, or have been lost on the way.

[1 Namely, Magdeburg, Bremen, Hamburgh, and Lubeck, which still held out against the authority of the emperor.]

[2 See above, Letter XCVIII. p. 185.]

Dismiss all your fears, for I know for certain that the goods, in which a portion of the books was inclosed, have safely reached England. Besides, Richard's servant, to whom I gave in charge the letter and book for the king, came safe to his master, and has returned safe to Antwerp. This letter[3] of master Richard will, I doubt not, sufficiently inform you what he has done with the book and letter for his majesty.

Hooper, I imagine, is too fully engaged to have any leisure for writing. His last letter to me was on March 29th, and with it I received a packet for you, which I immediately took care should be forwarded to you by Valentine Nüssbaum, a citizen of Basle. He has not written to me since. He is certainly a bishop, and I wish he may constantly watch over the Lord's flock. The letter I have now received from you I will take care shall be forwarded by post, and it will reach Antwerp within eight days. The bearer of this to you is an honest and trustworthy person, and was a servant of mine a year ago. If you can shew him any kindness, should he require it, I shall be much obliged to you. There is no news, except that I hear the Diet of Augsburg[4] will be prorogued to the 24th of this month. Every thing is quiet in England. Among us some turbulent mass-priests paraded the streets by night in arms, but were very near being beaten by the townsmen, had not the authorities made a timely appearance. Doctor John Tischell[5], the patron of the papists, was wounded. Should these mass-priests persevere in these disturbances, I hope it will turn out to the furtherance of the word of God. They are raising their crests, as long as they perceive the emperor so industriously endeavouring the re-

[3 See above, Letter CXXIII. p. 268.]

[4 The Diet at Augsburg was opened by the emperor on the 26th of July. Sleidan, XXII. 489.]

[5 Sleidan says, in his History of the Reformation, as to the tumults, at Strasburgh, in 1550: "It was thought that the bishop, who had always been looked upon as a man of a mild and peaceable nature, that loved his ease, did not act thus so much out of his own inclination, as at the instigation of his friends, who represented to him that this occasion of recovering his jurisdiction was not to be slighted, and that unless he prosecuted it, he might also incur the emperor's displeasure. In all these transactions he made use of one Christopher Welsinger, a civilian, who had sometimes studied at Wittemberg. But the chapter of the cathedral church of Strasburgh employed as their advocate one *John Tischell*, a doctor of the laws." Sleidan, XXI. 480.]

establishment of their errors. May the Lord grant you his favour and peace! Amen.

My wife very dutifully salutes you and yours. May you and all your family be preserved in safety! Salute all our learned friends. Farewell.

Yours,

BURCHER.

P. S. The Louvainists[1] have again published their Confession of Faith. Among other things they prohibit the people from reading the holy bible and the gospel. A new and unheard of inquisition[2] too is to be established through the whole of lower Germany. Pray ye the Lord to preserve his people! I have determined to go into England after the next Frankfort fair, on a visit to my friends, whom I have not seen for twelve years. If I can be of any use to you there, I am entirely at your service.

LETTER CCCXV.

JOHN BURCHER TO HENRY BULLINGER.

Dated at STRASBURGH, *Sept.* 1, 1550.

GREETING. I was exceedingly delighted, my very dear friend and master, Bullinger, at your having received a letter from Hooper[3], by which you were informed both respecting the books and the king's favourable reception of them. I shall receive the expression of your gratitude from Froschover with many thanks, and will make a suitable return whenever an opportunity shall be afforded me. When I send letters by the post, the cost is ten kreutzer for every ounce, which is equivalent to two German loths; besides the carriage from hence to Spires, which amounts to at least a batz for each packet, with an addition of one half, if they are above the ordinary weight. We have had no positive intelligence about the disturbances that have arisen in French Flanders. May the Lord grant us his grace, that in whatever way Christ and his kingdom may be advanced, that of antichrist

[1 The divines of Louvain drew up thirty-two articles of religion, and published them by the emperor's licence in 1545. They were replied to by Luther, Op. II. 542. See Sleidan, XVI. 343, and Seckendorf, III. 589.]

[2 See above, p. 417, n. 4, and Sleidan, XXII. 498.]

[3 See above, Letter XXXIX. p. 88.]

may be diminished! I willingly undertake the office you impose upon me, of receiving the letters and books from Froschover, and of forwarding them to England. It will be no trouble to me, but a very great pleasure; for I am anxious to do a service to you and to all Zurichers: for I consider myself as an Anglo-Zuricher. The books therefore and the letters I will either most carefully deliver in person, or will forward them to the individuals to whom you have addressed them. I wonder however that you have not sent a copy to the bishop. But it is of little consequence, for I will present him in your name with the copy which you gave me. I have sent your letter to doctor Mont at Augsburg; for he is there with the English ambassador, though he is to return hither at the end of this month. My business calls me away, and will not permit me to delay any longer. I pray you, therefore, to excuse this my short letter. We have no news; should I hear of any, I will communicate it when at Frankfort. Farewell, with all your family. My wife most dutifully salutes you and yours. All our brethren are in good health.

Yours,

BURCHER.

P. S. I cannot find the book of the Louvainists, but it shall be sent from Frankfort. Please to forward this letter to Winterthur.

LETTER CCCXVI.

JOHN BURCHER TO HENRY BULLINGER.

Dated at FRANKFORT, *Sept.* 14, 1550.

GREETING. Your two letters, my dear friend, I have received with much pleasure; nor will your request occasion me any trouble whatever. I have received the books and packets of letters from master Froschover; and I will take care with all diligence that they may be delivered to the parties for whom they are intended, and I take this charge upon myself.

It is a false and groundless report which is circulated respecting fresh disturbances in England. I send you the Inquisition[4], as they call it, put forth by the Louvainists, and

[4 See the preceding page, n. 1.]

written both in Dutch and German. There is no news here worth relating. I have read over the emperor's proposals to the states of the empire: he urges nothing more earnestly than that the rebels should be punished, and his religion be established. He urges, too, the renewal of the council at Trent. Their answer is published, but I have not yet seen it. They say that the emperor is severely suffering from ill health. I am glad that you have made a treaty with the confederates, and especially that you have obtained possession of the fortress. This will certainly be of great advantage to the state. May God enlarge your territory, and preserve you from all defilement of this present life! Amen.

Salute your wife and all our learned friends in my name and in that of my wife. I will not forget to present your salutations to your friends and acquaintance in England. Farewell.

Yours,

BURCHER.

LETTER CCCXVII.

JOHN BURCHER TO HENRY BULLINGER.

Dated at STRASBURGH, *Nov.* 21, 1550.

GREETING. I returned from England eight days since, my very dear Bullinger, where I left all our friends and acquaintance safe and well. The state of England is such, that we can perceive the simple truth is beginning to revive there. The word is preached in some places clearly, in others more obscurely; but both in public, during the performance of divine service in the churches, and also individually, in the hearts of many who set themselves up for gospellers, there is a snake in the grass. There is a contest between the godly and the pretended and false brethren about the dregs of the habits and of other ceremonies; and while these things are agitated, the fold of Christ is neglected. Some there are who have assumed to themselves too much licence, both in oppressing the poor, and also as regards a manner of life altogether impure; and this under the cloke of the word of God and the gospel of Jesus Christ. Many others have the truth at heart, and under the guidance of the word of God are really advancing to a perfect and a christian life. We must pray for these that they may persevere; for the others, that they may be brought to a better way of living. Let thus much suffice respecting the general state of England: I now come to private matters.

The king is daily making progress, as in age, so also in the knowledge of the word of God, and in distinguished virtues. He received with the greatest satisfaction both your letter and the book you had dedicated to him. I gave them to Hooper, as you requested; he to some one of the household, by whom they were delivered to the king. I doubt not but that you will receive the thanks of the king himself some time or other. I delivered or sent all the other books and letters to the persons for whom they were intended. I return you my lasting thanks for the book you gave me. Hooper is sufficiently comfortable, except that he is not on good terms with the bishop of London[1]. Hooper claims to be inaugurated only by the imposition of hands; the bishop contends on the contrary, that he must submit to popish ceremonies, or at least to those agreeing with the popish doctrine, namely, that he must carry the bible[2] on his shoulders, and put on a white vestment, and that thus habited and bearing the book, he is to turn himself round three times. This controversy does no little injury to the christian commonwealth; and the result of the tragedy is expected with some apprehension. The papists are rejoicing at the disagreement between these chief ministers of the word of God, and are hoping that from this controversy the overthrow of the gospel will ensue. Wherefore it would not be out of place, if both parties were reminded of their duty by yourself and the leading preachers of the truth of the present day. Peace might possibly be the result. Or you might more conveniently state your opinion to the king respecting profane ceremonies of this kind. But now, letting this pass, I come to master Richard and his family. He is alive and well, together with his wife and dear children, and desires his best salutations to his friends. Time does not allow me to write more. This letter of Hooper will supply what I have omitted. Farewell. Salute your wife from me.

Yours,

BURCHER.

[1 See above, p. 486, n. 1.]

[2 See Liturgies of Edward VI. (Park. Soc.) p. 185.]

LETTER CCCXVIII.

JOHN BURCHER TO HENRY BULLINGER.

Dated at Strasburgh, *Dec.* 28, 1550.

Perpetual health in the Lord! I pray for you, and for your family, and for all Switzerland every blessing of the present year: and that the word of God may abide and flourish with you, to the praise of the name of God, and the honour of Jesus Christ, and the benefit of all Christendom. Amen. Amen.

Since you ask my opinion, my very dear friend Bullinger, whether I think it advisable for you to write to the king, I shall not hesitate to declare it in few words; nor do I doubt but you will receive with candour what I am about to say. Great evil is impending over the Church of England, and I know that all worthy and godly persons are exceedingly distressed. This evil, however, may easily be either removed or mitigated by your authority, and that of your church, if you will write to the king. Hooper is striving to effect an entire purification of the church from the very foundation. Other bishops, on the contrary, who nevertheless are men of learning and professors of the truth, are ashamed of this, because they will not open their eyes to their own errors. Hence they contend with all their might to have him entangled in the same superstitious ceremonies with themselves. They charge him with insubordination, because he positively refuses to admit any other rite of consecration than what the apostles adopted. They first of all persuaded the king, that he condemned the vestments and things of the like kind as evil in themselves abstractedly considered: and when they could not gain their object by this means, they invented another falsehood, namely, that he had allowed the vestments, tonsure, and the like ceremonies adopted by the bishops, to be things indifferent. But Hooper did neither the one nor the other: for he neither condemned the vestments as evil in themselves, nor would he allow that the vestments and tonsure of the bishops were matters of indifference, and endurable in the church of God. The controversy now rests with the king to determine, who if he be clearly instructed by you as to the judgment that must be formed of it according to God's word, I have no doubt but that it will be of great advantage to religion. I do not, however, consider it either necessary or expedient for you to write expressly upon the matter now in dispute; but only as to what ceremonies may be allowed in the church, and to what extent; lest you might probably seem to have been suborned by Hooper to write on his behalf. You now have my opinion, and, should you think proper to write a letter, I will forward it by a courier without any expense to yourself. I have lately received a letter stating that the controversy is not yet ended. Hooper has John à Lasco and a few others on his side; but against him many adversaries, among whom is Bucer; who, if he possessed as much influence now as he formerly did among us, it would have been all over with Hooper's preferment, for he would never have been made bishop. I fear this may still be the case, and the bishop of London is striving by all possible means that it may be so. Master Christopher Mont has been for nearly these last six months at Augsburg, and has not yet returned. He is daily expected. Farewell. My wife dutifully salutes you and yours. Salute her also from me.

Yours,

BURCHER.

LETTER CCCXIX.

JOHN BURCHER TO HENRY BULLINGER.

Dated at STRASBURGH, *Jan.* 6, 1551.

GREETING. A letter hast just been brought me from England, my very dear Bullinger, which in part announces mournful tidings, though chiefly those of a more pleasing character. The mournful intelligence relates to the death of Paul Fagius, who departed this life not long since, that is, on the 23rd of November. The joyful news is this, that two christian men, namely, the bishop of Ely[1] and the marquis of Dorset, have been chosen into the great council of England. Richard [Hilles] and his wife are both in good health. The

[1 Thomas Goodrich, lord chancellor. See Strype, Mem. II. ii. 160.]

leaders of the rebellion have suffered punishment. The reports respecting the protector are all vain and false; for he has not yet been brought to execution. Another rumour, too, had reached us, but it is a false one, concerning a renewed rebellion in England. The messenger is waiting, and will not allow me to write more. I sent all your letters into England. In future, I pray you, send as few thither as you can; for they are not conveyed without great expense. What, however, you write to Richard, I will gladly forward at my own charge. Farewell. Communicate this letter to the English, to whom I have not now leisure to write.

J. BURCHER.

LETTER CCCXX.

JOHN BURCHER TO HENRY BULLINGER.

Dated at STRASBURGH, *Jan.* 21, 1551.

GREETING. Your letter, my honoured Bullinger, reached me two days since, and I forwarded to the post on that very day both the king's letter and that for Hooper. I most carefully gave them in charge to my singular good friend master Richard, that by his means they might be delivered to the king and to Hooper; and I well know that by reason of our ancient intimacy he will not decline this service. I approve of the argument of your letter to the king, nor do I doubt but that it will be for the advantage both of Hooper and of religion. The bishops have enjoined silence upon Hooper, accusing him, as my friend Thomas Knight writes me word from England, of heresy. I forward you his letter, which can be translated into Latin by the assistance of master Butler, (to whom commend me a thousand times.) You will thence perceive what are Satan's plans, whom we must resist with all our power. I request that, as you have it in your power to be of great service to our reviving church, a document may be delivered to the king by the common consent of yourself, Calvin, and other learned men, that he may be rightly instructed in this controversy. Otherwise, as you perceive, the truth is in danger; and as you have so greatly exerted yourselves in its defence, you must not now suffer it to be destroyed in England. I send you the news I have received respecting the war in Saxony, as it has been written to me by a friend at Cologne. He adds in his letter, that this inscription is carried in the hand of a man arrayed in cloth of gold, represented on their standard: "If God be for us, who can be against us?" They carry also, on another standard, a picture of a virgin, and a serpent painted before her, whom she addresses in these words: "Get thee away, Satan!" How true this may be, I cannot say; but it was told me by an honourable and trustworthy man. Should you require my assistance in any way, I am entirely at your service. My wife earnestly salutes you and yours. Salute her also from myself. I wish to yourself and family, and all my friends at Zurich, a happy, quiet and peaceable new year. May the Lord in his mercy bestow upon you and upon all kingdoms the peace of Jesus Christ! Farewell.

Yours,

BURCHER.

LETTER CCCXXI.

JOHN BURCHER TO HENRY BULLINGER.

Dated at STRASBURGH, *Aug.* 3, 1551.

HEALTH in the Lord, and a happy life! Two days since I directed a letter which I had received from England, addressed to you, to be sent by a messenger of Constance to Valentine Nüssbaum, a merchant at Basle. I safely received yesterday the letter that you sent by Frisius; that for Hooper I forwarded by the post. But as letters cannot be sent backwards and forwards without some expense, you will have the kindness to take this circumstance into your consideration. An ounce is conveyed for five kreutzers from Spires to Antwerp, exclusive of the charge of the courier from hence to Spires; which, as it may somewhat exceed the tariff, is not usually less than a batz. Our people are so given to making money, that they are quite unmindful of the duties of liberality, and will not do anything without straightway calling out for money, money. Wherefore they will sometimes look down with contempt upon the regulated price, and refuse to take charge of any letters unless you pay according to the covetousness of the demander. I should be loth to trouble you with this matter, were it not that such numbers of letters are brought to me from all quarters. I promise you my duty, fidelity, and diligence, and I will spare no exertion in looking out for a courier. But I will afterwards make out an account of what shall have been paid, and will forward it to you by some convenient opportunity. I know that you do not wish me to be at any loss. As for those I have already sent, I will make you a present of the postage, and that willingly, because I know that in them you have consulted the benefit of my country and of good men. As to those which you may forward in future, I will write upon them the weight and cost, if you wish them to be sent by post. But if you write word for me to send them by a neighbour without any charge, they will be detained longer, but may for the most part be forwarded in the course of a month. Therefore, if you receive letters from others to be sent by the post, receive at the same time the amount of the postage. Thus much have I thought good to write to you respecting letters: I now come to other matters.

Peter Martyr has published a book on the Eucharist[1], to which he has annexed his disputation with our people at Oxford. I will send you this book, if I conveniently can. My countrymen too have been celebrating the praises of the deceased Bucer, both in verse and prose. I wish you had seen their zeal and piety towards one however undeserving: and that you may see them, I have inclosed the book in this letter. The death of Bucer affords England the greatest possible opportunity of concord. The leading men of England are desirous of a successor not less learned than himself, to supply his place. For my own part, I desire one who may be more sincere and steady. If you know any one qualified for so important an office, pray inform me. I make no doubt but that he could easily be advanced to this high eminence, by the help of some individuals with whom I am acquainted, and who have conversed with me upon the subject. Whoever he may be, he will not want for friends and honour;

[1 See above, p. 478, n. 1.]

but as truth is generally wont to have hatred for her companion, so he must expect nothing but evil from those who are evil. Provide, if you can, for our country and our religion. The place is open to a man of learning, if he is on our side. The truth has prevailed. I hear nothing certain about the Magdeburghers. England is quiet. A pestilence, called the sweating sickness, has been prevalent in London. More than nine hundred died in one week; but the plague and wrath of God, by his blessing, is now abated. May the Lord grant us his grace! Diligently salute your wife, children, and all our learned and godly friends.

Yours,

J. B.

P.S. A friend has written me word to-day from Cologne, that the Magdeburghers[2] have sallied forth, and obtained a most important victory, and have taken from the enemy a great quantity of provisions of every kind.

It is reported among us for certain, that the Magdeburghers deceived the enemy by an extraordinary stratagem on the 15th of June. They sent out young men in women's clothes to gather forage, and added a guard of soldiers to accompany them. The enemy, supposing them to be really young women, made an attack upon them, as though certain of their prey. The pretended females made a shew of flight, the guard hastened to their defence. At last the young men threw off the mask, and appeared in arms. They attacked the enemy, and forced him to retreat. About eight hundred of the soldiers of Maurice fell in action. After this victory having become somewhat more elated, they again attacked the enemy, when they brought into the city three or four wagons laden with the slain bodies of the Magdeburghers. It is reported, however, that not less than five hundred of the enemy were slain. This statement is given by the messenger who has come hither from Magdeburgh. Communicate this, I pray you, to my friend master Sebastian.

[[2] For an account of the siege of Magdeburg, see Robertson, Charles V. B. x. Sleidan, B. xxii.]

LETTER CCCXXII.

JOHN BURCHER TO HENRY BULLINGER.

Dated at STRASBURGH, *Aug.* 10, 1551.

GREETING. I send you, my dear Bullinger, as I wished to do in my last letter, the disputations of Peter Martyr, and his treatise upon the eucharist. I was unwilling to deprive you any longer of so great a pleasure. I know not, however, whether you have received them before: should this be the case, I have nevertheless discharged my duty. You will commend the diligence and labours of one who is most learned in every way. He had a sharp contest with very shrewd and perverse opponents; yet he notwithstanding gained the victory, which is certainly a ground of rejoicing to all good men. Could Cambridge be similarly distinguished by one like him, how happy would our England then be! Some of our leading men in England are desirous that Musculus[1] should be appointed in the place [of Bucer]. But he, as I hear, rejects the terms that are offered him. But I dare answer for it, that if he will undertake this office, he will not be less in favour with the king and with all good men than Bucer himself was. Nor will he find the Cambridge men so perversely learned as master Peter found those at Oxford. For the scholars of that university have been always suspected of heresy, as they call it, by the ancient members, learned and unlearned: by which you may easily judge that their studies have always been of a purer character than those at Oxford. For from thence came forth Cox, Hooper, and (whom I ought to mention in the first place) Cranmer, and other most learned men of that class. And there is no reason why Musculus should be so averse to this vocation; for it is more honourable to render service to a kingdom than to a city. Wherefore, laying aside all natural misgivings, he would act, in my opinion, the part of a Christian, if, having been so often invited, he would at last consent. Should he refuse, he will hardly escape the suspicion of cowardice and lukewarmness. For the rest, I doubt not but that you will communicate with him upon the subject. If he is to be persuaded, let me know; and I will take care that due provision be made for his

[1 See above Letters CLXI—CLXIII.]

journey, besides whatever else may be necessary. I salute your wife and children. Salute all our friends. Farewell. I acquainted you with all the news I had to communicate in my last letter sent from hence to Valentine Nüssbaum three days ago; since which nothing has taken place. Farewell.

Yours wholly,

JOHN BURCHER.

P. S. I am most anxious to see your book, wherein you have replied to the last calumnies of Luther, together with the book of the said calumnies annexed[2]. Some persons have your reply, but are not in possession of Luther's book: wherefore I wish them both joined together, that both the calumnies and errors of Luther and your answer may be seen at the same time.

LETTER CCCXXIII.

JOHN BURCHER TO HENRY BULLINGER.

Dated at STRASBURGH, *May* 1, 1553.

GREETING. The son of Erasmus Fabricius[3] of pious memory has given me your most agreeable letter, my most esteemed Bullinger. Should I have it in my power to be of use to him, or any other [of your friends], I shall never be wanting: for any one who comes hither from you will be most acceptable, even on the ground of his being a Zuricher. I have made arrangements at Frankfort, that the letters and books for the English should be forwarded to England. I have received your discourses on Jonah, with which my wife is much delighted. We have long since received that little

[2 The books here referred to were on the sacramentarian controversy. That of Luther is entitled *Brevis confessio de cœna Domini,* which Melancthon in a letter to Bullinger calls 'atrocissimum scriptum.' Bullinger published an 'Apology,' which he annexed to the tract written by Luther, and sent to the leaders of the protestants in Germany; and by way of a further explanation of his opinions, he wrote shortly afterwards a tract entitled *Absoluta de Christi Domini et Catholicæ ejus ecclesiæ sacramentis tractatio,* the sale of which, Seckendorf states (III. 31), was forbidden in Saxony. An edition was published in London in 1551. See Melchior Adam. Vit. Bullingeri, p. 485.]

[3 Erasmus Fabricius was one of the canons of Zurich. Gerdes. Hist. Ev. I. 270.]

sum of money, as I lately wrote you word. The young men did not bring the parcel to master Wolfgang of Worms, but inclosed it with other things of theirs, which will not be brought hither before our fair. As soon as I receive them, I will safely send them you. Master Christopher Mont is alive and well; he has been absent some time, which has occasioned his silence. I saluted him in your name, and desired him to write, which he promised he would do.

We have some positive intelligence here, which I willingly communicate, that you may rejoice together with us. In the room of the deceased master Hedio[1], we have obtained a man who is not only learned, but a disciple of the true religion, and who professes and publicly lectures in divinity. He opposes the Lutherans, and all those who attribute to Christ's human nature properties which belong only to his divine nature. The Lutherans confound the two natures of Christ, if not in words, yet in reality. He opposes them publicly, and boldly charges them with error. I wish their eyes might be opened, lest while seeing they should become blind.

Of the affairs of Germany and the war I hear thus much. The princes and commissioners of the emperor and Ferdinand are to meet at Frankfort on the 16th of May to settle their disputes. I wish this may be accomplished. Albert, marquis of Brandenburgh, has slain some soldiers of the ecclesiastics[2], about four hundred, as some say, others about five hundred. He plundered others after they had taken an oath that they would not serve either against the emperor or himself for the space of three months. In England, by the blessing of God, all things are quiet. Our king has now sent, for the second time, ambassadors to the emperor and the French king to put an end to the war. I wish it were effected. I will write to you, as soon as I know the result. Salute your wife and dear children in my name and that of my wife. Salute all our learned and godly friends. Farewell. Salute my friend Butler a thousand times, together with my dear gossip.

Your most devoted

JOHN BURCHER, *Anglus.*

[1 Caspar Hedio died Oct. 17, 1552, and was succeeded by Jerome Zanchius in his pastoral duties at Strasburgh.]

[2 *Pfafforum*, orig. About this time Albert invaded the bishopricks of Bamberg and Wurtzburg. Sleidan, XXIV. 578.]

LETTER CCCXXIV.

JOHN BURCHER TO HENRY BULLINGER.

Dated at STRASBURGH, *July* 8, 1553.

GREETING. A most painful report, my dear Bullinger, has reached us, respecting our most christian king; (for it is fitting to attribute to this real christian the title of "most christian," rather than to another, who assumes that title without any pretensions to it.) This report at first alarmed me exceedingly; and I should scarcely have believed it, had not our common friend, master Mont, who has been summoned by the English ambassadors, at the king's command, to the emperor's court at Brussels, confirmed it in a letter to myself. He wrote both to me and to others on the 24th of June, that the English ambassadors had arrived at Brussels, and brought word that the king was suffering under severe illness, but by the blessing of God was so far recovered as to be out of danger. God therefore must be praised, and entreated to preserve this our sovereign very long among us. The whole church of England implores our great and gracious God in united prayer both for his restoration to health and long preservation. I entreat you also to commend both our king and church to God in your continual prayers. Mont writes word moreover, that Therouenne[3] has been taken by stratagem: negotiations for peace were going on between the citizens and the emperor, and commissioners were sent to arrange the terms, when a cessation of hostilities took place. Meanwhile, during their conference, the emperor's troops made a sudden attack upon the city, and effected an entrance on that side where they had previously battered down the walls with their cannon: they slew about five hundred soldiers, set fire to the city, and took away prisoner the son of the constable[4]. So that the proverb respecting the good faith of the Carthaginians may now be justly applied to that of the Spaniards.

[[3] Therouenne is about six miles south of St Omer's. It was taken and plundered on June 21. See Sleidan, XXV. 580, and Robertson, IV. 124.]

[[4] This was Francis, son of the duke de Montmorency, constable of France. He was the governor of the city.]

Thus much have I thought worth writing to you, my dear Bullinger. Salute a thousand times in my name and that of my wife your wife, children, and all our learned friends. Farewell.

Yours,

JOHN BURCHER.

LETTER CCCXXV.

JOHN BURCHER TO HENRY BULLINGER.

Dated at STRASBURGH, *Aug.* 16, 1553.

GREETING. What I wrote in my former letter, my honoured Bullinger, is daily confirmed, and more than confirmed, by the statements of some excellent men. That monster of a man, the duke of Northumberland, has been committing a horrible and portentous crime. A writer worthy of credit informs me, that our excellent king has been most shamefully taken off by poison[1]. His nails and hair fell off before his death, so that, handsome as he was, he entirely lost all his good looks. The perpetrators of the murder were ashamed of allowing the body of the deceased king to lie in state, and be seen by the public, as is usual: wherefore they buried him privately in a paddock adjoining the palace, and substituted in his place, to be seen by the people, a youth not very unlike him whom they had murdered. One of the sons of the duke of Northumberland acknowledged this fact. The duke has been apprehended with his five sons, and nearly twenty persons of rank; among whom is master Cheke, doctor Cox, and the bishop of London, with others unknown to you either by name or reputation. It is thought that these persons gave their consent and sanction, that Jane, the wife of the duke's son, should be proclaimed queen: should this prove to be the case, it is all over with them. The king of France has sent word to the city of Calais and to Guisnes, for the citizens to remove,

[1 At the time of king Edward's death it was strongly reported that he was poisoned; but it is hardly necessary to say that Burcher in this and some other matters was far too credulous. It is not however in general necessary to enlarge on these points, as they are sufficiently set to rights by other letters. See above, p. 365, n. 2.]

and leave the city and camp at Guisnes at his disposal; for that it was promised him by the English council. The duke and his fellow-prisoners are supposed to have been guilty of this shameful deed. Forces are collecting in England to defend the city and territory. I am afraid lest your Swiss should be sent against us. You see, my dear friend, how you are deprived of all your expectation respecting our England: you must consider therefore what you should determine upon respecting your son. My house[2] is open to him, and my services shall not be wanting. Farewell, and diligently, I pray you, salute all your learned men. I am exceedingly obliged to you all for the kindness you have shewn me.

Yours,

BURCHER.

LETTER CCCXXVI.

JOHN BURCHER TO HENRY BULLINGER.

Dated at STRASBURGH, *March* 3, 1554.

GREETING. I doubt not, my esteemed Bullinger, but that the report of the rebellion of disturbed and afflicted England has already reached you; the origin, progress, and result of which the bearer[3] of this letter will acquaint you with. I pray you to receive him with kindness; for whatever you shall do for him, you may consider as being done for Christ. He is a man not only learned, but pious and godly, and now an exile from England for the word of God and the testimony of Jesus Christ. Welcome him, I pray you, to your house and hospitality; for he will only remain with you until he shall have conferred with some learned men upon some controverted points of religion. He is quiet, and satisfied with so little, that I cannot sufficiently admire his parsimonious way of living. Your experience will confirm the truth of what I am writing. But he will not live with you at your expense, for he has wherewith to provide for himself. He has moreover

[2 See above, p. 511, n. 2.]

[3 This was probably "the learned and pious Mr Lever, once master of St John's College in Cambridge, and a great preacher in king Edward's days." Strype, Grindal, 274. See Letters LXXVII. and CCCLII.]

given not a few proofs of his learning. There are some learned and pious sermons published, which he preached before the late king and the nobility. To say no more, you will learn, my Bullinger, from your own experience, what kind of a man he is: wherefore I entreat you not to allow him to fail of obtaining your assistance.

And now to mention a few things which you will be glad to hear. It is stated that the rebels have put to death three hundred mass-priests[1]. They were successful at first, but their leader, I hear, was at length taken prisoner. It is rumoured among other things, (but the rumour is uncertain,) that the duke of Suffolk had joined the rebels, and was with them. I wish this may prove a false report. I have heard too, that the queen has beheaded his daughter Jane, together with her husband; that Jane, I mean, who was proclaimed queen. But I will write you word whatever I may hear. You must now excuse my being brief, for the bearer of this will acquaint you with all the circumstances. Farewell. Your son, by the blessing of God, is alive and well.

You know me,

[BURCHER.]

LETTER CCCXXVII.

JOHN BURCHER TO HENRY BULLINGER.

Dated at STRASBURGH, *Sept.* 3, 1554.

GREETING. The noble and learned Antony Cook, induced by the reputation of your country and learning, is about to pass through your city on his way to Italy. I wish him to find that my recommendation has been of some advantage to him. He was a fellow-labourer with [Sir John] Cheke in instructing the late king, and lived for some time with me at my house very piously and courteously.

I have sent back to you my servant Joachim. Do not pay him any thing for your son's tabling, unless you can do so without any inconvenience or loss to yourself. I will take care to provide clothes for your son as he may want them, and neither shabby nor too expensive.

[1 See above, p. 514.]

The noble bearer will be able to tell you the news from England better than I can. The emperor has sustained a great defeat[2], as I wrote you word in my last letter. The soldiers who survived the slaughter, and are daily passing disarmed through the city, bear evidence of the fact. May the Lord provide for you all! My wife salutes you in return.

You know the writer,

[BURCHER.]

LETTER CCCXXVIII.

JOHN BURCHER TO HENRY BULLINGER.

Dated at PINCZOV, *Nov.* 4, 1557.

PERPETUAL health in Jesus Christ our Lord! I doubt not, my dear friend and master, but that you are anxiously expecting the agreeable intelligence of my safe arrival in Poland. By the blessing of our great and good God I reached Cracow about eight days since, happy, safe and well, and proceeded from thence to Pinczov. I found that excellent man, and your loving friend, master John à Lasco, in good health. He received me, by reason of your recommendation, with the greatest kindness, and has diligently pleaded my cause[3] by letter with the Duke Palatine of Wilna. I doubt not but that I shall obtain the licence; and on this account I am to go in a few days direct to Wilna to the duke himself, and also to the king's majesty. I shall have for my fellow-traveller master William Barlow, formerly bishop of Bath in England, whom master à Lasco wishes to accompany me. From Wilna I will diligently write you an account of my proceedings.

There is no news, excepting that relating to the victory of the king of Poland over the Livonians[4]: but it may rather

[2 The engagement referred to took place on August 13, 1554. See Robertson, Charles V. B. IV.]

[3 The object of Burcher's visit to Poland, as appears by a subsequent letter, was to obtain permission to establish a brewery, or rather to instruct others in the art of brewing.]

[4 William de Furstenburg, grand master of the knights sword-bearers in Livonia, had imprisoned the bishop of Riga, Sigismund's cousin, and massacred the envoys whom he sent to demand the release of his kinsman. Sigismund was aiming to wreak vengeance on them, when they submitted and formed an alliance with Poland. See above, p. 599, n. 2.]

be called a surrender than a victory, although they were compelled to lay down their arms. The terms of peace are these. The Livonians had engaged to pay the expenses of the war, namely, forty thousand pieces of gold, but the king has liberally excused them. They are to provide a certain fixed number of cavalry for the king's service, whenever he may require them. The number is not ascertained, though some persons think it is four thousand. They are to give up to the king of Poland the individuals who murdered the royal ambassadors. Whatever they may have taken either by violence or stealth from the duchy of Lithuania, they are to restore. So much as to the conditions of peace.

Moreover, since I know that you are anxiously expecting the certain and avowed opinion of Melancthon respecting the humanity of Christ, I send you this, which master à Lasco has given me to copy. It is selected and taken by word of mouth from his lectures. And this it is which the Lutherans wished him to recant at Worms. May the Lord give him grace plainly and openly to defend the truth! The truth here in Poland, by the blessing of the great and good God, is deeply taking root. Master à Lasco is boldly instructing the nobles. He has to-day discoursed for two hours at a nobleman's table, upon the true and genuine interpretation of the words of Christ: "This is my body." He has converted many, and maintains the real, and not the Lutheran interpretation. We must pray the Lord to give him strength. He has just been with the prince of Cracow, who is seventy years old, whom he has brought truly to acknowledge that the pope is antichrist. Nor does any thing make him hesitate, except the misapplication of church property, and the right understanding of the Lord's supper. They will easily be brought to agree, that the property of the church shall be converted to pious uses; and master à Lasco hopes that he will gradually come to the true understanding of the words of Christ. Commend them both to the Lord in your prayers: for if he can gain him over, there is great hope of the whole of lesser Poland. Farewell with all your family. Communicate, I pray you, what I have written to masters John Wolf, Sebastian, your sons-in-law, and the gentlemen of Poland [now at Zurich], to all of whom I desire my dutiful salutations.

Yours, BURCHER.

P.S. I commend my wife to your kind protection.

LETTER CCCXXIX.

JOHN BURCHER TO HENRY BULLINGER.

Dated at CRACOW, *Feb.* 16, 1558.

GREETING. I feel assured, my esteemed friend and master, that you are anxiously expecting a letter from me, by which you may learn where I am, and how my affairs are going on. I am endeavouring to instruct the brewers here at Cracow, of whom there are at least five hundred, in the art of brewing. But the want of my licence, which I am daily expecting from Wilna, has hitherto hindered me. For though the king's majesty has granted me this privilege, yet it could not receive the sign manual and be sealed with the seal of the kingdom during my stay; for on the day after the licence was granted, the king went away to hunt, and does not intend to return before Lent. It seemed, therefore, more expedient for me to go to Cracow, and there ascertain what hope there might be in that city of success in the manufacture, than to waste this whole time in idleness at Wilna. And I find some persons here who gainsay, and think it impossible, while others are desirous of acquiring a knowledge of the art. The delay of the licence is the only impediment, but this I am expecting from day to day; for immediately after my departure, the king returned to celebrate the obsequies of his deceased mother[1]. And I gave my business in charge to one upon whom I could depend, namely, to master John Mantzinsky, a Polish nobleman, and secretary to the duke Palatine of Wilna. He faithfully promised to take care that, as soon as the king returned, the licence should be signed with the sign manual, and sealed with the great seal. This same Mantzinsky was studying at Zurich in the year 1547, which gave me hope of his fidelity and diligence. He is well acquainted with master Theodore and yourself, and desires his respects to you both. And thus much of my private affairs.

[1 Bona, daughter of John Galeazzo Sforza, duke of Milan, and of Isabella of Arragon, was married to Sigismund, king of Poland, in 1519. She left Poland in 1555, and died at Bari (in the kingdom of Naples) in 1557. Krasinski, Ref. Vol. I. 278.]

The word of God and the gospel of Jesus Christ is by the blessing of God taking deeper root every day; and I do not hear of a single man of learning, who does not abominate the Lutheran errors. Master John à Lasco is actively labouring in the Lord's vineyard; and enforces no subject with greater earnestness, than the pure doctrine of the Lord's supper. They hold their meetings, and sacred assemblies, but in the houses of the nobles. I have not seen any church purified [from popery], except only in Pinczov, where the word of God had its first beginning. For that brave nobleman of Pinczov, Nicolas Olesnicki[1], a man certainly deserving of great praise, began the opposition to antichrist and the papists. The duke Palatine of Wilna has sermons in his house, and baptism, and the Lord's supper, and many of the citizens of Wilna assemble there. He alone, among the nobles of Poland, bears the heat and burden of the Lord's vineyard. But he is much spoken against for patronizing the Jews, by whose bribes, they say, he suffers himself to be corrupted. Should this be true, it will occasion not a little stumbling at the word of God. I wish he could be admonished to consult both his own interests and the gospel of Jesus Christ.

I have many things to write respecting the people of Poland and Lithuania, their manners and customs, which I defer till I return to you. Thus much, however, I think right to add concerning their modes of religion. In Poland there are Jews, papists, and gospellers. In addition to these, there are in Lithuania Armenians, Tartars, Russians, Turks, and Muscovites. The Tartars acknowledge a God, creator of heaven and earth, but they worship moreover the sun, moon, and stars. The faith and religion of the Turks is well known to you. The Armenians, Russians, and Muscovites are of the Greek church and faith. They acknowledge as their head

[1 The first direct attack on the Roman Catholic establishment was made by Nicholaus Olesnicki, lord of Pinczov, who, induced by Stancari, turned out the monks from a convent in his town, ejected the images from the church, and established there a public protestant worship, according to the tenets and rites of Geneva. He was, in consequence, summoned before the ecclesiastical tribunal of Cracow, the result of which was simply to oblige him to promise the restoration of the convent to the monks whom he had ejected. See Krasinski's Reform. in Poland, I. 166, &c.]

the patriarch of Constantinople, and are more happy than the papists in allowing communion in both kinds, and retaining the marriage of the clergy. They perform their sacred worship too only in the old Ruthenian[2] language. They allow pictures, but not images, in their churches; but they place candles before them, and reverence and adore them just as the papists do. Their churches are divided into three parts, the upper, middle, and lower. The upper division they call, as the Jews do, the Holy of Holies, and no one enters therein save the priest and deacon. The unmarried part of the congregation occupy the middle division, and those who are married occupy the lower, not being allowed to enter into the middle division, till they shall have been introduced by the priest. They pray standing, and bowing down their heads to the very ground, as the monks do: they sign themselves with the sign of the cross, repeating these words, *Gospodi Pomilui*, which means, "Lord, have mercy upon us;" and thereupon they sign and bow themselves. If any one laughs at their ceremonies, they immediately turn him out of the church, and sweep and clean the place where he stood. They bury their dead with great noise and howling; they array them in new clothes and shoes, and pour on their heads two cups of wine or beer. The corpse, moreover, receives a letter from the priests, and half a groschen from his friends; and is to present the letter and money to St Peter, that the porter may immediately open for him the gates of heaven. They allow of no sermon, no teaching, and adhere to their ceremonies as tenaciously as the papists.

In Muscovy God has raised up another Luther, or rather a Zuingle. He reproved their errors, and was arrested, and was to have been burnt for the truth's sake, had not the great duke of Muscovy prevented it. For when the accusation was brought before him by his bishops, he decided that the prisoner was not deserving of death, and ordered him to be released. On his dismissal he went into Lithuania with some monks who had joined him, and there he was very kindly received by the Palatine of Wilna. At length, on the invitation of the duke of the Ruthenians, he is promulgating the truth in that nation. He has set forth a confession of faith in all respects agreeable to ours. A person has promised to send it me, in

[[2] See above, p. 600, n. 1.]

which case I will either bring or send it to you. We ought to be exceedingly thankful to Almighty God that, without any intervention of man's teaching, he has by his holy Spirit opened, even to the Greeks, the kingdom of his Son and of the truth. For this person is entirely unacquainted with the Latin, and every other language, in which, in our time, it has pleased God to reveal his Son.

I have this news to communicate, that the Tartars have within these few days invaded Russia, and plundered and laid waste more than five hundred villages and hamlets. They have carried off, as it is reported, together with an infinite quantity of plunder, thirty thousand prisoners, men, women, and children. They retired without any loss, nor is this nation affected in the least by this event.

On the 4th of December last, as I was journeying towards Wilna, I beheld a remarkable appearance and form of the sun. And I was not the only one who observed it; for my companions also, namely, master William Barlow, and master George Black, the son of Francis Black, noticed it at the same time. We left our lodging on that morning three hours before day; and as we were journeying on horseback, a great light arose, at one time towards the south, and at another time towards the west, and now towards the north, in appearance like the rising sun, and this too, out of the clouds which at that time covered the sky. At length, the clouds were all driven away, and the sun arose in a clear and serene sky, and sent forth its beams towards the west, resembling a comet. A yellowish pillar had appeared on each side, except that towards the sun a kind of light shone forth like that of a rainbow. Towards the west they terminated in a pyramid. And this appearance did not speedily vanish, but lasted steadily for three whole hours. This circumstance certainly reminded me of the coming of the Son of God, whom I assuredly expect to appear very shortly. May the Lord give us grace to repent and wait for him with confidence! Farewell.

Yours,

BURCHER.

LETTER CCCXXX.

JOHN BURCHER TO HENRY BULLINGER.

Dated at Cracow, *March* 1, 1558.

Greeting. Some time since, my dear friend and master Bullinger, I sent you a letter from this place, to which I added others to master James Zwickius and to my wife. If they have not yet come to hand, they may be inquired after from master John Lyner of Saint Gall; for I transmitted them to him. But now, when I had no occasion to write, our common friend master Utenhovius arrived, and earnestly desired me to write in his stead. For he has gone away from this place towards Prussia with master à Lasco, and was in too much haste to admit of his writing. Peter Paul Vergerio[1] (I wish he were really either a Peter or Paul) has laid before very many of the Polish nobility some grievous accusations respecting master à Lasco and Utenhovius. For they are accused by him of having written to you in a very uncandid and unchristian manner respecting him and his intended mission into Poland. And he is not satisfied with having written thus privately to the nobles, but he threatens to place the vindication of his innocence before the public: and because those holy and pious men see that great confusion is impending over the churches of Poland, they are anxious that it should be calmed and settled by the counsel, authority, and exertion of the people of Zurich. Do you therefore use your utmost endeavours, with your usual watchfulness and circumspection, that he may give up his intended defence. And he must not only be exhorted to give it up, but must be persuaded to remain at home, and lead the churches committed to his charge from the less pure doctrines of the Lutherans to the true and perfect acknowledgement and confession of both natures in Christ. For it is assuredly not the part of a christian man to quit his certain and manifest calling in search of a worldly employment, and one too which may prove injurious to sound doctrine. God has sent him among the Lutherans, that he might convince them of their error; not that he should either consent to their errors, or

[1 Respecting Vergerio, see above, p. 499, n. 2.]

introduce them into well ordered churches. He promised the whole church that he would not introduce the Confession of Augsburg, but I hear that he is meditating a worse, with the name only changed; namely, that of the Waldenses corrupted by Luther[1]. Poland does not need a deputation either from him or any one like him. The churches, by the blessing of God, are settled happily and after a christian manner; nor do I perceive any one among us who savours of Lutheranism. It belongs to you, therefore, to recommend the man to give up his apology and legation. For I greatly fear that, should he not change his mind, he will gain for himself indelible disgrace and eternal condemnation. But, forasmuch as there has been afforded him some grounds for his "apology" from the letters written to you by master Utenhovius, the latter prays and entreats you to be kind enough to order a copy of all which he wrote concerning Vergerio to be faithfully taken, and forwarded to himself: for he thinks he did not write any thing worthy of a public apology.

My own affairs continue in the same state as heretofore. For though there are some persons who desire to obtain a knowledge of the art of brewing, yet I am afraid of imparting it before I have received the patent. I believe there is no other reason of its delay, except my inability to remunerate the trouble of the persons concerned. And certainly nothing has more hindered or will hinder this affair of mine, than the circumstance of my not having wherewith to pay in fees and give in presents. For all things are torpid in the courts of princes without a bribe; and I am afraid lest I should at last be compelled, through poverty, to return without the accomplishment of my object. Your kindness will perhaps mention this to master James Zwickius, that he may know how impossible it is to effect a matter of so much importance with so little means.

I commend my wife to your kindness, and pray you to continue towards her that paternal regard, with which you have hitherto honoured us both, in this unfavourable juncture

[1 In 1533 Luther prefixed a preface to the confession of faith of the Waldenses, whom, after inquiry, he regarded not as heretics, but sound though imperfectly instructed Christians. See Seckendorf, III. 62, 63, and a letter of Musculus to Melancthon in Gerdes, Misc. Gron. VII. 119.]

of our affairs. I know she is much distressed at my long continued absence; but she will, I hope, comfort herself with the thought that every thing will turn out to the glory of God, if not to my individual benefit. I will perform the duty of a faithful husband; let her not forget the duty of a good wife and mother of a family.

Remind John Billinger of the promise he made to your kindness. He has promised me fidelity; let him shew fidelity to himself and to me[2], which will not be the case unless he abstain from drunkenness and evil company, and study to live upon a very little during his absence. Farewell.

LETTER CCCXXXI.

JOHN BURCHER TO HENRY BULLINGER.

Dated at CRACOW, *March* 16, 1558.

GREETING. Within these few days, my dear friend and most esteemed master Bullinger, I wrote to you at the bidding and exhortation of our common friend, master Utenhovius, respecting a subject which, though not a pleasant one, was yet necessary and of the greatest use in preserving the peace of the rising church of Poland.

As I have some suspicion of the honesty of the carriers, I now repeat the matter in few words. The inveterate enemy of the cross and gospel of Christ is envious of the peace, success, and prosperity which this holy and newly-formed church has hitherto enjoyed. He perceives his empire daily diminishing, and the assemblies of believers increasing. And as he finds that he cannot hinder this happiness by the instrumentality of his papists, strenuously as they are exerting themselves for the kingdom of their prince, he is exciting disturbances and dissensions among those who wish to appear and be regarded as members of the same church. Peter Paul Vergerio, a man who is in other respects well qualified to contend with the power of popery, has not conducted himself with becoming moderation in some private disputes with certain members of the church of Christ. And taking ill the holy and paternal admonitions, which masters John

[2 This sentence is in German.]

à Lasco and Utenhovius desired should be gently offered, dearest Bullinger, by yourself, he has written to this place to many of the religious nobility of Poland, bringing severe accusations against them both. For he complains that he has been unworthily treated by the letter written to you, and gives out that he will vindicate himself by a public "apology," which he threatens shortly to publish. These holy men perceive the triumph that these things will occasion to their enemies, and the distress it will cause to all the pious and good; wherefore they desire them to be composed and settled by your advice and influence. They pray you to make the man aware that he will do himself no good by the proposed apology, but that rather the peace of the church will be disturbed, and himself convicted of want of moderation. He doubtless does not perceive the evil he is bringing upon himself. For if the things that can be written about him should go forth, he will lose the reputation which he has hitherto enjoyed, not only with the church of Poland, but with all other churches. And they must of necessity come forth, if he publish his apology. And Utenhovius does not think that he wrote any thing so severe, as to call for a public defence rather than a private expostulation. But since he has kept no copy of what he wrote, he requests you to cause whatever letters may refer to Vergerio to be faithfully transcribed, and forwarded to this place as soon as possible. And he wishes you not only to write these things, but whatever other things may be of use against this attack, to confirm the peace of the church, and to defend his own innocence. And to this end will serve whatever can be said respecting the ambitious views of Vergerio. For it is believed as a fact, that he would rather by all means compass an appointment as ambassador in Poland, than be called to his present function by a voice from heaven. And I wish he would desist both from his legation and his apology. For I do not see what else he could effect by his legation, than what Bucer formerly introduced into Basle and Berne, namely, dissension scarcely to be effaced by much labour[1]. He promised the church that

[[1] In reading charges like the present, it is necessary to bear in mind the conciliatory character of Bucer; and that his repeated endeavours to effect an agreement between the Lutherans and Zuinglians respecting the doctrine of the Eucharist laid him open to the odium of his opponents and the distrust of his friends.]

he would not attempt to introduce the confession of Augsburg: but he endeavours to introduce, under a changed name, instead of the Augustan confession, that of the Waldenses corrupted by Luther. Do you prevent, as effectually as you can, these his unworthy attempts. These are the things that masters John à Lasco and Utenhovius, and together with them the entire church of lesser Poland, ask at your hands.

My affairs still remain in the same position. I am eagerly expecting my patent, on the obtaining of which there will be no small hope of some profit. For there are both some nobles and citizens of Cracow, who brew their own beer, and who are desirous of instruction in that art. On the other hand, there are some who make it their business to throw every obstacle in my way, and use all their endeavours to make me relinquish my pursuit. I shall think however all my difficulties surmounted, if I obtain the patent; if not, I shall have lost my labour and my pains. Nothing has done more injury to this business of mine, than the unreasonable parsimony of mistress ab Ulmis. For it is certain that unless there had been a lack of presents for distribution among the clerks, I should long since have obtained both my patent, and no despicable advantage from it. Respecting my affairs there is now some doubt, whether the seal of the kingdom of Poland can be obtained; especially as my opponents, who claim the invention of the art for themselves, have promised the chancellor five hundred florins to obtain a patent for them. But this is my chief comfort, that the king's majesty has long since granted me this privilege. God grant that he may some time or other send it me confirmed with his seal. Communicate, I pray you, these things to master James Zwickius, if he come to see you. I commend my wife to your fidelity and protection, nor do I less commend to your kindness my kinsman, John Billinger. Let him be admonished, I pray you, by you, both of his pledge and promise made to you when my affairs were unfortunate. For certainly, were he not wanting in inclination, he could restore me to my former condition. But this will never be the case, unless he give up his habit of drunkenness: for by that he consumes what might be of assistance to me, and is preparing for himself a premature death.

I beg my remembrances to your most amiable wife, your

son Henry, and your whole family. Salute very much in my name master Peter Martyr, and all your sons-in-law. May your state and whole church be kept in safety! Farewell. Dated as above.

If you would send your letters hither with safety, you may forward them to St Gall, to ***[1] Von Ustadt. For there is a citizen here, by name Hector Von Ustadt, a kinsman of Vadian. If they are sent to him, they can always be safely forwarded either to me or to master John à Lasco. Again farewell.

Yours, you know who,

JOHN BURCHER, *Anglus.*

LETTER CCCXXXII.

JOHN BURCHER TO HENRY BULLINGER.

Dated at CRACOW, *Oct.* 27, 1558.

GREETING. I wrote to you, my dear friend and master Bullinger, from Vienna, both respecting the debt of your sons, and the uncandid and unchristian conduct of my relative, Christopher Rotaker, towards me. Your sons are indebted to me a sum which I certainly should not have demanded at present, unless extreme necessity had compelled me to it. The other, Rotaker, contrary to the duty of a Christian, not to say, of a preacher, is contriving how to retain possession of my property, which was kindly lent to him by my wife, without my knowledge and in my absence, for the relief of his wants. Should necessity require it, repay, I entreat you, to my wife the money owing by your sons; and remind, I beg of you, my relative Christopher of his duty as a Christian and a minister. For if he do not restore to my wife the sum that he all but fraudulently extorted from her nearly a year since, he may be assured that I shall seek to recover my property by law as soon as I return home. I have hitherto refrained from

[1 The meaning of this sentence, which is written in old German, is somewhat doubtful, owing to the difficulty in decyphering the original MS.]

taking any notice, lest I should turn the conversation of every body upon ourselves, and we should become the town's-talk. And I did this the more readily, because he himself requested it, and promised to deal honourably with me. But when I asked for this, on my departure from home, he almost refused to give me an answer. Let him pay the twenty florins that he owes me to my wife, from whom he extorted them, and I shall not object to wait for the payment of the debt of my kinsman John Billinger, until he has met with a sale for the bows. Manage this affair, I pray you, with him for my sake.

I forgot to write to you from Vienna respecting your son Christopher[2]. He had departed for Venice just before my arrival. The reason of his departure was, that he could not obtain a situation in the emperor's bakehouse. An uncertain rumour is spread abroad here respecting the queen of Hungary, the widow of Wida, and sister of the king of Poland. For two days since there was a general report of her having been put to death by some Hungarian noblemen, whose relatives she had beheaded for having attempted to betray her with her son Ferdinand, and deliver them into the hands of the emperor. But it is now reported that she has betaken herself, together with her son, to a well-fortified castle, and is there besieged by the Hungarians. The Muscovites have entered the frontiers of Livonia, and have taken five fortified places and some cities; and they are now besieging the town and port of Revel[3]. They had sent an embassy to the king of Poland to render them assistance. Answer was returned, that if they would observe as fixed and inviolable the conditions of peace to which they bound themselves last year, the king was willing to deliver them from the enemy at his own expense. The ambassadors decided upon referring this answer to their sovereign.

A certain Julius, an Italian, who lived at Zurich, first with master Frisius, and afterwards with master Sebastian, because he could not be placed over the royal library, or sent to Paris to study (though it was in his power to obtain a frugal, christian, and liberal education elsewhere), has returned, to his

[2 Bullinger's son Christopher died in 1569 in the service of the prince of Orange.]

[3 Revel is the capital of Esthonia, on the gulph of Finland, 220 miles from Petersburgh, and 160 from Riga.]

monkery as a dog to his vomit. And the knave still adheres to his knavery[1], as I beheld with my own eyes.

The queen here is suffering under a dangerous disorder, so that there hardly remains any hope of her life; she has however recovered in some small measure. The Diet is proclaimed, according to the custom of the Poles, for Elizabeth's day; but it will be postponed by reason of the queen's illness. For the king is daily expected here, who would otherwise have been at Petrikow[2], where the Diet was to have been held.

The pope's legate[3] was received here with kindness by his own friends, and with ridicule by ours. For as he made his entry, the trumpeter, the city watchman, sounded on his trumpet the melody, "Uphold me herein by thy word:" some of the nobles made a noise with horns, like the bellowing of herdsmen, along the way by which he entered; while others shouted in an extraordinary manner, whereby he might easily understand how acceptable his arrival was to the people of Poland. The bishop of Cracow had cited a preacher of the gospel to appear before his tribunal. He arrived here two days since, and, accompanied by a large attendance of nobles, came unexpectedly upon the bishop as he was sitting at his cups with the pope's legate, and demanded of him the reason of his citation. The bishop, astounded at the number of the nobles, replied, that he knew nothing at all about it. The nobles then, after having warned him against molesting in any manner or summoning any of their preachers for the future, went their way.

I gave your book to master John à Lasco, who returned you his lasting thanks, not only for the present, but because it was dedicated to the palatine of Wilna. He is taking care that the palatine's book shall be elegantly bound, and, should an opportunity offer, I am to present it; if not, I shall send it; for the place where he is now staying is forty miles distant from hence. I have found out master Lælius[4], to whom I

[1 This sentence is written in old German.]

[2 Petrikow is a town in Poland, about 80 miles from Warsaw.]

[3 Namely, Aloysius Lippomani, bishop of Bergamo, and one of the presidents of the council of Trent. See Biogr. Univ. Art. *Lippomani.*]

[4 Lælius Socinus, of whom Bullinger writes to Utenhovius, June 24, 1558: "Habes vivam epistolam, D. Lælium Socinum Senensem Italum. Hunc tibi peramanter et diligentissime commendo." Gerdes, III. 436.]

gave your letter. Farewell, and salute your family and all your learned friends respectfully in my name.

Yours,

BURCHER, *Anglus.*

P. S. There is not much hope of my making any profit here by this trade of mine. For my licence is not sealed with the Polish, but with the Lithuanian seal, which is only valid in Lithuania.

LETTER CCCXXXIII.

JOHN BURCHER TO HENRY BULLINGER.

Dated at CRACOW, *Nov.* 30, 1558.

GREETING. After I had finished and sealed my last letter, I received the letters of masters à Lasco and Utenhovius, in which they desire to apologize for not having written individually to all the ministers at Zurich. For the want of time was an hinderance to them both, and to one of them, in addition to want of time, a very unfavourable state of health; for master à Lasco, who has been almost always under severe suffering from his usual disorder during the whole time of my being here, has for these eight days past been much more grievously and dangerously attacked. Let him therefore be commended to our good and gracious God in the prayers of the church at large.

They have in their letters imposed upon me this office, that I should entreat all the ministers of our church to send an united letter to the king's majesty, to admonish him touching both his kingly duty and his religion. They think it expedient too, that other princes should be admonished (for instance, the lord palatine of Wilna and the lord of Cracow) to persevere with diligence in what they have begun. They think that if the nobles of Christendom can be stirred up to this by a general letter, no slight benefit will ensue. Do you act as it becometh Christians. For the time is certainly arrived, in which the kingdom and truth of Christ can be advanced, if our indifference or cowardice do not prevent us from advancing where the hasty and shameless audacity of our adversaries has impelled them to rush headlong. The king is of an easy and tractable disposition, and may without difficulty be brought over to our opinions. Of this indeed he gave, not long since, an instance by no means to be overlooked, in that he could not be prevailed upon by the bishops to banish the gospellers to another place during the time of the Diet. I beg, entreat, and implore you by Christ, and by the salvation of your souls, not to neglect this opportunity. Master John Gualter ab Ulmis can forward your letters to this place with speed and safety. It would, moreover, tend to the advancement of the gospel, if you would make honourable mention of masters John à Lasco and Utenhovius both to the king and princes; nor should they be forgotten in writing to the nobility. And if it be allowed to mix secular concerns with things so sacred, I could wish that I myself and my affairs should at least be recommended to the princes and the nobility. Farewell in Christ our only Saviour! In haste, as above.

Your most devoted,

JOHN BURCHER, *Anglus.*

LETTER CCCXXXIV.

JOHN CALVIN TO LADY ANNE SEYMOUR[1].

Dated at GENEVA, *July* 15, 1549.

As the most illustrious princess, your mother, has lately presented me with a ring as a token of her good-will, and this too uncalled for by any desert of mine, it would be very unbecoming in me to refrain from some expression of gratitude, that may at least bear testimony of my respect. But again, when language is wanting to enable me to discharge the duty that I owe her, nothing appears to me more becoming than that I should invite you to my assistance, most noble lady, and who are not less distinguished by your virtue than by your birth. For as you will be, beyond all others, a suitable interpreter to your mother, you will also according

[1 Notices of this lady and her mother are given above, p. 340. See also, p. 365, n. 4.]

to your exceeding kindness readily perform this office; and the rather, because, unless I am mistaken, you are persuaded that it will not be disagreeable to her: for I understand that you have been made aware, from her conversation, of her friendly disposition towards me. Wherefore, if my request has also any influence with you, I would earnestly entreat you to condescend to offer her my humble salutation, with all reverence; so at least as she may understand that the present, with which she honoured me, was not bestowed upon an ungrateful person. Moreover, I dare venture to use more freedom with you, because I have been informed that you are not only adorned with a liberal education, (which is very unusual in a lady of such birth and station,) but that you are so conversant also in the doctrine of Christ, as to afford an easy access to his ministers, in the number of whom, if I am not mistaken, you acknowledge myself. It remains for me to exhort you to persevere in so happy a course. For although, as I understand, you have entered it of your own accord, (and I hope the Lord, who has given you this inclination, will give you also constancy to persevere even unto the end;) yet forasmuch as, in the midst of so many obstacles and hinderances from the world, and likewise in so great infirmity of our flesh, incentives are never superfluous, you will take my exhortation in good part. Certainly, among so many excellent gifts, with which the Lord has seen fit to endue and accomplish you, this is by far the most important, that he has held out his hand to you from your tender youth, that he might lead you to his Son, the author of eternal salvation, and the source of all good: wherefore it becomes you to endeavour with the greater zeal to follow with alacrity him who calls you, especially when he has at the same time afforded you aids, which we often perceive not only the daughters of princes, but princes themselves, to stand in need of. Salute for me your brother, a youth of noble disposition, and the ladies your sisters. May the Lord daily enrich you all with his blessing, and manifest himself to you as your constant guide through the whole course of your life! Farewell, most excellent and honoured lady. Geneva. July 15, 1549.

Your true and most obedient servant,

JOHN CALVIN.

LETTER CCCXXXV[1].

JOHN CALVIN TO THE LORD PROTECTOR OF ENGLAND.

[Without place or date.]

My lord, that I have so long delayed to write to you has not arisen from want of inclination; but I have abstained from doing so to my great regret, from the fear that, during the late troubles, my letter might have occasioned you some new annoyance. I now thank my God that he has afforded me the opportunity which I have hitherto been waiting for. And I am not the only one who rejoices in the happy issue which God has given you out of your affliction, but likewise all true believers, who desire the advancement of the kingdom of our Lord Jesus Christ; inasmuch as they know the pains and trouble you have taken that the gospel might be restored in all its integrity, and that all superstitions might be overthrown; and are nothing doubting but that you are ready to do the like for the time to come, according as you may have the means.

As to yourself, my lord, you have not only to acknowledge the goodness of God in stretching forth his hand for your deliverance, but you must also keep his visitation in remembrance, that you may turn it to your profit. I am aware of the regret you may feel, and how you may be tempted to make a like return to those whom you consider to have sought to do you a greater mischief than has happened to you; but you know the remonstrance of St Paul upon this, namely, that we have not to fight against flesh and blood, but against the hidden devices of our spiritual enemy. Let us not therefore wait trifling with men, but rather turn our attention to Satan, to resist all his machinations against us. And as there is no doubt but that he has been the author of the mischief that has been devised against you, to the end that by this means the progress of the gospel might be hindered, and every thing, in fact, be thrown into

[1 The originals of this and the following letter, written in French, are preserved in the library at Geneva. This appears to have been written shortly after February 6, 1550, on which day the duke of Somerset was set at liberty. See above p. 464, n. 1.]

confusion; so, my lord, by forgetting and pardoning the wrongs of those whom you may consider to have been your enemies, apply all your endeavours to repel the malice of him who has made use of them, by loving them even when they have sought your destruction. This nobleness of mind will not only be acceptable to God, but will render you more amiable before men. I have no doubt but that you will give this subject due consideration: but if your kindness extends so far, so much the more ought I to feel confidence that you will favourably receive what I am now saying upon it, as knowing that I have no other motive for giving you such exhortations, except the regard that I entertain for your welfare and honour. And indeed it is so difficult a virtue to overcome one's passions, so as to return good for evil, that we cannot be too much exhorted to that effect, even when the Lord has ordered the matter better than many persons supposed.

You must bear in mind, my lord, the example of Joseph. It would be difficult to find, in the present day, such a mirror of integrity: nevertheless, perceiving that God had turned to his good all the evil that they had devised against him, he resolved to shew himself a minister of the goodness of God towards his brethren who had persecuted him. This triumph will be more excellent than that which God has afforded you already, when he preserved and protected both your person, your property, and your honour. Nevertheless, my lord, you have also to consider, that if God has thought fit to humble you for a little time, he has not done so without cause: for however unblameable you may have been with regard to men, you know that before this great heavenly Judge there is no one who does not find himself guilty. See how the saints have regarded the chastisements of God, bending the neck, and bowing the head under the correction. David had walked very uprightly, yet he nevertheless acknowledges that it was good for him to have been humbled by the hand of God. As soon therefore as we perceive ourselves to be chastened in any way soever, it is good for us to enter into ourselves, and thoroughly examine our life, to discover the sins that were concealed from us: for whenever too great prosperity dazzles our eyes, so that we do not perceive why God is correcting us, there is surely reason to pay him at least as much respect as we should to a physician; for it belongs to him to discover our inward evils that were unknown to ourselves, and proceed to their cure, not according to our wishes, but according as he knows and judges what is proper. What is more, he must sometimes make use of a preservative remedy, not waiting till we are already fallen into disease, but previously providing against it. God, having placed you in a position of high dignity beyond your ordinary rank, has done great things for you, and which will possibly be more estimated after your death, than they are now valued in your life-time; and above all, he has caused his name to be magnified by you. Now the most virtuous and excellent characters are in greater danger than any other persons, of being tempted to forget themselves. You know, my lord, what is recorded of the holy king Hezekiah, that after having performed such memorable actions, as well for religion and the service of God, as for the common advantage of his country, his heart was lifted up. If God has chosen to prevent this in your case, it is an especial favour that he has done you, even if he had no other motive for it than that he might be glorified in your deliverance, and that he might be known both by yourself, and by all mankind in your person, as the true protector of his people. That alone ought to suffice you.

It remains, my lord, that since he has given you the upper hand of your enemies, you return him such homage for this blessing, as is justly due to him. If we are recovered from a dangerous disorder, we ought to be doubly careful to bless and glorify our gracious God, just as if he had granted us a second life. You ought not to do less in the present case: your zeal in exalting the name of God, and in restoring the purity of his gospel, has already been great; but you know, my lord, that in a matter so important, when we have done all in our power, we shall still have fallen short, by a great deal, of all it requires. However, if God, in binding you anew to himself, has intended by these means to encourage you to perform your duty better than you have ever done before, and to take pains and apply all your endeavours to the advancement of the holy work that he has begun by you, I no longer doubt but that you will perform it; but I am also confident that, knowing the kind feeling by which I am induced to exhort you, you will receive it with kindness, as you have been wont to do. When the honour of God has thus recommended this proceeding to you, above all it is certain that he will watch over you, and over all your family, to diffuse therein his graces more abundantly; and he will make you feel the value of his blessing, for this promise will never fail us, "Them that honour me I will honour," [1 Sam. ii. 30]. True it is, that those who do their duty best, are oftentimes the most molested by many attacks; but it is enough for them that God is with them for their deliverance. But greatly as it is for your interest to look up to God, and to be contented with rendering him your willing service; it is nevertheless, my lord, a great consolation to you to see the king so favourably disposed as to prefer the restoration of the church and of pure doctrine to every thing else; as it is an admirable virtue in him, that at such an early age the vanities of this world do not hinder the fear of God and the true religion from ruling in his heart: as it is too an especial blessing for his kingdom, so likewise should it be a great comfort and satisfaction to you, that you are doing him the chief service which he desires and demands of the heavenly King, the Son of God. Having, my lord, most humbly commended myself to your good grace, I implore our gracious God, that having you in his holy keeping, he may increase in you more and more the gifts of his Holy Spirit, and make them serve to his glory, so that we may have every reason to rejoice.

LETTER CCCXXXVI.

JOHN CALVIN TO KING EDWARD VI.

Dated at GENEVA, [*Jan.* 1, 1551].

SIRE. If I had to make excuse to your majesty for the liberty I have taken in dedicating to you these books which I herewith present to you, I must have found an apologist to address you on my behalf. For my letters would be so far from possessing any influence for this purpose, that they would have required a new apology for themselves. In fact, as I should never have taken upon myself to address to you the commentaries which I have published in your name, so I should not presume to write to you now, were it not for the confidence I have already entertained that both my letter and commentaries would be favourably received. For since, regarding me as of the number of those who exert themselves in advancing the kingdom of the Son of God, you have not disdained to read what I had not expressly dedicated to your majesty; I have thought that if in serving Jesus Christ, my master, I should equally bear testimony to the especial reverence and affection that I bear you, I could not fail to meet with a favourable and courteous reception.

What is more, sire! as I feel assured that my letters will be received by you as I desire, I shall make no difficulty in praying and exhorting you in the name of him to whom you yield all authority and power, to take courage in the pursuit of what you have so well and happily begun, as well in your own person, as in the state of your realm. It is that the whole may be consecrated to God, and to our good Saviour, who has so dearly bought us. For with respect to the general reformation, it is not yet so well established, as not to make it desirable to carry it still farther; and in fact it would be very difficult to cleanse at once so great a sink of superstition as we find in the papacy. Its root is too deep, and has long since extended too far, to come to the end of it so soon. But difficult or tedious as it may be, such is the excellence of the work, that one is never weary of the pursuit. I doubt not, sire, but that Satan is placing many hinderances in the way, to retard and cool your zeal. A great portion of your subjects are not aware of the good you are procuring them. The great, who are elevated in point of rank, are oftentimes too apt to consider the world, without any regard to God. And they daily raise up to themselves new combats which they never before thought of. Now I have good hope, sire, that God has endued you with such magnanimity and firmness, that, notwithstanding all this, you will not be wearied or enfeebled. But the thing is in itself of such extreme importance, that it well deserves the exertion of all human power to accomplish it. And even when one shall have come to the end of it, there will yet remain some work to be done.

We see that in the time of good king Josiah, who had the especial testimony of the Holy Spirit, that he had performed every duty of an excellent prince, in faith, zeal, and all holiness, nevertheless the prophet Zephaniah shews that there still remained some remnants of former superstitions even in the city of Jerusalem. Thus, sire, though you are most laboriously engaged with your council, you will never be able entirely to eradicate all the evil which so well deserves to be corrected. But this ought to be a great motive to animate and encourage you, and even if you cannot effect all that would be desirable, it is a very abundant consolation, when you see that the exertion made by this good king is a service well-pleasing to God; in such wise that the Holy Spirit magnifies the reformation effected by him, as if there had been nothing left to blame in it. Only then, sire, aim at the mark which is set before you in the example of this holy king, so that it may be testified of you that you have not only destroyed impieties which were repugnant to the honour and service of God, but also that you have abolished and rased to the foundations every thing that tends only to the nourishment of superstition. For when God wishes to commend to the utmost those faithful princes who have restored and re-established the purity of his service, he especially adds, that they also brake down the high places, that the memory of the idolatrous worship might be destroyed.

It is true, sire, that there are certain things indifferent which we may lawfully bear with. But we must always observe this rule, that there must be sobriety and moderation in ceremonies, so that the light of the gospel be not obscured, as though we were still under the shadows of the law: and then, that there be nothing inconsistent with, and unconformable to, the order established by the Son of God, and that the whole may tend and conduce to the edification of the church. For God does not allow any one to sport with his name, mingling frivolities among his holy and sacred ordinances. Now there are manifest abuses which are not to be endured; as, for instance, prayer for the dead, placing before God in our prayers the intercession of saints, and adding their names to his in taking an oath. I doubt not, sire, but that you have been informed of these things: I implore you in the name of God to persevere, so that every thing may be restored to its proper integrity.

There is another point, sire, which ought to be especially regarded by you, namely, that the poor flocks be not destitute of pastors. Ignorance and barbarism have pressed so heavily in this accursed papacy, that it is not easy to obtain, at the first attempt, persons fit and qualified to discharge that office. However, the thing is well worth taking pains about; and let your ministers, sire, keep their eye upon it, that the food of life may be afforded to the people, as it ought to be. Without that, all the holy and good ordinances you can make will avail but little to reform their hearts in good earnest.

In fine, forasmuch as schools are the seedplots of future pastors, it is quite necessary to keep them pure and unmixed with any weeds. I say this, sire, because in your universities, as they tell me, there are many young persons supported by exhibitions, who, instead of affording good hopes of being of service to the church, rather shew symptoms of a desire to injure and overthrow it, not concealing the fact of their being opposed to the true religion. Wherefore, sire, I again implore you in the name of God, that you be pleased to give some order upon this subject, so that the property which ought to be as it were sacred, be not converted to a profane use, and to the nourishment of venomous beasts, whose only desire it is to poison every thing for the future. For by these means the gospel will always be driven back by the schools, which ought to be as it were the pillars of it.

Meanwhile, sire, all right-minded persons praise God, and feel themselves greatly obliged to you, for having graciously been pleased to grant churches to your subjects who speak the French and German languages, as far as respects the use of the sacraments and spiritual discipline. I hope that the licence you have been pleased to afford them will have its effect. Nevertheless, sire, I cannot refrain from again entreating you, knowing as I do how necessary it is, not only for the peace and satisfaction of the well-disposed, who desire to serve God and to live peaceably in obedience to you, but also to keep in order vagabond and dissolute persons, if they have retired into your realm.

I am well aware, sire, that you have at your command persons of the most accurate information, who can inform you of these things by word of mouth far better than I can by writing; and also that in your council you have persons endued with wisdom and zeal to advance whatever may be expedient. I doubt not but that, among others, the duke of Somerset will exert himself in the advancement of what he has been faithfully employed upon till now. But I believe, sire, that all this will not hinder you from receiving with kindness whatever you know to have proceeded from the same source.

In fine, sire, while I am fearful of having already wearied you by my excessive prolixity, I pray you that, in this respect as well as others, you will be pleased to excuse and to pardon me of your gracious kindness, to which I most humbly supplicate to be commended, having implored our good God and Father to maintain you in his holy protection, to defend you by his Spirit, and to cause his name to be glorified by you more and more. From Geneva this [Jan. 1, 1551.][1]

LETTER CCCXXXVII.

JOHN CALVIN TO ARCHBISHOP CRANMER[2].

Dated at [Geneva about *April*, 1552.]

Most illustrious lord, you truly and wisely judge that in the present disturbed state of the church no more suitable remedy can be adopted than the assembling together of godly and discreet men, well disciplined in the school of Christ, who shall openly profess their agreement in the doctrines of religion. For we see by what various devices Satan is endeavouring to abolish the light of the gospel, which, having arisen upon us through the wonderful goodness of God, is shining forth in every quarter. The hireling dogs of the pope are barking unceasingly, that the pure word of Christ may not be heard. Impiety is every where boiling forth, and raging with such licentiousness, that religion is little better than an open mockery. Those who are not avowedly hostile

[1 The date is not given. Simler places it as above, as being the day when Calvin dedicated to king Edward his Commentaries on Isaiah.]

[2 This is probably the answer to Letter XIV. It is here inserted in its proper order, instead of being given in the Appendix, as at first intended. The original is printed in Cranmer's Remains, Park. Soc. Ed. p. 432. Calv. Ep. p. 100. Ed. Genev. 1575.]

to the truth indulge themselves nevertheless in a wantonness which, unless it be checked, will occasion to us sad confusion. Nor does this disease of foolish curiosity and intemperate audacity prevail only among the common people; but, what is more disgraceful, it is becoming too rife even among the order of the clergy. It is too well known by what reveries Osiander[1] is deceiving himself, and fascinating certain other persons. The Lord, indeed, as he has been wont to do from the beginning of the world, is able wonderfully, and by means unknown to us, to preserve the truth from being rent in pieces by the dissensions of man. Nevertheless he would by no means have those persons inactive, whom he himself has placed on the watch; since he has appointed them his ministers, by whose aid he may purify sound doctrine in the church from all corruption, and transmit it entire to posterity. For yourself, most accomplished prelate, it is especially necessary, in proportion to your more exalted position, to bestow all your attention upon these matters, as you do. And I do not say this, as though I considered it needful to spur you on afresh, who are not only outrunning us of your own free will, but are also of your own accord urgent in exhorting others; but that I may encourage you by my congratulations in so happy and excellent a course of action.

We hear indeed that the gospel is making favourable progress in England. But I doubt not that you find it there also to be the case, what Paul experienced in his time, that when a door is opened to receive pure doctrine, there forthwith arise many adversaries. But though I am aware of the number of champions you have at hand well qualified to confute the lies of Satan, yet such is the wickedness of those parties whose great business it is to create confusion, that the diligence of good men in this respect can never be deemed either excessive or superfluous. I know too, in the next place, that your care is not confined to England alone, but that you are at the same time regardful of the world at

[[1] The peculiar dogma of Osiander was, that the righteousness by which believers are justified, is the essential righteousness of the divine nature infused or communicated by the indwelling of the Deity in them. Calvin refutes this notion in his Institutes, Book III. ch. xi. § 5, &c. See also Melancthon, Consil. II. 158, Melch. Ad. Vit. Osiandri, 228. Fabric. Hist. Biblioth. P. IV. p. 232.]

large. Then not only is to be admired the generous disposition of the most serene king, but also his rare piety in honouring with his favour the godly design[2] of holding an assembly of this kind, and in offering a place of meeting within his realm. And I wish it could be effected, that grave and learned men from the principal churches might meet together at a place appointed, and, after diligent consideration of each article of faith, hand down to posterity a definite form of doctrine according to their united opinion. But this also is to be reckoned among the greatest evils of our time, that the churches are so estranged from each other, that scarcely the common intercourse of society has place among them; much less that holy communion of the members of Christ, which all persons profess with their lips, though few sincerely honour it in their practice. But if the teachers conduct themselves with more coldness than they ought to do, the chief blame rests with sovereigns themselves, who either from being entangled in secular matters disregard the welfare of the church and all godliness; or, satisfied each of them with his own individual tranquillity, are not touched by any feeling of concern for others. Thus it is that, the members being scattered, the body of the church lies torn to pieces.

As far as I am concerned, if I can be of any service, I shall not shrink from crossing ten seas, if need be, for that object. If the rendering a helping hand to the kingdom of England were the only point at issue, that of itself would be a sufficient motive to me. But now, when the object sought after is an agreement of learned men, gravely considered and well framed according to the standard of scripture, by which churches that would otherwise be far separated from each other may be made to unite; I do not consider it right for me to shrink from any labours or difficulties. But I hope my want of ability will occasion me to be excused. I shall have sufficiently performed my duty, if I follow up with my prayers what shall be undertaken by others. Master Philip [Melancthon] is too far off for letters to go backwards and forwards in a short time. Master Bullinger has probably replied to you already. I wish my efficiency corresponded to the ardour of my inclinations. However, what I declined to do at the

[2 For some valuable information respecting this design, which originated with Melancthon, see Jenkyns, Pref. to Cranmer, p. civ. &c.]

beginning, the very difficulty of the case, of which you are sensible, compels me to attempt; that is, not to exhort you only, but implore you to persevere, until at least something be effected, if all things do not turn out according to your wish. Farewell, most accomplished and sincerely revered prelate. May the Lord continue to guide you by his Spirit, and give his blessing to your holy endeavours! Geneva.

LETTER CCCXXXVIII.

JOHN CALVIN TO KING EDWARD VI.

Dated at GENEVA, *July* 4, 1552.

SIRE. Much as I ought to fear being troublesome to your majesty, and for this reason abstain from writing to you more frequently, I have nevertheless taken the liberty to send you a short exposition that I have made upon the 87th Psalm, in the hope that you would be pleased with it, and that the perusal may be very profitable to you. As I was expounding it one day in a sermon, the argument appeared to me so suitable to you, that I was immediately induced to write out the whole, such as you will see it, when it shall please your majesty to devote a single hour of your time to that purpose. It is true that I treat the subject in general terms, without a personal address to yourself, but I have only had reference to you in writing it; and in effect, in appropriating it, as your prudence may dictate, to your own use, you will find it to contain a lesson and a doctrine very profitable to your majesty.

You well know, sire, what danger there is to kings and princes, lest the height to which they are elevated should dazzle their eyes, and amuse them here below, causing them to forget the kingdom of heaven; and I doubt not but that God has warned you of this danger that he might preserve you from it, and that you will guard against it a hundred times better than those who experience it without being aware of it. Now in the Psalm before us is set forth the grandeur and dignity of the church, which ought in such wise to draw over to itself both great and small, that all the riches and honours of the world cannot hold them back, nor keep them from aiming at this object, namely, to be enrolled among the people of God. It is a great thing to be a king, especially of such a country; yet I have no doubt but that you esteem it incomparably better to be a Christian. It is therefore an inestimable privilege that God has made you, sire, a christian king, to the end that you may act as his vicegerent in maintaining the kingdom of Jesus Christ in England. You see then, that in acknowledging this especial benefit, which you have received from his infinite goodness, you ought to be very zealous in employing all your powers to his honour and service, affording an example to your subjects to do homage to this great King to whom your majesty is not ashamed to subject yourself in all humility and reverence under the spiritual sceptre of his gospel. If you have hitherto so acted that we have wherewith to glorify God on your behalf, this psalm will serve at all times for your encouragement and support. Meanwhile, sire, I entreat you that this brief writing may serve me as a protestation and testimony to your majesty of the great desire I have to employ myself in doing more, when the means shall be afforded me.

Sire, after having most humbly commended myself to your grace, I implore our good God to fill you with the gifts of his Holy Spirit, to guide you in all wisdom and virtue, and to make you flourish and prosper to the glory of his name. Geneva, July 4, 1552.

JOHN CALVIN.

LETTER CCCXXXIX.

JOHN CALVIN TO LORD JOHN GREY[1].

Dated at Geneva, *Nov.* 13, 1554.

Though it cannot be, most noble sir, but that the misfortunes of your house, so distressing and deplored by all good men, must have inflicted a doubly severe wound upon yourself, and must even now occasion you the most lively

[1 Lord John Grey was brother of the duke of Suffolk. He was sent to the Tower, Feb. 6, 1554, during Wyat's rebellion, and condemned as a traitor, but afterwards obtained a pardon. Strype, Mem. III. i. 136, 145.]

sorrow; I am nevertheless assured that, as is befitting a christian man, you have always stood firm and unmoved, and still continue to do so, under this excessive weight of trials. For though we sometimes perceive that godly minds, through the infirmity of the flesh, are grievously shaken even by lesser calamities, yet the faith that reposes upon Christ can never be entirely overthrown. Wherefore, I have no doubt but that when you were carried away in that stormy tempest, you had your anchor fixed in heaven, and that you bravely endured, and firmly sustained, the fury of those waves which might otherwise have overwhelmed you a hundred times. But something of more importance yet remains, that you should carry on the warfare of the cross even unto the end. For the Lord has not exercised you with such severe conflicts for a short time only, that you may afford an example of an exalted mind; but also that after this calamity, by which the greatness and splendour of your fortune is come to nought, you might pursue the remainder of your course with a calm and equable placidity of spirit. Moreover, he has designed also to bring you to the practice of that rule which Paul prescribes to us by his own example, that you may learn how to bear a lowly condition no less than a high one: and in proportion as this virtue is more difficult and seldom to be met with, if you make an advance in it, the loss occasioned by this shipwreck will be compensated in no small degree.

But though I congratulate the most illustrious duke your brother, and your excellent niece, a lady whose example is worthy of everlasting remembrance, to both of whom it was given, even in death itself, to commit their triumphant souls into the hands and faithful keeping of God; yet in the midst of so many most distressing tidings it has always afforded me no common comfort, to have heard that you have been snatched from the very jaws of death, and are still preserved to us in safety. The anxiety I had felt owing to the false report of your death, was first relieved a short time since by Immanuel Tremellius and his son-in-law Antony[1]; who, while speaking in commendation of your liberality and numerous

[[1] Antony Rodolph Chevalier. He was Hebrew professor at Strasburgh, and afterwards at Cambridge, where he succeeded Tremellius in 1569, on the recommendation of Archbishop Parker. See Strype, Ann. I. ii. 552, and Zurich Letters, Series II. p. 97, n. 1.]

offices of kindness towards them, added, that in the ruin of this most noble family they had great reason to deplore their own loss as individuals. They complained among other things, that on the first bursting forth of this storm they were deprived of those means whereby they had hoped to derive some alleviation of their poverty in their exile. Now, since you are restored, they implore that kindness from you which they have in so many ways experienced, if there be any hope and any possibility of recovering that means of support which they so greatly stand in need of. And though the recommendation of their learning and godliness will abundantly suffice without any request of mine, yet having full reliance on your favourable disposition towards me, I did not think I ought to refuse them this service, and I have no doubt but that you will easily pardon my boldness. Farewell, most noble and illustrious sir, and my most honoured master. May God, the Father of Jesus Christ and ours, defend you with his protection, guide you by his Spirit, sustain you by his strength, and enrich you with all heavenly benediction! Geneva, Nov. 13, 1554.

Yours,

JOHN CALVIN.

LETTER CCCXL.

THE PROVOST AND COUNCIL OF BERNE TO KING EDWARD VI.

Dated at BERNE, *Dec.* 14, 1549.

GREETING. Your ambassador, master Christopher Mont, has delivered to us your royal majesty's letter[2], from which, and also from what he afterwards told us, we perceive the exceeding kindness and benevolence and sincere friendship of your majesty towards us; for all which we offer abundant thanks to your majesty, with the assurance that when time and opportunity shall require, we shall be most ready to

[2 Simler speaks of the king's letter to Berne being the same as that to Zurich, given above, p. 1.]

return the obligation in like manner. But that your majesty may be acquainted with our feelings and intentions respecting these matters, the friendly regard towards us of your most serene father of happy memory, as well as that of your majesty, has been, as it ever will be, most gratifying to us; and if we have rendered to your majesties any duties and services, they have proceeded from a willing mind. It shall therefore be our duty, in which we desire to be most forward, to devote our care and attention to all the affairs and concerns of your majesty, (especially for the sake of the bond of the christian religion,) and to render you our grateful service, benevolence, and friendship. With respect to a future council, we doubt not but that your majesty has perceived long since the state in which the affairs of Christianity and evangelical religion continue among us and in our churches, since the public disputation[1] that was held here; in which state, by God's blessing, we have finally purposed and determined to continue. Nevertheless, should it happen that a general or a national council be appointed, and held in the Spirit of the Lord, to which a safe and free conduct shall be granted to all persons, both in going and returning, and in which the sacred scriptures of the old and new testament shall alone have place, and be regarded as the standard; we shall not, as becometh Christians, refuse to comply with this, and doubt not but that other Christians will do likewise. Wherefore we do not think that there is any necessity, or that it is worth while to introduce other consultations, considerations, or bonds; earnestly entreating your majesty to commend us to you, and to be pleased to take these things in good part. And may your majesty happily live in a peaceable, prosperous, and lengthened government of your most flourishing kingdoms, and in the propagation and defence of the christian faith! Dated Dec. 14, 1549.

[[1] This disputation was held in 1528, from the 7th to the 26th of January, inclusive, one day only excepted. The proceedings were published at Zurich, two months after its close. See also Scultetus, 122, &c. Gerdes, II. 338, &c. Ruchat, II. 29—202, and Bucer's dedication of his commentary on St John to the magistrates and ministers of Berne.]

LETTER CCCXLI.

CHRISTOPHER FROSCHOVER[2] TO HENRY BULLINGER.

Dated at OXFORD, *Nov.* 19, 1550.

GREETING. Grace and peace from our Lord Jesus Christ! I have been long in doubt, most reverend lord and father, and my mind has been almost distracted by various cogitations, namely, by pondering with myself whether I ought to undertake so great a charge as to address your dignity with my unpolished letter. At length, when I saw our countrymen John ab Ulmis and John Rodolph Stumphius frequently writing to you, and understood that their letters were kindly received by you, I was then induced to send you that brief epistle. And truly but for this reason, and that your exceeding courtesy had encouraged me, and your beneficence invited me, I should have kept my hand from my pen. I have, however, a good hope that you will receive my letters with the like kindness. Nevertheless, I must deprecate the charge of presumption in one so insignificant as I am, writing to so distinguished an individual as yourself. But as I have nothing very suitable to write about, I will briefly acquaint you with my present condition.

As soon as I left Zurich, I went to the Hesse family at Marpurg, where I remained half a year, and so much the more gladly, when I perceived that Philip Fallenberg, who derived no small advantage from your commendation of him, was coming down to me. Afterwards, however, when that Burcher, who is trading at Strasburgh, had determined upon a journey to England, I was sent thither with him, and am now staying in the university of Oxford with our townsmen, namely, John ab Ulmis and John Rodolph Stumphius, the latter of whom I have joined in his lodging, and partly in his studies. I have now, I think, said enough upon this subject; for I doubt not but that you have long since heard the circumstance from my uncle. And that I may not keep you from your occupations longer than is becoming, and that

[2 Christopher Froschover was a learned printer at Zurich. He boarded some of the English exiles in the time of the Marian persecution. Strype, Mem. III. i. 232.]

you may not become weary of attending to me, I will adopt a Laconic conciseness, and tell you in one word what I wish. I beg therefore, and entreat you, that when you write to master Peter Martyr, you will in the course of your letter thank him in my name for having so courteously noticed me, and promised me all his influence and assistance; and you may add a commendation of me, by which he may be confirmed in his favourable opinion. I request you therefore, again and again, to condescend to do me this service, and by no means to suffer your patronage to be wanting. Should I obtain from you this kindness, I shall be more closely bound and united to you, and most ready to do you every service in my power. Meanwhile, however, I must ask your forgiveness for the freedom of my request.

What is now doing here, and what has been done, you will more easily learn from the letters of others, for at the time of my writing this I have scarcely been a month in England; for which reason I have possessed neither the opportunity nor the ability of acquiring much information. You must however consider what I have written, whether you approve it or not, as proceeding from the best feeling, and from a mind entirely devoted to your service; and should you, in fine, meet with any thing in my letters which offends your dignity, you must impute and ascribe it to my youth, and with your usual kindness and good sense bestow your forgiveness. Should I learn that this present letter is acceptable to you, you shall have, by God's blessing, a better and a more correct one in future. You may read this when you are at leisure from more important engagements. Salute your sons individually in my name. Farewell, and may the Lord Christ long preserve your dignity in safety, to the restoration of true godliness, and the advancement of good learning! Dated at Oxford, Nov. 19, 1550.

Your most respectful and attached,

CHRISTOPHER FROSCHOVER.

LETTER CCCXLII.

CHRISTOPHER FROSCHOVER TO RODOLPH GUALTER.

Dated at OXFORD, *Feb.* 21, 1551.

GREETING. Whereas, most dear and honoured master, I am beforehand in interrupting and disturbing by my trifling letters you and your sacred occupations and fruitful studies, in which I know you to be engaged, to the great advancement of useful learning; you must not impute it to my boldness, but to your courtesy which is every where spoken of, and which, together with your abundant benefits and my consciousness of the service I owe you, has suggested to one of the meanest of mankind this confidence, namely, that you shall not seem to have bestowed your favours upon an ungrateful and thankless person. For though my destinies may rage against me, and render me most miserable, they never shall or can make me ungrateful. But as I had nothing of importance, and as nothing occurred worthy or fitting to write to you about, I thought it would be best for me to give you an account of my studies. Be assured therefore that I have directed all my labour and diligence to the learning of languages, Greek and Latin for instance, since nothing can be more useful or more appropriate to my calling. But yet, as we know by experience, that an elegant, terse, and polished diction is the greatest recommendation to a man, I do not neglect that best of all guides to eloquence, namely, the exercise of my pen. Moreover, as our studies, and all the actions of mankind produce more abundant fruit, and daily make improvement, when united with the knowledge and fear of God, I am right, I think, in adding to my studies the godly lectures in divinity of master doctor Peter Martyr. Besides too, as every one knows the great advantage that arises to study from a friendly intercourse with learned men, I took the liberty in my last letter of requesting from you an introduction to master doctor Peter Martyr, a man most learned in every way, and who is a great patron of literature. And I have an entire confidence that you will not be wanting to me in this act of generosity, especially when you know it to be so necessary to myself, and so easy for you to perform.

As to the state of England, I did not know what to write; for it is in the enjoyment of the greatest tranquillity. Good learning is every where flourishing, in spite of the opposition of the patrons of former ignorance; and true religion is triumphing by the aid of the king and the bishops. Silence is imposed upon those Romanist brawlers whose tongues are only made for slander, although they sometimes raise a wonderful stir. This, however, is not in open warfare, but they effect every thing by artifice and trickery. The bishop of Winchester[1], who had assumed a reputation for true piety when he last gave an account of his faith, and could not be induced to agree in all respects with the other bishops, is cast into prison and deprived of his bishoprick. The papists are now labouring under great unpopularity; so great indeed, that I very often wonder at their perverseness, who, having been so frequently warned, yea, often too turned into ridicule, do not come to their senses. But these appearances portend that true religion will continue to be in a most flourishing state. For thus arose the Roman empire; thus was advanced the glory of the Jews; thus it arose, thus it was extended. In fine, there is nothing excellent that has not sprung from difficulties at the beginning.

It is rumoured here that the French are again raising troops against England, with the view of seizing upon another barbour[2] for their ships. Tidings are daily brought to us from Germany, but, as I guess, not without a great mixture of falsehoods: wherefore, lest I should be deemed a liar myself, I forbear to enumerate them. But should any thing come to light in future, I will inform you of it as quickly and as frequently as possible, provided only you take in good part what I have now written, not as being worthy of your attention, but such as came unpremeditated into my mind.

[1 For the circumstances attending the imprisonment and deprivation of bishop Gardiner, see Foxe, Acts and Mon. VI. 24, &c. Strype, Mem. II. i. 372, &c.]

[2 Sir James Croft was sent to Ireland in February 1551, to look after the condition of that kingdom, especially the havens and other places which certain the king's enemies intended to invade there. And a fleet of ships was sent forth to guard some havens on the south side towards France. Orders also were taken for strengthening the castle, and other important places in the isle of Jersey against the French. See Strype, Mem. II. i. 441.]

For this intense cold, by which I am frozen, has made me so inactive, and stupid, and listless in writing, that I may well seem, as they say, to have been feeding on wild animals[3]. For I must freely confess that nothing in England so disturbs and troubles me as the severity of the winter, and the season of Lent, or of fasting. They allege the ancient custom of the country, which I too should approve of, if my stomach did not require something else. But, not to detain you any longer from your studies, let this suffice for the present, while I beg and pray you in the mean time to interpret every thing for me with candour according to your singular kindness. We are anxiously expecting the arrival of Cellarius. Salute in my name that most excellent and amiable lady your wife. May Christ, the only hope of godly minds, preserve and support you in good health, and pressing forward towards the things of heaven! Dated at Oxford, Feb. 21, 1551.

Your reverence's most attached,

CHRISTOPHER FROSCHOVER.

LETTER CCCXLIII.

CHRISTOPHER FROSCHOVER TO RODOLPH GUALTER.

Dated at Oxford, *May* 28, 1551.

Greeting. Your letter, most honoured master, of the 19th of April has come to hand, than which nothing more delightful could have happened to me, and from which I perceived the extent of your kind feeling towards me. This I more especially discovered in your so diligent commendation of me to that most renowned of scholars, master doctor Peter Martyr; which has certainly rendered him not only a friend, but, I should say, the greatest friend to me, and a most active patron and supporter: whereby any one may perceive the extent of his regard for you, which is certainly very great. But forasmuch as I am unable to return you due thanks for your most friendly services in my behalf, I have

[3 *De fera comedisse.* It was thought of old that the flesh of wild animals rendered the eaters thereof stupid.]

been endeavouring to think upon the way by which I may escape the imputation of being ungrateful; namely, by cherishing in grateful recollection and remembrance those benefits of yours which are too great and splendid for my slender and inadequate ability to repay: and this, I hope, will be most of all agreeable to yourself. I am daily expecting master Christopher Hales, who has already promised you by letter that he will serve me for your sake in any way he can. For, as I have been told by his servant, he is about to visit Oxford, and to remain here for some time, for the purpose of conversation with learned men; and he will not, I trust, be an undesirable friend to me, but rather a patron, and your influence will be of great service in this respect. Moreover, I am no less sensible of your paternal feeling towards me, in that you so faithfully exhort me to study, that I may not disappoint the hopes entertained of me; and especially, that I may be regarded as one desirous of godliness, forasmuch as we all know by experience that the advantages of person and fortune are of no value without a zeal for religion. The remembrance of your exhortation will never suffer me to forget my duty: it will admonish me day and night, and, as I hope, be effectual in enabling me to preserve and sustain the opinion that has sometimes been entertained respecting me.

I would now explain to you the whole state of my affairs, were it not that I should detain you too long from your engagements: this one thing however I would not have you ignorant of, that I have determined next spring to travel into France with my friend Stumphius, who is recalled by his father; and to remain there, if my uncle will allow me, for some months, that I may also obtain some acquaintance with French affairs. I sent you an account of my studies in my last letter, which you received, I suppose, after the fair. The church of England is daily strengthened more and more in the knowledge of the true faith, though she has suffered a severe loss[1] in the death of master Bucer; for she might still have been greatly benefitted by his learning. You know, I suppose, who have been invited over from Germany to supply his place; among the

[1 The opinion here expressed may be noticed in contrast with that of John Burcher, given above, p. 678.]

number of whom are our friend Bibliander, Musculus, Melancthon, and some others, who, however, I hope, will remain in Germany. And in this respect the English are in my opinion justly worthy of censure, that they are endeavouring to draw away from Germany its men of learning, that they may be able in the meantime to live at ease themselves; for if we diligently look into the facts, we shall find that they have men of higher talent for the most part than the Germans. This however might be permitted, unless it were done to the injury of others, as it is in this case. For we perceive the church of Germany and the house of God to be at this time in such a state, as especially to need the guidance of men of that character, lest it should altogether sink under the threatened overthrow.

In conclusion, I entreat you with your accustomed kindness to put a candid interpretation upon everything concerning me, and not only to regard the thing itself, (I mean my letter,) but the mind of the writer, which is certainly most zealous towards you. We were anxiously expecting the arrival of George, who, as I understand, is gone to Padua. I congratulate him very much on his being engaged to be married. Be pleased to give my most respectful salutations to your wife, and likewise to all your family. Farewell, most honoured master, and may God long preserve you to us in safety! Commend me to you. Dated at Oxford, May 28, 1551. In haste, just as I am about to depart for Cambridge.

Your most devoted and obedient Son,

CHRISTOPHER FROSCHOVER.

LETTER CCCXLIV.

CHRISTOPHER FROSCHOVER TO RODOLPH GUALTER.

Dated at LONDON, *Aug.* 12, 1551.

GREETING. At length, most beloved master, I am learning by daily experience, that no greater misfortune can happen to a grateful mind, than the inability of making a return, however trifling, to those to whom one is indebted for the greatest kindness. And this is altogether the case with me in respect to yourself; whose immense benefits whenever I revolve in my mind, and anxiously look about to see whether I can anywise repay your exceeding kindness, in part at least, if not altogether, so often am I angry with my fates, and complain of them for having placed me in this situation, where I cannot even in the smallest degree recompense those favours, by which you have obliged me, so that you might perceive them to have been conferred upon a grateful recipient. And this is especially the case, when I call to mind that fatherly recommendation, by which you were pleased to commend me to that most excellent man, master doctor Peter Martyr: for I perceive it to have been not of an ordinary character, but so complete, as to render that most godly man not only my friend, but also my especial patron. Moreover, when I call to mind that very pious exhortation in which you advised me to the pursuit of all honourable studies, I feel a vast fire, as it were, within me; for my mind burns to return the obligation, while at the same time it occurs to me, how little my slender ability, and how much your kindness, is able to accomplish: whence I may be allowed to form the conjecture that your mind is still affected towards me as ever, from your being so desirous that I should be exercised and employed in honourable studies. But the only method afforded me of returning the obligation is by paying the greatest regard to your advice, and the rule of conduct you have laid down; and by trying myself by it, as gold brought to the touchstone, lest I should seem to have slighted the admonitions of my most revered master; which, as long as the breath of life animates this body, shall not be the case. Wherefore, since otherwise I am defeated in two ways, and am unable to return any obligation, much less an equivalent, I shall not cease to do what alone is in my power, namely, to bear in remembrance, to love, to thank you with all my strength, that I may not altogether seem ungrateful.

Master Christopher Hales, who was coming, as we hoped, to Oxford, has not yet arrived; but I think I know the reason, namely, these turbulent times which have lately visited England. For not long since the disease, which we call the English sweating sickness, pervaded the whole country. It has relaxed in some measure, but not without causing great mortality. About two thousand men died at

London; at Cambridge two hundred, where also the duke of Suffolk died, together with his younger brother, and many other distinguished characters, whose names do not occur to me. I am glad for these and also for many other reasons, that our young men have left England; for they staid with me at Oxford during these last three months, and certainly at no small expense. For the price of every thing is daily increasing more and more, and this by reason of the diminution of the value of money[1]. This has hitherto been much debased, and being ordered to be restored, by the proclamation of the king's majesty and his whole council, has lost a fourth of its value, to the great detriment of the people. I accompanied our friends to London, and there took leave of them. I could neither see the king, nor have an interview with Hales. You will learn from Joshua what is going on here. I would have written more, had they not hastened their departure. Do you, most distinguished sir, and much honoured master, receive with a candid mind what I have now written, and continue to love me as you have done. Salute, I pray you, most respectfully from me that excellent lady your wife, and all your family. Farewell, most reverend master. Dated at London, from Byrchman's printing office, Aug. 12, 1551.

Your honour's most devoted,

CHRISTOPHER FROSCHOVER.

LETTER CCCXLV.

—— TO [HENRY BULLINGER.]

[Without place or date.[2]]

VERY sad tidings have lately been written to me by my friends from England, of which, as I doubt not but that they are

[1 A proclamation was made, July 9th, that the testourns or testons, which passed for twelve-pence, though scarce half so much in intrinsic value, should go at nine-pence, and in August it was again reduced from nine-pence to six-pence. Strype, Mem. II. i. 486. K. Edward's Journal in Burnet, III. 218, 219.]

[2 The name of the writer of this letter is not given. The letter itself was probably written at the close of 1549. For a full account of the circumstances herein mentioned, the reader is referred, once

also reported among you, and disfigured and exaggerated by excited feelings of alarm, I shall communicate to your reverence a true but succinct account, by giving you a particular statement of the distressing facts. The nobility of the kingdom of England, perceiving with much sorrow and indignation that those defences, which King Henry VIII. of pious memory had erected at very great expense for the fortifying and preservation of Boulogne, were now taken after a slight struggle by the king of France[1], and that the loss and destruction of those forts had arisen from the negligence and penuriousness of the lord Protector, called together the Londoners by sound of trumpet on the 8th of October, and commanded the heralds to make proclamation that no one should from henceforth render obedience to any letters or orders issued by the above named Protector, the duke of Somerset, even though they should be confirmed under the king's hand and seal: for that his most negligent administration had occasioned the utmost disgrace and irreparable injury to the kingdom, inasmuch as, disregarding the matured and strenuous charge of the noble and honourable council, as also the complaints of those governors who had charge of the garrisons in the parts beyond sea, he neglected to fortify and furnish with supplies those same garrisons, with such care and diligence as his duty required; so that by his neglect and omission they have been taken by the French, to the perpetual disgrace and danger of the realm. The king's money too, which he ought to have expended upon the defence and fortification of the kingdom, he had lavished in these times of war upon most sumptuous buildings[2], and has defrauded

for all, to Burnet, II. 215, &c. Strype, Mem. I. 282, &c. Foxe, VI. 282, &c. Soames, III. 479, &c., and the authorities quoted by them.]

[[1] It was one of the articles objected to the duke of Somerset, that he would not suffer the king's pieces of Newhaven and Blackness to be furnished with men and provision; albeit he was advertised of the defaults, and advised thereto by the king's council; whereby the French king was emboldened to attempt upon them. Burnet, IV. 301.]

[[2] Namely, Somerset house, in the Strand, for which it was said that the duke procured architects from Italy, and compelled some bishops (those of Worcester, Lichfield, and Llandaff,) to resign the houses belonging to their respective sees, that he might obtain a convenient site for his own palace.]

of their due pay for many months the king's army, anxious to fight both against the Scots and the French, at home and abroad, at the risk and danger of their lives, in defence of the king's majesty, and for the maintenance and increase of the honour of the realm: and therefore they (the council) moved by these evils, both as nobles of the kingdom, and also as appointed by his father as guardians to the son, were compelled by their duty and allegiance to remove the protector from the government, and to take it upon themselves with due care and solicitude; lest, when hereafter called upon to give up an account of their guardianship, they should render themselves liable to a heavier accusation than they shall be able to reply to. That they therefore enjoined all the subjects of the most serene king, not to interfere or bestir themselves in the matter: for that this change was made for no other cause than from a regard to the public welfare. The people having been forewarned by this proclamation, tranquillity followed throughout the kingdom.

At the time these things were taking place in London, the protector, who had the king in his power in Windsor castle[3], being first deserted by all the nobility, (and the king afterwards being brought to London by the council,) was at length conveyed a prisoner to the Tower of London on the 16th of October, together with three other persons, who alone were partakers in, and cognisant of, all his actions. This is a true and succinct account of the change that has taken place in England. And I know, first from the private letters of my friends, and next from the proclamations published under the king's seal, and confirmed by the subscription of all the nobility and royal councillors, that it did not originate in any ambitious motive, or in a dislike or hatred to religion; but that it was occasioned by the just grief and indignation arising from the loss of the garrisons and forts which had been erected by King Henry of pious memory, at very great expense, for the preservation of Boulogne: so that the necessity and welfare of the kingdom

[3 The duke removed the king to Windsor Castle by night, being apprehensive that the palace of Hampton-court, if attacked, would be found capable of offering very little resistance. The archbishop of Canterbury, sir Wm. Paget, and secretary Smyth, were at Windsor likewise. Soames, III. 482.]

compelled those persons, whom both their private and public character, and the weight of the charge entrusted to them, obliges to act in a case of this kind, to take more accurate order in the administration of affairs. By this explanation of the change you will be able to comfort both yourself and your friends; for I know that most groundless and false representations are every where made respecting it, according to the inclination of each individual who spreads the report.

LETTER CCCXLVI.

FRANCIS BOURGOYNE[1] TO JOHN CALVIN.

Dated at LONDON, *Dec.* 4, 1550.

[EXTRACT.]

You have been informed, I suppose, long since both by my letter to my brother, and that of Utenhovius to yourself, that our Josiah, the king of England, made most courteous inquiry of me concerning your health and ministry. To which when I had made such reply as in my judgment I considered worthy of you, he sufficiently declared both by his countenance and his words, that he takes a great interest in you, and in every thing belonging to you. Mention was incidentally made of the letter which you once sent to be delivered to his uncle, the then protector of the kingdom, and which he declared to have been exceedingly gratifying to him. From that time, therefore, I have thought it would be well worth your while, if, availing yourself of this opportunity and subject, (unless you have, it may be, something better, or see more deeply than I do,) you would send him such a letter as would add spurs to a willing horse. The king supports and encourages pure religion and godly and learned men to the utmost of his power, and would effect much more if his age allowed him.

[1 Francis Bourgoyne was minister of the church of Corbigny in the diocese of Autun, from whence he was banished by the persecutions of the clergy there in 1547. He resided some time at Geneva. See Beza, Hist. des Eglises Ref. de France, I. 65.]

LETTER CCCXLVII.

FRANCIS BOURGOYNE TO JOHN CALVIN.

Dated at LONDON, *Jan.* 22, 1552.

GREETING. Unless complaint afforded relief to distress of mind, and especially such complaint as is poured into the bosom of a christian friend, I should far rather choose, my very dear sir, with Timon[2], to hide myself in some silent corner than to give utterance to a single word; or, if I must make the attempt, I should employ my pen in writing an elegy rather than a letter. But as I entertain such an opinion of you, that I think there is no one who sympathizes in a more christian manner with the misfortunes of the distressed, and as I am, too, in some measure apprehensive on my now recalling you to my remembrance, that I have hitherto been more tardy in the duty of writing to you than I ought to have been, I have determined to be no longer silent. Therefore, that I may in the first place explain to you the cause of my grief, hence arise our tears, hence arises the all but universal distress, that on this very day, about 9 o'clock, the duke of Somerset of pious memory, when hardly any person looked for or suspected such an event, was led out publicly to execution[3]. I myself, for certain reasons, was not present at the sight; but many of our friends, with whom you are well acquainted, met me in the street immediately after the event had taken place, and related to me in order, but not with dry eyes, what they had seen and heard. Among them was our godly preacher master Richard[4], Utenhovius, and very many of that class: some of whom, understanding English, carefully noted almost every word of the dying nobleman. They tell me, among other things, that he said to the people standing around him, "I am about to die, good people, and confess that I justly deserve to die for having offended against the laws of my country and the

[2 Of Athens. See Shakspeare's play of that name.]

[3 For other notices respecting the execution of the duke of Somerset, see the Index, and especially Foxe, Acts and Mon. VI. 293.]

[4 Richard Vauville, respecting whom see above, p. 339, n. 2.]

king's commands; from obedience to which, as they are made for all, it was neither just nor reasonable that I should be exempted. But I profess that by the goodness of God there remains to me this testimony of commendation and innocence, that I have hitherto conducted myself without blame in the cause of religion, and in my duty to my king and country: for God and my conscience is witness, that I have used all my endeavours and exertions to this end, that the cause of religion, the education of the king, the welfare and security of the realm might be consulted and provided for in the best possible way. Whence it is that I shall undergo this death with an undisturbed and ready mind, feeling assured, as I now heartily implore my God, that the crimes which I have acknowledged are forgiven me, as I now freely forgive all persons all their offences against me. But let it be the care of you all, and which I earnestly entreat from every one of you, to pray the Lord for me, and not through grief and excitement at this my punishment to raise any disturbance, or even to wish that my life could be restored, which I do not myself desire to be prolonged; and besides I would rather that each one of you would bear this with the same equanimity and fortitude, as I am now content to have myself and my case thus dealt with. Moreover, obey the king and his nobles and councillors in all things. Let God and the gospel of Jesus Christ hold, as is fitting, the chief place in your regard; and if at least you would profit by my example, shew careful obedience to the laws of your country, civil and political, and never violate them."

They state that he spake all this, and whatever else he said, with a look and gesture becoming the firmness of a hero, and the modesty of a Christian; that he was splendidly attired, as he used to be when about to attend upon the king, or to appear in public on any especial occasion; that he gave the executioner some gold rings which he drew from his fingers, together with all his clothes; only to a certain gentleman, the lieutenant of the Tower of London, in which he had been confined, he gave his sword and upper garment. What weeping, and wailing, and lamentation, followed upon the death of this nobleman, is as difficult to describe as to believe. It is stated by some persons who belong to the household of some of the councillors, and who are not altogether unacquainted with the affairs of court, that by the royal indulgence the capital punishment had been remitted, with a free pardon, while the duke was yet in prison, and that the whole council sent to inform him of it more than once; but when he rejected with contempt the grace and kindness that was offered him, (I know not whether in reliance on his own innocence, or on the favour of the king and of some other parties, or on his own influence, and wealth, and rank, or on some other delusive persuasion,) the whole council were at length so irritated by this conduct, that they determined that they would no longer endure that excessive arrogance of the man, which made it quite evident that should he be released from imprisonment, he would not, for the sake of avenging himself, refrain from raising disturbances and tumults, and intestine commotions that would endanger the whole kingdom. Besides, as it is probable that none of them would be so safe and secure, as not hereafter to apprehend some impending mischief from a prisoner whom they had unanimously condemned to death, especially the primary authors of this calamity, their minds could never be satisfied unless by the removal of one whom they were afraid of when alive. And thus was realised the saying of Sinon in the poet[1],

> "On one devoted head
> They seek to launch the vengeance that they dread."

But however this might be, it is quite evident, in my opinion, that the deceased nobleman, like other men, was not without his faults, and those perhaps more grievous than could be passed over by God without punishment in this life: wherefore I conclude from hence that God would have the wonderful mystery of his hidden judgment to be made known; and upon a more accurate consideration of the subject, I can scarcely doubt but that you and all godly persons will be of the same opinion. This man was endowed and enriched with most excellent gifts of God both in body and mind, as I am well aware you have in great measure been informed by others. But is not that, I ask, the best gift, that God has chosen the light of the gospel to shine forth by his instrumentality throughout this kingdom, that the Son of God has presented himself to the people of Britain, as it were by

[1 Virg. Æn. II. 130.]

his hand? I do not now mention how God had so exalted him, from being born in a private station, that as the late king's brother-in-law, the brother of a queen, the uncle of the present king, he had no one here superior to him in any degree of honour; and then especially, when appointed lord protector of the realm, he was all but king, or rather esteemed by every one as the king of the king. I omit to tell you how wonderfully God preserved him from capital punishment, when those great disturbances, of which you have heard, were stirred up against him. Though I am acquainted with many other circumstances of the same kind, for the sake of brevity I pass them over. I know assuredly, and have ascertained in many ways, that he did not always use these mercies of God, as a Christian should do, but rather, that he grievously and wickedly abused them, although I think that you never knew any of these things, or could have any suspicion of them. Master à Lasco himself, with whom you are acquainted, can bear sufficient testimony, among others, that during almost the whole time when we were both of us here together, he had become so lukewarm in the service of Christ as scarcely to have any thing less at heart than the state of religion in this country. Nor indeed did he retain in this respect any thing worthy of commendation, excepting that, as far as words go, he always professed himself a gospeller when occasion required such acknowledgement; but yet so that he could not in reality be found fault with by any one, for shewing himself opposed to good and christian actions. But not even this can be allowed him from the time I have now mentioned, that he seriously and heartily employed his authority for the advancement of godliness; and I fear, as far as I have been able to discover the disposition of the man, that if it had been more for his interest to have followed a different course, he would some time or other have made his recantation. For when he manifested certain instances of his liberality and munificence both to yourself, and also very lately to your friend Nicolas for your sake, and to many other persons professing godliness, I know with greater certainty than I could wish, that this was done more for the sake of pleasing man than God; and that it was rather on this ground, that he was unwilling to lose the reputation which he had acquired, than from a sincere regard to godliness. This indeed was not altogether unknown to me, when I was lately with you at Geneva; but as I did not yet despair but that, while he was living, Christ would be preached on every opportunity by his authority more than he had ever been before; and even that he might be induced to reform his life, and repent, which I always believed would be effected rather by you than by any other person, so greatly did he esteem you, (for which reason also I exhorted you the more to write to him, particularly as I suspected that, having been somewhat estranged from him through that messenger of mine, you no longer thought proper to do so,) I considered it best to be silent with you on the subject.

It was notorious to every one in this kingdom that he was the occasion of his brother's death, who, having been convicted on a charge of treason which no one could prove against him by legal evidence, and of which when brought to execution he perseveringly denied the truth, was beheaded owing to his information, instigated by I know not what hatred and rivalry against his brother. Who is there, that, knowing this to be the case, must not forthwith conclude that the awful denunciations and judgments of God against Cain in the fourth chapter of Genesis may be applied in the present instance? And, as I have diligently been informed by those who saw and heard these things, after that murder had been perpetrated, our duke was no longer like himself, but began to labour under those misfortunes which I have above hinted at. And not long after there followed those disturbances which made him, from being the lord protector of the kingdom, a miserable prisoner universally detested and despised. And a certain godly and honourable lady of this country, with whom I am acquainted, is reported to have exclaimed upon that occasion, "Where is thy brother? Lo! his blood crieth against thee unto God from the ground." In fine, that very act, for which he was last of all thrown into prison, was both unworthy of a Christian such as he professed himself to be, and also sufficiently shews that the most part of the crimes, which I have laid to his charge, have their foundation in truth. For he was himself the head and author of a certain conspiracy against the whole of the royal council, and more particularly against the duke of Northumberland, lately called the earl of Warwick, whom he pursued with the most unrelenting hatred, as having been foremost in depriving him of the rank of protector, and being himself regarded from that time by the king's councillors as occupying that office; the duke of Somerset, I say, gained over some accomplices in this conspiracy even from among the council itself, (who are now in prison awaiting the king's pleasure respecting them,) by which it was agreed among them, that on the duke of Northumberland being dispatched (together with any of his friends who should oppose their views) either by violence, or in secret, or in any other way, they should place the entire administration of the kingdom in their own hands, but that the duke of Somerset should be invested with the chief authority, or even be restored to the office of protector.

I know there is now no occasion for me to follow up the details of this and of his other actions to greater length, and shew you how diametrically opposite they are to the word of God, and the profession of Christianity. For you will yourself, with your usual discrimination, not only understand this, but likewise all my feelings, and the object of all that I have said. I think therefore that, for the sake of brevity, I must now conclude, that, though I look upon this punishment to have been inflicted upon this deceased nobleman by a certain necessity for divine judgment, yet, since at his death he manifested some favourable marks of christian penitence, I consider that God has not only chosen in this case to make known to us the mystery of his judgment, but also that of his infinite mercy, by which he kills and makes alive, brings down to the grave and brings back; whereby he would have the body to be destroyed for the salvation of the soul, and that one should be cast down in this life, whom he chooses to be exalted in a future one. And the consideration indeed of this circumstance, though it should afford no small comfort to me and to every one, yet cannot at once divest me of all sorrow at his death. And indeed I should be more than ordinarily cruel and unfeeling, could I bury so recent a calamity in immediate oblivion. Yet two reasons are presented to my mind which increase my regret: one of them is, that we have lost so great a man, and one who was not so entirely corrupted but that there remained some hope both of his reformation, and also that the interest of the gospel would in any case be advanced by his authority and protection, since there is certainly the greatest scarcity and want of such characters in this country. Then, also, it seems to me to be a cause of the greatest lamentation and sorrow, that his life, imprisonment, and execution, were, and are, and will be, a stumbling-block to many persons, to the great contempt and injury of the gospel and of godliness.

I now proceed to certain other matters[1]. The lord archbishop of Canterbury, master à Lasco, Utenhovius, Richard the minister of our church, having received your letters through me, requested me, on my writing to you, to make their excuses, that, for various reasons, they have not forthwith returned an answer; and also to salute you most dutifully in the name of them all, with the promise that they will all of them write to you when they have more leisure, and more important subjects to write about. London, Jan. 22, 1552.

Yours,

FRANCIS BOURGOYNE.

LETTER CCCXLVIII.

VALERANDUS POLLANUS[2] TO JOHN CALVIN.

Dated at LONDON, *March* 7, 1552.

GREETING. An intimate friend of mine, a learned and godly man, has advised and urgently entreated me to advertise you, at the first opportunity, of the circumstances I am about to mention. He understood, he said, you were exceedingly distressed at the death of the duke of Somerset, as I dare affirm that all godly persons are in this country; and that even the chief nobility themselves have not witnessed so great a fall of a character so illustrious without

[1 As the passage next following refers only to the private affairs of the writer, it was not thought necessary to procure a transcript.]

[2 Valerandus Pollanus was minister of the church of Strangers at Glastonbury, which fled from Strasburgh by reason of the Interim. He translated into Latin the Liturgy they used, and published it in Feb. 1551. See Strype, Mem. II. i. 378, &c.]

the greatest sorrow of mind. But these are examples of the judgments of the Lord, by which all persons are reminded that they should fear the Lord, cherish true godliness without hypocrisy, and not abuse to their own lusts the doctrine of the gospel. But my informant added, moreover, that you had some intention of writing, I know not what, against our people respecting his death, and even to the king himself; to which I, who well know your discretion, replied, that it could not be the case. He persisted, however, in urging me to write to you upon the subject, that you may not inconsiderately publish any thing, by which a fresh flame may be rekindled, or the minds of certain parties be irritated against the professors of the gospel. If I had a messenger at hand, I would now lay before you the whole case, though I had rather relate the whole affair by word of mouth to some one upon whom I could depend. For I have no doubt but that many persons make various statements, according as they are individually affected, while but few are made with judgment. If any one has had reason to grieve at this great calamity, it is surely myself, who have experienced by manifest proofs, that he entertained a regard both for me and for my little church which I had gathered together in his duchy[1] a year ago. But when I consider the providence of God, and the severity of his judgments, first of all upon his own people, and then upon those who are aliens from his election; here I restrain myself, and am content to commend his church and the whole ministry to him in continual prayer, that every one of us, aided by his Spirit, may rightly be employed in his house, and, mindful of our calling, entirely devote ourselves to the edifying of his church. Want of time compels me to conclude against my wishes. Farewell, and salute all your fellow-ministers and all godly persons in my name. If I can

[[1] The duke of Somerset, to whom the dissolved abbey of Glastonbury was granted, settled Pollanus and his congregation there, with a promise to buy wool and necessaries to carry on their manufactures, and allotted them rooms for their dwelling, and ascertained certain proportions of land for feeding of their cows. Upon the misfortunes of the duke, these men's industry came to a stand for a time, but in Nov. 1551, they received farther encouragement from the privy council. See Strype, Mem. II. i. 381.]

in any way be useful to you, I offer you all my services. London, March 7, 1552.

Your ever most attached pupil,

VALERANDUS POLLANUS.

If you think this letter worthy of a reply, send your answer to my friend master Richard, minister of the French church in London; for I shall shortly be obliged to return to Glastonbury, where God, by the instrumentality of the duke, and lately too by that of the king, has appointed me the superintendent of the foreigners' church.

LETTER CCCXLIX.

HENRY BULLINGER TO JOHN BURCHER.

Dated at Zurich, *June* 28, 1549.

Greeting. I have duly received, Burcher, your letters of the 30th of May and the 1st of June[2], and I thank you for your fidelity and attention. I should very much like to see the book of the Anglican religion[3]. You will therefore exceedingly oblige me by procuring me a copy. Should you receive any letters for me from England, I pray you to see that they be safely forwarded to me. If you have received any certain intelligence respecting our friend Hooper[4], and likewise how Bucer is conducting himself in England, I beg you will let me know; as also, lastly, how our friend Richard [Hilles] is going on, and what is the present state of your kingdom. You probably know what the emperor is doing, or where he now is. As for ourselves here, we have not heard anything about him. That nobleman of Ghent, ab Utenhoven, far exceeded your commendation of him. He is without his equal, and I thank you that by your instru-

[2 These letters are given above, pp. 651, 653.]

[3 Namely, the Book of Common Prayer, first published in May, 1549. See the Liturgies, &c. of Edward VI. Parker Soc. Edit.]

[4 Hooper was at this time chaplain to the duke of Somerset, and a famous preacher in London. See above p. 65.]

mentality and that of my friend Hooper I have contracted an intimacy with one who is in every way so distinguished. I have nothing farther to communicate respecting our affairs in Switzerland, than that every thing is quiet among us; except that those states which have made an alliance with France are at some little disagreement among themselves, by reason of there being many among them who still disapprove that alliance[1]. But there is the greatest harmony among the christian cities, who with one consent renounced that alliance. Some other states have also renounced it; but those which have admitted it are not on bad terms with those which have refused, although they wished that all would act as they themselves have done. Among other things, these words are inserted in the treaty: "and should the king's majesty aforesaid require assistance for the subjugation of the city of Boulogne, and the dominions of the Boulognois in Picardy, the confederates are bound to afford it, as has been before suffered by others of our free provinces[1]." You see whither these sanguinary princes are endeavouring to drag us along with themselves. Oh! I wish the king of England would send a short letter to all the Swiss, not with a view of making any request, but only with that of vindicating and defending his right, and, in fine, exhorting them not to persist in waging war against one who had done nothing to deserve it.

Farewell, my Burcher, and diligently write me an account of every thing. Farewell again and again. I am exerting myself to procure the payment of the salary of your wife's brother, and shall repeat my endeavours to-morrow. The Lord knows how I shall succeed. I bid farewell also to your wife. Salute all our friends and sisters in England. Zurich, June 28, 1549.

Yours, you know who,

[HENRY BULLINGER.]

[[1] See above, p. 68.]

LETTER CCCL.

HENRY BULLINGER TO THEODORE BEZA.

Dated at [ZURICH], *Aug.* 30, 1553.

GREETING. The youth who brought me your most welcome letter found me engaged in a great variety of business, so that I have hardly had it in my power to write this in reply. You have been informed by our friend Gualter what is to be done with the boy. I am sure that he will be a father to him, and I myself will not be wanting to him, were it only for the sake of my friend Calvin.

The day before yesterday I received a letter from Bassefontaine the king's envoy, written at Soleure on the 27th of this month; who mentions among other things, that an English[2] nobleman lately passed through that city on his way to Rome, whither he was sent by [queen] Mary to recal that Reginald Pole, who is too well known both to you and to myself: for that English Athaliah desires the benefit of his presence and his counsel. Scarcely has any other thing so much distressed me as this English affair. I am hourly expecting more certain information, of which I will not fail to let you know. Oh! how truly wretched are the times into which our good Lord has thought fit for us to enter! Let us earnestly implore his mercy, that he may shew pity upon us and upon his most afflicted church. But where is our Martyr? Where John à Lasco? Where is Hooper, bishop of Worcester? Where is Cranmer, archbishop of Canterbury? Where is the duke of Suffolk? Where are numberless other excellent men? Lord, have mercy upon them! I cannot easily express how greatly these things distress me.

The French fleet has pillaged and set fire to many towns in Calabria. They have taken and burnt the cities of Aliaca in Sicily, and Nori in Sardinia, and are now laying siege to Elba in the Mediterranean, belonging to the duke of Florence. In Germany every thing is in a most grievous and

[2 The person entrusted with the message to cardinal Pole was John Francis Commendone, chamberlain to the pope, and afterwards cardinal. See Burnet, III. 334. Soames, IV. 61, &c. and the authorities there quoted.]

deplorable state. But what is your most honourable senate of Geneva going to do with that blasphemous wretch Servetus? If they are wise, and do their duty, they will put him to death, that all the world may perceive that Geneva desires the glory of Christ to be maintained inviolate. Farewell, my very dear friend. Salute for me Calvin, Viret, Farell, and all good men. August 30, 1553.

Yours,

BULLINGER.

LETTER CCCLI.

HENRY BULLINGER TO JOHN CALVIN[1].

Dated at ZURICH, *Oct.* 15, 1553.

IT is wonderful, my honoured master and dearly beloved brother, how greatly I desire to hear of the state of your affairs, by a letter from yourself. I well know that my opinion against Servetus and the assurance of my approval have been laid before you. And at the same time our most honourable senate wrote to yours, seriously exhorting them to put a stop to this pestilence. What reply has been made by other cities and ministers of churches, I do not yet know[2]. We pray God in the mean time to preserve and defend your church.

As to the state of affairs in England, you will learn it from the inclosed letter[3] sent to me within these few days, from a prison in London, by the godly bishop of Worcester and Gloucester, whom I suspect by this time to have been removed from this world. He writes me word that divine things are trodden under foot, and that human things have the pre-eminence. The duke of Northumberland is executed, the duke of Suffolk was thrown into prison, but, being innocent, was discharged shortly afterwards; but having been

[1 The reply to this letter is given in Calvin's epistles, p. 127. Ed. Genev. 1575.]

[2 Copies of Servetus's appeal were transmitted to the churches of Zurich, Berne, Basle, and Schaffhausen. Their replies are given in Calvin's epistles, pp. 116—122.]

[3 This letter is given above, p. 100.]

attacked by disease, he is reported to have departed to the Lord. That most excellent man, the archbishop of Canterbury, is deposed, and Pole is appointed in his place. They are now holding the parliament after the queen's coronation. It began to-day.

Of masters John à Lasco, Martyr, Cox, Sidall, and the other most godly servants of God and very dear brethren, I have not any certain information. Should you learn anything from your friends, either better or worse, do not fail to let me know. May the Lord visit our people, and soon cast down the crown of antichrist! He permits many things, that his tried ones may be approved. Let us pray the Lord to preserve his people in these sad commotions, and to beat down Satan under his feet. Farewell for ever with all the ministers and brethren our fellow-labourers. In the greatest haste. Zurich, Oct. 15, 1553.

Yours,

BULLINGER.

LETTER CCCLII.

HENRY BULLINGER TO JOHN CALVIN.

Dated at ZURICH, *March* 26, 1554.

GREETING. I return you my best thanks, honoured master and very dear brother, as well for your most friendly letter as for the present you have made me of a copy of your book[4]. Haller, to whom you had sent it, has only forwarded it to me within these eight days, so that I have not yet been able to read it through, as I have been entirely occupied during the whole of last week with the duties of the pulpit. I have, however, taken a cursory view of it, and perceive that you have inserted my letter, and at the same time made honourable mention of our church; for which I thank you. I have no doubt but that you handle

[4 This book appears, from a letter of Calvin to Bullinger, dated Feb. 23, 1554, to have been his "Refutation of the errors of Servetus." Calv. Ep. p. 385.]

every thing with the most perfect faithfulness. I only fear that your book will not be so acceptable to many of the more simple-minded persons, who nevertheless are much attached both to yourself and to the truth, by reason of its brevity, and consequent obscurity, and the weightiness of the subject. And indeed your style appears somewhat perplexed, especially in this work. Nevertheless I acknowledge that all good men are much indebted to you, and that those who are more learned are exceedingly so. I know that you will kindly take this freedom of mine; for I love you from my heart.

I have inclosed in this letter the answer I made to the Scotsman whom you commended to me. You will return it to me when you have an opportunity. I commend to your kindness and hospitality these two Englishmen, one of whom, Thomas Lever[1], used to preach before the king; the other is an individual of rank. The former is a learned and very godly man. They have been my guests about a fortnight, and I am greatly delighted with their piety. They have expressed their intention of remaining in your town for some time. I pray you therefore to be pleased, if you can, to shew yourselves faithful and friendly hosts. Whatever kindness you may shew them, I shall consider as conferred upon myself; nay, rather, you will confer it upon Christ. I hope that you have long since received my books upon "The grace of God justifying us for Christ's sake by faith only;" for I sent it for you to master Haller. Farewell, and ever remember me in your prayers. All our fellow-ministers are well. The emperor is preparing for a serious war with the French; and the Germans, divided into many parties, are suffering the punishment of their ingratitude. Zurich, March 26, 1554.

Yours,

BULLINGER.

[[1] See above, Letter LXXVII. where Lever refers to this letter of introduction. See also, Lett. CCCXXVI.]

[The following is the inclosure referred to in the above Letter.]

An answer given to a certain Scotsman[2], in reply to some questions concerning the kingdom of Scotland and England.

1. Whether the son of a king, upon his father's death, though unable by reason of his tender age to conduct the government of the kingdom, is nevertheless by right of inheritance to be regarded as a lawful magistrate, and as such to be obeyed as of divine right?

That person is, in my opinion, to be esteemed as a lawful king, who is ordained according to the just laws of the country. And thus it is clear that Edward VI. of happy memory was ordained. For his father on his death-bed appointed him king, and so claimed for him the right of sovereignty, which they say is hereditary. The states of the kingdom acknowledged him, as they testified by his coronation. They provided him with councillors, endued as he was with great gifts of God; nor was any thing wanting to that kingdom, which is wont to be looked for in the most prosperous kingdom elsewhere. He was therefore a lawful sovereign, and his laws and ordinances demanded obedience; and he ruled the kingdom after a more godly manner than the three most wise and prosperous kings of that country who immediately preceded him.

2. Whether a female can preside over, and rule a kingdom by divine right, and so transfer the right of sovereignty to her husband?

The law of God ordains the woman to be in subjection, and not to rule; which is clear from the writings of both the old and the new Testament. But if a woman in compliance with, or in obedience to the laws and customs of the realm, is acknowledged as queen, and, in maintenance of the hereditary right of government, is married to a husband, or in the meantime holds the reins of government by means of her councillors, it is a hazardous thing for godly persons to set themselves in opposition to political regulations; especially as the gospel does not seem to unsettle or abrogate hereditary rights, and the political laws of kingdoms; nor do we read that Philip

[2 Simler conjectures either Knox or Goodman to be the Scotsman here referred to. It was probably the latter. See below, p. 771. n. 1.]

the eunuch, by right of the gospel, drove out Candace from the kingdom of Ethiopia. And if the reigning sovereign be not a Deborah, but an ungodly and tyrannous ruler of the kingdom, godly persons have an example and consolation in the case of Athaliah. The Lord will in his own time destroy unjust governments by his own people, to whom he will supply proper qualifications for this purpose, as he formerly did to Jerubbaal, and the Maccabees, and Jehoiada. With respect however to her right of transferring the power of government to her husband, those persons who are acquainted with the laws and customs of the realm can furnish the proper answer.

3. Whether obedience is to be rendered to a magistrate who enforces idolatry and condemns true religion; and whether those authorities, who are still in military occupation of towns and fortresses, are permitted to repel this ungodly violence from themselves and their friends.

The history of Daniel, and the express command of God Matt. x., and the examples of the apostles in Acts iv. and v., as also that of many of the martyrs in ecclesiastical history, teach us that we must not obey the king or magistrate when their commands are opposed to God and his lawful worship; but rather that we should expose our persons, and lives, and fortunes to danger. This power is the power of darkness, as the Lord saith in the gospel. And Eusebius records, in the ninth book and eighth chapter of his Ecclesiastical history, that the Armenians took arms against their lawful sovereigns the Roman emperors, who desired to force them to idolatry. And this conduct of theirs is not reproved. Those very Armenians, many years after, by reason of the ungodliness of the kings of Persia, slew their ungodly commanders, and revolted to the emperor Justin, as is recorded by Evagrius. [Eccl. Hist. v. 8.] For the holy scripture not only permits, but even enjoins upon the magistrate a just and necessary defence. But as other objects are often aimed at under the pretext of a just and necessary assertion or maintenance of right, and the worst characters mix themselves with the good, and the times too are full of danger; it is very difficult to pronounce upon every particular case. For an accurate knowledge of the circumstances is here of great importance; and as I do not possess such knowledge, it would be very foolish in me to recommend or determine any thing specific upon the subject. For even Paul, we read, made use of the Roman soldiery against those who plotted against him, and was right in doing so: yet at another time, though under almost the same or similar circumstances, he is recorded to have used only the arms of patience, and none else. There is need therefore, in cases of this kind, of much prayer, and much wisdom, lest by precipitancy and corrupt affections we should so act as to occasion mischief to many worthy persons. Meanwhile, however, death itself is far preferable to the admission of idolatry.

4. To which party must godly persons attach themselves, in the case of a religious nobility resisting an idolatrous sovereign?

I leave this to be decided by the judgment of godly persons, who are well acquainted with all the circumstances, who look up in all things to the word of God, who attempt nothing contrary to the laws of God, who obey the impulses of the Holy Ghost, and who are guided by circumstances of place, time, opportunity, persons, and things, without making any rash attempt, and who can therefore be directed more safely by their own sense of duty than by the consciences of others. But I would advise them, above all things, that those causes may be removed, on account of which hypocrites are predominant; iniquities, I mean, that we may become reconciled to God by a true repentance, and implore his counsel and assistance. He is the only and the true deliverer; and, as we read in the books of Judges and Kings, and the ecclesiastical histories, has never been wanting to his church. Let us lift up our eyes to him, waiting for his deliverance, abstaining in the meantime from all superstition and idolatry, and doing what he reveals to us in his word.

LETTER CCCLIII.

HENRY BULLINGER TO CERTAIN ENGLISHMEN[1].

Dated at *Zurich*, *Aug*. 24, 1554.

Greeting. Our Lord Jesus Christ not only requires

[[1] The title of this letter at full length is, "The Letter of the

believers to befriend his banished ones themselves, but also to procure for them the favour of all godly persons, and by pleading their cause in all quarters to aid them in every possible way. For this reason we do not hesitate to commend to your kindness your English exiles, whom our most honourable magistrates here have taken into their protection, and to whom we wish well from our hearts. They have hitherto lived among us in the sincere fear of God, in true godliness, in constant prayer, in godly discipline, and in purity and innocence of life. They have, as far as we know, afforded no occasion of offence to any one; they have not injured or been troublesome to any one; they are beloved by all godly persons; they are so devoted to, and so greatly profit by, their literary and theological studies, that it is impossible not to expect from them the most abundant fruit. Should they go on as they have begun, there is no doubt but that they will be a benefit and advantage to the renowned kingdom of England. For though England at this present time neither regards nor requires them and their progress in learning and godliness, we nevertheless entertain the hope that other and happier times will at length arrive; especially when we see that changes in kingdoms are of very frequent occurrence, and in a word, that the grace of Christ is denied to none, so that the man who has lately been a most active persecutor of Christ and his gospel, may soon perhaps become a most zealous preacher of the gospel.

You will therefore, honoured friends and brethren, act with the greatest wisdom as well as godliness, by not withdrawing your support from the deserving and hopeful members of Christ, who stand in need of your assistance. You know what praise and honour in the sight of God and men Obadiah, the governor of the house of the ungodly king Ahab, procured to himself, because, at the utmost risk both of his life and property, (living as he did in those most perilous times, when queen Jezebel purposed to destroy all the prophets of God, either by the sword, or to make them perish with hunger,) he fed even whole schools of the prophets in caves and secret places. And indeed these

Ministers of the church of Zurich on behalf of the English exiles in the city of Zurich in the time of the Marian Persecution, to the English." It is without any address, and signed by Bullinger in the name of the rest.]

your countrymen are so far from abounding in luxury, that they seem to the most carful observers to deny themselves even what is necessary for their support, and live far too sparingly. And I wish that many among ourselves had the same power of shewing kindness to them, as we should otherwise have the inclination; for they would then be richer than they are at present. But inasmuch as God has blessed you, and has not only bestowed upon you more ample means, but has also afforded you this seasonable opportunity of benefiting your countrymen; your charity will understand how acceptable a sacrifice you will offer to God, and how greatly you will improve your own circumstances, if you continue to shew liberality to these your countrymen, who are true members of Christ. For you are aware that Paul, the holy apostle of Christ, in more than one place calls the collection made by the rich, on behalf of those who were in banishment and poverty by reason of the gospel of Christ, "an odour of a sweet smell, a sacrifice acceptable, well-pleasing to God." [Phil. iv. 18.] The same apostle too adds: "My God shall supply all your need according to his riches in glory by Christ Jesus." And again, in another place: "God is able," he says, "to make all grace abound towards you, that ye, always having all sufficiency in all things, may abound to every good work; as it is written, He hath dispersed abroad, he hath given to the poor; his righteousness remaineth for ever." [2 Cor. ix. 8, 9.] And the Lord Jesus himself expressly declares in his gospel: "He that receiveth you, receiveth me; and he that receiveth me, receiveth him that sent me. He that receiveth a prophet in the name of a prophet, shall receive a prophet's reward; and whosoever shall give to drink unto one of these little ones a cup of cold water only in the name of a disciple, verily, I say unto you, he shall not lose his reward." [Matt. x. 40—42.] For the same Lord declares in another place: "I was an hungered, and ye gave me meat; I was thirsty, and ye gave me drink; I was a stranger, and ye took me in; naked, and ye clothed me," &c. "Verily, I say unto you, inasmuch as ye have done it unto one of the least of these my brethren, ye have done it unto me." [Matt. xxv. 35, 40.] And Christ our Lord promises to such persons all manner of blessing, and a happy life. And we read also that David sung: "Blessed is the man that considereth the poor and needy; the Lord will deliver him in the time of trouble. The Lord preserve him and keep him alive, and make him blessed upon the earth, and not deliver him into the hand of his enemies. The Lord comfort him upon his bed of languishing; thou wilt make all his bed in his sickness," &c. [Ps. xli. 1, &c.] All the words of God are true, stedfast, and undoubted. For heaven and earth shall pass away, but the eternal word of God shall never perish, nor shall one jot or tittle fall from it.

Believing therefore in these most certain declarations of God, earnestly endeavour, brethren and friends beloved in the Lord, by a plenteous sowing and liberal contribution to prepare for yourselves against that day an abundant harvest, and one that will satisfy you for eternity, through Christ our Lord. Fare ye well, and receive this our exhortation with kindness as from your friends and brethren. Zurich, Aug. 24, 1554.

HENRY BULLINGER,

In the name of all the pastors, readers, and ministers of the church of Zurich.

LETTER CCCLIV.

HENRY BULLINGER TO JOHN CALVIN.

Dated at [ZURICH,] *Sept.* 9, 1554.

[EXTRACT.]

LEVER is in good health, as, thank God, are also the rest of our English; but they are exceedingly grieved, and not without reason, at the ingratitude of their afflicted country. You know that she has admitted the Spaniard, who has handselled his government with the blood of two noblemen whom he has beheaded. They fear lest those most holy bishops, Latimer, Cranmer, Ridley, Hooper, &c. have been cut off by this time. I see that we must pray unceasingly for that most afflicted church.

LETTER CCCLV.

HENRY BULLINGER TO JOHN CALVIN.

[Without place or date.]

[EXTRACT.]

My friends write me word that those excellent men and my very dear brothers, master Latimer, and master Ridley bishop of London, were burned in the sight of Cranmer[1], who testified however that this punishment was more grievous to him than death itself, namely, that he was not offered to the Lord on the same funeral pile with his brethren. He was led back in chains to prison, and it is supposed that he also is by this time reduced to ashes.

They say that the emperor is about to sail into Spain, but that he will previously place on Philip's head the crown of England; for they think he will visit that country in the course of his journey. The Lord protect his faithful people, and recompense the bloody men on their own heads!

LETTER CCCLVI.

ROBERT HORN AND OTHERS[2] TO THE MAGISTRATES AT ZURICH.

Dated 1554.

Forasmuch as we are exiled, most honourable magistrates, from England, our beloved country, and for the sake

[1 Strype's account is somewhat different. He states that Ridley and Latimer were brought forth to their burning, (Oct. 16, 1555); and, passing by Cranmer's prison (in Bocardo) Ridley looked up to have seen him, and to have taken his farewell of him; but he was not then at the window, being engaged in dispute with a Spanish friar (Soto). But he looked after them, and, devoutly falling upon his knees, prayed to God to strengthen their faith and patience in that their last, but painful passage. Strype, Mem. III. 1, 529. Foxe, VII. 548.]

[2 The signatures to this letter are probably those of the twelve persons who, according to Laurence Humphrey's account in his Life of Jewel, dwelt together, like brothers, and with great glee, in the house of Froschover. See Strype, Mem. III. i. 232.]

of that light of divine truth by which she was lately distinguished, we humbly request of your worthiness, that we may be permitted to sojourn in this most famous city, relying upon and supported by your sanction, decree, and protection against the violence of those, should any such be found, who would oppose and molest us. The Lord knoweth, for whose sake we have left our all, that we seek for nothing besides himself. And for this reason chiefly we have unanimously and with ready minds come to this place, where he is most sincerely preached and most purely worshipped. This being the case, we entertain the hope that, as you are most zealous defenders of the true Christian religion, so you will protect us by your authority, who by reason of the same are exiled and homeless. May the Lord Jesus long preserve you and this your illustrious state in safety and prosperity! Your most humble petitioners,

ROBERT HORN[1].	RICHARD CHAMBERS.
MARGERY HIS WIFE.	THOMAS SPENCER[6].
JAMES PILKINGTON[2].	HENRY COCKRAFT.
THOMAS LEVER[3].	MICHAEL RENIGER[7].
JOHN MULLINS[4].	LAURENCE HUMPHREY[8].
THOMAS BENTHAM[5].	WILLIAM COLE[9].

[1 Dean of Durham, and afterwards bishop of Winchester.]

[2 Fellow, and afterwards master, of St John's College, Cambridge, and bishop of Durham.]

[3 Master of St John's, Cambridge, and afterwards prebendary of Durham, and master of Sherburn Hospital.]

[4 Afterwards archdeacon of London, canon of St Paul's, and rector of Bocking.]

[5 Fellow of Magdalene College, Oxford, and afterwards bishop of Lichfield and Coventry.]

[6 Afterwards archdeacon of Chichester.]

[7 Afterwards chaplain to queen Elizabeth, and prebendary of Winchester.]

[8 Afterwards regius professor of divinity at Oxford, and president of Magdalene College; dean of Gloucester, and lastly, of Winchester.]

[9 Fellow, and afterwards president, of Corpus Christi College, Oxford.]

LETTER CCCLVII.

RICHARD COX AND OTHERS TO JOHN CALVIN[10].

Dated at FRANKFORT, *April* 5, 1555.

GREETING. After that our very dear brother Thomas Sampson had communicated to us sometime since the letter that you wrote to him touching our common controversy with certain brethren, we considered it a mark of our duty and regard to you to inform you, as early as possible, of all that has been done, and with what design. But though it may perhaps seem to you somewhat late to write to you, when the matter is altogether brought to a termination; yet we implore you by Jesus Christ, not to suppose that the delay has arisen from any desire unduly to undervalue your authority. For it both is, and ought to be, most highly esteemed and regarded, not only by ourselves, but by the world at large. But since your reverence was many days' journey distant from us, and because there was great hope that all that controversy could be settled with less inconvenience between the brethren themselves, we were unwilling to disturb your most important meditations by our trifling and domestic concerns. But though we are very loth to suspect our brethren of any thing that savours of insincerity, we are nevertheless somewhat afraid that the whole affair and case has not been set before you with sufficient explicitness. For neither are we so entirely wedded to our country, as not to be able to endure any customs differing from our own; nor is the authority of those fathers and martyrs of Christ so much regarded by us, as that we have any scruple in thinking or acting in opposition to it. And we have not only very frequently borne witness to this by our assertions, but have at length proved it by our actions. For when the magistrates lately gave us permission to adopt

[10 Calvin's reply to this letter is printed in his Epistles, p. 158. Ed. Genev. 1575. A translation of it is given in the Brief Discourse of the troubles begun at Frankfort, p. 51, (Reprint, 1846,) a constant reference to which treatise is necessary for the full understanding of this and the subsequent letters.]

the rites of our native country, we freely relinquished all those ceremonies which were regarded by our brethren as offensive and inconvenient. For we gave up private baptisms, confirmation of children, saints' days, kneeling at the holy communion, the linen surplices of the ministers, crosses, and other things of the like character. And we gave them up, not as being impure and papistical, which certain of our brethren often charged them with being; but whereas they were in their own nature indifferent, and either ordained or allowed by godly fathers for the edification of our people, we notwithstanding chose rather to lay them aside than to offend the minds or alienate the affections of the brethren. We retain however the remainder of the form of prayer and of the administration of the sacraments, which is prescribed in our book, and this with the consent of almost the whole church, the judgment of which in matters of this sort we did not think should be disregarded. With the consent likewise of the same church there was forthwith appointed one pastor, two preachers, four elders, two deacons; the greatest care being taken that every one should be at perfect liberty to vote as he pleased; except only that by the command of the magistrate, before the election took place, were set forth those articles lately published by the authority of king Edward, which contained a summary of our doctrine, and which we were all of us required to subscribe. For what kind of an election, they said, must be expected, unless the voters shall previously have agreed as to doctrine? Certain parties, who had before manifested some objection, subscribed to these articles of their own accord. Some few declined doing so, of whose peaceableness nevertheless we entertain good hope.

We have thought fit to write thus fully to your kindness, that you might ascertain the whole course of our proceedings from ourselves. Our liturgy is translated into French, and the articles above mentioned have very lately been printed at Zurich. Did we not suppose that they would easily be met with among you, we should take care that copies should be forwarded you. But we pray your kindness not to imagine that we have aimed at any thing else throughout this whole business, and this we testify before the Lord, than the purification of our church, and the avoiding of most grievous stumbling-blocks which otherwise seemed to be hanging over us. May the Lord Jesus very long preserve your piety to us and to his church! Farewell. Frankfort, April 5, [1555.]

Your piety's most devoted

English exiles,

RICHARD COX[1].	EDMUND GRINDAL[6].
DAVID WHITEHEAD[2].	JOHN BALE[7].
RICHARD ALVEY[3].	ROB. HORN.
THOMAS BECON[4].	THO. LEVER.
EDWIN SANDYS[5].	THO. SAMPSON[8].

LETTER CCCLVIII.

DAVID WHITEHEAD AND OTHERS TO JOHN CALVIN[9].

Dated at FRANKFORT, *Sept.* 20, 1555.

As we were awaiting the arrival of certain of our brethren, to whom your letter seemed especially to apply, we were prevented from answering it, most learned Calvin, so early as either the case itself required, or as you probably expected.

[[1] Richard Cox had been tutor and Almoner to Edward VI., dean of Christ Church, and privy councillor. He was afterwards bishop of Ely, and died in 1581.]

[[2] David Whitehead was recommended by Cranmer for the see of Armagh. He was sequestered for nonconformity in 1564.]

[[3] Richard Alvey was made prebendary of Westminster in 1552. Strype, Mem. II. ii. 274.]

[[4] Thomas Becon had been chaplain to Cranmer, and was afterwards prebendary of Canterbury, and rector of St Stephen's, Walbrook. See the biographical notice prefixed to the Park. Soc. Edition of his works.]

[[5] Successively bishop of Worcester and London, and archbishop of York. See his works, Park. Soc. Edition.]

[[6] Successively appointed to the sees of London, York, and Canterbury. See his works, Park. Soc. Edition.]

[[7] Bishop of Ossory.]

[[8] Afterwards dean of Christ Church. For a notice of the other writers see above, p. 752.]

[[9] This letter is in reply to one from Calvin to Richard Cox and others, dated May 31, 1555, a translation of which is printed in the Troubles of Frankfort, p. 51, 1845, reprint. See Calv. Ep. p. 158. Ed. Genev. 1575.]

But now, since all hope of their coming to us is taken away, it has seemed good to us who are here, to make at length some reply; partly indeed, lest by our silence we should seem unmindful of our duty to you, and partly, lest we should seem to betray our excellent cause. And, first, we desire you to be fully persuaded of this, that we regard you with entire veneration and love, both by reason of your singular godliness, and also of your especial preeminence in the most valuable attainments. But we consider it as a matter of exceeding regret, that our late letter was not altogether satisfactory to you in removing all your scruples. This, however, we must ascribe to those parties to whom you appeared to be a fit object for them to endeavour to deceive, and one whose authority they might shamelessly abuse for the purpose of disturbing our church. For it seems very evident to us, that they would never have ventured to raise such a disturbance, had you not refrained in that letter of yours from pouring as it were cold water on the flame. Your letter was to them like the club of Hercules, by which they easily believed that they could beat down all their opponents. And, indeed, your name ought deservedly to have influence both with us, and with all godly persons. But if you had been well acquainted with their devices, if you had been sufficiently aware of their boldness and wicked designs, we have no doubt but that you would never have suffered them to come near you, much less to impose upon you as it were in so barefaced a manner. Indeed we consider it impossible to entertain any doubt of your candour and impartiality, as soon as our case shall have been clearly made known to you, and their artifices exposed. But though your letter is not a little annoying to us, inasmuch as it seems to brand us and bring us in guilty of such great offences, yet we hope that you have another ear in reserve for our reply. Receive, therefore, these few remarks in answer to your letter.

These friends of yours complain that "we are too precise in enforcing the English ceremonies, and unreasonably partial to our own country[1]." These, indeed, we pertinaciously

[[1] Calvin says, "For certain of my friends found themselves grieved that you would so precisely urge the ceremonies of England, whereby it might appear that ye are more given and addicted to your country than reason would." Troubles of Frankfort, p. 51.]

retain, as knowing them to be very godly: this, however, has never been done by us in a precise manner; for we have abandoned some of them for the sake of your friends, which might at that time have been piously adopted. But we make this concession to the love of our country, to which, forsooth, we are too much inclined. These, your friends, however, are altogether a disgrace to their country; for whatever has been bestowed from above upon our country in this respect, with exceeding arrogance, not to say impudence, they are treading under foot. You must know that we do not entertain any regard for our country which is not agreeable to God's holy word. Neither in the mean while are we so ungrateful to our country, nor have we so cast off every feeling of humanity, as rashly to despise the benefits which God has bestowed upon it. Nor have we such a mean opinion of the judgments of our countrymen, who resisted ungodliness even unto blood, as that by reason of the clamours of individuals, possessing no weight whatever, we should brand them with the foulest marks of papistical impiety. You "heard the reasons which would not allow us to depart from the received form[2]." You heard them, indeed, but not from us, and probably not all of them. And, indeed, we have very little doubt but that you would easily refute them: but we are confident that the best reasons of our conduct will stand good before the judgment-seat of God. You say that "it offended you that there was no concession or relaxation made to them on our parts[3]." And you might justly have been offended, had no concession been made. But as this is a barefaced and impudent falsehood of theirs, you can judge for yourself in what light they must have regarded you. You object to us "lights and crosses[4]." As for lights, we never had any; and with respect to crosses, if we ever made use of them, these friends of yours have not

[2 "I confess that, I heard certain reasons alleged on your behalf, which would not suffer you to depart from the received order, but they might be soon and easily confuted." Calvin's letter, as above.]

[3 "Now, as I counselled my own friends which dissented from you, somewhat to yield, if they might conveniently, so it offended me that there was no concession or relaxation made on your parts." Calvin, as above.]

[4 "Verily no man well instructed, or of a sound judgment, will deny, as I think, that lights and crossings or such like trifles sprang or issued out of superstition." Calvin, as above.]

imposed upon you. But consider again in what estimation they must have held you, when they presumed to assault you with so many manifest falsehoods. They also falsely lay it to our charge before you, that we wished to "burden the church with trifling and unprofitable ceremonies[1]." Our ceremonies are very few, and all of them of no little use towards the advancement of godliness. But it is no wonder that our ceremonies appear redundant, and even burdensome, to those persons who exclaim against the public reading of the word of God as an irksome and unprofitable form. But from those words of yours it is quite evident, that you are entirely ignorant of almost all the circumstances of our case. For we have nothing, we are well assured, which either in your judgment, or in that of any godly man, will appear to be either unprofitable or injurious. But you are right in restraining yourself[2]; or you would otherwise, as the mountebanks do, fight to no purpose against things which have no existence. We are quite ready to give you an account of the ceremonies we make use of here, whenever you please; and, whatever our cavillers may have muttered against them, we have more reason, we think, to apprehend the dissatisfaction of many persons by reason of their fewness rather than of their number.

To return now to the other points of your letter. "All good men[3]," you say, "will allow the pastors and other ministers to be elected by the common voice, so that others do not complain that a part of the church has been oppressed fraudulently and with crafty practices." This assertion is certainly a stinging one, and would have wounded us severely, had not its point been blunted when it fell upon us. Nay, we allow it to be a thunderbolt; but it has not reached the

[1 "Neither do I see to what purpose it is to burden the church with trifling and unprofitable ceremonies, or, as I may term them with their proper name, hurtful and offensive ceremonies, when as there is liberty to have a simple and pure order." Calvin, as above.]

[2 "But I keep in and refrain myself lest I should seem to begin to move a new contention of that matter which, as you report, is well ended." Calvin, as above.]

[3 "All good men will allow the pastors' and other ministers' elections with common voices, so that none complain that the other part of the church was oppressed fraudulently and with crafty practices." Calvin, as above.]

object at which it was aimed. It is neither a novelty to us, nor a matter of surprise, that men, conscious of being in the wrong, will at length proceed to assert what is untrue. But it certainly turned out contrary to all our expectation, that you should so lend your ears to them, as to incline in some measure to that party. For what kind of an election ours was, we call to witness God, our conscience, our whole church, and the very magistrates themselves, of whose authority and advice we always availed ourselves. But we will explain to you at another time, if we are compelled to do so, the means by which others have attempted to undermine the church, and consequently to overthrow it; what indirect artifices they have made use of, and by what turbulent proceedings they have laboured after their own exaltation; and also, what a heavy charge that is which you seem to insinuate, that we have abused the lenity of the magistracy[4]. We wish, however, that those persons who are filling your ears with these calumnious and slanderous accusations, had never abused our lenity, the kindness of the magistrates, and your authority, which has given them no small encouragement to stir up this controversy. God forbid that we should abuse any persons whatever, much less those excellent magistrates who have deserved so well of us. But if you could bring your mind to believe that we were so lost to shame, how could you possibly think that the magistrates, discreet and worthy men as they are, would either be so stupid in regard to our cause, as not to find out our trickeries, or that they would suffer them, when detected, to go unpunished, and even regard us with greater kindness than before? In detecting the artifices of your friends, which, nevertheless, they knew how to devise and manage with much more ingenuity than we do, they were of such quick scent, that they immediately smelt them out, and their opinion of them is no secret.

But leaving these things, let us return to the business of Knox, wherein you greatly desire godliness and brotherly

[[4] "It standeth your wisdoms in hand to consider, that how much commodity the goodness of the senate doth deserve, so much envy shall you be guilty of, or charged withal, if you have abused their lenity or gentleness, which were so well affected towards your nation." Calvin, as above.]

love on the part of those who were implicated in it[1]. We will, therefore, briefly and truly explain to you the history of the whole affair. There were, at that time, certain parties in our church, who, instructed by long practice and experience, were able easily to foresee and conceive beforehand in their minds the evils that were either already impending over our church, or might happen to it in future. These persons understood that Knox had published a certain book[2], which they perceived would supply their enemies with just ground for overturning the whole church. For there were interspersed in this publication atrocious and horrible calumnies against the queen of England, whom Knox called at one time the wicked Mary, at another time a monster. And he exasperated king Philip also by language not much less violent. When these men had read this infamous libel, attached as they are to true religion and to our church, they considered it neither profitable nor safe to ourselves that Knox should be received with favour by our church. One of them, therefore, called upon the intimate friends of Knox, and pointed out to him that it would be most advisable for Knox to leave the church, and depart to some other place; and this he earnestly recommended him to do. Not succeeding in this, our friends, having more closely considered the danger which without doubt was hanging over them, thought it right to proceed in a different way. The matter was at last brought before the magistrates, with no other view than that Knox might be ordered to quit the place. When the magistrate was made acquainted with the case, and had also discovered that the emperor was defamed in that pamphlet; considering that a man of this kind might easily occasion danger, not only to our church, but also to his state, he ordered him to leave the city.

Thus you have the whole affair as it really took place; nor

[1 "This one thing I cannot keep secret, that master Knox was in my judgment neither godly nor brotherly dealt withal." Calvin, as above.]

[2 This book was entitled "An Admonition to Christians." The substance of it was first preached in Buckinghamshire. Nine places therein were laid to the charge of Knox, in one of which he called the emperor "no less an enemy to Christ than was Nero." See McCrie's Life of Knox. Fuller Ch. Hist. II. 412. Soames, IV. 564. Troubles of Frankfort, 44. The whole account is given in Strype, Mem. III. 1. 406.]

would we for the sake of our friends evade the subject, by holding back any thing, or obscure it by our relation of it. Something was conceded to Knox. For our party had observed some other things in him, which we have now purposely forborne to mention, but which induced them to desire his departure.. But these clearly were the reasons which drove our friends to this step, and it was altogether in this way that they got rid of that affair. But what an occasion for disseminating falsehoods these authors of confusion thence laid hold of, what dreadful language they uttered, what disturbance they excited, must be matter of wonder to every one who is unacquainted with their character: especially when they even prevailed upon you to write concerning men who were in every respect innocent, that "it had been better for them to have remained in their own country, than to have brought over to a distant land the firebrand of unjust severity[3]." If those who occasioned Knox's departure from hence had been in any way known to you, you would assuredly have dealt more gently with them. For scarce any man living is more remote from cruelty than, by the grace of God, those persons both are and have been. Certainly, when an account of what they had done was demanded of them by our pastor, they gave such a straightforward statement, that, scrupulous as he is in every thing else, he had nothing whatever to find fault with. For you cannot but be aware, how unbecoming it would have been in us impotently to rage in half-muttered abuse against magistrates; not, perhaps, because they do not deserve it, but because of the office imposed upon them by God. This we can assure you, that that outrageous pamphlet of Knox's added much oil to the flame of persecution in England. For before the publication of that book, not one of our brethren had suffered death: but as soon as it came forth, we doubt not but that you are well aware of the number of excellent men who have perished in the flames; to say nothing of how many other godly men besides have been exposed to the risk of all their property, and even life itself, upon the sole ground of either having had this book in their possession, or having read it; who were

[3 Calvin's letter adds, "quæ nolentes quoque inflammet," to set on fire those that would not be kindled.]

perhaps rescued from the sword at greater cost and danger of life than the others offered their necks to it. But enough of these things.

You piously exhort us that, if we perceive that the minds of some parties are wounded not without cause, we should endeavour to make amends for the injury. But when you have left no stone unturned to heal those persons who have inflicted their wounds upon themselves, and have nevertheless lost all your pains, what can you possibly do for them? You say that you have "diligently admonished those who are minded to leave us, that their departure should not rend asunder the agreement of the brethren[1]." We wish that your wisdom had foreseen this, and that the authority of your letter had not given encouragement to the former quarrel, before you had heard the other side of the question. We wish that your sagacity had anticipated what was the tendency of their designs, namely, to open faction, to say nothing more. For they themselves now presume to write that they are ready to maintain the lawfulness of their secession from our church. We certainly hoped, indeed, when we wrote to you, that our reconciliation would have been lasting; and your friend Whittingham, with all the rest of his party, except three or four, had given in his adhesion to our church. But oh! like true Proteuses, they now make subterfuges, and shamefully desert us, under I know not what pretence. We know not whence this change of sentiment has arisen; but we leave you to judge what opinion must be entertained of those persons who tell you that they leave the church solely on account of ceremonies which even they themselves dare no longer affirm to be ungodly, or can prove to be at variance with the word of God, or in any way unprofitable. We pray God to bestow upon them a better mind; and we earnestly entreat you no longer to mix yourself up in so hateful a business, lest some disparagement should arise to your reputation, which we desire should at all times be most honourable and holy. May the

[[1] "When I heard that the one part was indeed to depart from thence, I earnestly admonished them, as it became me, that if they could not well remain there, the distance of place should not dissipate or rend in sunder their brotherly agreement; for I feared much lest that some privy grudge of the former contention remained." Calvin, as above.]

Lord Jesus preserve you as an especial ornament to his church!

Frankfort, Sept. 20, 1555.

Your admirers,

DAVID WHITEHEAD, Pastor.	RICHARD ALVEY.
RICHARD COX.	HENRY PARRY.
THOMAS BECON, Minister of the Word of God.	BARTH. TRAHERON.
	THOMAS COTTISFORD.

LETTER CCLIX.

DAVID WHITEHEAD AND OTHERS TO HENRY BULLINGER.

Dated at FRANKFORT, *Sept.* 17, 1557.

HEALTH IN CHRIST JESUS. Others inscribe the monuments of their genius to men of rank, by whose authority they may obtain protection, or by whose wealth they may become enriched; but you, most learned and most excellent sir, consecrate your most godly studies to the miserable and afflicted churches of the exiles, from whom no human support or worldly advantage can be expected. In this truly you have followed the rule of perfect charity, which seeketh not her own, but the things of others. For you have not sought for any benefit to yourself, but the comfort of the churches groaning under the cross; placing your hand as it were under the burden, and partaking and sympathising in our calamities. And this purpose of your most compassionate mind you have, as far as we can judge from ourselves, most abundantly accomplished. For having been introduced through the door opened by you into the revelation of the Lord concerning his churches, as if to behold an object immediately present before our eyes, we have derived indeed very much comfort, both from the will of Almighty God, by whose permission and allowance these things are taking place, and also from this your kindness and favour, whom we regard as a messenger of God to us. For which your deservings towards us, as you in no wise expect any return from us, so we are unable to afford any other, except that (as is the duty of men who are not ungrateful) we return you our most hearty thanks to the utmost of our power, and will in the mean time entreat God the Father of our Lord Jesus Christ in our earnest and constant prayers, that he may be pleased evermore to defend and preserve to his flock such a pastor, and to his afflicted church such a comforter. Dated at Frankfort, Sept. 17, 1557. Your piety's most devoted, the minister, elders, and deacons of the church of the English exiles at Frankfort on the Maine.

DAVID WHITEHEAD.	JOHN HALES.
JOHN WILFORD.	WILLIAM MASTER.
THOMAS SOWERBY.	GREGORY RAILTON.
JO. TAVERNER.	EDMUND SUTTON.

LETTER CCCLX.

WILLIAM WHITTINGHAM[1] TO JOHN CALVIN.

Dated at FRANKFORT, *March* 25, [1555].

THE occasion that ought to bring us the greatest comfort from your most important letter[2], has in a manner thrown us into the greatest anxiety and distress. For when there seemed likely to be no end to such noisy contentions, and on that account it was ordered by the magistrate that

[1 William Whittingham was concerned with Knox, Goodman, and others, in the translation of the Geneva bible. He likewise translated some of the Psalms in Sternhold and Hopkins's version. He was ordained at Geneva, and on his return to England was made dean of Durham through the interest of the Earl of Leicester. He died in June, 1579. For a further notice of him, see the references in the index to Strype, and the introduction to the Troubles of Frankfort, of which book he is supposed by Professor M'Crie to have been the author.]

[2 This is probably the letter to Knox and Whittingham, dated Jan. 20, 1555, printed in Calvin's Epistles, p. 158. Ed. 1575, and translated in the Troubles of Frankfort, p. 34. London reprint.]

we should comply with all the rites of the French[3] church, (unless there should happen to be any thing that might justly be found fault with;) this circumstance so much offended some parties, that, leaving the contest about ceremonies, they betook themselves to forensic accusations. For master Knox, being most unjustly charged before the magistrate with high treason, has been ordered to quit the place, not without the regret of all good men, and even of the magistrate himself. He is, therefore, on his way to you, and will explain the whole matter in order. This only I can speak from experience, that nothing ever occasioned greater distress and shame to good men, than this wickedness has done. But I cannot now relate these things by reason of my grief, and he will himself explain them better and more fully in person, as well as all other matters, of which I will describe the progress and result more at length after the fair. Farewell in Christ, and with your wonted affection aid us by your prayers and counsel. Frankfort, March 25, 1555.

WILL. WHITTINGHAM[4].

[3 "The 22d of March master à Glauberg came to the English church, and shewed the congregation that it was commanded them by the magistrates, when by his procurement the church was granted, that they should agree with the French church both in doctrine and ceremonies, and that they understood how the falling from that order had bred much dissension among them." Troubles of Frankfort, as above, p. 43.]

[4 The following is an extract from the council book of Geneva in reference to Whittingham's return to England, dated May 30, 1560. "William Whittingham, citizen, in his own name and that of his company came to thank the magistrates for the kind treatment they have received in this city, and to state that they are required to return to their own country in order to minister to the church there; but that they entreated their worships still to regard them as humble servants of the republic, and promised that in every thing and every place, wherever they might have the means of doing service either to the state, or to any inhabitants of this city, they would exert themselves to the utmost of their power. They requested, too, a certificate of their life and conversation during their residence in this city, and gave in a register of those of their countrymen who came to dwell therein, by way of a perpetual remembrance. It was decreed that they should have honourable licence to depart, together with a testimonial of the satisfaction we have had in them; and that they be exhorted to pray for us, and to act in their turn towards foreigners, as we have done to

LETTER CCCLXI.

WILLIAM WHITTINGHAM TO JOHN CALVIN.

Dated at FRANKFORT, *Sept.* 21, [1555].

SUPPOSING that this letter will scarcely reach you much sooner than I shall arrive myself, I do not write so fully as the subject itself requires, and as I could wish. For I have sent off all my baggage, and am hastening to you as speedily as possible. With respect to those who are at Basle[1], we are in hopes, that, after a mutual conference, they together with us will both enjoy your valuable assistance, and not only rejoice in that divine benefit, but will embrace and cherish it. I shall very soon, I hope, converse with you in person about your letter to our friends, and our own departure, and other matters. Master St Andrew has zealously conducted himself here, and to the great and common benefit of the churches. Master John à Glauberg[2] has made honourable mention of you, as he ought to do, and requests me to salute you most diligently in his name, as, being at this time especially engaged in a multitude of affairs, he is unable to write to you. All our friends salute you, reverence, and most deservedly esteem you. May Almighty God very long preserve you, both to his own glory, and the common comfort both of ourselves and all others! Frankfort, Sept. 21.

Your disciple,

WHITTINGHAM.

them; that they be always disposed to look with affection upon this city, and that those who are now citizens or subjects be still regarded as such for the time to come."]

[1 "God of his mercy .... hath not only at Basle moved the magistrates' hearts towards us in granting us a church, but also at Geneva, where as God's word is truly preached, manners best reformed, and in earth the chiefest place of true comfort." Whittingham to a friend in England. Troubles of Frankfort, p. 49.]

[2 John à Glauberg was one of the chief senators of Frankfort, by whose favour and mediation a church was granted to the exiles in July, 1554. Fuller, II. 407. Troubles of Frankfort, p. 6.]

LETTER CCCLXII.[3]

JOHN FOXE TO BONIFACE AMERBACH.[4]

Dated at BASLE, *Nov.* 25, 1556.

HEALTH with much peace in Christ! The book[5] of common places inscribed to the young men of your university, as I was unable to present it to them individually, I send and deposit, most honourable lord rector, and ornament of the university, with you in the name of the whole body: not that it contains any thing worthy of you, or adapted to their use, but that there might exist some memorial of my regard towards them. I should not dare request you to receive it with courtesy and kindness, much less to honour it with your patronage, were not the subject itself deserving of it. But, as there is scarcely any thing of this sort in the common affairs of life, however useful it may be of itself, which does not require some patron or other, how much greater occasion have I for the aid of your patronage in the present instance; which if you will grant me, you will perform an act, if not suited to my labours, at least worthy of your own kindness. Basle, Nov. 25, 1556.

Yours in Christ,

J. FOXE.

[3 This letter is from the collection of Mr Burkhardt at Basle.]

[4 Boniface Amerbach was the son of a famous printer at Basle, where he was made professor of civil law, in which he gave lectures for twenty years. He died in 1562.]

[5 This book is inscribed, Locorum communium Logicalium tituli et ordinationes 150, &c. Basil, 1557. 4to. Foxe was at this time engaged in a printing office at Basle, as corrector of the press.]

LETTER CCCLXIII.

CHRISTOPHER GOODMAN[1] TO PETER MARTYR.

Dated at GENEVA, *Aug.* 20, 1558.

How dear I have ever been to you, my honoured master, I have more frequently and happily experienced in the fact itself, than I could now, if I had leisure to do so, express in writing. And, what has been very gratifying to me, I abundantly perceived from your last letter, which I received about the end of June, that it would not be your fault if I did not continue in the same degree of favour with you. Wherefore if on this account the letter of so insignificant an individual as myself has been so acceptable to you, yours on the other hand cannot but be most acceptable. For though I greatly desired to have your opinion, which in that business would have been equivalent to that of many others, yet I acknowledge your paternal regard for me, and appreciate it as I ought to do. But it does not become me to conceal from your piety what displeased me. I know indeed that I have your free permission to enter on this subject, in such a way however that, whatever it be, it may be submitted to your paternal correction and judgment, as it is right it should be. First of all then, it has always been my opinion that we should aim at nothing with greater earnestness than the defence of truth, whatever the controversy may be, or by whomsoever it may be taken up; whether they stand on our side as friends, or against us as avowed opponents; provided only all rashness and bitterness of spirit be removed. And as the never sufficiently admired sentiment of a heathen writer leads us to this, when in matters of secular interest he prefers truth to his dearest friends, and men of most honourable character[2]; how should we be led to

[1 "Christopher Goodman, son of William, an Englishman, of Chester, has been gratuitously admitted a citizen at his own request." Extract from the council-book of Geneva, dated June 1, 1558. He was concerned in the Geneva translation of the bible. See many references to him in the index to Strype.]

[2 Arist. Eth. I. 6.]

desire it in sacred learning, where its majesty and authority are most conspicuous! And as it is right never to spare our most bitter enemies the papists, so also according to our ability should we remove the ignorance of our brethren. This is the case whenever the truth, openly brought forth by the diligence and authority of learned men, is made manifest to the contemplation of all. I know indeed that such persons will always incur the dislike of many, and sometimes too that of their friends: but since it has ever been the property of truth to be viewed with hatred by the generality, such persons are to be regarded, in my opinion, with greater praise, in proportion as they have more frequently endured the opposition of men; because truth should never be left destitute of its proper support, and exposed to the reproaches of the wicked. Then it very often comes to pass in practice, that when we seek to benefit either party by our silence, we benefit neither; God so ordering all things, to whom due obedience is not rendered as often as entire respect is not paid to truth: forasmuch as in the cause of religion, as you know, no third party is allowed, but we are required therein always to be either hot or cold, and must either gather or scatter; provided only that in our proceedings moderation and charity may be preserved between brethren as far as possible.

For which reason, as I deny not that I had much to regret in that Frankfort controversy; so indeed, though it occasioned me great uneasiness in common with the rest, I do not now repent of having stood forth and laboured with others in that cause, which has been the chief occasion of that happy agreement and solid peace which by the great blessing of God we enjoy in this place[3]: which I persuade myself never would have occurred, if for the sake of the other party it had been permitted to contaminate the purity of religion with the dregs of popery which they wished to force upon us. For by such conduct we should deservedly have been called traitors to the truth, and that too against our own convictions; and those who have so pertinaciously endeavoured to load the free consciences of the brethren with unprofitable ceremonies and paltry ordinances of man, would

[3 Goodman left Frankfort about Sept. 1555, for Geneva, and was chosen with Knox as pastor of the church in that place.]

not so readily have been brought to an acknowledgement of their offence. If Paul and Barnabas had given place to the brethren who came from Jerusalem to Antioch, and had not withstood the doctrine of those persons with all their might, what a pestilence would have spread throughout all the churches! And if Peter, James, and the rest had refused to deliver their opinion to Paul and Barnabas when they asked for it, how would they themselves have been otherwise than cruel to the brethren, and faithless before God? They thought fit therefore so to condescend to the infirmity of their brethren, as yet meanwhile not to withhold their sentiments on the side of truth. And as to the contention which then seemed evil and calamitous, it was shortly afterwards evident how necessary it was to those churches, and useful to us who come after them. Since therefore they are set before us as an example in those things which relate to God, we may safely imitate them; not only that we may boldly contend for the truth, whether it be against open enemies, or against those who wish to be called brethren; but also that we may not refuse our support, whenever it is demanded with simplicity and for the sake of arriving at the truth. And though in this case it may be difficult to avoid the imputation of being contentious, yet when our conscience bears witness to us that we are averse from strife, and that we do not regard the opinions of men, but the cause of the contention itself, we must faithfully discharge our duty, and leave the event to Almighty God, who will defend his own cause.

I do not write thus as not having received your so friendly reply with a feeling of kindness, nor as presuming to dictate, especially to your prudence, which I venerate, what I think ought to be done; for I well know how incompetent I am for this office, and how greatly I need an adviser myself. Neither do I write with a view of extorting from you the opinion for which I asked, though I greatly desired it, as I still continue to do: but as, whether it had been in my favour or the contrary, it would have been most gratifying and profitable, (for your sanction would not so much have confirmed me in that opinion, as your dissent, had it existed, would have recalled me to a more careful examination of the subject;) so I only proposed to your consideration what seemed to me proper to be done in this business, not taking the decision upon myself, but leaving it, as I ought, to you alone. I requested the judgment of master Calvin, to which you very properly attach much weight, before the book was published, and I shewed him the same propositions[1] which I sent to you. And though he deemed them somewhat harsh, especially to those who are in the place of power, and that for this reason they should be handled with caution, yet he nevertheless admitted them to be true.

There is no news here but what I think you must be acquainted with: for I know that you have received information of what has happened to the church of your countrymen among us, and especially concerning our friend Silvester, for whose case I grieve not a little; not because I do not hope well of him, but because he has given occasion for being deservedly suspected of so awful an heresy. I pray God speedily to purge his church from such a pestilence, and entirely to deliver our friend Silvester, altogether restored to us, from the suspicion under which he is still labouring.

Master Whittingham salutes you, and heartily thanks you for your kind mention of him in your letter. Salute, I pray you, in my name Julius and his wife, Jewel, Parkhurst and his wife, Aylmer, Frensham, and Ulmis. May the Lord Jesus evermore strengthen you by his Spirit, and very long preserve you in safety for the benefit of his church! Geneva, Aug. 20, 1558.

Your disciple,

CHRISTOPHER GOODMAN.

[[1] These are probably the propositions sent to Bullinger, which with his reply are given above, p. 745.]

APPENDIX.

I. ACCOUNT[1] OF CERTAIN ENGLISH MARTYRS.

Extract from an anonymous letter dated in 1555.

1. JOHN HOOPER, Rowland Taylor, John Rogers, Laurence Saunders, John Bradford, true ministers of God, in whom with the constant preaching of the word was also united a godly innocence of life illustrating the same, were on account of evangelical truth boldly asserted by their lips, as it was truly believed in their hearts, condemned to the flames. Hooper at Gloucester, Taylor at Hadleigh in Suffolk, Rogers at London, Saunders at Coventry, Bradford at Manchester in the county of Lancaster, were committed by their cruel tyrants to be burned at the stake on the last day of February; and these most innocent lambs of God, thus led to the slaughter, could neither be subdued by threatenings, nor softened by blandishments, so as not to confirm with their blood the doctrine of Christ, which they had truly professed before both by their living and preaching. For they chose rather to refuse the Queen's pardon, which was repeatedly offered them, and set before them too in the very juncture of their undergoing martyrdom, than deny their profession of the truth. Wherefore, having manfully and resolutely rejected a pardon, and setting life itself at nought, having first exhorted others to embrace the truth, they thus most victoriously completed their warfare.

2. The magistrate to whom Saunders was given in charge, and who was ordered to put him to the torture, was so moved by the integrity and constancy of the man, that he

[1 The name of the author of this statement is not preserved. The transcript is made from the original document, Arch. VI. 113, 2251. John Hooper and Rowland Taylor were committed to the flames on the ninth, John Rogers on the fourth, Laurence Saunders on the eighth of February, and John Bradford on the first of July, 1555. A full account of them all is given in Foxe, Vol. VI. Book xi.]

could not execute with a safe conscience so tyrannical a command of the queen, neither would he do so. He was therefore accused, arrested, and committed to prison.

3. Thomas Rose[2], who has now been for many years a constant preacher of the gospel, having secretly assembled some brethren on the first of January, administered to them in a godly manner, and according to Christ's institution, the supper of the Lord, preceded by a sermon, in which because he prayed for the conversion of the queen in this way, either that God would soon convert her, or remove her yoke from the necks of the godly, he was adjudged a traitor by the bishop of Winchester, as guilty of treason, and is kept in prison with all who communicated with him, twenty-eight in number, who are all of them condemned to the flames, unless perhaps the above-named Rose be forced to undergo that more cruel kind of death usually awarded to traitors.

4. Two godly virgins, and one sober matron, behaved themselves in the presence of their tyrants with so much modesty, holiness, religion, and firmness in the cause of the gospel, that they were regarded with admiration by all good men; but our tyrants thought proper to condemn them to the flames.

5. The queen has issued a proclamation[3] for the apprehension and punishment of heretics, according to the statute *ex officio*, as the canonists call it; and for the examination of books of suspected doctrine (as they call it), that the parties, with whom they may be found, shall either be punished capitally, if they choose to disown their contents, or condemned to the flames, if they think fit to defend them.

6. The emperor and his sister are at Antwerp with three thousand troops; for what purpose, or with what intent, is unknown.

[2 For an account of Thomas Rose, see Foxe, VI. 579.]
[3 This proclamation is given in Foxe, VII. 127.]

II. AD HENRICUM BULLINGERUM.

[See page 114, for a translation of this Letter.]

S. P. Quando accepi librum D. mariti mei, Compater amantissime, cupiebam, sicut mihi mandabat per suas literas, ut ederetur ante has nundinas. Quare misi illum D. Petro Martyri, ut hoc curaret Argentinæ. Hoc excusavit propter doctrinam de Eucharistia, quæ non ibi est recepta. Possit hic imprimi cum bona venia Senatus; sed melius est ut tu ipse librum prius revideas, atque istic imprimi cures. Quia autem non ignoro memoriam illius esse tibi sanctissimam, non dubito, quin æque nunc sis illi hac in re gratificaturus, ac si viveret: imo vivit jam ille cum omnibus sanctis martyribus, et Christo suo martyrum capite; ego vero hic morior, donec Deus me rursum illi adjungat. Habeo gratiam pro sanctissimis tuis literis. Ego certe jam opus habeo talibus consolationibus et vestris precibus. Rogo te igitur per sanctam amicitiam sanctissimi martyris mariti mei, quo nunc orbata vitam hanc mortem esse duco, ne me deseras. Ego non sum illa quæ possim reddere paria; sed Deo præstabis obsequium gratum, qui vobis viduas imprimis commendat. Ego et Rachela mea tibi agimus gratias pro elegante xenio misso in novo anno. Saluta optimam uxorem tuam, commatrem carissimam et omnes amicos. Bene vale. Francofordiæ, xi. Aprilis, 1555.

Tui amantissima commater et soror in Christo,

ANNA HOPER.

Rachela tua mittit tibi nummulum Anglicum, in quo effigies sunt Ahab et Jezebel.

INDEX.

A.

Abel, a popish priest, executed for denying the supremacy, 209.
Abel, John, 541 *n*.
Adam, Michael, 641.
Adams, John, martyr, 41 *n*.
Æpinus, John, notice of, 616 *n*.
Agricola, Julius, 383 *n*.
Albright, Ann, martyr, 175 *n*.
Alen, 150.
Alexander, Peter, 67.
Allen, Edmund, notice of, 541 *n*.
Altars removed from churches, 79, 466.
Alvey, Richard, an exile, 755 *n*.
Ambleteuse, camp near, taken, 658 *n*.
Amerbach, Boniface, notice of, 766 *n*.
Amerius, an assumed name of Robert Barnes, 616 *n*.
Ammian, 379.
Ampton, sir Edward, 340 *n*.
Anabaptists, 65, 87.
Ancher, Ant., mayor of Dover, 614.
Andernach, Quinter, 27 *n*., 54.
Andrè, St, M. le Mareschal, 497 *n*.
Anglus, Michael, an assumed name of M. Coverdale, 245 *n*.
Anna of Oldenberg, patroness of John à Lasco, 513.
Anne of Cleves. See *Cleves*.
Argyle, bishop of, 429.
Arians, disputes of, with the strangers' church in London, 574.
Arnstadt, convention at, 528 *n*.
Arragon, Catharine of, 548 *n*.
Arragon, Isabella of, 689 *n*.
Arschot, duke d', son of, wounds the prince of Spain at a tournament, 61.
Articles, the Six, 527 *n*; of 1552, 594.
Arundel, sir Thomas, 33 *n*, 577 *n*, 579 *n*.
Askew, Ann, martyr, 41 *n*.
Attyn, Thomas, 170.
Audley, Thomas, lord, 36 *n*, 317 *n*.
Augsburg, diet of, 669; taking of, 456 *n*.
Augustine quoted, 327.
Austin Friars, church of the, granted to the foreign protestants, 565 *n*.
Aylmer, John, notice of, 275 *n*.

B.

Babington, warden of the Fleet, 101 *n*.
Bale, John, bishop of Ossory, 755 *n*.
Bambergh, bishop of, 682 *n*.
Banks, John, 292, 296, 297.
Barlow, William, bishop of Bath and Wells, 76, 171, 687.
Barnes, Robert, martyr, 207, 209, 616.
Barsham, Henry VIII. walked barefoot from, to Walsingham, 610 *n*.
Basil, St, monks of, persecuted, 600.
Basle, exiles at, 765 *n*.
Batt, 621.
Bavaria, Lewis, duke of, 526 *n*; William, duke of, *ib*.
Baxterley, 361.
Baynton, sir Edward, 36.
Beach, John, executed, 317 *n*, 614 *n*.
Beaton, cardinal, 37, 240.
Becket, Thomas à, image of, set up outside Mercer's chapel, 177 *n*; shrine of, 610 *n*.
Becon, Thomas, notice of, 755 *n*.
Bedrot, 607.
Belenian, Nicholas, martyr, 41 *n*.
Bentham, Thomas, notice of, 752 *n*.
Bergzabern, 247.
Bernardine, wife of, 55. See *Ochinus*.
Berne, disputation of, 718 *n*.
Bernher, Augustine, notice of, 360 *n*.
Berwick, 429, 434.
Bexley, rood of, exposed, 604, 606, 609.
Beza, Theodore, 153.
Bible, reading of, prohibited, 356 *n*.
Bibliander, Theodore, notice of, 11 *n*.
Bigamy, proclamation against, 263 *n*.
Bill, William, 150 *n*.
Billinger, John, 695, 697.
Binder, 621.
Bizarro, Peter, notice of, 338 *n*.
Black, Francis, 692.
Black, George, 692.
Blackness, fort of, 728 *n*.
Blaurer, Ambrose, notice of, 392 *n*.
Blaurer, Thomas, 635 *n*.
Blesilla, 5 *n*.
Bocher, Joan, burnt for heresy, 560.

Boleyn, Ann, slanders respecting, 553.
Bona, queen of Poland, 689 *n*.
Bonar, castellan of Bietz, 602 *n*.
Bonner, Edmund, bishop of London, imprisoned, 69, 80, 660; Hooper's controversy with, 70; conduct of, before the commissioners, 557 *n*.
Bopfingen, surrender of, 638 *n*.
Boulogne, attacked by the French, 652; surrender of, 398 *n*, 410, 559.
Bourchier, earl of Essex, death of, 221 *n*.
Bourgoyne, Francis, notice of, 730 *n*.
Bourn, Gilbert, bishop of Bath and Wells, notice of, 368 *n*.
Boyneburgh, George à, 612 *n*.
Bradford, John, martyr, 171, 772; rescues Gilbert Bourn, 368.
Bradgate, 275 *n*, 429 *n*.
Brandenburgh, Albert, marquis of, 58 *n*, 113, 682.
Brandon, Charles, duke of Suffolk, 36 *n*.
Brandon, Henry, duke of Suffolk, 454 *n*, 496 *n*.
Brandon, lord Charles, 454 *n*, 496 *n*.
Bremen, 561; resists the Interim, 668 *n*.
Brentius, John, 543.
Bristol, mint at, 649.
Brown, George, the first protestant archbishop in Ireland, 428 *n*.
Brown, Thomas, martyr, 175 *n*.
Brussells, visit of Charles V. to, 60.
Bucer, Martin, views of, respecting the divorce of Henry VIII., 551 *n*; respecting divorce in general, 666; on the eucharist, 544 *n*; on the vestiarian controversy, 488, 495, 585; dismissed from Strasburgh, 649, 651; invited to England, 19; arrives, 652; resides at Lambeth, 67; holds Lutheran opinions, 61; lectures on Ephesians, 81, 339, 401, and on the Sixth of John, *ib.*; illness of, *ib.*, 543; death of, 5 *n*, 490, 662; account of his funeral, 492 *n*; statement of his property, 362 *n*; sir John Cheke's opinion of, 666 *n*; Burcher's ditto, 662, 666.
Bucer, widow of, 28 *n*; letter of, 363.
Bugenhagius, 513 *n*.
Bullinger, Christopher, notice of, 699 *n*.
Bullinger, Henry, dedicates a book to Henry VIII., 611; to the duke of Suffolk, 3 *n*, 82 *n*; to Edward VI., 88, 560 *n*.; treatise of, on Christian perfection, 6 *n*; on justification, 744; on the eucharist, 681 *n*; reply to certain queries about the government of women, 744; advice to his son, 511 *n*.
Burcart, Francis, envoy to Henry VIII. from the German princes, 612 *n*.
Burcher, John, 246, 259 *n*, 687.
Buren, count de, takes Darmstadt, 639.
Butler, John, notice of, 311, 621 *n*.
Byrchman, John, 344.

C.

Cadwell, friend of ab Ulmis, 424.
Caius, Thomas, 415 *n*.
Calais, surrender of, 139 *n*.
Calvin, John, commentaries on 1 Cor. objected to by Hooper, 48; agrees with Bullinger respecting the eucharist, 121 *n*, 267; controversy with anabaptists, 622 *n*.; with Servetus, 743 *n*.
Cambridge, favours religion, 680.
Capito, Wolfgang, 15 *n*, 520, 524, 553 *n*.
Caraffa, cardinal, 149 *n*.
Cardmaker, John, prebendary of Wells, and martyr, 171 *n*.
Cards, allowed only at Christmas, 285 *n*.
Carew, sir Nicolas, notice of, 625 *n*.
Carew, sir Peter, 132 *n*, 133 *n*.
Carlos, don, son of Philip II., 510 *n*.
Carnisprivium, 627.
Caroli, accuses Calvin, 622 *n*.
Cassilis, Gilbert Kennedy, third earl of, taken prisoner at Solway Moss, 239 *n*.
Catechism, set forth by Ponet, 142 *n*; by Cranmer, 381 *n*.
Catharine of Arragon, 548 *n*.
Catmer, Joan, martyr, 175 *n*.
Cechelles, or Secelles, 112, 114.
Cecil, William, 77 *n*.
Cellarius, 372, 424, 723.
Chamberlain, sir Thomas, 568 *n*.
Chambers, Richard, 128, 155 *n*.
Charlemagne, statue of, at Zurich, 192.
Charles V, treaty of, with Henry VIII, 36 *n*; recalled on his way to England, 133; defeat of by the French, 687.
Châtillon, the lord, commissioner for peace with France, 563, 565.
Cheke, sir John, 81, 117; knighted, 438 *n*; tutor of Edward VI, 465; the king's regard for him, 456 *n*; apprehended, 132 *n*, 684; recantation and death, 132 *n*.
Chelius, Ulric, 27 *n*, 364.

Cheney, Richard, archdeacon of Hereford, 373 *n.*
Chevalier, Antony, notice of, 716 *n.*
Chichester, Sampson, bishop of, maintains the pope's supremacy, 208.
Chimere, what, 585 *n.*
Christina, wife of the landgrave of Hesse, 666 *n.*
Church, Greek, described, 691.
Church, Strangers', discipline in, 587.
Cleobury, personates lord Devon, 133 *n.*
Clergy, marriage of, allowed by parliament, 377. Account of, in 1550, 547.
Cleves, Anne of, 205, 529 *n*, 627.
Cleves, duke of, 240 *n.*
Cleves, Sibill of, 529 *n.*
Cobham, George Brook, lord, 264.
Cochlæus, John, notice of, 244 *n.*
Cockraft, H., exile at Frankfort, 752.
Coinage, gold, new, in England, 53.
Colbach, margrave of, 258.
Cologne, Herman, archbishop of, 540 *n.*
Collins, martyr, 200 *n.*
Commendone, Francis, sent to recal cardinal Pole, 741.
Commissioners for religion, 590.
Common prayer, book of, 331.
Consensus Tigurinus, 121 *n*, 479 *n.*
Constance, reported destruction of, 385, 435; conduct of Charles V. towards, 385 *n*, 641 *n*, 642 *n.*
Consubstantiation, rejected by the Swiss divines, 50 *n.*
Convocation in 1551, 444; in 1553, 508 *n.*
Cook, sir Antony, 686.
Cope, Henry, 664.
Cornwall, rebellion in, 654.
Cottesford, exile at Frankfort, 763.
Courtenay, Edward, lord, death of, 133.
Courtenay, Henry, Marquis of Exeter, 207, 625 *n.*
Coverdale, Miles, 245, 247, 483, 505.
Cox, Richard, almoner to Edward VI, 82; deprived of his preferments, 373; patron of John ab Ulmis, 384; commissioner in the disputation on the eucharist, 391 *n*; arrested on the death of Edward VI, 684; exile, 753.
Cracow, prince of, 688; bishop of, 700.
Cranmer, Thomas, early opinion of, respecting the eucharist, 13 *n*; change of views, 71, 323, 383 *n*, 388; declaration of, against transubstantiation, 371 *n*; catechism set forth by, 381, 643 *n*; conference of protestant divines recommended by, 502 *n*; declaration of, against the mass, 505 *n*; alleged recantation, 173 *n*; deposed, 743; imprisoned, 505; sent to Oxford, 515; martyrdom of, 143 *n.*
Croariensis, Andrew, 437, 500.
Croft, sir James, 722 *n.*
Crome, Dr, 80, 211, &c.
Croydon, earthquake near, 433.
Cruciger, Caspar, 602 *n.*
Crumwell, Thomas, lord, 15, 611, 202.
Crumwell, Gregory, lord, 240 *n*, 496 *n.*
Culpepper, executed, 226 *n.*
Curio, Cælius Secundus, 89 *n*, 595.
Curtop, James, notice of, 89 *n.*
Cyprian quoted, 234 *n.*

D.

Dacre, Thomas, lord, executed, 220 *n.*
Darmstadt, taken, 639.
Dasipodius, 509 *n.*
Decades of Bullinger, 123 *n.*
Delœnus, or Delvin, Walter, 587 *n*; minister in the strangers' church, 575.
Devonshire, rebellion in, 66, 410, 654.
Divorce, proclamation respecting, 263 *n*; lectures of P. Martyr upon, 404; Bucer's opinion respecting, 665.
Dorset, Henry Grey, marquis of, 76; duke of Suffolk, 437, 454 *n*; privy councillor, 675; titles of, 406, 409.
Dowdall, George, archbishop of Armagh, 428 *n.*
Downton, William, servant to bishop Hooper, 292 *n.*
Dryander, Francis, 77, 348 *n*, 535.
Dudley, lord Ambrose, 374 *n.*
Dudley, lord Guildford, condemned, 374 *n*, 507 *n*; executed, 686.
Dumbarton, the queen of Scots sails from, 643 *n.*
Dunbar, taken by the English, 645.
Duren, taken by the imperialists, 633 *n.*

E.

Eblie, Conrad, 225.
Edinburgh, pillage of, 37 *n.*
Eding, Adrian, 583, 589.
Edward IV, a natural son of, committed to the Tower, 220 *n.*
Edward VI, letter of, to the senate of Zurich, 1; proclaimed, 257; character of, 321, 543, 646; illness of, 593, 683; death of, 100, 272; report of his at-

tempted assassination, 648; of his having been poisoned, 365 *n*, 684.
Eliot, Nicolas, 225, 378, 611.
Elizabeth, princess, 76, 278 *n*.
Enghien, duke d', one of the French hostages, 559 *n*.
England, state of religion in 1539, 624; in 1550, 635, 672.
Enno, count of East Friesland, 513 *n*.
Enzinas, Francis, 348 *n*. See *Dryander*.
Eucharist, disputation respecting, 478 *n*.
Eusebius quoted, 228 *n*, 229 *n*.
Eustochium, 5 *n*.
Exeter, marquis of, beheaded, 207.
Exiles, English, settle at Berne, 162; at Vevay, 167; at Arau, *ib.*; expelled from Wesel, 163, 168; from Basle, 164 *n*; names of some of those at Zurich, 752, and Frankfort, 755, 767.

F.

Faber, Martin, 539.
Fabricius, Erasmus, 681.
Fagius, Paul, dismissed from Strasburgh, 538, 651; invited to England, 329; account of journey, 331, 332; death of, 549, 675; son of, 355; educated by Cranmer, 32, 332.
Faith, Louvaine confession of, 671 *n*.
Falckner, Henry, 216, 241.
Falcon, Michael, 638.
Fallenberg, Philip, 719.
Farell, William, 328, 548, 622 *n*.
Farrar, Robert, bishop of St David's, and martyr, 76, 645 *n*.
Farringdon, Hugh, abbot of Reading, executed, 317 *n*, 614 *n*.
Ferdinand of Austria, crowned, 182 *n*.
Fetherstone, executed, 209 *n*.
Fillol, sir William, 340 *n*.
Filmer, Henry, martyr, 242 *n*.
Finch, John, 605.
Fitzpatrick, Barnaby, notice of, 423 *n*.
Fleming, John, lord, 239 *n*.
Fontaine, Nicolas de la, prosecutor of Servetus, 622 *n*.
Foster, Isabel, martyr, 175 *n*.
Fowler, John, sent to the Tower, 648 *n*.
Foxe, Edward, bishop of Hereford, 15 *n*; ambassador to Smalcald, 520 *n*.
France, treaty with, 480; protestation of, against the council of Trent, 497 *n*; arms against the emperor, 590.
Francis, Thomas, notice of, 420.
Frankfort, Troubles of, 753, &c.
Froschover, Christopher, 216, 502, 719.
Furstenburg, William de, 687 *n*.

G.

Gaming, Haddon's opinion respecting, 282, &c.
Garbrand, 68.
Gardiner, Stephen, envoy to the emperor, 37; imprisoned, 80, 256, 384 *n*, 722; released, 367; writes against Bucer, 254 *n*; book of, de vera obedientia, 298 *n*, 347; challenges Hooper to a disputation, 80; preaches at Paul's Cross, 298; performs mass at the funeral of Edward VI., 368 *n*; obtains leave for P. Martyr to quit England, 507 *n*; death of, 301 *n*.
Garner, John, minister of the French church at Strasburgh, 112.
Garrard, Thomas, martyr, 209 *n*, 632.
Geneva, council book of, extracts from, 764 *n*, 768 *n*.
Gilgate, Philip, 341.
Glaris, 628.
Glastonbury, abbey of, granted to the strangers, 738 *n*; its revenue, 627 *n*; abbot of, executed, 627.
Glauberg, John à, 765 *n*, 766.
Glencairn, earl of, taken prisoner by the English, 239 *n*.
Goodman, Christopher, citizen and pastor at Geneva, 769 *n*.
Goodrick, Thomas, bishop of Ely, 76; chancellor, 444 *n*; privy councillor, 675 *n*; ambassador to France, 497 *n*.
Gray, lord, taken prisoner, 239 *n*.
Green, Bartlett, martyr, 175 *n*.
Gresna, archbishop of, 597.
Grey, lady Jane, 278 *n*; translates a book into Greek, 427; execution of, 154, 515, 686; character of, 433.
Grey, lord John, notice of, 715 *n*.
Grey, lord Leonard, beheaded, 220 *n*.
Grey, Henry, duke of Suffolk, 3 *n*; account of his family, 304, &c. See *Dorset, marquis of*.
Grey, lord, of Wilton, disperses the rebels in Oxfordshire, 391.
Grindal, Edmund, 755.
Grynæus, Simon, 552 *n*, 523.
Gualter, Rodolph, 504; visits England, 124 *n*; his book on Antichrist, 174.
Guisnes, 685.

H.

Haddington, siege of, 388; taken, 264*n*.
Haddon, James, 103, 289*n*; argues against transubstantiation, 295*n*.
Haddon, Walter, executor of Bucer, 361; replies to Osorius, 365*n*.
Haines, Dr, dean of Exeter, 391*n*.
Hales, Christopher, 83, 686, 724.
Hales, sir James, 154, 177.
Hales, John, 19*n*, 189, 764.
Haller, 153.
Hamburgh, holds out against Charles V., 668*n*.
Hampton Court, 76.
Hardenberg, Albert, notice of, 538*n*.
Harding, Thomas, 304*n*, 309*n*.
Harvel, Richard, 158.
Heath, Nicolas, lord chancellor, 175; disputes with Cranmer, 323, 645*n*; imprisoned, 80; attends the duke of Northumberland at his execution, 367*n*; character of, 530*n*.
Hedio, Caspar, notice of, 50*n*, 682.
Heilbrunnen, 638.
Helding, one of the framers of the Interim, 383*n*.
Henry II. of France, burns five persons for religion, 655; makes war with England, 656.
Henry VIII. progress of, to York, 219; marries Catharine Parr, 242; visits our lady of Walsingham, 609*n*; invades Scotland, 634*n*; death of, 257*n*.
Heresy, inquiry into at Brussels, 417*n*, 670; proclamation against, 773.
Herlinus, 509*n*.
Hertford, earl of, made duke of Somerset, 256*n*; and lord protector, 258.
Hesse, Philip, landgrave of, imprisoned, 52, 58; bigamy of, 666*n*; Hooper's character of, 58.
Hilles, Gershom, 243.
Hilles, Richard, persecuted for religion, 230; frequents mass, 345.
Hilsey, bishop, exposes the images in St Paul's, 606.
Hoby, sir Philip, 379*n*; envoy to France, 497*n*; sent to bring over king Philip, 511.
Holbeach, bishop, 576*n*; favours the reformation, 76; commissioner in the disputation on the Eucharist, 391*n*.
Hooper, Ann, 63, 576; quits England, 110; Latin letter of, 774.
Hooper, John, resides with Cranmer, 24; doubts respecting attendance at mass, 39; satisfied by Bullinger, 40; conference with Gardiner, 35*n*; sufferings during journey to England, 41; doctrine of, respecting the Eucharist, 47; and divorce, 64, 416, 422; his father, a papist, 75; uncle of, favourable to religion, 86; preaches in London three or four times a day, 108, 557; lectures on Daniel, and the sixth chapter of St John, 73; on Titus and the Psalms, 75; on Nahum and Zechariah, ch. iv., 88; on Jonah, 75*n*, 185; nominated bishop of Gloucester, 87, 559; consecrated, 271; imprisoned in 1551, 107*n*; in 1553, 100*n*, 505; sufferings in prison, 102*n*; condemned, 171; martyrdom, 772; Hilles's character of, 251; controversy on the habits, 466, 571, 583, 674; a commissioner for the reformation of ecclesiastical law, 503*n*.
Hooper, Rachel, 50*n*.
Horn, Margery, exile at Zurich, 752.
Horn, Robert, invited to Frankfort, 128; exile at Zurich, 751; and Frankfort, 755; notice of, 752.
Howard, Catharine, 201; beheaded, 226.
Howard, lord William, imprisoned, 226.
Hubert, Conrad, 27*n*, 364.
Hume castle taken by the English, 387, 651; retaken, 387*n*.
Humphrey, Laurence, notice of, 752*n*.
Hungerford, lord, beheaded, 226.
Huntley, lord, prisoner at Pinkey, 43.
Hurtzel, Peter, 225, 235.

I.

Ignatius, 146.
Images, abolished, 377; not allowed in the Greek church, 691.
Injunctions of Crumwell, 231*n*.
Inquisition, of Brussels, 417*n*, 670.
Interim, the, 18*n*, 540, 649; account of, 383*n*; opposition to, 470*n*, 650; received at Strasburgh, 667.
Ireland, earl of, 423.
Isengrenius, 218.

J.

James V. of Scotland, death of, 235*n*.
Jedburgh, castle of, taken, 387.
Jerome, St, 5*n*.
Jerome, William, martyr, 209, 632.

Jersey, 722*n*.
Joachim, elector of Brandenburg, 640*n*.
Joachim, servant to Burcher, 686.
Jonas, Justus, the younger, 22.
Judæ, Leo. See *Leo*.
Juliers, invaded, 633.
Julius, a monk of that name, 699.
Julius III., pope, 344*n*.
Justiniani, Bernard, notice of, 228*n*.

K.

Kelly, Walter, 170.
Kelso castle, taken by the English, 387.
Kent, rood of grace in, 604, 606.
Kingston, sir Antony, notice of, 442*n*.
Kneeling at the Lord's supper objected to, 591.
Knight, Thomas, 357, 676.
Knightley, sir Richard, 341*n*.
Knox, John, 591, 592; banished from Frankfort, 760; pastor at Geneva, 769*n*; admonition to Christians, 760*n*.

L.

Lacels, John, martyr, 41*n*.
Lactantius quoted, 233*n*, 234*n*.
Lambert, John, martyr, 175*n*.
Langhern, Richard, 170.
Lasco, John à, 187*n*, 262, 483*n*, 512*n*, 560*n*; invited to England by Cranmer, 17*n*; arrival, 560; a friend of Hooper, 95; at Frankfort, 131; commissioner for reforming the ecclesiascal laws, 503*n*; illness, 516; disputes with Bucer respecting the eucharist, 572; writes on this subject, 578; marries, 581; visits Poland, 592; interview with king Sigismund, 596; preaches at Wilna, 600, 608.
Lashford, Joan, martyr, 175*n*.
Latimer, Hugh, summoned before the council, 371*n*; forbidden to preach, 215; renounces transubstantiation, 322*n*; bishoprick offered to, 465; exposes the images at St Paul's, 607; resigns his bishoprick, 204*n*; imprisoned, 505; sent to Oxford, 515; martyrdom of, 143*n*, 154, 751.
Lavater, Lewis, 251.
Leipsic, siege of, 258*n*.
Lenglin, Joseph, 534.
Lent, strict observance of, 723.
Leo Judæ, notice of, 235*n*, 623*n*.
Lever, Thomas, 151, 685*n*, 744; at Wesel, 160; Arau, 167; Zurich, 752; Frankfort, 755.
Lignitz, duke of, 513*n*.
Lindisfarne, 435*n*.
Lindsey, sir Walter, 237*n*.
Lippomani, Aloysius, reception of, at Cracow, 700.
Lisle, 220*n*.
Lisle, the lord, marries lady Ann Seymour, 565*n*.
Lismanini, notice of, 602*n*.
Lithuania, various religions in, 690.
Livonia, war of with Poland, 599*n*, 687*n*; invasion of, by Russia, 699.
Lomas, John, martyr, 175*n*.
Longueville, duke of, 633*n*.
Lord's supper, mode of celebrating in 1549, 72; dispute concerning, 391; decree at Trent respecting, 24*n*; kneeling at, objected to, 591.
Louvaine, divines of, confession of faith by, 671*n*.
Lubeck, 668*n*.
Luther, Martin, dissuaded Melancthon from coming to England, 616*n*; want of firmness towards the landgrave, 666*n*; controversy with Bullinger, 681*n*; opinion of the Waldenses, 694*n*; Hooper's character of, 46.
Luttrell, sir John, 496*n*.
Lyner, John, 693.

M.

Magdeburg, siege of, 668*n*, 679.
Main, marquis du, 559*n*.
Major, George, notice of, 26*n*.
Mammæa, 6*n*.
Mantzinsky, John, 689.
Marbach, 251, 663.
Marcus Antonius, an assumed name of bishop Gardiner, 30*n*.
Marpach, 534.
Marpurg, 719.
Marshall, Richard, dean of Christchurch, 373.
Martin, Dr, disputes with Ponet, 116.
Martyr, Peter, defends Lutheranism, 61; Hooper's commendation of, 97; illness of, 99; expenses of journey to England, 541*n*; cautious views of, 544*n*; opinion respecting the habits, 487, 585; duties of, at Oxford, 481; disputation on the eucharist, 344*n*; patron of Froschover, 723; confined

to his house, 369; obtains leave to depart, 372; invited to Zurich, 137*n*; succeeds Pellican there, 509*n*, 518; lectures on the Romans, 401; in a commission for reforming ecclesiastical laws, 447, 503*n*; opposition to, at Strasburgh, 509*n*.
Martyrs, English, account of, 772.
Mary, queen, 366*n*; terms of marriage with Philip, 510.
Mary, queen of Hungary, 133*n*, 417*n*; notice of, 343*n*, 509.
Mason, sir John, 370.
Mass, abolished in England, 377; a priest imprisoned for celebrating, 467.
Masters, Dr William, 419, 764.
Matravers, 612, 618.
Matthias, 44.
Maudlin, Dr, 202*n*.
Maurice, duke, 258.
Maxwell, earl, 239*n*, 429.
Medman, Peter, 538.
Megander, 633.
Mekin, Richard, martyr, 221*n*.
Melancthon, Philip, 688; invited to England by Cranmer, 17, 21; views of, respecting the eucharist, 544*n*; want of firmness, 666*n*.
Metz, taking of, 456*n*, 590*n*.
Michael Anglus, an assumed name of Coverdale, 245*n*.
Micronius, Martin, 587.
Money, depreciation of, 727*n*.
Mont, Christopher, 528, 671, 675, 717.
Montague, lord, notice of, 625*n*; son of, attainted, 207.
Montmorency, Monsieur, hostage from France, 559*n*.
Montmorency, Francis, prisoner, 683.
Morison, sir Richard, 147, 391*n*.
Muhlberg, battle of, 260*n*.
Mullins, John, exile at Zurich, 752*n*.
Muscovy, reformation in, 691.
Musculus, Wolfgang, 335*n*; invited to England, 680; his "Proscerus", 572*n*.
Myconius, F., envoy to England, 612*n*.

N.

Negelin, Matthew, notice of, 333*n*.
Negroo, sir Peryn, 496*n*.
Nevill, sir Edward, notice of, 625*n*.
Nevill, sir John, heads the northern rebellion, 219*n*.
Nevinson, Christopher, 150, 391.
Norfolk, duke of, committed to the Tower, 42*n*, 256, 639; released, 367; privy councillor, *ib.*; invades Scotland, 237*n*, 634*n*.
Norfolk, duchess of, confined in the Tower, 226.
Norlingen, surrender of, 638*n*.
Northampton, William Parr, marquis of, 88, 93*n*, 497*n*.
Northumberland, duke of, commended by Hooper, 99; executed, 367*n*, 742.
Norton, Thomas, 512*n*.
Nüssbaum, Valentine, 644, 667, 669.

O.

Oath of supremacy, form of, objected to by Hooper, 81*n*, 566; altered, 559*n*.
Ochinus, Bernardine, 334; expenses of journey to England, 541*n*.
Œcolampadius, 46; opinion of, respecting the divorce of Henry VIII., 551*n*.
Oglethorpe, Owen, 124, 187.
Olesnicki, Nicolas, notice of, 690*n*.
Oliphant, lord, taken prisoner, 239*n*.
Olivetan, Peter, notice of, 622*n*.
Oporinus, 106, 595*n*, 638.
Orange, prince of, invades Juliers, 633*n*.
Order of Holy Communion, translated by Coverdale, 31.
Origen, 6*n*.
Osiander, dogma of, 712*n*.
Osorius, 365*n*.
Ostend, John van, martyr, 578.
Oughtred, sir Antony, 340*n*.
Oxford, expenses of study at, 190, 194; studies of, 419, 424, 459.
Oxfordshire, rebellion in, 391.

P.

Paget, sir William, 77*n*, 661, 729*n*.
Palmer, sir Thomas, imprisoned, 577*n*.
Parker, archbishop, 361.
Parliament, meetings of, 468*n*, 508*n*.
Parnell, Thomas, 617*n*.
Parr, Catharine, 242*n*.
Parry, Henry, exile at Frankfort, 753.
Partridge, sir Miles, executed, 579*n*.
Partridge, Nicolas, 124, 608*n*, 626, 637.
Passau, peace of, 456*n*.
Paula, 5*n*.
Paul III., pope, 344*n*.
Paul IV., pope, 149, 599*n*.
Pellican, Conrad, 138*n*, 509*n*.
Person, Antony, martyr, 242*n*.

Pest, siege of, 634.
Peterson, William, 217, 381, 604.
Petre, sir William, 77 *n.*
Petrikow, 700.
Pflug, Julius, 383 *n.*
Philip II. at Brussels, 52; excesses of, at Antwerp, 175; arrives in London, 177; demands to be crowned, 180.
Philips, Walter, 373 *n.*
Phrygio, Paul Constantine, 554 *n.*
Pictures in the Greek church, 691.
Pighius, Albert, 325.
Pilkington, James, exile, 752 *n.*
Pinkey, battle of, 43.
Poinings, sir Thomas, 36 *n.*
Poland, various religions in, 690.
Pole, cardinal, 741; arrives in England, 347; archbishop of Canterbury, 743.
Pole, Henry de la, notice of, 625 *n.*
Pollanus, Valerandus, notice of, 82 *n*, 737 *n*; pastor at Frankfort, 111; baptizes his son in the Rhine, *ib.*
Polsted, 612, 618.
Ponet, John, bishop of Rochester, 87 *n*; catechism by, 142 *n*; controversy with Dr Martin, 116.
Ponet, Maria, 118.
Pope, league against the, proposed by Henry VIII., 612 *n.*
Powell, execution of, 209.
Powis, lord, 496 *n.*
Pownall, Robert, 170 *n.*
Preachers in London, persecuted, 171.
Preaching forbidden, 645 *n.*
Predestination, disagreement of Hooper and Traheron respecting, 406; Martyr's views of, 506.
Pretie, John, 170.
Proclamation respecting heretics, 773.
Procopius, 146.
Protestants, foreign, restricted as to ceremonies, 569; restrictions removed, 570; church government, 571.
Purgatory disproved by P. Martyr, 378.

R.

Radzivil, Nicolas, palatine of Wilna, 597 *n.*
Railton, Gregory, exile, 764.
Rands, Henry. See *Holbeach.*
Rappenstein, Andrew, 225.
Ratisbon, conference at, 37.
Reading, abbot of, executed, 627.
Rebellion of sir T. Wyat, 513.
Redman, Dr, notice of, 150, 264; his death-bed declaration, 151.
Reformatio Legum, 584 *n.*
Reniger, Michael, notice of, 374 *n.*
Rescissio alienationum, 149 *n.*
Revel, besieged by the Russians, 699.
Rich, lord chancellor, 263 *n.*
Richelius, 364.
Ridley, Nicolas, bishop of Rochester, 76; translated to London, 79 *n*, 185 *n*; visitation of, 187; controversy with Hooper, 91 *n*, 486; reconciliation with, *ib. n*; disputes on the eucharist, 323; sent to Oxford, 515; martyrdom, 143 *n*, 154, 751; opposition of, to the German church in London, 586.
Riga, bishop of, 687.
Ripen, 621 *n.*
Robinson, archdeacon, summoned before the council, 264 *n.*
Rochford, lady, beheaded, 226.
Rochet, what, 585 *n.*
Rogers, John, martyr, 171, 772.
Rood of grace in Kent, 604, 606.
Rose, Thomas, persecution of, 773.
Rossem, Martin van, 633 *n.*
Rotaker, Christopher, 698.
Rotenberg, surrender of, 638 *n.*
Roustius, 421.
Roxburgh castle, taken, 387.
Russia, invaded by the Tartars, 692.
Ruthenians, 600, 691.

S.

Sacrament of the Lord's supper, disputation respecting, 322 *n.*
Saints, swearing by the, objected to by Hooper, 416.
Sala, Margaret de, marries the landgrave of Hesse, 666 *n.*
Salisbury, countess of, 220 *n*, 625 *n.*
Salkyns, William, 345.
Sampson, Thomas, translates Gualter's book on Antichrist, 176; exile at Frankfort, 755.
Sandys, Edwin, exile, 755 *n.*
Sapidus, 51, 509 *n*, 605.
Saunders, Laurence, martyr, 171, 772.
Saverne, 49 *n.*
Saxony, duke Maurice of, 456 *n*, 650.
Saxony, elector of, prisoner, 58 *n*, 260 *n.*
Scepper, admiral, sent to carry off the lady Mary, 568.
Schintzius, 628.

Schmutz, Alexander, 396 *n*, 402; fellow of St John's, Oxford, 449 *n*.
Schuendi, Lazarus, 58 *n*.
Schwenckfeldt, Caspar, 513 *n*.
Scory, bishop, 371 *n*.
Scots invade England, 237.
Scots, Mary queen of, carried into France, 387 *n*, 643 *n*.
Servetus, Michael, 742 *n*.
Seymour, lady Anne, 340, 565 *n*.
Seymour, lady Jane, notice of, 2 *n*.
Seymour, Thomas, lord, sent to the Tower, 477; beheaded, 55 *n*, 648 *n*.
Sharrington, sir William, 649 *n*.
Shaxton, Bp, forbidden to preach, 215.
Siculus, George, 325.
Sidall, Henry, 311, 369.
Sigismund, king of Poland, 596; war of, with Livonia, 599 *n*, 687 *n*.
Silesia, duke of, 650.
Silvester, 771.
Simler, Josiah, godson of Bullinger, 261.
Sion house, 2 *n*.
Six Articles, bill to moderate, 204 *n*.
Skinner, Ralph, 313.
Sleidan, John, 54 *n*.
Smalcald, council at, 521.
Smith, Agnes, martyr, 175 *n*.
Smith, sir Clement, 341 *n*.
Smith, Richard, disputes against P. Martyr, 478 *n*.
Smith, sir Thomas, 77 *n*, 497 *n*, 729 *n*.
Socinus, Lælius, 700.
Sole, Joan, martyr, 175 *n*.
Solway moss, raid of, 239 *n*.
Somerset, duke of, sent to the Tower, 6, 69 *n*; conspiracy against, 76; set at liberty, 464 *n*, 636; privy councillor, 559 *n*; tried, 440, 728; executed, 441 *n*, 449, 579, 731; grants Glastonbury Abbey to Pollanus, 738 *n*; account of his children, 339, &c.
Somerset, duchess of, imprisoned, 342 *n*, 577; released, 367.
Somerset house, 728 *n*.
Somersetshire, rebellion in, 66.
Somerville, lord, taken prisoner, 239 *n*.
Soto, Peter de, confessor to Charles V., 58 *n*.
Sowerby, Thomas, exile, 764.
Spain, prince of, wounded at a tournament, 61.
Speke, sir Thomas, 496 *n*.
Spencer, Thomas, exile at Zurich, 752 *n*.
Spon, Huldric, 425.
Stanhope, sir Edward, 340 *n*.
Stanhope, sir Michael, 77 *n*, 579 *n*.
Stokesley, bishop, 231 *n*.
Strange, lord, 340 *n*.
Strasburgh, mass rejected at, 49 *n*; restored by the bishop, 657 *n*, 661 *n*; disputes at, respecting the Interim, 470 *n*, 471 *n*; receives it, 667; sickness at, 659.
Stumphius, John, 311; accompanies Hooper to England, 57; studies at Oxford, 64; antistes at Zurich, 98 *n*.
Sturmius, James, 372, 531 *n*.
Sturmius, John, 51, 509 *n*.
Suffolk, Henry, duke of, 454 *n*, 496 *n*.
Suffolk, Henry Grey, duke of, 3 *n*, 742; executed, 154, 290 *n*, 305.
Sultzer, Simon, 297.
Sun, remarkable appearance of, 692.
Surrey, earl of, executed, 42 *n*, 257.
Sussex, earl of, sent against the gospellers, 179 *n*.
Sutton, Edmund, exile, 764.
Suvermerians, 50 *n*.
Sweating sickness, 94, 496, 575 *n*, 679.
Swerder, William, notice of, 247 *n*.
Switzerland, five cantons of, allied with France, 68, 653, 656, 740; civil war in, 552 *n*.

T.

Tartars, invade Russia, 692; religion of, described, 690.
Taverner, Jo., exile at Frankfort, 764.
Taylor, Rowland, martyr, 175 *n*, 772.
Terentianus, Julius, 365.
Tertullian, quoted, 229 *n*.
Testwood, Robert, martyr, 242 *n*.
Therouenne, taken by stratagem, 683 *n*.
Thirlby, Thomas, envoy to Charles V, 37; bishop of Norwich, 185 *n*, 430; disputes with Cranmer, 645.
Thunsen, William, 261.
Thynne, sir John, 77 *n*.
Tischell, John, 669.
Tomkins, Thomas, martyr, 113 *n*.
Torvillanus, 157.
Toul, surrender of, 590 *n*.
Tracy, Richard, 613.
Traheron, Bartholomew, 316 *n*, 326; tutor to the duke of Suffolk, 465; exile at Frankfort, 763.
Tremellius, Immanuel, 535, 716.

Trent, council of, 23.
Tripartite History, notice of, 228*n*.
Tudson, John, Martyr, 175*n*.
Tunstall, Cuthbert, envoy, 374.
Turpin, Thomas, 170.
Tybald, Thomas, 16*n*, 520*n*.

U.

Ukraine, 600*n*.
Ulmis, Conrad ab, 458.
Ulmis, John ab, studies at Oxford, 70; patronized by the marquis of Dorset, 84; takes an M.A. degree, 450.
Ulric, duke of Wirtemberg, 543*n*.
Universities, Bucer's account of, 546.
Ustadt, Hector von, 698.
Ustazades, 198.
Utenhovius, John, notice of, 56, 653; resides with Hooper, 562; elder of the strangers' church in London, 572.

V.

Vadian, Joachim, 11*n*, 13*n*.
Valteline, 517.
Valys, de, 42.
Vane, sir Ralph, 577*n*; executed, 579*n*.
Vauville, R., minister of the French church, 339*n*; marriage of, 565*n*.
Velsius, Justus, 132.
Venice, the gospel preached at, 357.
Verdun, taken by the French, 590*n*.
Vergerio, Baptist, bishop of Pola, 499*n*.
Vergerio, Peter Paul, bishop of Capo d' Istria, 603*n*, 693, 695.
Vermilia, wife of P. Martyr, 582.
Villegagnon, Monsieur de, carries the queen of Scots into France, 643*n*.
Viret, 548.

W.

Waldenses, Luther's opinion of the, 694*n*.
Wallachia, king of, 650.
Wallop, sir John, 496*n*.
Walsingham, shrine at, 609*n*.
Warne, Joan, martyr, 175*n*.
Warner, Francis, 355.
Warwick, earl of, commands at Pinkey, 43; favours the reformation, 76, 82; opinion of the mass, 439; warden-general of the north, 454*n*; illness of, 89, 409. See *Northumberland.*
Welsinger, Christopher, 669*n*.
Went, John, martyr, 175*n*.
Wentworth, lord, 139*n*.
Werdmuller, Otho, 415*n*.
Werdmuller, Valentine, 85, 561*n*, 563.
Westchester, bishop of, 80.
Weston, Hugh, attends the duke of Suffolk at his execution, 303*n*; succeeds Cox at Westminster, 373.
Westphalus, 513*n*.
White, bishop, 175; writes against P. Martyr, 479*n*.
Whitehead, David, preacher at Frankfort, 128*n*, 763, 4.
Whiting, abbot of Glastonbury, executed, 317*n*, 614*n*.
Whittingham, W., 370, 764*n*, 765*n*.
Whittle, Thomas, martyr, 175*n*.
Wibrandis, wife of Bucer, 364.
Wida, king, widow of, 699.
Wildbaden, 654.
Wilford, John, exile at Frankfort, 764.
Willock, John, 393, 314.
Wilna, Palatine of, 597, 599, 690.
Wilson, Dr, maintains the pope's supremacy, 208; pardoned, 211.
Windsor castle, 76.
Wirtemberg, duke of, a patron of Brentius, 543*n*.
Wladislaw, 596.
Wolfe, Reginald, notice of, 523*n*, 609*n*.
Wood, Hugh, chaplain to lord Hungerford, 202*n*.
Woodrooffe, 610.
Wormulus. See *Werdmuller*.
Wullock, Andrew, 401.
Wurtzburgh, bishop of, 682*n*.
Wyat, sir Thomas, 36*n*, 513*n*.

Y.

Yong, John, 151.
Young, Thomas, precentor of St David's, 373*n*.

Z.

Zanchius, 553*n*, 682*n*.
Ziegler, 428.
Zinkia, hostess of Hooper at Zurich, 55, 70, 562.
Zolle, Matthew, 250.
Zuinglius, Ulric, 33*n*, 551*n*, 552*n*, 556*n*; son of, his death, 250*n*.
Zwickius, James, 693.

Praise for Intersection of Intensity

This book clearly transcends most views on the subject of giftedness and exceptionality as relating to the psychological, developmental and neurobiological factors that affect this special population. Patty crossed a precipice in her work that most would not venture to go over. Patty begins the process of laying the foundation to move all of us towards a far deeper and more complex understanding of the gifted person's struggle with their humanity. She takes on what most, in the field of gifted would hesitate to embrace. Her work demonstrates how those who venture into the world of giftedness should never compromise on facing the complexities of the gifted. And as you read her work do not lose sight of her deep passion and commitment to those who are gifted.

—Andrew Mahoney, M.S., L.P.C., Founder
Center for Identity Potential Identity Potential LLC

The author has courageously written a book which is destined to be a foundational text in the study of trauma as it affects gifted individuals over the lifespan. While the book is written for clinicians, I believe that practitioners, researchers, advocates, parents, and gifted adults can benefit from the research and recommended strategies designed to better understand trauma, its development, and impact on the life experiences of the gifted. The text is very well written and follows a format which enables the reader to continuously be reminded of previous discussions and closes each chapter with reflective questions that may be used in book study sessions, class discussions or individually. I anxiously await the author's future publications regarding trauma, identity, and the psychosocial needs of special populations of gifted learners.

—Joy Lawson Davis, Ed.D., Diversity/Gifted Education/
Teacher Ed Scholar, Author and Professional Development expert

With Intersection of Intensity, *Patty Gently has given us an important contribution to the field of gifted psychology. It is essential for gifted people to understand how traumas, both acute and developmental, affect a person's access to their authentic gifted expression across the lifespan. Equally essential is understanding how to heal those traumas and how someone can recover their capacity for joy, connection, support, wholeness, and meaning in their gifted experience. Having Patty's words of guidance and wisdom on their path to healing, gifted readers will find comfort, hope, direction, and practical answers for the 'how' of facing, healing, and growing from painful pasts. The book is an excellent primer for laypeople and helpful resource for professionals in the field of gifted psychology and gifted education. It is also an important guide for parents, carers, partners, friends, and employers wanting to best support the gifted people in their care. The field of gifted psychology is richer with this contribution. Thank you Patty!*

-Jennifer Harvey Sallin, Psychologist, Founder of InterGifted and Host of the Conversations on Gifted Trauma Podcast